...And On the Sixth Day God Created the Horse

A beautiful 365-day journey of horses throughout history

By
Sheri Grunska

All rights reserved. No part of this publication may be reproduced, distributed, or transmitted without the author's expressed consent. Published 2022, Copyright 2022 © Sheri Grunska. Cover images purchased through Shutterstock.

The author has researched every story to the best of her ability to make sure each story, account, and historical event is accurate. All resources, references and links can be found at the back of this book. A huge thank you is given to all the historians and writers throughout the centuries, who have researched and written articles that made it possible for a book like this to be written.

Edited by Cindy Lambert

Book cover design by
Stoney's Web Design
www.stoneyswebdesign.com

You can find all of Sheri's books at www.probarnmanagment.com and also sold on Amazon and other book outlets.

Dedication

This book is dedicated to all the people past and present who have loved and cared for horses during the harshest of times, and during times of peace and prosperity. The horse will always remember the kindness given to him, even if it was for a few fleeting moments.

Why I wrote this book

The horse is one of God's greatest masterpieces, filled with strength, majesty, color, and personality, all wrapped up in this exquisite creature. I realize more and more the enormous impact horses have had on people's lives throughout history. But it wasn't until I started writing this book that I fully saw the magnitude the horse has had on civilizations and their accomplishments, past and present. You are about to embark on a year-long journey that I know will forever change how you look at the horse.

Horses have always been a huge part of our fabric, and without them, our world would be a much different place. As I started doing the research for this book, I often had a lump in my throat as I began to take in the full scope of what horses have endured throughout the centuries and what their contribution or fate truly was. No one could imagine or prepare the horse for what he would endure for thousands of years. It would show the very best of humanity and the absolute worst. The learning curve was massive, and new problems evolved as man craved more. As man was figuring out his relationship with the horse, the mistakes that were made often led to mental or physical injury and even death for many equines.

Thank goodness that with each new generation, there were men and women who God genuinely gifted with a deep understanding of what the horse needed for his wellbeing. Those people went on to teach others and pass along valuable knowledge to the next generation. This was all to create a better work and living environment for the horse. It was a slow process, but with each century, things did improve for these majestic animals.

Up until a hundred years ago, the horse was the work truck and the Ferrari. It powered boats and machines, vehicles, and equipment. They are the forgotten heroes and have always been a beast of burden of warfare for every civilization that has conquered or been conquered throughout history. I am encouraged that this book will leave you changed in how you view these amazing animals, as it did for me after I was done writing the manuscript.

I now fully see God's complete and perfect creation when he created the horse, knowing they would be working side by side with man. Adding a splash of color to each horse and a personality to match their size and job, God created perfection. For many of us, we now consider our horses a part of our family, and just like our dogs, they share in the biggest moments in our lives. Get ready for a journey of true historical accounts and stories that will make you smile, and even tear up at times. You will begin to see the wonder of these magnificent equines in a much deeper way.

My prayer is that you will enjoy this book as much as I did writing it, and that you will begin to see the enormous contribution horses have given people throughout the ages. What an incredible gift the Lord gave humans when he created the horse. Savor each page and let each true account and story sink in. For then, you will begin to see the horse in ways you never imagined. Enjoy the ride!

And to all the beasts of the earth and all the birds of the sky and all the creatures that move along the ground – everything that has breath of life in it – I give every green plant for food. And it was so. God saw all that he had made, and it was very good. And there was evening, and there was morning – the sixth day.

Genesis 1:30-31

Table of Contents

~January 1~ **Horse-Powered Locomotive** 24

~January 2~ **Incredible Legacy** 25

~January 3~ **The Bond** 26

~January 4~ **Industrial Revolution** 27

~January 5~ **Medical Evacuation** 28

~January 6~ **Trigger** 29

~January 7~ **The Perfect Design** 30

~January 8~ **Angels Among Us** 31

~January 9~ **The Norse Horse** 32

~January 10~ **The Russian Troika** 33

~January 11~ **The Marsh Tacky** 34

~January 12~ **Little Bighorn** 35

~January 13~ **The Queen's Horses** 36

~January 14~ **Ponies At The Poles** 37

~January 15~ **The Harness** 38

~January 16~ **The First Fire Horse** 39

~January 17~ **Losing Their Jobs** 40

~January 18~ **Ship In Distress!** 41

~January 19~ **Leroy** 42

~January 20~ **Bring In The Big Guns** 43

~January 21~ **The Rodeo** 44

~January 22~ **Logging** 45

~January 23~ **Pit Ponies** 46

~January 24~ **Horse Latitudes** 47

~January 25~ **A Time To Reflect** 48

~January 26~ **Tea Horse Road** 49

~January 27~ **Horse Training** 50

~January 28~ **Mercury** 51

~January 29~ **It's Now Against The Law** 52

~January 30~ **Kings Rode Stallions** 53

~January 31~ **The Status Symbol** 54

~February 1~ **It's In The Genes** 55

~February 2~ **Marengo** 56

~February 3~ **The Bell Mare** 57

~February 4~ **Koumiss** 58

~February 5~ **Tremendous Machine** 59

~February 6~ **Mexican Charro Horse** 60

~February 7~ **It's A Hanging Offense!** 61

~February 8~ **First Natural Horsemanship** 62

~February 9~ **Doctor Peyo** 63

~February 10~ **The Earliest Olympics** 64

~February 11~ **A Long Day** 65

~February 12~ **Strongest Of Them All** 66

~February 13~ **Jousting** 67

~February 14~ **Campdrafting** 68

~February 15~ **Horseshoes** 69

~February 16~ **The Cavalry Blacks** 70

~February 17~ **The Playful Beast** 71

~February 18~ **The Riderless Horse** 72

~February 19~ **Merlin** 73

~February 20~ **Milk Delivery** 74

~February 21~ **The Bedouin Legend** 75
~February 22~ **Jim Key** 76
~February 23~ **Deep Scars** 77
~February 24~ **Nelson & Blueskin** 78
~February 25~ **Warhorses Missing** 79
~February 26~ **Snow & Mud** 80
~February 27~ **World War One** 81
~February 28~ **The Arabian** 82
~March 1~ **Rex** 83
~March 2~ **Seine Fishing** 84
~March 3~ **Hawaii** 85
~March 4~ **Medical Advancements** 86
~March 5~ **They Never Forget** 87
~March 6~ **The Artillery Horse** 88
~March 7~ **Mustang** 89
~March 8~ **That Amazing Nose** 90
~March 9~ **Snowman** 91
~March 10~ **The Horse Action Saddle** 92
~March 11~ **Guns A Blazing** 93
~March 12~ **Endurance Racing Today** 94
~March 13~ **Spanish Riding School** 95
~March 14~ **The Wagon Train** 96
~March 15~ **Horses & Farming** 97
~March 16~ **The Wedding Gift** 98
~March 17~ **The 80-1 Longshot** 99
~March 18~ **Jigitovka** 100

~March 19~ **The Games As We Know Them** 101
~March 20~ **The Roping Horse** 102
~March 21~ **Circuit Riding Preacher** 103
~March 22~ **Ancient Egyptian Horses** 104
~March 23~ **Mini-Me** 105
~March 24~ **Bucephalus** 106
~March 25~ **Ice Harvesting** 107
~March 26~ **The Newspaper** 108
~March 27~ **The Cattle Drive** 109
~March 28~ **Ban'ei** 110
~March 29~ **The Boat Ride** 111
~March 30~ **The Trolley Car** 112
~March 31~ **Mounted Drill Team** 113
~April 1~ **The Sacrifice** 114
~April 2~ **Police Horse Training** 115
~April 3~ **The Makeover** 116
~April 4~ **Warrior** 117
~April 5~ **Mounted Orienteering** 118
~April 6~ **Airborne** 119
~April 7~ **The English Saddle** 120
~April 8~ **Polo** 121
~April 9~ **Mongol Derby** 122
~April 10~ **Time To Retire** 123
~April 11~ **Stunt Doubles** 124
~April 12~ **The Samurai** 125
~April 13~ **The Thoroughbred** 126

~April 14~ **The Icelandic Horse** 127
~April 15~ **Public Health Hazard** 128
~April 16~ **The Four Horsemen** 129
~April 17~ **Horse-Pulling** 130
~April 18~ **Hunting On Horseback** 131
~April 19~ **Falconry On Horseback** 132
~April 20~ **Horse Car On Rails** 133
~April 21~ **The Mule** 134
~April 22~ **Stroller** 135
~April 23~ **Mister Ed** 136
~April 24~ **Military Maneuvers** 137
~April 25~ **Jesse** 138
~April 26~ **Those Beautiful Eyes** 139
~April 27~ **Horse Powered Wine** 140
~April 28~ **Rescuing Each Other** 141
~April 29~ **The Aussie Police Horse** 142
~April 30~ **Ship Ahoy!** 143
~May 1~ **The Trainer** 144
~May 2~ **A Time To Honor** 145
~May 3~ **The Religious Ceremony** 146
~May 4~ **Ancient Rome** 147
~May 5~ **Feeding Horses** 148
~May 6~ **Diphtheria** 149
~May 7~ **Pony Express** 150
~May 8~ **Jack & Jack** 151
~May 9~ **Chetak** 152

~May 10~ **Figure** 153

~May 11~ **Reining** 154

~May 12~ **Trading For Power** 155

~May 13~ **Ancient Greek Life** 156

~May 14~ **The Quest For Wood** 157

~May 15~ **Horse Of A Different Color** 158

~May 16~ **The Carousel** 159

~May 17~ **Humble Beginnings** 160

~May 18~ **The Best Horses** 161

~May 19~ **Opening The American West** 162

~May 20~ **The Flood** 163

~May 21~ **Skepticism Of The Automobile** 164

~May 22~ **The Stagecoach Horses** 165

~May 23~ **South Of The Sahara** 166

~May 24~ **The Space Shuttle** 167

~May 25~ **Carriage Driving** 168

~May 26~ **The Insane Disguise** 169

~May 27~ **The Police Horse** 170

~May 28~ **Forest Service Mustang** 171

~May 29~ **Vanning** 172

~May 30~ **The White Horse** 173

~May 31~ **The Saddle** 174

~June 1~ **Jappaloup De Luze** 175

~June 2~ **Time For A Change** 176

~June 3~ **The Buffalo Hunt** 177

~June 4~ **Horses In The Bible** 178

~June 5~ **Traveller** 179
~June 6~ **The Only Wild Horse Left** 180
~June 7~ **To All The Old Cow Horses** 181
~June 8~ **Sharing The Roads** 182
~June 9~ **Horse Camping** 183
~June 10~ **In Times Of Desperation** 184
~June 11~ **The First Speed Limits** 185
~June 12~ **Sport Of Kings** 186
~June 13~ **The American Indian Horse** 187
~June 14~ **The Western White House** 188
~June 15~ **Miracle Twins** 189
~June 16~ **Horse Crazy Celebrities** 190
~June 17~ **Doma Menorquina** 191
~June 18~ **Women And Horses** 192
~June 19~ **The Meat Eater** 193
~June 20~ **La Voltige** 194
~June 21~ **"Blue" Lakota Warhorse** 195
~June 22~ **Horse Galloping Ceremony** 196
~June 23~ **Real Horsepower!** 197
~June 24~ **Equine Reenactors** 198
~June 25~ **This Armor Is Heavy!** 199
~June 26~ **Chinese Horse Proverb** 200
~June 27~ **Modern Day Packhorses** 201
~June 28~ **Harness Racing** 202
~June 29~ **Left Or Right Handed** 203
~June 30~ **Cincinnati** 204

~July 1~ **Belle And Sundance** 205
~July 2~ **The Movies** 206
~July 3~ **Old Wives Tales** 207
~July 4~ **Light Horse Troop** 208
~July 5~ **The Posse** 209
~July 6~ **The Good Death** 210
~July 7~ **Making People Laugh** 211
~July 8~ **Palomo** 212
~July 9~ **Equine Therapy** 213
~July 10~ **Love In A Tiny Body** 214
~July 11~ **War Paint** 215
~July 12~ **The Cutting Horse** 216
~July 13~ **Amish** 217
~July 14~ **Medicine Hat Horse** 218
~July 15~ **The Last Pit Pony** 219
~July 16~ **The Hunter/Jumper** 220
~July 17~ **A Very Special Horse** 221
~July 18~ **Shetland** 222
~July 19~ **Chincoteague** 223
~July 20~ **Copenhagen** 224
~July 21~ **Tithes, Taxes And Rules** 225
~July 22~ **Riding The Rails** 226
~July 23~ **Old Billy** 227
~July 24~ **Horse Whims** 228
~July 25~ **Horsepower** 229
~July 26~ **Sandy** 230

~July 27~ **Chariot Racing** 231
~July 28~ **The Capture** 232
~July 29~ **Chemical Warfare** 233
~July 30~ **Tent-Pegging** 234
~July 31~ **The Disney Horses** 235
~August 1~ **Mackinac Island** 236
~August 2~ **Babieca** 237
~August 3~ **The Parade** 238
~August 4~ **Never Forget** 239
~August 5~ **Horses Act 1535** 240
~August 6~ **The Horse Stable** 241
~August 7~ **Expectant Mothers** 242
~August 8~ **Gulf Of Mares** 243
~August 9~ **Fantasia** 244
~August 10~ **Barge Horses** 245
~August 11~ **Kasztanka** 246
~August 12~ **The Ferryboat** 247
~August 13~ **A Horsemen's Prayer** 248
~August 14~ **Bits** 249
~August 15~ **Road Rage** 250
~August 16~ **Fire Horse No. 12** 251
~August 17~ **Xenophon** 252
~August 18~ **Forty Belgian Draft Horses** 253
~August 19~ **The Jinx** 254
~August 20~ **World War Two** 255
~August 21~ **Harvesting The Sea** 256

17

~August 22~ **The Farm Horse** 257

~August 23~ **Circus Maximus** 258

~August 24~ **Black Jack** 259

~August 25~ **Lewis And Clark** 260

~August 26~ **The Shunting Horse** 261

~August 27~ **The Gelding** 262

~August 28~ **Vonolel** 263

~August 29~ **Faithful Until Death** 264

~August 30~ **Dream Alliance** 265

~August 31~ **Horses In Art** 266

~September 1~ **Barrel Racing** 267

~September 2~ **Horse Manure Crazies** 268

~September 3~ **Where To Put Them All** 269

~September 4~ **Big Game And Fast Cats** 270

~September 5~ **Long Live The Friesian** 271

~September 6~ **Horseball** 272

~September 7~ **How Many Hands?** 273

~September 8~ **Star** 274

~September 9~ **Face Protection** 275

~September 10~ **The Fox Hunt** 276

~September 11~ **Vehicle Names Inspired By…** 277

~September 12~ **Surprising Statistics** 278

~September 13~ **Unusual Inventions** 279

~September 14~ **Horses Of The Civil War** 280

~September 15~ **Queen Of Diamonds** 281

~September 16~ **Colonial Life** 282

~September 17~ Chernobyl's Wild Horses 283
~September 18~ The Horse Trail 284
~September 19~ The Ultra-Race 285
~September 20~ Pick-Up Horse 286
~September 21~ Twenty-Mule-Team 287
~September 22~ Buzkashi 288
~September 23~ The Shahzada 289
~September 24~ The Fire Horse 290
~September 25~ Silver 291
~September 26~ Search And Rescue 292
~September 27~ Off To School 293
~September 28~ The Circus Horse 294
~September 29~ Packhorse Librarians 295
~September 30~ The Vaquero Tradition 296
~October 1~ Holiday Horse Shortage 297
~October 2~ The Omnibus Horse 298
~October 3~ The Horse Phase 299
~October 4~ The Unique Relationship 300
~October 5~ The Farrier 301
~October 6~ Branded For Life 302
~October 7~ The Horse's Prayer 303
~October 8~ Big Ben 304
~October 9~ The Shire 305
~October 10~ Ghost Horses Of The Desert 306
~October 11~ To Pace Or Trot 307
~October 12~ A Second Chance 308

~October 13~ **Funeral Horses** 309

~October 14~ **The Requisition** 310

~October 15~ **Therapy Horses For Veterans** 311

~October 16~ **The First Equine Veterinarians** 312

~October 17~ **The Bathing Machine** 313

~October 18~ **Uniting Over Horses** 314

~October 19~ **The Musical Ride** 315

~October 20~ **The Bond** 316

~October 21~ **Winter In The City** 317

~October 22~ **Cloning** 318

~October 23~ **The Treadmill** 319

~October 24~ **Combined Driving** 320

~October 25~ **The Golden Horse** 321

~October 26~ **Train Race** 322

~October 27~ **Hollywood Horses** 323

~October 28~ **Sefton** 324

~October 29~ **Sea Biscuit** 325

~October 30~ **The Horse Logo** 326

~October 31~ **Retirement** 327

~November 1~ **Horses In Mythology** 328

~November 2~ **Wells Fargo Stagecoach** 329

~November 3~ **Baśka** 330

~November 4~ **Shipping Warhorses** 331

~November 5~ **The Hairless Horse** 332

~November 6~ **The Rescue Of 5000** 333

~November 7~ **What Bravery Looks Like** 334

~November 8~ The Scythian's Horse 335
~November 9~ "The Galloping Horse" 336
~November 10~ The Outrider 337
~November 11~ Hot/Cold/Warm 338
~November 12~ The Beer Wagon 339
~November 13~ Horse Fighting 340
~November 14~ Today's Logging Horse 341
~November 15~ Horse Bells 342
~November 16~ Bess 343
~November 17~ Old Charley 344
~November 18~ Making House Calls 345
~November 19~ The Steeplechase 346
~November 20~ The Colonial Pacer 347
~November 21~ The Brumbies 348
~November 22~ Today 349
~November 23~ Cortés 350
~November 24~ The Last Fire Horse 351
~November 25~ Extinct Equines 352
~November 26~ That Beautiful Mane 353
~November 27~ Horse Of A Different Color 354
~November 28~ Horse Soldiers 355
~November 29~ The Mounties 356
~November 30~ The Lesson Horse 357
~December 1~ Pinto 358
~December 2~ Horsehair 359
~December 3~ Coconut Roll 360

21

~December 4~ **Eventing** 361

~December 5~ **Side-Saddle** 362

~December 6~ **The Western Saddle** 363

~December 7~ **Horse Diving!** 364

~December 8~ **The Show Stealer** 365

~December 9~ **Phar Lap** 366

~December 10~ **Laws That Still Exist Today** 367

~December 11~ **Lipizzaner Rescue** 368

~December 12~ **American Quarter Horse** 369

~December 13~ **Sleigh Racing** 370

~December 14~ **After The War** 371

~December 15~ **Seeing-Eye Mini** 372

~December 16~ **Skijoring** 373

~December 17~ **Strep & Strangles** 374

~December 18~ **Wild Horse Annie** 375

~December 19~ **Bill The Bastard** 376

~December 20~ **The Christmas Party** 377

~December 21~ **The White House Stables** 378

~December 22~ **The Show Horse** 379

~December 23~ **Those Beautiful Spots** 380

~December 24~ **The Livery Stable** 381

~December 25~ **Return Of Horse Power** 382

~December 26~ **Helping Prisoners Heal** 383

~December 27~ **Because Of The Horse** 384

~December 28~ **Epic Fail** 385

~December 29~ **Dressage** 386

~December 30~ **Half Man/Half Beast** 387
~December 31~ **What Will I Be?** 388
References/Sources 390

~January 1~
Horse-Powered Locomotive

The horse-powered treadmill has been around for thousands of years, but the real power was unleashed once man figured out how the gearbox and shafts would connect to whatever they wanted moved. Now it gave man the freedom to go bigger and better with the use of the horse, and instead of just making grain, man would travel by the horse-powered treadmill on rails. It was called the horse-powered locomotive.

In 1827, the South Carolina Railroad was looking for a horse-powered locomotive that would travel the rails. They ran a competition, and the winning design would receive $500. Engineer Christian Edward Detmold won the competition with his horse-powered locomotive called the Flying Dutchman. It consisted of a single carriage and at the center of the carriage was a treadmill that a horse would stand on and walk to make the locomotive move forward. The Flying Dutchman debuted in 1830, and it carried 12 passengers and hit an average speed of 12 miles per hour while the horse walked the entire time. During that same time, another style of horse-powered locomotive called the Cycloped was put to the test in 1829 against a steam-powered locomotive. Unfortunately, the treadmill was structurally weak and as the horse was walking, he fell through and they were disqualified from the trial. It was not mentioned what happened to the poor horse. In 1851, at the Crystal Palace in London, Italian engineer Clemente Masserano, unveiled a horse-powered locomotive called the Impulsoria. At the center of the locomotive stood four horses (in two pairs), standing on an inclined treadmill. The horse-powered locomotive traveled 7 mph, but with some minor changes, it was believed it could reach up to 20 mph and outrun the newly invented steam engine. In the end, the steam engine locomotive became the preferred choice, and I am sure the horses were glad about that!

~January 2~
Incredible Legacy

The beautiful foal was born in Kentucky on March 29, 1917, and they named him Man o' War because he was born during World War I. Mr. Belmont, his owner, was a soldier in the war and his wife, Mrs. Belmont, named him My Man o' War, but to all the people close to him, he was simply known as Big Red.

As a yearling, Man o' War was sold to Samuel D. Riddle for $5,000, and if things didn't work for him as a racehorse, Riddle would have him trained as a show jumper. Man o' War was 16½ hands tall, weighed 1,125 lbs. and became one of the greatest racehorses to ever live. He broke numerous racing records and won 20 out of 21 starts. Man o' War only lost one race to a horse named, Upset. To this day that particular race is still considered shocking and controversial in the world of horse racing. It was a genuine upset, and that is where we get the term "upset" for the underdog who wins a sports competition. It all started with this one horse race and a big loss for a champion Thoroughbred.

Man o' War's best friend was a horse called Major Treat. Wherever Man o' War traveled, Major Treat was by his side. They were closely attached to each other throughout their lives. Man o' War died quietly in his stall on November 1, 1947. He was 30 years old. His funeral was broadcasted nationwide on the radio, and during the service, nine eulogies were given! The New York Times called him a superhorse, and he could quite possibly be the greatest Thoroughbred ever to race.

Do you give the horse its strength, or clothe its neck with a flowing mane? Do you make it like a locust striking terror with his proud snorting? He paws fiercely, rejoicing in its strength and charges into the fray. He laughs at fear, afraid of nothing. The quiver rattles against his side along with the flashing spear and lance. In frenzied excitement he eats up the ground; he cannot stand still when the trumpet sounds. Job 39: 19-25

~January 3~
The Bond

Colonel Henry Commager wept like a baby when his horse Big Frank, his partner of several significant battles, died in 1862. Big Frank was tall with big flanks, and some said he looked more like a draft ready to pull a plow, but his fierce personality was better fit for battle. They had been a team for years and the last few months of war had been exhausting and painful for the both of them. They had shared many experiences like the time when they were on a steamer in the Chesapeake Bay when the ship collided with another boat and it sent a few soldiers and horses into the dark grungy water. The men were rescued but there were no horses in sight. About five hours later, and fifteen miles downstream, they saw what looked like a small boat in the dark. It turned out to be a horse swimming towards Colonel Henry Commager's vessel. It was Big Frank! He had survived. Months after Big Frank's rescue out of the water, the horse charged while under fire into a ditch near Fort Wagner during a night assault with bullets flying in every direction. He had been the only horse to make it. When Big Frank died from exhaustion after surviving so many battles it crushed the Colonel.

There is no way we can possibly comprehend the bond between a soldier and his horse. Not only were these men fighting wars, but they were entrusted to care for this animal that was solely devoted to them during such dark times. One military veteran gave his horse a military funeral in his back yard. Another warhorse was named after the soldier's wife. One general, who loved his horse so much, would ride the horse in parades after the war. Then one day, the horse was found poisoned and dead. He was soon buried, only to be exhumed later on, decapitated and then mounted. The bond can be so tight that it can bring a man to his knees and, at times, even cause him to do the strangest things for the love of his horse.

There is no secret so close as that between a man and his horse.

~January 4~
Industrial Revolution

The horse became the "living machine" that helped transform how cities operate and, in fact, was monumental in the success or the failure of a business or city. As the Industrial Revolution was taking shape, the horse was used for every part of business and personal life. This great animal would bring the United States and Europe into a new way of life, but while the Industrial Revolution was still in its infancy stage, the horse was still king of the road.

As steam and coal powered machines took over, the horse's jobs would start to change. The combustible engine came along and soon the automobile and tractor would dislodge the horse from farms, public transport, and wagon delivery systems, and it would eventually sever the city life from the rural life. Without the horse, people would either become city dwellers who rarely came in contact with a horse, or they would live far out in the country where they were disconnected from the busyness of the city. The two worlds would become very far apart. But before the reset of city and rural life became permanent, the horse would become king one more time.

The horse soon pulled coal-fired machines at the railway stations and became known as the "shunting horse." The horse could move goods and people anywhere the locomotives could not, and horses could easily travel the muddy or uneven roadways, that motorized vehicles could not. And so, as more railroads, canals, ferries and ports were being built, they needed more horses to collect and distribute both goods and factory workers. The horse along with farriers, wagon and carriage builders, horse tack and leather makers, became the backbone of 19th century life. Together they helped usher in the Industrial Revolution and work themselves and the horse out of jobs. The new way of life was hard for many people and the horse's role was now uncertain.

~January 5~
Medical Evacuation

During the Renaissance period in Europe, ambulances were actually horse-drawn carriages and wagons. When horses began to be used for transporting the sick or injured, the idea spread throughout all of Europe. Since the Renaissance period, horses have played a massive role in saving countless lives. As the Napoleonic Wars (1700's) began, Dr. Dominique Jean Larrey, a French surgeon in Napoleon Bonaparte's Grande Armée, was working close to the battlefields and saw first-hand the need for immediate medical care. He took notice of the old heavy wagons that were stationed at the rear of the army and felt they were greatly inadequate. Dr. Larrey designed a new lightweight horse-drawn wagon that could move fast across the battlefield to quickly pick up injured soldiers and deliver them to the field hospital for medical care. These wagons became known as "Flying Ambulances," which were appropriately named because of the speed at which the horses could move across the battlefield.

During the American Civil War, the first recorded horse-drawn ambulance materialized around 1862. At first, the ambulances were two-wheel carts before evolving into four-wheel designs that were better suited for the injured, and could quickly take wounded soldiers to steamboats and medical tents for further attention. During the First World War I, field horse-drawn ambulances were needed for medical evacuation of the injured soldiers. Horse-drawn ambulances were heavily relied upon to evacuate the wounded when motorized transport was not possible. Since much of the terrain or roadways were in poor condition, the military quickly found it easier and faster to have a horse-drawn ambulance waiting and ready to go, especially during the rainy, muddy season. These horses endured great hardship as they saved countless lives, and their bravery is truly unsurpassed.

~January 6~
Trigger

He was foaled on July 4, 1934, and was named Golden Cloud. Little did anyone know at the time that this independence baby would grow up to represent so much of what made America great. He was a Thoroughbred-Cross golden palomino that graced the western films of the 1940's and 1950's alongside his famous owner Roy Rogers.

Roy Rogers purchased Golden Cloud for $2500.00 after he rode him for a movie. It is said that he instantly fell in love with the horse. After he purchased him, he quickly changed his name to Trigger. While on set, another actor told Rogers, "Roy, as quick as that horse of yours is, you ought to call him Trigger." The name fit him perfectly, and as the stallion rose to fame, everyone knew the name Trigger. The golden palomino was beautiful and often referred to as "The smartest horse in the movies." Roy Rogers decided to keep him a stallion, though he never bred a mare his entire life. Rogers chose not to breed Trigger because he was worried that he would lose his sweet disposition and find mares more interesting than the movies! Trigger appeared in eighty-eight movies, over a hundred episodes on television, and even had stunt doubles for some of the action scenes! Roy Rogers would often trailer Trigger to hospitals and walk him up the stairs and into the hospital so that the children could have a chance to see the legendary stallion, and help to bring a smile to each of their faces. Rogers also trailered Trigger to large events and stood outside where the children that couldn't afford a ticket could see him for free.

Trigger lived out his golden years at Roy Roger's ranch and died at 30 years old. After his death, Rogers had Trigger preserved, mounted in a rearing position, and put in his museum so the public could see and enjoy the famous stallion.

~January 7~
The Perfect Design

The horse transformed the world once man could harness his speed and power. Man was blessed to have such an incredible beast to use at his whim and if man could learn to be kind to this amazing animal, then his equine partner would return his allegiance in hard work and little complaint. Unfortunately, history has often shown a different life for the horse. All that horses have ever asked for in return for their hard work is safety, shelter, plenty of good food and fresh water to drink. Would this prove to be a fair trade throughout the centuries? Your answer will be determined as you read on through the pages ahead.

We have 6,000 years of history with the horse and only 100 years of history with the automobile! When I really think about it, it sends shivers down my spine. Horses have contributed to the human race in many different roles throughout history. What started as a good food source for the early civilizations has ended up as a horse used for leisure and enjoyment for people of the present day. When horses became domesticated, they transformed the world, and with each century, the horse's role has continued to evolve. The horse was the prefect animal to take on the demands of man and survive through it all, even with equine deaths too numerous to count throughout the centuries. Because of the horse's anatomy, physiology, and sociability, it would survive where other mammals could not. The horse being a herd animal, quickly learned there was a pecking order with man, just like in his herd. He could eat and run without the need to regurgitate and masticate his food, unlike the cow or deer. He was born a fast mover, and his body was perfectly designed for man to sit upon. God's creation of the horse is completely perfect.

God made the horse from the breath of the wind, the beauty of the earth and the soul of an angel. ~Author unknown

~January 8~
Angels Among Us

She was bred to be a racehorse and her breeding was part Jeju, a local breed of South Korea. Her breed was known for its hardiness and she would prove that to be true. During the 1950-53 Korean War, a United States Marine bought the little mare from a racetrack for $250.00 from a boy who needed cash to buy his sister an artificial leg. Little did the Marine know at the time that this horse would become one of America's greatest equine war heroes.

The mare became a pack animal to carry ammunition for the Marines in 1952. The Marines named her Reckless after the recoilless rifle for which she carried ammunition. The rifle was called "reckless" because it was extremely hazardous to handle. Reckless was the only horse with the Marines at that time and she became very attached to them, and they also to her. During the ending stage of the Korean War, Reckless played an important role during a five-day battle. Reckless made 51 trips to supply Marines with ammunition in one day while walking through rice paddy fields and steep mountain terrain. Reckless learned to do this primarily unassisted with enemy fire all around her. She would drop off the ammunition, and then carry injured soldiers back to safety on the trip back down. The Marines believed Reckless was an angel among them. She was promoted to Sergeant and from that time on, she was called Sergeant Reckless. She earned two purple hearts for injuries she received during the war. She was also credited with saving countless lives of soldiers. After the war, she came home to the U.S. to live the rest of her days at Camp Pendleton. Sergeant Reckless died in 1968 and was buried with full military honors.

Be strong and courageous. Do not fear or be in dread of them, for it is the Lord your God who goes with you. He will not leave you or forsake you. Deuteronomy 31:6

~January 9~
The Norse Horse

During the 2nd century AD, the Scandinavian people known as the Norsemen or Vikings had a love affair with their horses that went far beyond caring for the animals. To the Vikings, the Norse horse was religion in their pagan world, and the horse was worshipped in life all the way through until its death. The horses of Iceland worked as pack horses, were ridden for battle, used for farming and even entertainment, which included horse fighting. But their uses went way beyond that. They were an answer to the prayers to the Norse gods, and the people made sure the horse was raised to mythological levels.

To the Norse people, the horse was believed to carry a man to his afterlife after he died, so it was often practiced to bury the horse in full tack along with the deceased man. This practice was established by King Danr of Denmark, who asked to be buried with his horse fully saddled. The Norse had sacred horses that they used for their pagan sacrifice because the horse was so revered and valued among the people. The offering of sacred horses to the gods was a way of sending messages and requests to the gods. When the horse was sacrificed, the blood was saved and read to foretell the future. There would be a feast of horsemeat following. It was believed that certain colored horses were sacrificed to different gods to keep them satisfied. For example, a black horse was sacrificed to the Finno-Ugric god of disease and misfortune to keep the god at bay in his underworld. As Christianity started to spread and came to Iceland, the pagan rituals and practices changed throughout the subsequent centuries, and the sacrifice and eating of the sacred equines pretty much disappeared. The relationship between the Norse and their horses evolved into a legendary mythical status that we are familiar with today, with Pegasus being one of the most famous mythical horse.

~January 10~
The Russian Troika

A Russian Troika (Trio in Russian) is a cart or sled that is pulled by a trio of three horses standing side by side harnessed together. The Troika is a unique way of harnessing a team of horses and, in fact, it doesn't exist anywhere else in the world. The Troika is almost as fast as a car with the right horses!

The Russian Troika team of three horses moves at different gaits. The horse in the middle (korennik in Russian) moves at a trot and needs to be the biggest and strongest horse. The two trace horses on the sides (pristyazhnyye in Russian) maintain a canter taking the middle horse with them in whatever direction they are moving. Such a team of horses can cover vast distances at a very fast pace. Many people believe that the fastest Troikas are pulled by Orlov Trotters (horses specially bred for speed). It seems like it would be a complex set-up for a team of three horses, but through the centuries, it has proven to be very efficient and fast.

It is not known for certain who invented the Troika, but many say it was around the 17th century. The development of the postal service contributed to the creation of the Troika and a trio of horses traveling at different gaits. In Russia, the distance between cities is very far and the roads are often in poor condition year-round. It could take weeks to receive mail, especially during the wet muddy seasons in fall and spring. Both endurance and speed were important for the horses transporting mail, and by pulling a Troika, the mail could be delivered much faster without exhausting the animals. It proved to be very successful.

Today, you can still see trios of Orlov Trotters pulling decorated Troikas for rides or racing, and it is an important symbol of Russian history and innovation. The Orlov Trotter is the oldest trotting horse breed in Russia.

~January 11~
The Marsh Tacky

The Marsh Tacky horse is known in some southern states as "The little horse that helped win the American Revolution." This strong and gentle little horse is also the official state heritage horse of South Carolina. Now if you are wondering why you have never heard of the Marsh Tacky before, you are not alone. I hadn't either until I did some deeper digging, and what I uncovered was fascinating.

The Marsh Tackies are now considered a rare breed of horse, but during the Revolutionary War, they were the preferred choice of mount for the cavalry. The Marsh Tackies originated on the Sea Islands off the Atlantic Ocean along the Eastern Coast waters. It is said that the horses descended from the Colonial Spanish horses brought to the coast of South Carolina in the 16th century. That was when the Spanish attempted the first European settlement in the Americas at Santa Elena, which is now present-day Parris Island.

The Marsh Tackies were used as pack horses and traded with the Native Americans. Due to their hardiness and the ability to do quite well in very hot and humid weather, and the swamplands didn't bother them at all, they soon became the first choice as cavalry mounts. The Marsh Tacky breed was also popular with the guerilla soldiers under Francis Marion, also known as the "Swamp Fox," whose victories in the Revolutionary War helped turn the tide for the patriots. The British soldiers were riding big heavy warhorses, and their horses struggled greatly through the muddy swamps of South Carolina, while the Marsh Tackies moved the patriots through the heavy swampland easily.

While the Marsh Tacky was an integral part of the Revolutionary War they are now very rare, with less than 500 horses in existence. Through much hard work and dedication to preserving the breed, the Marsh Tacky is slowly making a comeback.

~January 12~
Little Bighorn

Comanche was a mixed breed horse that was purchased in St. Louis by the U.S. Army in 1869 for the price of $90.00. Captain Myles Keogh took a liking to the horse and bought him for his mount. They were stationed on the western frontier, and together, they faced the Native American tribe called the Comanches. Keogh named his brave horse after the tribe, and it stuck.

Comanche soon became respected and known throughout the troops, as a reliable and courageous equine companion in the heat of battle. Comanche was shot in his hind quarter with an arrow during one of the first battles, but continued to carry Captain Keogh through the fight. Later, a huge battle took place at Little Bighorn that would be one the bloodiest defeats for the U.S. Army. Up against a combined force of Lakota, Cheyenne, and Arapaho tribes, the 7th cavalry regiment was annihilated. Comanche was found badly wounded and barely standing after the fighting had ended. The horse was given special medical attention and is often referred to as the only survivor of Little Bighorn. Unbelievably, Comanche had been shot seven times and survived each war wound. Historians have noted that there were a few other horses barely alive, but Comanche was the only horse to receive medical treatment and go on to live a long life. Comanche was given the honorary title of "Second Commanding Officer" from the U.S. Army, and the warhorse retired in 1879. He died in 1891 at 29 years old with the best care a horse could receive. Upon his death, he was given a full military ceremony with the highest military honors for bravery.

"This one isn't just any old horse. There is nobility in his eye, a regal serenity about him. Does he not personify all that men try to be and never can be? I tell you my friend; there is divinity in a horse, and especially in a horse like this. God got it right the day he created them." ~*Michael Morpurgo*

~January 13~
The Queen's Horses

The Queen of England has been riding horses since she was a little girl. Her father, King George VI, gave the Queen a pony when she was four years old, and the pony was named Peggy. Even in her nineties, she still likes to take a hack out in the field! It has always been known that the Queen loves horses, but there are so many interesting facts about her fondness for horses, and the horses that are part of the royal family.

The Royal Mews at Buckingham Palace are the Queen's stables, where all of the horses are kept that are used for royal parades and events. It is one of the most beautiful stables in the world, and nothing is spared for the care of the horses. The Queen chooses a name for each horse that lives there, and you will only find Windsor Greys and Cleveland Bays at the royal stable. The Windsor Greys pull the carriages for the Queen, and the royal family. During Victorian times, the Windsor Greys were kept at Windsor, hence the name Windsor Greys. The Cleveland Bays are used for picking up high commissioners and ambassadors visiting the Queen. The Queen owns many racehorses, having inherited them from her father, King George VI. The Queen breeds Thoroughbreds and Shetlands, Highlands, and Fell ponies. When the Queen was young, she would ride side-saddle for the ceremonial events, and from 1969 to 1986, the Queen would ride her favorite horse, Burmese. The Royal Canadian Police gifted the Queen with the black mare, and she fell in love with her instantly.

Throughout her long and amazing equestrian life, you can find many beautiful images of the Queen with her horses, talking softly to them or brushing her hand down their neck to tell them they are safe. To see the Queen of England share her love of horses with the world is truly a sight to behold.

"I should like to be a horse." ~ *Queen Elizabeth II*

~January 14~
Ponies At The Poles

Horses have played a monumental role in exploration to some of most desolate places on earth. The North and South Poles were no exception when it came to using horses to reach the ends of the earth. The use of horses for reaching the poles started with Norwegian Fridtjof Nansen. Nansen had discovered that horses could survive in freezing climates, if they had enough food. This was proven in 1893 when Siberian horses were used to pull a sledge 3000 miles across the frigid landscape in Siberia. The Siberian horses were heavy coated, and the extreme negative temperatures did not bother them at all. In 1894, the first Russian horses were used for polar exploration. They pulled 700-pound sledges in temperatures of -30 degrees. One explorer wrote, *"The ponies proved by far the most useful animal for sledge dragging. They were hardy, and when the supply of oats and hay was exhausted, easily accustomed themselves to eating dry dog biscuit or polar bear meat."*

Anthony Fiala, in 1903 led an expedition into the vast Arctic Circle. He employed U.S. cavalrymen to take care of his Siberian horses. In 1907, Sir Ernest Shackleton took along horses for his exploration of Antarctica. Shackleton turned to the British Army for advice because he knew there would be no grazing for the horses. These experts knew that other cultures fed their horses protein and fodder. They invented a meat-based ration for Shackleton's horses to help him reach the pole. In 1912, Danish explorer Johann Koch was determined to cross the inhospitable landscape using Icelandic horses. When they set off in March of 1913, the temperature was -40 **degrees and** quickly dropped to -50 degrees, but the cold did not hurt the horses. He fed his horses special protein-based food and equipped them with special equine snowshoes that had been used in Scandinavia for centuries. It was said, *"As draught horses, the ponies have achieved miracles."*

~January 15~
The Harness

The horse was domesticated somewhere around 4000 BC. By 2400 BC man had put a harness on the horse for working the fields and pulling wagons. The first harness resembled a yoke used for oxen but was poorly suited to the horse's anatomy and was realized quickly that it would pinch the horse's windpipe. During the 5th century, the Chinese developed the full-collar harness. It was rigid but padded, and it conformed well to the shape of the horse's body without interfering with their breathing. Lines and traces, or different lengths of wood could be attached from the collar to any number of tools, including plows, carts, and wagons. The harness gave the horse something to lean on as he moved forward, which literally harnessed his power and strength. A harnessed horse now had strength to do the work of fifty men, and it transformed the way man was able to do things forever.

The use of horses in farming improved with the development of the full-collar harness and better designed plowing equipment. Soon the horse became a familiar sight, working every job on the farm. They were used to pull farming equipment like harrows and plows through the fields, and to transport crops. The strength and speed of the horse allowed farmers to work larger areas of land in a shorter amount of time. The combination of improved farming equipment and the use of raw horsepower resulted in better crops. Farmers went from growing only enough food for their own livestock and family, to producing surpluses which they could then barter or sell. Surpluses contributed to the development of larger towns and cities, which gave farmers a central location in which to sell their excess fruits and vegetables.

The development of the equine full-collar harness changed man's life in ways never imagined, and the horse became just as important to farmers as they were to the military.

~January 16~
The First Fire Horse

In 1832, New York Mutual Hook and Ladder Company No. 1 was one of the first fire departments to purchase a fire horse. Many of the fire stations were short firefighters, possibly due to the yellow fever epidemic that hit the country hard. Even so, most firemen were unsympathetic to having a horse pull their fire equipment. So much so that one evening an unknown anti-equine person snuck into the stable, shaved the horse's mane and tail, and painted a white stripe down the horse's back hoping to embarrass the firefighters as they went out on a call.

As steam engines gained popularity, they also grew in size and weight. Firefighters reluctantly accepted the need for horses. At first, the horses were kept down the street from the station. When the alarm sounded, it took valuable time to fetch the horses that were stabled down the road and then harness them to the engine. It didn't take long before the horses were living at the station, and the hesitancy to accept them as part of the crew was replaced by a deep affection for the courageously brave equines.

Not every horse was cut out to be a fire horse. The horses needed to be strong, obedient, and extremely fearless. They needed to stand patiently and calm at the fire scene, while flames blazed high into the air, and the firefighters spent long hours fighting the fire. A fire horse needed to be able to handle the pressure of this type of work, and these horses would be called out day or night no matter the weather. It was a sad day for the firemen when a fire horse could no longer do his job due to age or health. Many retired fire horses continued to work for the city in new jobs that were less strenuous, like delivering goods or pulling junk wagons. At times, the fire horses would forget their new roles and charge down the streets hauling a wagon after hearing a fire bell. It was said, "Once a fire horse, always a fire horse," and it was proven true many times!

~January 17~
Losing Their Jobs

During the 1920's, the number of horses used in the workforce in America peaked at about 25 million. Around the same time, gas-powered tractors slowly came on the scene, and by the 1960's had peaked at nearly five million. It was estimated that one tractor would replace about five horses working on a farm. It was around 1945 when horsepower was replaced by tractor power, and the workhorses started losing their jobs. New technology with bigger tractors and the comfort of enclosed air-conditioned cabs made life for the farmer easier. They could plant and grow more acreage and not have to use valuable farmland to grow feed, like hay and oats for the horses to eat. The mechanical advancements were a wonderful thing for the farmer but also left uncertainty for the horses that lost their jobs. A new era of horse ownership was rushing in, and the days of workhorses were fading away except for a few small pockets of communities like the Amish, who, to this day, use horsepower for everything from farming their fields to traveling to town, or a neighbor's house to visit.

Since I live on a farm with an old dairy barn that now stables horses, I often think about my husband's grandfather and great-grandfather, who owned draft horses to work the land, and farm the fields each year. Since owning horses and caring for them daily, even during the harsh winters of Wisconsin, I have a newfound respect for the farmers and workhorses of yesteryear. Even though the farm horses of decades ago had a hard life, I still catch myself romanticizing about those huge draft horses standing quietly in the barn waiting to be tacked up for a long day of work ahead, and I still get goosebumps just thinking about it.

God must have smiled and opened a generous hand when he gave to man the horse. ~Author Unknown

~January 18~
Ship In Distress!

On January 12, 1899, the Lifeboat Station volunteers and the Lifeboat horses were about to do something that had never been attempted before. It would involve eighteen horses pulling a massive lifeboat over hills and winding roads, a total distance of thirteen miles, to launch in rough waters to aid a ship in distress.

The Forrest Hall was a 1,900-ton ship sailing from Bristol to Liverpool and had 18 people aboard, but had run into extremely bad weather. It had been under tow, but the cable had snapped and the rudder broke away. At 7:52pm, the Lynmouth Lifeboat Station received a telegram reporting that the Forrest Hall was drifting ashore at Porlock Weir. The violent weather prevented the crew from launching from the Lynmouth lifeboat station to aid the ship. It was proposed that the lifeboat be taken overland and launched from Porlock Weir itself, where it was more sheltered. This was a 13-mile trek which would be a massive undertaking. The Lifeboat Louisa was 32 feet long and weighed 10 tons.

Eighteen draft horses were brought in from local farmers and hitched up to the Louisa. Six men were sent ahead with shovels to widen parts of the road. By the time they started pulling the heavy lifeboat with the horses, it was dark and the weather had worsened. After a very tough climb up Countisbury Hill, they had to stop to repair a carriage wheel. This gave the exhausted horses, time to rest. The most dangerous part was ahead for the horses. The men had to control the boat down the steep hill into Portlock. At one stage, the boat was dragged on skids as the road was too narrow for the carriage and could not be widened. Finally, the men were able to safely navigate the horses down the hazardous terrain of Portlock Hill, after breaking down part of a wall to let the lifeboat and horses through. The lifeboat was launched, the men on the ship were rescued, and overnight eighteen horses became heroes.

~January 19~
Leroy

In 1976, Bicentennial fever had taken over the United States. It was America's 200th birthday, and people everywhere were feeling very patriotic. One of the ways American citizens were exploring their rich heritage and roots was to travel across the U.S. and see the vast landscape of America.

During this time of celebrating our freedoms, two men came up with an idea they called the Great American Horse Race. It was dreamed up by two horse lovers, Chuck Wagoner and Randy Scheiding and the race would offer a more historical experience. Birthed on the idea from the early settlers who lacked trains and automobiles, the race would be on horseback and it would give people a way to see America the way it was experienced a hundred years earlier. The route was very nostalgic, incorporating bits of the Oregon Trail, the Pony Express Trail, and even the Donner Party's doomed journey. The race would be 3,500 miles over fourteen weeks, and farther and longer than any organized race had been done in recent history. And the winner would receive $25,000!

By the start of the race, 91 teams (horse and rider) had registered. Each person was allowed two horses for the journey, and the variety of breeds registered for the race was amazing. There were Quarter Horses, Arabians, Thoroughbreds, Appaloosas, and Icelandic horses, to name a few. And then there were two mules named Lord Fauntleroy (Leroy) and Lady Elouise who were owned by Virl Norton. The race turned out to be more grueling than any participant expected, with tired horses and many injuries. Norton's mule, Lady Elouise, became lame and was pulled from the race, but Norton continued with Leroy alone. Many riders and horses dropped out of the race. When Norton and Leroy finally crossed the finish line, they were tired and Norton had no idea how they had done. It turned out Leroy the mule had won by a landslide!

~January 20~
Bring In The Big Guns

Sometimes our trucks and vehicles are no match for the winter snow and ice. Once in a while, we need help getting unstuck. Help can come from a tow truck, or if we are really lucky, help may come in the form of giant draft horses!

I was strolling through the internet when I came across a video from a few years back that took my breath away. It was somewhere in the upper Midwest and the entire area had been hit by heavy snow and ice. An eighteen-wheeler had hit the ice and gone off the side of the road, and lodged the semi into a crevice. The wheels were just spinning and the truck was not going anywhere. The truck happened to get stuck in a rural area where a man who owned large Belgian draft horses lived next door. The driver of the truck and the man started talking, and before long, they decided to try and pull the semi out with a team of the man's Belgian draft horses. What was so amazing is that they videotaped it for all to see.

The massive gentle giants were hitched up and brought over to the front of the semi. Then the man hitched up the team with a rigging attached to the semi and gave a call to his horses. The horses perked up when they heard the command. Slowly the horses started to move forward using every bit of strength they had. Inch by inch the semi crept forward and soon it became dislodged from the snow and ice. The strength and willingness of the horses was remarkable.

I must have watched that video several times, and each time it gave me goosebumps. Then I started looking up other videos on my computer, and realized there were many videos of draft horses pulling out delivery trucks, mail trucks, semis, and tankers! With each one I watched, I just smiled because I was watching something beyond beautiful. And I thought to myself, sometimes you just need to bring in the big guns!

~January 21~
The Rodeo

Before there were rodeos, cowboys working out on the ranches would test their horses against other cowboys from other ranches. The meaning of rodeo actually dates back to the Spanish word "rodear," which means "to encircle." As families moved out West and were influenced by the Spanish, their culture started to rub off and soon small informal competitions began popping up between ranches to see who the best cowboy was and, of course, who had the best horse. Back in the 1800's and early 1900's there wasn't nicely built enclosed arenas like we have today. Sometimes these competitions would be set in an arena encircled by wagons or, later on, motorized vehicles. The earliest forms of rodeo competition appealed to local ranchers and cowboys because it gave them the chance to bring their ranching skills to town for people to see and show off the versatility of their horses. The horse truly made the cowboy great and the cowboy knew that.

Rodeo has grown from the days of parking vehicles or wagons in a circle to keep the horses and cattle enclosed, to a multi-billion dollar industry with high earnings for the cowboys. The horses are a huge part of rodeo and are participants in all the events except bull-riding, and these horses are not just your average equines. They are true athletes in every sense of the word. They are intelligent, fast and know their job inside and out. Whether it's roping a calf and keeping the rope tight as the cowboy jumps off to tie the calf's legs, or the pick-up horse that is ready at a moment's notice to help the cowboy get off his bronc, the horse is what has made rodeo one of the most loved sports to watch. Rodeo has come a long way since the early days, but one thing that hasn't changed is the horse and his willingness to give his all for his cowboy or cowgirl, especially when he knows exactly what his job is. These horses are nothing short of spectacular and true athletes in every way.

~January 22~
Logging

Until the early 19th century, oxen were the choice of animal to use in lumbering operations. They were cheap and could survive on just about any type of native forage, which made it much easier to move them from one place to the next without hauling food along. The horse was much faster, but the initial expenses to purchase the horses, harnesses, and the feed were much higher. However, with the growing logging operations, the need for an animal that could move the logs faster trumped the overall cost of purchasing and feeding horses. In came the big boys, the Percherons and Clydesdales to get the job done, and soon thousands of draft horses were being used in the logging industry.

Logging with horses was very dangerous work for the men and horses. Unstable trees and falling branches were just some of the common hazards that injured or killed logging horses. The loggers worked in harsh conditions, and so did their equine coworkers that waited quietly while the trees were being downed. The days would start early in the morning with the horses being fed, brushed, and tacked up. Then they would head out to the job site. The size of the trees depended much on the area, but no matter the size, the horses were on the job ready to move the heavy logs. Draft horses were known for their very calm disposition and not easily spooked, which was important with trees falling down around them. Snow covered roads and frozen ground made it much easier for the teams to pull the sleighs of cut logs to rivers to be floated downstream to timber mills.

It was said, *"A logging horse had to be much cleverer than a farm horse. A farm horse just needs to put one foot in front of the other while a logging horse, needs to look at where he is walking and maneuver around other trees, stumps, tight turns and uneven ground that could easily create problems when pulling logs. The logging horse had to think about what he was doing before he moved."*

~January 23~
Pit Ponies

Once man realized how coal could benefit them, the coal industry took off. With the turn of the 19th century came the Industrial Revolution, and coal mining was at the forefront. Soon coal was providing fuel for steam engines, transportation, and home heating. In the early years of mining, women and children worked the mines alongside the men until laws were passed to protect the women, as well as boys under the age of ten. As the need for coal increased, horses and ponies replaced men for moving the heavy carts filled with coal. Large draft horses all the way down to very small ponies worked in the mines and they were all affectionately known as "pit ponies."

In one of the world's most dangerous working environments, the horses and ponies were pushed every day to move coal carts and wagons. The area in which these pit ponies worked was small and for the large horses, the room to move was very tight. The work was hard, extremely dirty, and hazardous, and it came with the constant danger of injury or death. The horses would live in the mines for years without ever seeing the light of day. The larger horses often scraped the tops of their heads on the low ceilings, and they had to learn to carry their head low. In really small tunnels they would sometimes get jammed in by their withers. Injuries often became infected in the dirty air and required veterinary treatment. Horses that were injured or sick were either cured or euthanized. Some miners were kind to the horses and treated them with the best care possible under such deplorable conditions. Many of the workers did not think the mines were the right place for horses and ponies, yet they were glad they were down there with them. Pit ponies were used in mines throughout the world until the 1970's. Now there are only a handful of mines in remote areas of the world still using horses as pit ponies.

~January 24~
Horse Latitudes

If you are a sailor, then you have probably heard the term "horse latitudes." But have you ever wondered where the name came from and what it has to do with sailing?

About 30 degrees north and south of the equator is an area referred to as the horse latitudes. It is an area of ocean where the winds fluctuate and diverge often, and either flow toward the poles (known as the prevailing westerlies) or toward the equator (known as the trade winds). Calm winds, bright sunny skies, and little or no rain are the result of an area of high pressure which creates the diverging winds. The consequence of these types of weather patterns result in a dead calm ocean where the wind is non-existent for long periods of time.

Horse latitudes is said to have originated from the 16th century when Spanish sailing vessels sailed to the West Indies. The ships would often become stalled for days or weeks at a time when they encountered high pressure and calm winds in this area of ocean water. Many of these ships heading to the Americas carried horses as part of their cargo. Unable to keep their ships moving due to the lack of wind, crews often ran out of water to drink. To conserve the water, sailors on these ships would have to do the unthinkable and sometimes push the horses they were transporting overboard. Horse latitudes were birthed from those tragic events.

It is said that nearly half of all the horses transported by ships on those early crossings met their death by being thrown overboard and drowning, or worse, being eaten by hungry sharks. Horse latitudes are still used today even though most sailors probably have never asked why or thought twice about it. But the horse, no matter how tragic their ending, still played a part in the sailors life during the earliest days of travel from Europe to the Americas.

~January 25~
A Time To Reflect

Many different breeds of horses were used during wartime throughout history, and they each contributed in ways that would be hard for us to imagine these days. They supported their soldier and went bravely into battle with chaos all around them. They watched their fellow equines fall and perish, and often become sick from exhaustion, starvation, and injury. They saw the tears and suffering of the soldiers and caretakers around them and they endured unbelievable hardship, sensed the danger, and felt the incredible stress of wartime. Some horses mentally couldn't handle it and went crazy, while others shut down but still managed to do their job. Many horses were too exhausted to put up a fight and worked until they dropped and died. With every battle that has taken place throughout history, the horse was a vital part of it and equally important to the soldier leading him. It was often said, a war couldn't be won without the horse and that was true up until World War II, when gas-fueled military machinery and fast warplanes took their place. Even then the horse played a big part in World War II as well.

Sometimes I look at the horses on my farm and smile, because I know they don't realize how good they have it and how spoiled they are. Their only concern is to make sure they are fed their grain and hay on time, and turned outside for the day. And when I am not on "their" time schedule, they often have a fit and act like impatient spoiled children and it often makes me laugh. The peaceful days they now live, can be contributed to the millions of horses that came before them and worked and died on the battlefield. And for that, we will be forever thankful.

The horse does one of two things – he does what he thinks he's supposed to do or he does what he needs to do to survive. ~Ray Hunt

~January 26~
Tea Horse Road

Thousands of years ago, a famous General Ma Yaun (14 BC - 49 AD) spoke this phrase, "Horses are the foundation of military power, the great resource of the State." His words sum up the importance of the horse and how they were of the highest value during the Han Dynasty (206 BC - 220 AD). Horses were considered a strong status symbol for the Chinese elite, and vital in portraying a strong military power. It was believed that a country could not be won without the horse, and the Han Dynasty would do whatever it needed, to breed the best horses for war.

The constant supply of good war stallions was considered essential to fighting the Xiongnu nomadic people located in today's Mongolia. China faced long periods of time in which good-quality warhorses were scarce. China also knew they had many quality goods that they could send out and trade for larger, sturdier horses to ride and breed. Soon bolts of Silk and Jade were traded for well-bred horses from the Mongolian steppes and Tibetan plateau. Even tea was used as a great trading commodity beginning with the Tang Dynasty, and the "Tea for Horses" market became very famous. The Ancient Tea Horse Road, which is in China, was a trade route that went through Yunnan, Sichuan, and Tibet. People in Sichuan and Yunnan traveled with pack horses to exchange tea for horses with people in Tibet, and the pathway was called the Tea Horse Road.

The Tea Horse Road was risky and dangerous. Transportation was especially difficult because of the narrow zigzagging roads that made traversing the high mountains a slow journey. They also had to cross fast-moving rivers that were very deep in areas. The only means of transportation during that time were the pack horses. It was once said, "The road was created by humans with their feet and horses with their hooves."

~January 27~
Horse Training

When the horse was first domesticated thousands of years ago, learning to train the horse for work, battle and riding was a learning experience in itself. Before man realized the horse was a gentle animal, his fear led to harsh training techniques to keep the horse under control. Thank goodness, throughout history there have been some very smart and intuitive people who saw the horse as a gentle beast and companion that only wanted to please its master. Those people trained their horses with patience and gentleness.

Horse breaking, or training, has some very interesting roots and history behind it. It is sometimes also called "starting or gentling" a horse. The horse's domestication has allowed us to harness the horse to do many things we would not normally be able to do. Researchers have studied artifacts from thousands of years ago and found evidence of bits and tack that was used on the horse. From these findings in different areas of the world, the equipment used on the horses was harsh in order to keep them under control. The horse was a war-machine and the warrior didn't have time to deal with an unruly animal or get hurt. Some cultures took a different stand and gentled the horse and formed a relationship with the equine. The drawings, artwork, bits, and tack show a much easier way of life for the horses of these other cultures. Later on, it became popular to break a horse by jumping on his back and letting him buck his way to exhaustion, as done in the old west with the wild horses. Over the last century, a new way of thinking has evolved with horse training, and natural horsemanship was born. Even though some earlier cultures understood and used a form of natural horsemanship, the horse was mainly used for battles during that time, whereas now, the horse is used mainly for enjoyment and competition. With time and knowledge the horse is finally being understood for the gentle equine he truly is.

~January 28~
Mercury

The foal was born in the spring of 2005 at Dyfed Shire Horse Farm. As a young gelding, he became part of the Household Cavalry Mounted Regiment. In October 2008, he began training to become one of the iconic drum horses for the Queen's Household Cavalry of England. This great horse was named Mercury.

To watch the Queens Household Cavalry Mounted Regiment is truly something special, and the horses that are chosen to be drum horses have an important job. This large draft breed needs to be strong, powerful, and good-natured to successfully perform in the Queen's processions. Mercury had it all. He was 17.2 hands tall and weighed over 1800 pounds. Mercury would carry his rider and a set of kettledrums during the Queen of England's Band of the Life Guard processions. As Mercury would walk through the streets along with the other horses and riders, his rider would play a set of very large drums that hung over each side of his body. Mercury was controlled by reins that were attached to the rider's feet instead of using his hands. This allowed the rider to play the drums with his hands and control the Mercury with his feet, which was all the more impressive.

Mercury towered over most of the other horses and was strong, which was needed since the drums alone weighed over three hundred pounds. He was known for his calm and very good-natured personality and he always willingly respected and responded to the cues he was being given by his rider's feet. Mercury became a celebrity and he represented well the traditions of the Royal Family that had been perfected for centuries. Mercury was nominated by The Household Cavalry Mounted Regiment to be inducted into the Warhorse Memorial Hall of Fame after he had sadly, and very unexpectedly, passed away after an accident. Mercury will always be remembered as one of the Queen's iconic drum horses.

~January 29~
It's Now Against The Law

It was 1866 in New York City. The driver of a large cart, filled to the top with coal, was whipping his horse without ceasing to make him pull the heavy load down the street, but the weak, emaciated horse was struggling to move even one more step. People walked by while looking the other way except for one man who stood there watching. The man was impeccably dressed and as he approached the driver of the coal cart, the man continued to whip the tired horse. This gentleman began to explain to the driver that it was now against the law to beat your horse.

Henry Bergh was a prominent man with a huge heart for animals. He traveled the world but when he came to America, he decided to make a difference for these "mute servants of mankind." On February 8, 1866, Bergh attended a meeting at Clinton Hall where he pleaded with the others in attendance to create laws to protect the horse. He went on to detail the practices he had witnessed in America. His audience included some of Manhattans most powerful leaders when he spoke these words, "This is a matter purely of conscience; it has no perplexing side issues. It is a moral question in all its aspects." His speech would set the wheels in motion to protect the horse. The American Society for the Prevention of Cruelty to Animals was created on April 19, 1866, and an anti-cruelty law was passed. From that day on, Bergh would spend his days checking on horses and their tack, saddles, and collars. He made sure there were no sores or torn flesh on the horses that were working. He supplied water tanks throughout the city so working horses could drink water daily. Bergh's efforts spread quickly to 38 states in the Union, and it all started with one horse and a man that cared enough to do something.

"I said, somebody should do something about that. Then I realized, I am that somebody." ~Author Unknown

~January 30~
Kings Rode Stallions

During the medieval period, it would have been beneath a king to ride a gelding. Instead he always rode a stallion. The knights of the king also only rode stallions for many reasons. Stallions were thick-necked, big bodied horses that were full of fire, and were also known to be more aggressive, in which, they were used as weapons when it came to fighting in battles. It was believed they had more endurance than most geldings and faced battle without fear. Since stallions were often hot-blooded with increased stamina, geldings were considered second rate and were used for menial jobs and for peasants to ride. The only time geldings were used for warfare during the medieval period, was for transportation when the Dragoons (cavalry soldiers) rode them to the battle site, and then hopped off their horses to fight on foot.

If a man wanted to get a woman's attention, he rode a stallion not a gelding, and definitely not a mare! A big prancing, snorting stallion was a sign of a man's masculinity. It was a symbol of his manhood. In some ways things haven't changed much in society when it comes to impressing a woman. Now instead of horses, a man will often try to impress the girl of his dreams with a beefed-up car with a lot more horses under the hood! By early modern times, it was the wealthy man with high social standing who would only be seen riding a stallion. This thought or belief about stallions, warfare, and manhood started to fade in the 1800's, as it was realized that many great geldings could handle the same work and were much less difficult to handle. The truth is that there were fewer horse accidents with geldings than stallions because geldings were usually easier to ride. But to this day, no one can deny the flash and fire of a beautiful stallion.

Then thundered the horses hooves – galloping, galloping go his mighty steeds.
Judges 5:22

~January 31~
The Status Symbol

Horses have played a notable role in man's ability to live, conquer, eat and travel, amongst other jobs that the horse was harnessed with. The horse has undeniably changed how man has done things, and has given man a new power early on that he did not possess before. Along with his strength that had been harnessed and tamed, the horse gave man one more thing—status in society. The horse now became a status symbol of wealth, power and military might.

During the medieval era, the horses owned by the Viking nobility and the rich and powerful, symbolized masculine honor. It was a man's world with men's rules and the horse strengthened their power and, in many ways, gave them spiritual status. The rich owned and rode horses (the best horses that could be found) while the rest of society, especially women, walked or used horses for less noble purposes like working the fields and millwork.

The lower-class commoners often rode their workhorses in an attempt to mimic the masculine prestige and honor that the upper class represented on their finely bred, groomed and well-cared for horses. The comparison of steeds between the two classes of people was often very far apart, and the results were never quite the same since the peasant's horses served practical and laborious jobs. The lower class horses were often tired, poorly groomed, and aged, where the upper class horses were full of fire with coats that glistened. Rather than being seen as respected citizens for their ability to own and ride horses, these lower-class people were equated with their horses and often viewed as "beasts of burden" themselves.

The horse really was the symbol of riches and power. And it was flaunted with a clear purpose, and to send a loud message about who a person was and their importance and status in society.

~February 1~
It's In The Genes

Throughout history, people have sought to achieve the perfect horse by breeding the best mares with the best stallions. Whether you believed that the traits you were trying to achieve came from the mare, as some early Arab tribes assumed, or from the stallion, which was often the thinking during the medieval period, we have not changed much in wanting to breed a horse as close to perfection as we can possibly reach. As for me, I love every part of the horse. I am attracted to color, markings, personality, eyes, and the shape of their head. I even find their legs to be beautiful and, of course, who doesn't love a big butt on a draft or Quarter Horse!

That is only the tip of the iceberg and scientists are now finding out how genes are essential in passing personality traits to the next generation of babies. What makes one horse more nervous or calm than another? Why is it that two horses of the same breed, size, and conformation can race, but one horse is always faster at the finish line? What makes one horse more aggressive, while another so easy-going and submissive? Why do some horses overreact to everything while others take the plastic bag floating across the arena in stride? Scientists have found that certain genes contribute to so many of these factors, which makes it very exciting if you are looking to breed a mare with the best qualities possible.

So much is still a mystery, which makes it even more beautiful because, after all, if we could control every part of the design of the horse, then it would take away from the total awesomeness and mystery of these amazing equines. What is even more incredible is that God took the time to create each individual horse with unique colors, markings, and traits. Even after thousands of years, the pallet of colors, the vast array of shapes, sizes, and personalities is still endless.

~February 2~
Marengo

Napoleon Bonaparte is one of those outstanding figures in European history, but many say he owes much of his military success to his horse, Marengo. At the beginning of the 19th century, any military endeavor had to involve the horse as a means of transportation and communication. For Napoleon, the horse that helped change history and catapult this leader to the top of his military career and political success was his favorite horse Marengo, a purebred Arabian imported from Egypt.

Marengo was said to be small but very powerful with great stamina and beautifully majestic. He stood about 14.1 hands tall and was light grey in color. He was named Marengo after the battle of Marengo on July 14, 1800. He was fast and extremely smart and carried Bonaparte into the battles of Austerlitz, Jena, Wagram, and of course, the Battle of Waterloo. He was ridden often on the 80-mile journey from Valladolid to Burgos, which he consistently completed in five hours. The stallion was injured eight times during his career, but it never slowed him down. Marengo was captured when the French were defeated at the Battle of Waterloo, and the horse was passed into British hands and sent to a farm where he was used as a breeding stallion. Marengo lived out his days with the best of care in quiet surroundings.

Marengo lived to be 38 years old (1793-1831), which is incredible, considering what he had endured during his battle years. When Marengo died in 1831, his skeleton was preserved and later given to the Royal United Services Institute. He will always be remembered as Napoleon's most loved horse.

You cannot lead a battle if you think you look silly on a horse.
~Napoleon Bonaparte

~February 3~
The Bell Mare

It takes a savvy mare to lead the pack, as some would say. When pack horses, donkeys, or mules were on a long trip, the cowboy would choose a very smart, dominant mare to lead the pack train of equines. The mare chosen was called a "bell mare," and she was not usually ridden, but instead used as a guide horse to keep the other horses and mules in line. A bell would be placed around the mare's neck, and she would be given the freedom to lead, and the other pack animals would follow the sound of her bell. This freed up the packer's hands rather than having to hold on to a lead rope and wrestle his animals through brush or rough terrain. The land was vast, and pack trains of horses or mules were a common sight, especially in the cavalry. These bell mares would naturally lead the horses and mules following behind them. This also allowed the men to explore and still know where their pack train was by the sound of the mare's bell. The idea of using a bell mare caught on, and packers found out quickly that traveling long distances or through steep and rugged terrain was much easier when using a bell mare. The packer could also rest and not worry about his pack team wandering off since they would not leave the bell mare.

Later on, during World War I & II, bell mares were used to lead the pack mules and horses off the ships at their destination overseas. The mules were known as "bell sharps" who were trained to follow the sound of the bell on the lead horse, which was always a mare. It was said that mules naturally refer to the horses as their superiors in the equine world, and the bell mare was dominant over most geldings. A soldier would often ride the bell mare, and as she walked, the sound of the bell around her neck would reassure the mules following behind her even if they couldn't see her. It was also noted that if a bell mare was killed during the war, you would often see pack mules grieving as they had lost their leader.

~February 4~
Koumiss

The horse has been used for everything you could imagine, but did you know that even the mare's milk was used to make an alcoholic drink? Horses were first domesticated on the plains of northern Kazakhstan some 5,500 years ago by people who rode them and even drank their milk. It was the beverage of the ancient Nomads and they called it Koumiss. Koumiss originated in Central Asia and Mongolia, where the nomadic people have been making this curative drink in complete secrecy since the pre-Christian era. Koumiss has a sour and sweet taste, and is known to be refreshing. People today, say it usually takes a few times to acquire a taste for the beverage, but for the native people, it is a deep-rooted part of their culture and they look forward to a cup. Asian nomads knew a lot about horses and realized early on that the mare's milk would satisfy their thirst on a hot summer day, particularly if they were somewhere along a steppe or in the mountains.

Authentic Koumiss is rich in proteins and microelements that are good for health and help satisfy thirst and restore the microflora of the gastrointestinal tract. Koumiss became known as a refreshing alcoholic drink, as the natural fermentation created a 3% or higher alcohol content. Since the 1850's, Koumiss has been used in folk medicine and, at one time, there were special clinics dealing in Koumiss therapy. It was highly popular among people and was said to cure pulmonary tuberculosis and other respiratory diseases, as well as anemia and some gastrointestinal disorders. Koumiss is still popular today in Kazakhstan, Uzbekistan, Tajikistan, Kyrgyzstan, Mongolia, and Bashkiria. The Mongolians still today celebrate the holiday of the first Koumiss every year. It's a day when mares feed their newborn foals for the first time each spring.

~February 5~
Tremendous Machine

There are a lot of famous racehorses, each with their own unique story. Some of these amazing Thoroughbreds came from great breeding mares and famous sires, and others hit the ground as an underdog with enough heart to take them to the top. One Thoroughbred that has always tugged on my heartstrings is a stallion by the name of Big Red, or more famously known as Secretariat.

It was said that Secretariat was built almost perfectly. He stood at 16.2 hands tall, weighed 1200 lbs. and was put together with nearly perfect conformation. To watch him run was a sight to behold. In 1973, Secretariat won the Triple Crown in racing which includes three legs of the race—the Kentucky Derby, the Preakness Stakes, and the Belmont Stakes. On top of it, he shattered the track records for all three races, which brought tears to grown men as they witnessed something so rare and beautiful happen right before their eyes. During the last race, the Belmont Stakes, which is the longest and most grueling of the Triple Crown races, Secretariat moved far ahead of the other horses on the track and his distance and speed kept increasing. As the crowds watched what was unfolding before their eyes, the announcer's spoke into the microphone and said Secretariat looked like a *tremendous machine*. He had won the race and the Triple Crown (the first one in 25 years!) and shattered track records that have never been broken since.

After many years as a breeding stallion and enjoying his fame, Secretariat was euthanized in 1989 at 19 years old due to a severe hoof disease. They did an autopsy and found his heart to be two times the size of an average equine heart and in perfect condition. It weighed 22 pounds, while an average Thoroughbred heart is around 9 pounds! He definitely was a tremendous machine and was all heart.

~February 6~
Mexican Charro Horse

Horses arrived in Mexico as early as the 1500's when the Spanish brought them on ships. The number of horses grew fast, and the people of Mexico learned to ride and become great equestrians with their own style and traditions. Ranch life was a big part of the Mexican culture, and soon competition between horsemen grew into what they called the Charreria, the Mexican version of a rodeo. The Charro (Mexican cowboy) fine-tuned his riding and ranch skills with his best horse, and these cowboys looked forward to the Charreria, a day of roping and riding events with their families.

Today's Charro horses need to have the skills once necessary for ranch life. A calm demeanor, intelligence, and strength were, and still are, more important than speed. The horses preferred by Charros are a combined breed of the American Quarter Horse, which descends from European Thoroughbreds and the horses derived from the stock brought over by the Conquistadors. In Mexico, the career of a Charro horse lasts around 12-15 years, if the horse is well cared for. For some of the retired Charro horses, unfortunately, they end up being sold to work new jobs pulling rickety garbage carts through city streets, or worse, end up at a slaughterhouse. Some of these horses have second careers in breeding or as therapy horses, and they are considered the lucky ones. Many of the Charros love their horses and make arrangements so their horse will be well cared for in retirement. Some help others in a positive way through therapy programs. They want to make sure the horses do not end up in bad situations. For the Charro, his horse is an extension of himself, just as the horse is deeply entwined throughout the history of Mexico.

"We were conquered by horses, we gained our independence with horses, we made our Revolution with horses and we continue to love horses." said Daniel Flores Yeverino.

~February 7~
It's A Hanging Offense!

Horse stealing in the Old West was a serious crime. It was said, "To take a man's horse from him, in some cases, was like putting a bullet through his head." Horses were the fastest way to travel and often the difference between life and death. A horse could get you where you needed to go much faster than on foot, and if your life or the life of a loved one depended on it, then having a horse became a means of survival. Horses were of such great value, and it was often young men who wanted to make quick money by selling horses and thinking they would never get caught. Because of the seriousness of the crime, the results were often the same for the person found guilty of horse thieving—death by hanging. The guilty man would be hung with a noose around his neck on a tree with a note often attached to his jacket or shirt that read, "Horse thief." There was no confusing what that man had done. It was a time in our history when the punishment was swift and harsh with the idea of sending a clear message to others who might have their eye on somebody else's horse.

Is it truth, myth, or maybe a little of both? The records found of judges approving the hanging of horse thieves in most states was not the norm. Usually it was vigilante groups who took the law into their own hands and hung the horse thief, and most people didn't buck the system no matter how brutal the punishment. Different states in the union had different laws on the books, including branding for horse thieves. Horse theft is still relatively common, with an estimated 40,000 horses a year being taken from their lawful owners. Stolen Horse International is one modern-day organization in the U.S. that works to reconnect stolen horses with their owners.

Treasures gained by wickedness do not profit, but righteousness delivers from death. Proverbs 10:2

~February 8~
First Natural Horsemanship

During a time when horses were being domesticated and used for battle in most countries, the African Numidian (modern day Algeria) people were way ahead of their time in training and riding their cavalry horses as early as 202 BC. It was commonplace for horsemen and the military to create and make harsh bits to control the horses they were riding. The Romans, who were heavily armored and had less ability to move and control their horse by other means, used bits that were sharp with jagged edges of bone that were very severe. Later, rigid metal bits were designed for a quick response from the horse without any thought to what it was doing to the horse's mouth. The Numidian people were unique in how they looked at the horse, and they chose to form a relationship with the horses they rode.

The Numidian horsemen rode without saddles or bridles and would instead put a simple rope around the horse's neck for control. At times they would also use a small stick to guide their horse. Unlike other cavalry of the time, they chose to ride without armor, except for a leather shield. Their main weaponry was the javelin or sword, which they would carry. It was their superior riding skills that would make up the difference for their lack of armor and heavy weapons. They became experts at warfare tactics and could easily frustrate less mobile armies. They were once described as "by far the best horsemen in Africa." The Numidian's warhorses were the ancestors of the Berber horse. These horses were smaller than the other horses of the period; however, they were much faster, especially over longer distances. The relationship the Numidian people had with their horses was unique for that time period. The horses were bonded with their riders and would follow them around wherever they went. You could say that they were the first people to use natural horsemanship on their horses.

~February 9~
Doctor Peyo

During a large part of his life, Peyo, a huge 15 year old stallion, and his owner Hassen Bouchakour, heavily competed in Dressage competitions throughout France and other countries. That was until a few years ago when something happened that would change the horse and his owner's life forever. Peyo went from dressage and equestrian shows around the world to visiting palliative care wards.

His trainer and owner, Hassen Bouchakour, knew there was something special about the stallion from the beginning. They would travel to a horse show, and Peyo would often inch his way towards a person and then gently nudge them with his head. It often seemed like the horse gravitated towards the people who were disabled. Bouchakour noticed this and decided to take Peyo to a therapy unit. There he discovered that the horse was very good at making sick people happy. They seemed to light up when they saw the gentle horse, and the horse seemed to sense it also.

After changing direction in his career as a trainer, Hassen and Peyo now spend their time visiting the sick several times a month at local hospitals. While many people may think a horse entering a hospital is unsanitary, the doctors and nurses take every precaution to ensure that Peyo is as clean as a whistle. He is bathed, and his tail and mane are braided. His hooves are greased, and his body is completely covered with an anti-bacterial lotion. Finally a blanket is put on him as one more precaution. It is only then that Peyo is allowed inside a hospital. Once inside, it is up to him which room he wants to enter. He tells his trainer which room by stopping at the door and raising his front leg. The horse seems to choose the rooms of those who are the sickest or dying. He'll stand near the patient and comfort them in their last moments. The doctors and nurses at the hospitals now affectionately call the stallion Doctor Peyo.

~February 10~
The Earliest Olympics

While the Equestrian Olympic Games as we know them today began in April of 1896, the modern games are based off of sporting events that were held every four years in Olympia, in the western Peloponnese. These equestrian games began in 776 BC with an invitation for athletes from all over Greece to compete. The very first competitions were basically races between men on foot, but horses quickly were added into the mix and the games really took off from there. The first horse/man competitions included:

- Tethrippon – a four-horse chariot race over 12 laps of the stadium (hippodrome) that eventually included a version for two-year-old horses where they ran 8 laps on the track. This race was the most popular and the most dangerous.
- Keles – a single horse race run over 6 laps. The horses needed to be fully grown and had a rider. Eventually a version for two-year-olds was included.
- Kalpe – a trotting or canter horse race for mares where the rider would start off on the horse but towards the end of the race, jump off and run alongside the horse holding onto the reins.
- Synoris – a two-horse chariot race run over 8 laps of the hippodrome that eventually included a version for two-year-olds over three laps.
- Apene – This was a two-mule chariot race that eventually died out because it wasn't as fast enough, and didn't excite the crowds as much as the electrifying horse-pulled chariot racing events.

These competitions were extremely dangerous, and many horses were seriously injured from the crashes. The high death rate of horses became a normal part of chariot racing. Unfortunately, these horrific crashes added to the excitement and popularity of these early Olympic events, and many of the owners and drivers gave little regard to the horses competing. If a horse was injured or died, they quickly bought in a new one to race.

~February 11~
A Long Day

Horses were a huge part of the agriculture landscape up until the mid-20th century, when motorized tractors and other equipment replaced the horse in most areas. But, it is important never to forget the incredible contribution the millions of horses have had in helping feed humans worldwide for centuries. Today there are still some groups of people who choose to use horses for farming as a part of their lifestyle, and in some of the poorest countries, horses are still pulling a plow and wagon. Before motorized tractors, each farmer had to sit down and figure out which fields he would use for specific crops, and a big part of the equation were the horses. After all, the horses had to be fed. That meant the farmer had to grow food for his horses, which took more money, time, and horsepower, and it became a never-ending cycle each spring and summer when it was growing season. Each farmer would own several teams of horses, depending on the size of his farm, which enabled him to work longer hours while rotating the horses out.

Each growing season, about five acres of productive land had to be allotted to every horse in the barn for raising oats, fodder, hay, and straw. The farmer's work was usually a race against time with weather and the growing season. A farmer typically had extra teams of horses in case one got injured or if they were in a race against the weather. The horse's weakest point was his endurance. A horse or team could only be relied on for about 15 miles a day if the conditions were right and the horses were strong and healthy. It was exhausting work pulling heavy equipment through rough, uneven, and even muddy ground. The work day didn't start out on the field but rather at the barn where the horses needed to be fed, brushed, watered, stalls cleaned, and bedded, and that was only the beginning. The farmer and horse were an incredible team that worked very long days side by side.

~February 12~
Strongest Of Them All

Man has been able to accomplish the unthinkable because of the draft horse. They have carried the medieval knights laden with heavy armor into battle and worked the fields to bring food to our tables. They have pulled wagons loaded with the goods that we use every day, and pulled our carts and carriages for our own personal gain, all while working long hours without complaint. Just watching them walk with their heavy hooves hitting the ground can give you a sense of how small and weak we are as humans and how beautifully made these huge equines truly are. There is something noble and majestic about draft horses with their massive body and gentle spirit that makes us fall in love with them even more.

It is said that the strongest horses are the Belgian, Shire, Suffolk Punch, Ardennes, and Percheron, but there are many others as well. Most of these breeds can be traced back centuries and some even further, each with a long, colorful history. Most of these draft breeds stand between 16 and 19 hands tall, but there have been some draft horses that have stood even taller in recent history. Depending on the breed, these gentle giants can weigh anywhere from 1800 to 2600 lbs. and pull many times their weight with ease.

For centuries, men have competed to see which teams of horses were the strongest, and today it has turned into a sporting competition that is very popular in most countries around the globe. Which horse is the strongest of them all? If you were to ask ten people who own heavy draft horses, you would probably get many different answers. But the one thing they will all agree upon is that they love their big drafts and consider them a huge part of their family!

Of all creatures God made at the Creation, there is none more excellent or so much to be respected as the horse. ~ *Bedouin Legend*

~February 13~
Jousting

When we think of King Arthur and his Knights of the Round Table, we often romanticize about the mighty steeds these warriors rode. During the Middle Ages (5th-15th centuries), knighthood was closely linked to horsemanship and the word "chivalry" comes from the French word "chevalier," meaning "skills to handle a horse."

Jousting was an extremely dangerous sport where both the knight and the horse often died from their injuries. In early jousting tournaments, men wore leather and chainmail armor and rode smaller horses. As the sport of jousting grew, heavier metal armor replaced the chainmail armor, and it was realized that the light horses couldn't handle the heavy weight of the armor. The massive cold-blooded horses of France soon became the preferred choice of mount. The two most common horses used for jousting during that period were not identified as a breed but instead a type. There were the warmblood "Chargers" and larger draft-cross "Destriers." Even though these horses were considered large for that time, they were actually smaller than our present-day draft horses.

As the armor became heavier to protect the knight, the target soon became the horse. If an opponent could take down the horse, then it would be a much easier win. Soon heavy metal was being designed to cover much of the horse (including his head) and this new barding (horse body armor) was extremely heavy. Then add the knight's armor, which often weighed over a hundred pounds, and then add the saddle, tack and the rider! Jousting armor was much heavier than battle armor. The horses used for jousting had a hard and often, short life in such a dangerous sport. Usually only the wealthiest could participate, knowing they could be without their horse by the end of the game.

The horse is made ready for the day of battle, but the victory rests in the Lord. Proverbs 21:31

~February 14~
Campdrafting

What exactly is Campdrafting, and what does it have to do with horses? I asked myself the same question when I first came across the term and what I uncovered sounded super fun! Campdrafting is an Australian equestrian sport that involves horses and cattle. It is believed to have originated in Queensland with the pioneering stockmen of the Australian bush in the late 1800's. Australian cattle stations were huge (much larger than the ranches in Texas), and cattlemen needed many horses to cover the miles and track cattle. It was a hard job in often harsh climates for both man and horse. Often the stockman or drover (a person who drives cattle to market) had to cut cattle out of a herd for different reasons, and before you know it, they were bragging about who had the best cattle horse. Soon it became a way for the stockmen to have some fun and friendly competition at the same time.

In a Campdrafting competition, the rider enters the ring or "camp" on horseback and at the other end is a group of cattle. It is a timed event, and once the buzzer goes off, he runs his horse to where the cattle are and cuts one cow from the herd. He then needs to turn the cow towards the judge two or three times to prove he has the cow under control. Then he guides the cow through a course of standing pegs which involves right and left turns of a figure eight pattern. After the figure eight, the rider pushes the cow through two pegs called "the gate." The course needs to be done in less than 40 seconds!

One of the most famous horses in Australian history was called Radium. He was an Australian-bred stock horse who was so successful at Campdrafting competitions that in 1913 at a Campdrafting event at Geary's Flat Bushman's carnival, Radium's owner was asked not to compete so that other riders had a chance of winning.

~February 15~
Horseshoes

Once man tamed the horse, he quickly realized he would use this animal to travel long distances for hunting and warfare, to pull wagons, and work the land. The horse changed how man did everything, but it was quickly realized that these huge powerful beasts easily got sore feet. It was a new problem for man, and the invention of the horseshoe to protect the horse's feet came into play. The old saying couldn't be truer—*No hoof, no horse.*

Thousands of years ago, horsemen in Asia developed booties made from hides and woven from plants. These booties would slip on the hooves and were used for therapeutic purposes. These primitive shoes provided protection for sore hooves and helped guard against future injury. In Japan, Waraji was a woven grass horseshoe that slipped over the horse's hooves and was tied on the top. After the first century, Roman horsemen started using a different kind of covering and protection on their horse's feet. The horseshoes were inspired by the sandals strapped to their own feet. These leather and metal "hipposandals" fit over the horse's hooves and fastened with leather straps.

Traveling to colder northern climates, the constant soft and wet ground of northern Europe overly softened porous hooves. Horses became plagued with soundness issues due to the ongoing wet conditions, and while traveling the European roads, horses had a very difficult time keeping their footing on the slick paths. Horsemen tried various ideas and, by the 6th century, began nailing metal shoes onto their horses' feet. It is not clear who actually invented the first nail-on horseshoe, but there must have been a learning curve along the way. Horseshoeing became standard practice in Europe around 1000 AD. The early shoes were cast from bronze and were very lightweight, with a scalloped outer rim and six nail holes. Horseshoes have come a long way in history.

~February 16~
The Cavalry Blacks

The Cavalry Blacks are the Queen of England's royal horses and still, today is an operational part of the British Army. The Queen's horses form the Household Cavalry Mounted Regiment, maintaining a world-famous tradition that dates back to 1660.

The regiment's mounts for the soldiers need to be solid black, and that is why they are endearingly called the Cavalry Blacks. Although if a horse has white socks or a star or snip, that is permitted. The only color exception is the trumpeter's horses and the drum horses, which are an altogether different color. Today there are 350 men and 280 horses that make up the ceremonial troops for state occasions and other royal duties.

The vast majority of Cavalry Blacks come from Ireland. Once or twice a year, a purchasing commission goes to Ireland to purchase younger horses that will replace the horses reaching retirement age, which is normally around 17 to 20 years old. The Cavalry Blacks must be able to carry a lot of weight for a long period of time. The horses are usually of warmblood breeding and resemble the old-fashioned heavier sport horse type—not the newer leaner horse we see today in competition. The Queen's horses need a longer period of training so there are no mishaps in front of the public. Once the horse has shown that he is ready, he is then dressed in full military tack along with his rider, and more training is required. The horses are young and unbroken when they are purchased and the trainers go slow and make sure each horse has the mental capability to be a Cavalry Black. They need to be calm and easy to direct; after all, the parades and crowds can be intimidating, and the horses need to be able to take it in stride. Since the 17th century, when the Household Cavalry was formed, there have been special horses chosen to represent the royal family and to protect and serve. When you think about it, it is pretty incredible.

~February 17~
The Playful Beast

When I think about our boarding stable and the horses that my husband and I have had the privilege of caring for throughout the years, certain horses always come to mind as the "players" at our barn. Some horses are happy leading a quiet life while others are the instigators of roughhousing and mischief. What is so nice about owning and caring for horses in the 21st century is that most horses today have a pretty easy life compared to the horses of the past. Even if they competed heavily on the show circuit or came off the track, by the time they are sold to new owners and make it to our stable, their lives have changed dramatically, and watching their playful side come to life is a wonderful thing to witness.

With the horse now being used for entertainment and less the beast of burden, the softer and funnier side of the equine has been allowed to blossom. Horses have always been social animals since the beginning of time, but they also needed to survive, and many of them were just trying to find food, water, and rest while enduring their situations.

Today we can appreciate the horse and how they communicate with each other. You have to wonder what they were saying to each other during times of war, throughout the ages. We can learn so much about the horse if we just take the time to watch them in their herds doing what horses do, which is eating, resting, grooming, playing, fighting and even pooping! There is a wealth of information to learn just by observing them. They are a very gregarious animal, and when everything lines up right in their life, along with plenty of hay, water, shelter, and safe surroundings, that is when the playful beast immerges, or should I say, it sure does for the geldings!

So today, I encourage you to grab a chair and bottled water, sit outside your horse's paddock and enjoy the show. There is nothing more beautiful than watching a horse just be a horse.

~February 18~
The Riderless Horse

To watch a horse being led in a funeral procession with a saddle on his back and riding boots facing backward in the stirrups, is something that most will never forget. In some ways, it's eerie and majestic at the same time. It is a beautiful symbol and a way to honor the person who served our country well. When did this tradition begin? It is mentioned that during the reign of Genghis Khan (1206-1227), a riderless horse was led to the burial site and sacrificed to be buried with his deceased owner. Thank goodness some traditions die out for the horse's sake!

Today we use a horse called the Caparisoned horse because he follows the Caissons (6-horses pulling the wagon and casket) with the boots facing backward to present a picture and symbolize the image of a fallen leader looking back on his troops for the last time. This American tradition began with our first President, George Washington when he died. Since Washington, many Presidents' caskets have been followed by the riderless horse. In our present day, it is also done for fallen police officers and military who are a colonel or higher in rank. It is a symbol of a rider that will ride no more, and it is emotional to witness.

The riderless horse is called to duty, not ever knowing the emotions he will stir up as he walks slowly behind the casket with his handler. He knows he needs to be quiet, calm, and listen to his cues from the person leading him, but he will never know the impact he will leave on the hearts of so many. To be chosen as a riderless horse for the death of a police officer, military person, or President will be an honor only bestowed upon that one special horse.

"Wherever man has left his footprints in the long ascent from barbarism to civilization, we find the hoofprints of a horse beside it."
~John Trotwood Moore

~February 19~
Merlin

Bullfighting is a sport that has been going on for centuries in Spain. It is a harsh and even cruel competition that involves a Matador who rides a horse into an arena with the goal of killing the bull who is waiting for him. It is not an easy sport to watch, and often the horse is gored in the game, which ultimately ends his life. But once in a while, you come across a story that has to be told because it shows the sheer loyalty a horse has for his rider under the harshest of situations.

Merlin was born a strong Lusitano colt, and as destiny would have it, he would follow a long line of bullfighting horses. Lusitano horses are possibly the oldest saddle horses in the world. The origins are from Portugal, but the breed is closely related to the Spanish Andalusian horse. As a stallion, he was brave and very smart, and his trainer saw something exceptional in the young horse. Merlin was fearsome and had the strength and athletic ability to move in exact precision of what he was asked without hesitation, which is vital for the sport of bullfighting, and he seemed to do it with ease. It was as if he knew what the bull was going to do before his rider.

What made Merlin famous would ultimately free him from the life of a bullfighting horse. During one particular bullfighting competition in front of thousands of people, Merlin was in the arena, and the matador had dismounted to fight the bull. Suddenly Merlin turned and aggressively attacked the bull to protect the Matador. It was something that had never been witnessed before and it changed the course of life for this brave stallion. Merlin became a hero overnight and his bullfighting days came to a complete halt. He would never again go into a bullfighting ring. He now enjoys his days hanging around mares and greeting the people who travel from all over to see the very courageous horse.

~February 20~
Milk Delivery

It may have been the 1950's, but many towns and cities were still delivering milk by the old-fashioned horse and wagon. The milk delivery horse had an essential role in history as these trusted equines have brought milk to people's homes in the cities and suburbs for nearly two hundred years.

The horses that were trained to pull a milk delivery wagon started their day long before most people got up. They would be fed very early in the morning and then brushed and hitched up at the crack of dawn to begin their delivery routes. Often these horses were stabled at the processing facility that produced the milk fresh each day, and the driver would go there early in the morning to get the horse or team ready for the daily deliveries. The horses knew their routes so well they could walk the route while the driver did his paperwork or even dozed off on the long country roads. They made the same turns on the same streets, and stopped at the same houses or apartments, and it didn't matter what the weather was like—the milk was delivered. The driver would grab the milk bottles out of the wagon and deliver them to each house while the horse walked slowly down the street unattended. The seasoned horse knew exactly what to do, and the driver hardly ever had to grab the reins.

In the colder states, where snow and ice were part of the wintertime landscape, milk delivery horses would often pull a large sleigh carrying the milk. This was often more dangerous on hills and when the roads were icy. Many of the horses had metal pegs on their shoes (these act like cleats on the shoe) to help the horse grip the icy roads. There was something very special about the delivery of fresh milk in a bottle to your doorstep each morning, and the clickety-clack sound of hooves going down the road made a person feel like everything was alright in the world.

~February 21~
The Bedouin Legend

From around 1500 BC, the Bedouin nomadic people of the Arabian Desert are said to be the original breeders of the refined Arabian horse that exists today. These horses adapted to their desert environment quite well, and most became warhorses for the tribes. The Bedouin people became extremely close with their horses, and often, the horses would sleep in the family tents to keep out of the harsh desert weather, but sleeping in the tents served a greater purpose—it prevented horse stealing.

It is said that the horses that lived in the same tents as their masters formed incredibly strong bonds with the people they lived and ate with. On top of it, many horses had greater family status than the children of the tribes! What was most unusual to the Bedouin people was that the mares were of greater value than the stallions, and the mares took priority in almost everything. Also, as a warhorse, mares were requested more often for riding into battle because they were believed to be extremely fierce. To be given a gift of an Arabian stallion was wonderful, but a gift of an Arabian mare was the greatest gift a Bedouin could receive.

According to a legend, after a very long journey in the sweltering hot desert, a Bedouin tribe released their mares to get water at a watering hole. To test the horses' loyalty, a horn was blown to call them back to their masters without getting a drink of water. They watched as only five mares out of many turned around and came back without ever drinking the water. Each of these loyal mares was given a unique name that would carry to each of their foals. These mares would be known as Al Kahmsa, which translates as "the five" and signifies purity of the bloodline for these Arabian horses.

And God took a handful of southerly wind, blew His breath upon it, and created the horse. ~Bedouin Legend

~February 22~
Jim Key

When he looked at the homely orphaned foal, he decided to name him Jim and give him his last name. The colt quickly became very attached to his owner, a former slave known as "Doc" William Key, who was a self-trained veterinarian. The colt wouldn't leave Doc's side and followed him everywhere. William Key was well known for his "horse whispering" and gentle hands on the horses he cared for at his clinic.

As Jim Key grew up, Doc noticed that the horse seemed to be exceptionally smart. After trying a few things with Jim, he realized that he could do math problems, spell names and even retrieve a coin from a glass jar filled with water. He could tell time, and sort mail, and skeptical audiences could give Jim instructions, and he would do the task without Doc giving any signals. Jim Key and his owner Doc soon became famous and started traveling about the country performing for people from all walks of life. Jim was billed as "The Smartest Horse in the World," but for Doc it was about so much more. Doc wanted to teach people to be kind to animals during a time when animals were often treated harshly. With Jim's popularity, Doc now had a platform to share his knowledge and love for all animals. He especially loved to bring Jim to perform in front of children, for they were the next generation of horse owners. Jim Key had a huge impact on many people of all ages. As many as two million children signed the pledge, "I promise always to be kind to animals and other sentient beings," and they also joined the "Jim Key Band Of Mercy." Doc and his horse, Jim Key, were a remarkable team, and together they taught the world so much during a time when it was desperately needed.

A great horse will change your life; the truly special ones will define it.
~Author Unknown

~February 23~
Deep Scars

Endurance racing has come a long way since the earliest recorded competitions. Unfortunately, the early years of racing were often extremely cruel and inhumane for the horses that were forced to run them. The earliest endurance racing competitions have left deep scars that are not easily forgotten. But it is important to read about the past, no matter how bad, so that the future of the sport and the care of the horses can be greatly improved.

In 1892, one of the most competitive rides in history had just finished in Europe. German and Austrian officers rode 360 miles in a race known as the Distanzritt (distance ride). Approximately 200 horses started the race, but by the end, 25 horses had died. Morphine was given to many of the horses to keep them going. One horse broke down but kept on for another 74 hours, allegedly under the influence of a narcotic. The winner in Berlin was an Austrian count who crossed the finish line only to have his horse drop dead. He had ridden his horse 360 miles in 71 hours.

In the United States, Buffalo Bill heard about the race and came up with the idea of the 1000-mile race to prove that cow ponies could outrun the European horses. Then in 1868, four men rode two horses (two men were on each horse) in a race from Brighton to Worcester in Massachusetts. The length of the race was 40 miles long and they never stopped once for food or water, and the horses were forced to run the entire distance. Both horses died. This race is what finally woke people up to the inhumane treatment of horses. Massachusetts soon passed its first animal protection laws and other states quickly followed. Times have changed, and the world of endurance racing is now very well-monitored by equine veterinarians and board members. Their primary goal and objective is to make sure the horses stay healthy throughout the entire race. Thankfully some things get better with time.

~February 24~
Nelson & Blueskin

George Washington had two beloved horses he rode throughout the Revolutionary War. It is said that his favorite was Nelson, a chestnut horse with white socks and blaze, who was born around the year 1763. In 1778, a friend named Thomas Nelson learned that Washington was having trouble finding a new mount to replace his horse. Thomas Nelson gifted him the chestnut horse, and Washington fondly named the horse Nelson. Nelson was 15 years old when he was sent to Mt. Vernon, Washington's home.

Washington preferred to ride Nelson rather than his other favorite horse, Blueskin (the grey horse that is portrayed in so many paintings with Washington praying), because Nelson was less skittish during cannon fire or the sounds of guns going off. Blueskin instead was often ridden for ceremonies and other appointments. Washington also chose to ride Nelson on the day the British army surrendered at Yorktown in 1781.

After returning to civilian life, both Nelson and Blueskin were retired from service. It is said that Nelson and Blueskin were never to be ridden again in thanks for their service. Blueskin had also been a gift to Washington, and after living at Mt. Vernon for some time, was returned to his original owner. Nelson became somewhat of a celebrity at Mt. Vernon as people would visit and want to see the famous horse. Washington's affections for Nelson were very evident to anyone who knew him. Washington would walk the grounds of his farm often, and when Nelson saw him, even in his senior years, he would nicker and run to him. Nelson died in the best of care in 1790 at Mt. Vernon at the old age of 27.

I had rather be on my farm, than be emperor of the world.
~George Washington

~February 25~
Warhorses Missing

During and after the Revolutionary War, horses often broke loose from their encampment or were stolen. During the 1770's, you would find many ads, along with rewards, in newspapers from men trying to retrieve their horses. It was much different than trying to retrieve your lost car! Here are a few examples, quoted exactly as they were written back then.

"Twenty Dollar Reward. Strayed or Stolen out of a pasture in Upper Makefield Township, Bucks County, in the night of the 18th of August. A brown horse, about 15 hands high, said to be nine years old. His mane is thick and bushy, and hangs to the near side, his tail has been set, and the hair at the end bob'd square off, shod before, is an imported horse, did formerly belong to the British light dragoons, and is a natural trotter."

"Strayed from the encampment of the 38th regt. on the 23rd. A dark bay mare, black mane and tale, her head sore, about 14 hands high, in good order, and trots all. Whoever will give intelligence of the said mare to Capt. Norman, 38th regt. or to the printer hereof, so that she may be found, shall receive a guinea reward. The New York Gazette, August 25, 1777."

"Three Guineas Reward. Stolen or strayed from Bedford Camp, about the middle of August, a bright Bay Mare, about 14 hands and a half high, with a small blaze on her forehead, and D.37th marked upon her left buttock, near the tail. Also a dark brown Mare, strong made near 13 hands and an half high, with a very large blaze in her forehead, both being the property of an Officer in the 37th regiment. Any person producing the above Mares, or giving information where they may be found, on applying to the Printer, shall receive the above reward. New York Loyal Gazette, September 23, 1778."

"A Bay Mare Marked T. M. 35th Regiment. It is requested, that the Officer who lately was at Mr. Burrough's, New-Town, Long-Island, with a Young Bay Mare, marked T. M. No. 35 on her back, will please to send her directly to Lieut. Murray, 35th, at Brooklyne-Ferry, as she is his property, and to prevent further trouble. Royal Gazette (New York), 30 May 1778."

~February 26~
Snow & Mud

For the people who lived in the northern climates where heavy snow turned to mud in the springtime, it was realized very quickly that the workhorses had a tough time trudging through the landscape since their legs and hooves would sink deep down into the snow and mud. Man has used snowshoes for thousands of years on smaller pack horses, but now they would try using larger snowshoes on their draft horses. The hardest part would be training the horses to walk with the large and very awkward wooden or metal frames tied to their hooves. There were books and articles written as early as the 1500's regarding snowshoes on horses.

One of the first known articles was written in 1565, describing how to put snowshoes and mudshoes on horses when needed. It explained how to place each individual hoof over a larger area to keep them from sinking into the deep snow or mud.

In 1888, James Mason Hutchings wrote in his book "In the Heart of the Sierras," a piece regarding snowshoes. *"Concerning the snowshoes...Each animal seems to have an intuitive knowledge of what they are for, as of the duties expected of them; for, carefully lifting the foot higher than he would under normal circumstances".*

In 1891, another article was written about horses and snowshoes, which said, *"They wore the ordinary Canadian snowshoes, oval in shape, and rather small. At first the horses were awkward with them; but after a time they learned the trick of spreading their feet apart, and seemed to understand the purpose of the unusual hoof gear."*

In 1872, the lumber and mattress-making businesses in Canada used marsh hay in many of their products. Horses wore wooden snowshoes strapped to their front feet while harvesting hay to prevent them from sinking into the marsh. It was exhausting work for the horses, especially with the wet soil and the large awkward wooden snowshoes they were forced to wear.

~February 27~
World War One

World War One was called the first modern war with technology that had not been used in previous wars. With the invention of the motorcycle and vehicle, one would think that the horse would be obsolete for use as a warhorse, but that couldn't be farther from the truth. Vehicles and motorcycles were in sparse supply considering the large number of men and supplies that needed to be transported. The horse's job was not over by a far cry, and the logistics of each army would have come to a halt without the strength of the horse.

The horses were responsible for carrying soldiers, moving ammunition, supplies, heavy artillery and, of course, the wounded. The supplies and artillery were extremely heavy, and a single gun could require 6 to 12 horses to move it. The massive number of horses needed for the war was staggering and proved to be very difficult to meet for both sides of the war. The British imported as many as one million horses from the United States and more from New Zealand and other countries. The conditions faced by the horses in the war were horrific. Many died of starvation, disease, exhaustion, and artillery fire. The British alone recorded 400,000 horses killed during the war, and tragically only one horse out of 136,000 returned to his homeland of Australia after the war.

Britain's Army Veterinary Corps included 27,000 men and 1,300 veterinary surgeons. The hospitals received over 750,000 injured horses to treat or euthanize during the war. Most did not make it. We owe so much to these horses that were not given a choice but faced the battle head on with courage and a willing heart.

Lord, if we should stumble, my horse and I, please pick him up first for he has carried me through heaven and hell. ~Author Unknown

~February 28~
The Arabian

When you mention the Arabian horse, no other description needs to be added for a person to develop a picture in their mind of the breed. The Arabian horse is definitely set apart in looks and origin, and the Arabian has been the seed of many breeds of horses throughout the centuries. The truth is, the Arabian horse has helped build the horses of today, and it all began somewhere between 2400 and 4000 years ago. There have been many cave drawings from thousands of years ago that depict the small defined body, the dished nose and muzzle, the short back, pointed ears and refined head.

Bedouin nomadic tribesmen were the first breeders of the Arabian horse. They roamed the deserts of the Middle East and became expert horsemen. Breeding outstanding horses was crucial to their survival and prosperity, and only the finest Arabian stallions and mares were allowed to reproduce. The Bedouin tribes kept strict records of certain bloodlines to make sure they were passed down to the next generation of horses, and every caution was taken to ensure stallions and mares were not mixed with horses of a lesser quality. Bedouins prized Arabian mares above all possessions. Mares were preferred and carried their masters into battle, and were revered for great courage, stamina, and loyalty to their owner. The Arabian mare was the greatest gift a man could receive, and the value of the mare was done through the tracing of the lineage on the mare's side—not the stallion.

In the United States, the Arabian Horse Association was established in 1908, and interest in these fiery horses exploded during the Chicago World's Fair when 45 Arabian horses were brought in from Turkey for the public to see. The registry started with only 74 registered horses, and today, they have over half a million registered Arabian horses.

~March 1~
Rex

The date was Saturday, June 2, 1923, and it was just another work day for the miners and Rex, the pit pony. Rex was waiting to pull the heavy load like he had done thousands of times before when suddenly there was a huge explosion of dirt and rock crashing down everywhere. The mine shaft was caving in and closed the hole completely, cutting off all access to the outside world. Three miners and Rex were trapped forty feet below. Many long hours went by, and the men could hear the drilling above and prayed they would be rescued before the gases killed them. A small pipe had been pushed through all the dirt and stone to reach the men. Soup was fed through the pipe and corn was dropped down for Rex, but the corn ended up clogging the pipe, so the men instead shared their soup with the pony. After three long days, the hole was finally large enough for the miners bodies to fit, and slowly they were hoisted to the top. The last man to crawl to safety looked back to see if he could see Rex. All he could hear was his soft whinny.

Safety engineers found that the shaft was too dangerous and unstable and decided to leave Rex to his fate. But soon there was a huge outcry from the town for Rex to be rescued at any risk, and the rescue effort went forward. Using a corn shredding machine with a blower and traction engine, fresh air was forced down the shaft for the pony. A larger pipe was inserted into the mine so children could drop food to Rex and talk to him. More than a dozen men worked on the hole, and finally, on June 12, they were able to reach Rex. It took seven more days to widen the opening so that the pony could be brought up. After 255 hours underground by himself, a miner went down to Rex and yelled up that he was alive! He put Rex into a leather sling and he was slowly hoisted to the top. He was alive and doing pretty well, considering his last ten days!

~March 2~
Seine Fishing

Commercial horse seining (a type of fishing) on the Columbia River played a vital role in the area's economy from the 1890's through the 1940's. Native Americans along the Columbian River used hand-operated seines to catch a large amount of fish at one time. A fish seine is a horizontal net with floats, which holds the line of the net at the water's surface. The net extends down in the water and then the weighted line can be pulled so that the net acts like a purse to catch Salmon and other fish. This was a successful way of catching large amounts of fish for the Native Americans, but it was also very tough physical work.

In 1895, a man by the name of R.D. Hume refined the technique by using horses to haul the seines. At the time, a total of 84 seines were being used, but the number increased to 100 by the 1920's with the help of the horse. A horse seine crew could employ from two to forty people and use up to seven teams of horses. The preferred heavy horse was usually the Clydesdales and Percherons. The fishermen would fish with seines only when the water was low enough that they would be able to bring the horses in safely. If the water became too deep where it was up to their chests and stomachs, they would lose all their pulling power. Then slowly, the horses would be directed to pull the fish-filled nets to shore. It was hard work for the horses and it took several horses to pull in one net.

In 1948, the horse seines came to an end as they were outlawed by what some called a "political" initiative petition in Oregon. Today on the Columbian River, you can still see a remnant of the floating horse barns in the water that could house over a dozen horses at a time. A way of life using horses to help in fishing had ended, even though this practice of using horsepower for fishing is still used in a few remote areas of the world today.

~March 3~
Hawaii

The horse was soon found in most civilizations throughout the world, but one of the most beautiful places on earth had to have the horses shipped in by boat. It was the Hawaiian Islands, and it was paradise for both man and horse. In 1793, Captain George Vancouver brought cattle on ships to the Big Island of Hawaii. King Kamemeha was so impressed with these new animals, that he placed a "Kapu" (taboo) on the slaughtering of cattle for ten years so they could multiply. Within a decade, large numbers of wild cattle were roaming the slopes of the Big Island, and the beef industry had begun.

In 1803, the first horses came to Hawaii. King Kamehameha was given a horse as a gift from an American trader named Richard Cleveland. Twenty years later, in 1823, saw the introduction of the first Mexican/Spanish vaqueros who became known as the Hawaiians cowboys, also called "Paniolo." Cattle ranching by this time had become a huge industry and the vaqueros taught the native Hawaiians how to ride, handle a horse, and rope, and soon the Hawaiians were becoming Paniolos for the cattle ranches. The horses that were brought to the island flourished and multiplied in the vast lush grassland valleys. The horse herds grew large, and many of the horses formed wild herds that still exist today.

In the Waipio Valley, "Valley of the Kings" on the Big Island, you will see the descendants of horses brought over by ship in 1803. Today the working cattle and horse ranches still exist and produce much of the beef for the Hawaiian Islands. You can also rent horses and ride through beautiful trails and vegetation just like the Paniolo did when they first arrived in the 1800's. Horses are still shipped to the islands and you can now find many working breeds on the ranches.

Mālama Lio - "caring for the horse."

~March 4~
Medical Advancements

The horse is a work of art that we can wrap our arms around and fall in love with every day. But the horse is more than just a pretty face! Equines have done so much for medical advancements, and it is definitely worth sharing how they have contributed in the medical field for the benefit of human health.

Horses helped cure Diphtheria and Toxic Bacillary Dysentery by producing an antiserum to the bacteria's toxins. In 1888, it was discovered that man could replicate the symptoms of a disease when it was injected into horses. The bacterium responsible for diphtheria worked well in the study, and in 1891 an antiserum to the toxin (known as an antitoxin) was developed while protecting the horses. Production of the antitoxin was soon achieved on a large scale using horses, which resulted in saving millions of children.

Both HIV (human immunodeficiency virus) and HPV (human papillomavirus) were discovered due to the research into similar viruses in horses. Lentiviruses, the class of retroviruses which include HIV, were known to cause diseases affecting the immune system in the early 1900's in which horses were used for the studies.

The Heart Catheterization was first developed in 1861 using horses! It was first thought to be an impossible idea because it would cause severe damage to the vessel. But through testing and trials, success followed with the help of the horse.

The study of animal cell lines and cell cultures, and the production of normal and cancerous tissues in horses allowed the discovery of reverse transcriptase—a viral enzyme that produces DNA from an RNA template. These studies between horses and humans have led directly to developing a recent vaccine for cervical cancer. By using horses, scientists could start understanding how tumor viruses work.

~March 5~
They Never Forget

Horses are beautiful and perfectly designed in so many ways. We love every square inch of our equine partners, and get all choked up if they nicker to us. We smile when we see them standing by the fence looking straight at us as we drive into the stable, and our heart skips a beat when our horse makes his way to the gate while the others stay back. It makes us feel like we have bonded with them and they haven't forgotten about us or who we are. The truth is they haven't!

A 2010 study on the horse's memory came up with some incredible information about their intelligence and memory. Not only do horses understand our words better than we initially thought, but they will remember if we have been kind to them or treated them harshly. If a person treats their horse with gentle hands, they will remember that person even if they are separated from that human for years. Horses also remember places very well, and if a particular place or situation (like a bad trailering experience) has happened to them, they will do their best to let you know that it makes them nervous.

The combination of a good memory and smart intellect can also be the perfect combination for a horse to get itself into compromising situations. They watch and learn how to open gates, unlatch stall doors and get themselves into situations that they need help getting out of. If you are the proud owner of one of these intelligent equines who knows how to open his stall door or gate—watch out! He will keep you busy for years to come and you will learn many new ways to secure everything at your stable. What an awesome blessing!

Horses forgive, but they never forget.

~March 6~
The Artillery Horse

Although the earliest relationship between man and horse was built primarily on the necessity to win battles, the horse was still a willing servant no matter what he was asked to do. With the invention of gunpowder, man began making larger and heavier artillery that needed to be moved to where the fighting was. That meant that the horse had a new and much more demanding job. He soon became harnessed to the artillery, and with that came a hardship like he had never known before.

As early as the Napoleonic Epoch, the horse was vital in moving field artillery close to the frontlines and then being able to quickly retreat at a moment's notice as the fighting went back and forth from offense to defense. The horses needed to be powerful and fast, but it was exhausting labor that often had horrific results. Moving heavy artillery with real horsepower would be the standard for the next few centuries until motorized vehicles came into play.

The massive number of horses needed for war created a unique challenge for the military. The horses had to be fed and watered, and replacement horses needed to be on hand when a horse was injured or killed (which was a constant). It was quickly realized that the artillery horse was an easy target, and if you took down the horses, then the artillery couldn't be moved. Sadly the life expectancy of an artillery horse was under eight months. The artillery horses suffered from disease and exhaustion, and it was typical for them to pull the heavy artillery up to 16 miles in a day, depending on how intense the fighting was. One of the biggest problems the military faced was the roads that were often wet and very muddy. The horses would sink down in the mud along with the artillery, and it became impossible at times, to get the horses or artillery out. Horses died right in their tracks as they collapsed from the work. Today we honor the faithful artillery horse.

~March 7~
Mustang

The Mustang is an American icon, and if you love horses, then it is worth learning about these beautiful equines that are woven deep into the fabric of the west. You can't think about the cowboy or Native American Indian without thinking about the Mustang horse. The word Mustang comes from the Spanish word Mesteno meaning "stray or ownerless" horse. The true Mustangs are directly related to the horses that Columbus brought over on his second voyage in 1493. Later in the 16th century, Spaniards, on their voyages to America and South America, brought many horses with them, but as horses escaped, they traveled and populated new areas. They came from the well-known Spanish horses of the time with a background of Jennet and Barb breeding. They were strong and full of stamina with strong Andalusian bloodlines. No other breed in the world at the time was more suited for what would evolve into the Mustang.

The first wave of wild horses originated in New Mexico and spread across lower Texas and the Great Plains. The swift spread of the wild horse herds began with the Pueblo Revolt of 1680, where the Native Indians fought off the European invaders. The early Mustangs were changing a culture and landscape quickly. Before the horse, the Native Indians traveled and hunted on foot. The distance they could travel was limited, but once they learned to tame and ride these horses, they could travel miles to hunt for food, and they became great warrior with these animals. They quickly became one with the horse.

Mustangs are not technically "wild horses" because they are derived from domesticated breeds of horses. The Mustang horses living today are considered feral and they are extremely tough and hardy, and many still roam throughout the Midwest. To see a herd of Mustangs is to gaze upon perfection.

~March 8~
That Amazing Nose

It would be safe to say that even a horse's nose is beautiful in the eyes of a horse lover. It is amazing how their huge nose and nostrils can detect the tiniest of mint candies when put in the palm of your hand. What I didn't know when I was writing this book was how good of a "smeller" horses actually have.

If you have been around horses long enough, then you know how frustrating it can be when you try to hide their medicine in molasses grain or applesauce, and they turn their nose up at it and then give you those disappointed eyes. Most of us have been there a time or two. Horses can smell much better than humans and use their nose along with their eyes to size up their humans and other people who might come near them. They use their nose to smell other horses, and when they smell the scent of another strange animal, they will stop dead in their tracks with eyes and ears forward on high alert. Stallions have the most heightened sensitivity to smell (sorry geldings!), and they can smell when a mare is in heat from far away. Horses will also react with an upper lip curl that makes them look like they are smiling, but they are just reacting to a strong or pungent smell. Sometimes a horse might react to a strange smell with fear if he cannot identify if the scent is friendly or dangerous to him.

So now, when you look at your horse and see his long nose and adorable muzzle, just remember that he has smelled you coming long before you had time to take in that wonderful horse smell we all love so much! He's got your scent, and in some weird way it makes me feel good to know that my scent makes him feel safe. Happiness does have a smell!

All of creation testifies to the power and presence of God.

~March 9~
Snowman

It was the early 1950's, and the tractor had quickly replaced horse-drawn farm equipment for farmers across the country. Most of the 25 million horses and mules that had been used for farm work were now out of a job. Many were sold privately, but unfortunately, many were taken to auctions where their next trailer ride would take them to the slaughterhouse. Such was the fate of one flea-bitten grey gelding.

It was a cold, snowy day when the gelding was loaded up on the truck, waiting to head for the slaughterhouse at only eight years old. The auction was over and no one wanted the horse. On that same day, Harry de Leyer drove off from the horse stable in Long Island, New York, to the same horse auction in New Holland, Pennsylvania, hoping to find inexpensive lesson horses. He got to the auction late due to vehicle problems and the auction was over. He asked someone if he could see the horses that were loaded on the truck headed to the slaughterhouse. De Leyer looked at the sad-looking horses and spotted the dirty grey gelding. After looking into his eyes and noticing something special, he bought the horse for eighty dollars, and named him Snowman.

Snowman quickly became a lesson horse and had a very gentle spirit, but most of all, De Leyer found out that Snowman loved to jump. The higher the rails, the more the horse seemed to love it. Just two years later, in 1958, Snowman was named the United States Equestrian Federation Horse of the Year, Professional Horseman's Association champion, and Madison Square Garden's Diamond Jubilee Grand Champion. The following year, Snowman achieved the impossible by returning to Madison Square Garden and winning the Open Jumper Championship for the second year in a row, beating out $100,000 dollar Thoroughbreds. Snowman became known as the eighty-dollar champion.

~March 10~
The Horse Action Saddle

The horse has inspired man to do the greatest of accomplishments, but the horse has also been the inspiration for some crazy inventions and propaganda that helped make some people very rich along the way. One of these inventions was the Vigor's Horse Action Saddle! Horatio Vigor invented the Action Saddle around 150 years ago, and it would change the world of indoor exercise forever. You can say it was the original home fitness machine. The wooden Horse Action Saddle simulated riding a horse and it could be adjusted to the different gaits of a horse, from walk to fast gallop! It was a wooden frame with springs inside, handlebars in front to hang onto, and "stirrups" that were the push peddles to make the contraption work. On top of the wooden box was a leather saddle that both men and women could sit on.

The invention may have been unique, but it was the marketing of the Horse Action Saddle that was truly amazing. It appears this saddle cured everything! Marketing posters claimed it "invigorated the system by bringing all the vital organs into inspiring action." The ads claimed it was a "Complete cure for obesity, hysteria, and gout and worked directly with the circulation and prevented stagnation of the liver!" It seems this wooden horse machine cured everything. The ads also mentioned "Open all windows when exercising for safety," which was the funniest part of all. Drawings of a man or woman finely dressed in formal attire sitting on the wooden horse exercising, appeared in all the printed ads, and the ads worked. People purchased the Horse Action Saddle for better health! The saddle was available for purchase, and it was also rentable in Mr. Vigor's gym in London. You could purchase an English saddle for men that came attached to the machine or a sidesaddle for women who wanted an "invigorating experience." No more words needed!

~March 11~
Guns A Blazing

When it comes to mounted shooting on horseback, it's easy to think about the old western movies where you had the good guys and the bad guys, and they would shoot it out while sitting on their horses. Now think of yourself riding a 1200-pound horse and blazing through a course, shooting up everything in sight!

Today, mounted shooting is a growing sport where both men and women compete while riding their horses and shooting at different objects in an arena while galloping as fast as possible. For many, it is an adrenaline rush. Mounted shooting is a sport that combines elements of an old-time Wild West Show along with the aspects of pole bending, barrel racing, reining, and other equestrian skills. This is all done while using two .45 caliber single action revolvers loaded with five rounds each of black powder blanks, to shoot balloon targets that are set in a special pattern or Old West type scenario called a "stage." There are many different patterns in competition depending on your skill level.

What about the horses? The majority of horses used for mounted shooting are of stock type, but Quarter Horses are often preferred. A good shooting horse has speed and athleticism, but it also needs to be calm and completely broke. For most classes, you're holding the reins with one hand and shooting a revolver with the other. If you're in the rifle class, you drop the reins entirely and guide your horse with your legs while shooting. Then there is the noise factor. Some horses never get over the sound of the gun going off, and those are the horses that are better suited for a different, quieter sport. When you find a horse that doesn't get bothered by the loud shots being fired and balloons being busted, then you have a keeper! Those horses are worth their weight in gold. When they say horses need to be bomb-proof in mounted shooting, they really mean it!

~March 12~
Endurance Racing Today

Endurance racing has come a long way from the 1800's when the horse's health and well-being were not considered by many of the riders, which led to horrific outcomes for many of the horses. Thank goodness those days are behind us, and worldwide, endurance racing is more popular than ever, keeping the horse's health and care a top priority during a race.

What makes endurance racing so unique is that there are different lengths of races depending on what you and your horse feel comfortable with. You can go slow and take your time or be extremely competitive and race to win. Either way, you get to see the amazing landscape all around you as you ride, and also meet some pretty nice equestrians and make new friends along the way. The best part above anything else is the time you spend with your horse on the trail. It will create a bond that is unbreakable.

The breed of horse that has excelled in this type of competition has always been the Arabian. It was as if they were created for this sport, and they seem to thrive on it. The Arabian horse is known not only for its grace and beauty but also great stamina in traveling long distances. Prized by the Bedouin people thousands of years ago, their adaptations for desert life make them well suited for modern-day distance events.

The American Mustang has endured natural selection, making them an excellent choice for endurance racing. Because they breed naturally out in the wild, strong traits are favored and passed on. In 2018, two Mustangs finished in the top 10 in the Tevis Cup Endurance Race. MM Cody and MM Woodrow finished 8th and 9th respectively while the 7 top placements were held by Arabians.

The beauty of today's endurance competition is that anybody can ride, and it doesn't matter what breed of horse you enter. What matters the most is that you have fun and enjoy the ride!

~March 13~
Spanish Riding School

The Spanish Riding School in Vienna, Austria, has a colorful history and in the middle of all it is the Lipizzaner horses. The idea of riding the horse in a way that would bring out his greatest beauty, strength, and bravery was slowly coming into man's thoughts back in Roman times, but warfare always took priority, and the need for fast horses took precedence over the finesse of proper riding. The birth of the Spanish Riding School dates back to the 16th century. The need for proper riding instruction for the military came about because soldiers now carried firearms.

The earliest training facility for the military was a wooden Spanish riding hall that, in the next few decades, grew (in-between the constant warfare of the time) into a larger and very formal training and riding stable called the Hoffberg Palace Complex. The complex provided a very prestige environment for the military.

The school was named for the Spanish horses that were highly desired. They were the Lipizzaner stallions. These beautiful horses were also known as the Imperial Whites and had the strength and personality to be trainable in the "art of riding." The horses used in the school needed to have powerful hind quarters to successfully make the jumps and movements that were asked of them.

The origin of these amazing white horses (they are born completely black!) goes back to the occupation of Spain by the Moors until 1492. The Moors did a lot of cross-breeding with Arabic and Iberian horses which developed into the powerful Spanish horses. It was soon discovered over the next hundred years that these Spanish horses had movements unlike the other horses of that time, and had the temperament and brains to pick up on their training easily. The Lipizzaner breed came out of the town of Lipizza, and in the 1580's, the Imperial Whites became the magnificent crown jewels of the Spanish Riding School.

~March 14~
The Wagon Train

For the settlers heading west in the 1800's, it was the dream of moving to new territory and starting a new life. But many would quickly learn that it was a hard and very dangerous way to travel. The wagon trains usually were pulled by horses, mules, or oxen and much would depend on the size of the wagon (Prairie Schooner) and the weight of the load. It was said that horses broke down the most during the long journeys, and the oxen had the easiest time pulling the heavy loads but were often unruly. Wagons trains could have up to 100 wagons following each other, and they did this for strength in numbers and protection while traveling through hostile territory. The wagon train could travel anywhere from 12 to 20 miles daily, depending on the terrain and weather. Each evening they would form a large circle so that they could keep their cattle and horses inside for safety, and it also created a barrier from human danger.

Captain John Baker led the first wagon train on May 1, 1841, to Brazos River, Texas, from Bell Buckle, Tennessee. The journey out west was often exhausting for the horses that pulled the wagons and many horses and people never reached their destinations. Often miscalculations in the trail maps, weather, sick or lame horses, thieves, and attacks by hostile people led to their sad fate.

Many wagon trains chose to travel north and south along the east coast. The Conestoga wagons were mainly used for traveling along the eastern trails and Canada due to the heaviness of the wagons. Each Conestoga wagon was pulled by four to six horses. At the time, the preferred breed was the Conestoga horse—named after the Conestoga tribe. These horses were gentle, strong, and could cover 12 to 14 miles a day with little trouble. The driver of the Conestoga wagon would usually drive the team by riding one of the rear horses or walking next to them.

~March 15~
Horses & Farming

By the 1900's, most farmers used draft horses for farm labor. The massive heavy horses plowed the fields for corn and oats, planted the crops, cultivated the fields, brought in the hay crop, and hauled manure and that was only the beginning of their jobs. Farms would not have been as successful without the help of the draft horses. By 1920, it is estimated that 25 million horses and mules were working on farms all across the United States.

The growing market for bigger farm equipment created a demand for stronger and larger horses to power the new and improved machinery that could cover more acres in less time. The horse, the farmer, and the machine became an unstoppable team out in the farm fields. Heavy draft horse breeding programs flourished in the late 1800's, and as the growing need for larger horses became essential, many saw a great financial opportunity in breeding draft horses for resale. During this time, many farms had more horses than people working, with each horse working an average of 600 hours per year. With the millions of horses being used on farms across the country, it was quickly discovered that there was a need to teach better equine care and education to farmers. Newly created agricultural and veterinary courses began educating farmers starting with the youth, which led to better breeding and care for the horses. The draft horses and farmers were now working larger fields which helped push and grow the economy all at the same time. The Percheron horse became a preferred draft breed of choice for farming due to their strength, size, and temperament. The Percheron got its name from the small French district of La Perche, which is in Normandy. In 1839, the Percheron was the first heavy draft breed to come to America and has remained one of the favorite draft breeds of all time.

"The wagon rests in winter, the sleigh in summer, the horse never."

~March 16~
The Wedding Gift

Historically, it was common for certain Native American tribes to give a horse as a wedding gift. When the groom gave the wife's parents a horse as a gift, it was a way of showing great honor to her family. It was also customary in many tribes for the man to provide a horse as payment for his bride. Though some traditions are no longer commonly practiced in modern Native American weddings, the giving of a horse as a gift is something that is still done in some wedding ceremonies across the country. The Sioux Indians took marriage and the value of the bride very seriously and it was typical of a Sioux man to offer between one and four horses to the father of the bride. On rare occasions, there have been circumstances where a Sioux man would offer up to 40 horses to the head of the family for his bride-to-be. In one remarkable occurrence, a Sioux man offered 100 horses to the father of the girl he wanted to marry!

In Mongolian tradition, when a man wanted to marry a woman, he would have two men ride out on white horses to talk to the young woman's family on behalf of the young man. Once they shared the intention of the possible groom-to-be with the family, they would leave and wait for the family to decide on the future of their daughter. If the family said yes, then the couple was now betrothed. Then the groom would send many betrothal gifts to the family over the coming weeks, but the most precious gift of all would be a white horse bearing a Khadag (sacred scarf) wrapped around his neck.

Trying to visualize the immense value of the horse in different cultures throughout the centuries can be challenging since we are only familiar with the modern-day conveniences we use today. But before the motorized vehicle, the horse would have been one of the most valued gifts a couple could receive because the horse made everything easier for the family to exist.

~March 17~
The 80-1 Longshot

If you are lucky, you will get to witness something beyond great in horse racing once in your life. For me, it happened while I was writing this book. The colt's name is Rich Strike, and he was the second longest shot in history to win the 148th Kentucky Derby on May 7, 2022. His odds were 80-1.

It was the first time in over two years that the stands at the Derby were completely full since the pandemic. The atmosphere was electrifying because life felt normal again and the country was trying to get back on its feet. Most people watching and placing bets anticipated the favorite horse to win. Except for one thing, the favorite horse didn't win, and the second longest shot in history won the race. What makes this horse racing story so much better is that it is truly a great underdog story.

Rich Strike was born on April 25, 2019. After two years of training, the horse showed no potential as he had lost all his races. He finally was put in a $30,000 maiden claiming race and was claimed by an Oklahoma businessman who had become disheartened by the racing industry, but wanted to give it one more shot. The colt's training changed dramatically in the first few months and he started to run with some real speed.

Rich Strike wasn't on the list to race in the Kentucky Derby, but D. Lukas scratched his horse just a few minutes before the closing bell on Friday morning. Rich Strike was entered just thirty seconds before the deadline. He was set to race on a jockey who had never ridden in the Derby, and a trainer that had never had a horse in the Derby. Rich Strike didn't know he was an 80-1 longshot. All he knew was what he was born to do, and that was run fast. He ran fast and gave his all and Rich Strike beat the top horses in a very fast field and will go down in racing history as the horse that proved nothing is impossible if you are just given a chance.

~March 18~
Jigitovka

For centuries, the Cossack military guarded the border areas of Russia. They were excellent horsemen and courageous warriors who handled a saber with great skill while sitting atop their warhorses. Today, the Cossack's fighting abilities are not needed in battle, but they have kept their military and horsemanship traditions alive through their performances.

The Cossacks are known for exceptional trick riding skills known as Jigitovka, meaning "skillful and brave rider." Jigitovka turned the Cossack rider into a powerful and deadly attack weapon. The Cossack warrior didn't think of his horse as a means of transport but instead a fellow warrior and trusted friend. Napoleon Bonaparte once said, "With just the Cossacks alone, I could conquer Europe." According to the 1899 Cossack service regulation, Jigitovka was mandatory for each Cossack to master because it developed courage and expertise in riding and warfare. It was even adopted by the Red Army cavalry in the 1920's.

After the Civil War ended many Cossacks who had fought the Communists were forced to flee the country, and many settled in Europe and United States. There, they showed off their horseback riding skills in performances as a way to earn money. Jigitovka quickly became popular in the U.S. and took root, and soon, they were performing at many rodeos as early as the 1920's. Soon, other venues across the country were also requesting them to perform.

In Russia, Jigitovka disappeared with the cavalry's dissolution in the 1950's. Still, Jigitovka lives on in sporting events and performances with the traditions of the Cossack regiments. The Azerbaijani Karabakh horses are famous in Russia for being the mounts used in Jigitovka. These horses are strong, steady, and have a wonderful temperament making them ideal for the complex riding maneuvers they perform.

~March 19~
The Games As We Know Them

In 1896, the Equestrian Olympic Games really took shape and developed into the modern day games involving the horse and rider. Equestrian competition made its debut in the modern Olympic Games in 1900 in Paris, France. The original riding disciplines in the Olympics were Polo, Grand Prix Jumping, High Jump, and the Long Jump. The High Jump competition was scored by the height at which the horse and rider jumped. The Long Jump competition involved the length at which the horse and rider could jump. The winning horse and rider cleared the distance of 20 feet!

The equestrian events disappeared for the next two Olympic Games as it was felt there was not enough interest. But they came back revamped at the 1912 Stockholm Games, where new equestrian events were added, and others were taken off the lineup. Count Clarence Von Rosen, a Swedish Cavalry leader, and distinguished horsemen is credited for saving the equestrian events as he worked non-stop to get the new equestrian events added to the Olympics. That is when history was made and equestrians have never looked back. The new events added were Dressage, Show Jumping, and Eventing, which are the same events we watch today. The Long Jump, High Jump, and Vaulting were discontinued early on.

The Equestrian Olympic Games have gone through many transformations throughout the years. Every person has their preferred riding discipline and would love to see their sport entered as part of the Olympic lineup. Undoubtedly in the future, just like anything else, the equestrian sports we love today might be reinvented tomorrow with new ones added, or present disciplines discontinued. The one thing we can be sure of is that nothing ever stays the same. Who knows, maybe one day, Chariot racing will return!

~March 20~
The Roping Horse

One of the rodeo events that directly evolved from the cowboy's ranch duties was team roping. Cowboys would brag about how quickly they could rope a steer and brand it or help the animal if it was injured in some way. This boasting led to many informal competitions between cowboys in the early days of ranch life. Of course, the cowboy really should have been bragging about his horse, after all, he would have never caught the steer without his horse!

The history of team roping began when cattle were brought to the continental United States in 1521 by Spanish explorer Ponce de Leon. He delivered a small herd of cattle to Florida, and from there, they spread out west, and the cowboy's way of life was born. Back in the day, cowboys didn't have the luxury of electric fencing or cell phones to call other ranch hands. They depended solely on their horse and other cowboys who rode the long days with them. When an animal was injured, they had to catch it in order to help it. This meant the cowboy needed to rope the animal. This is where they relied heavily on their horse to stand firm and keep the rope tight, so that they could have some leverage against the animal.

The roping horse is vital to the cowboy, and his success is very much determined by his horse. Roping horses need to be very smart, agile, and naturally coordinated. These qualities make a great "header horse" because they must have the strength to pull the steer so that the cowboy in the heeler position has a chance at roping the hind legs. This all takes place within seconds, so the "heeler horse" must also be coordinated and able to move quickly and effectively. The breed that is often the best choice for a roping horse is the American Quarter Horse. The Quarter Horse is fast and has a great mind to do his job well. Once he learns his job as a header or healer roping horse, nothing can stop him.

~March 21~
Circuit Riding Preacher

Horses helped spread the gospel in the old days before preachers used automobiles. Horseback riding preachers were called circuit preachers or saddlebag preachers. The circuit preacher carried whatever he could in his saddlebags and often rode alone through dangerous territories throughout America. The circuit preacher was a much different profession than the city preacher, only because he was always moving from one town to the next while covering many miles in-between. It would often take five or six weeks to cover their route and this meant they needed a steady, surefooted, and very smooth horse to ride that could carry them the entire way, no matter the terrain.

In 1790, a very unique breed of horse was created in the state of Tennessee. It became known as the Tennessee Walking horse. The most noticeable characteristic of Tennessee Walkers is their very quick and smooth "running-walk." This gait is inherited and the horse does not possess it naturally, which means the gait cannot be taught. It's truly in their genes. When performing the running-walk these horses will overstride, placing the back hoof ahead of their front hoof print. Traveling at speeds from 6 to 12 miles per hour, Tennessee Walkers can sustain this gait for long distances without becoming tired. The Tennessee Walker is also known for a very smooth canter known as the "rocking chair gait." This horse quickly became popular with many people. Slave owners traveled miles each day on horseback, keeping watch over their land and slaves, and the preacher traveled far and wide to preach God's word, perform weddings and burial services, and whatever else the Lord called them to do. No one knew at the time how much impact the Tennessee Walking horse would have on spreading the good news of Jesus Christ!

It is God that arms me with strength and keeps my way secure. Psalm 18:32

~March 22~
Ancient Egyptian Horses

The Ancient Egyptian royalty thought of the horse as part of their royal household and not just an animal to use for daily work. They were symbols of royal authority and were often worshipped after they would return from a battle. Rameses II had two favorite horses he referred to as "Victory in Thebes" and "Mut is Pleased," which is found on a Kadesh inscription—a hieroglyphic depiction of the Battle of Kadesh. That is how much he loved his horses. The royal kings gave their horses names referring to ancient Egyptian gods. Even though horses were not associated with religion, they were raised to a heavenly level.

Horses were viewed as essential in ancient Egyptian warfare since they were used to draw chariots in battle. For many decades, a pharaoh and his warriors were the only ones that could afford horses. Their art and storytelling showed how valuable and loved the Egyptian horses were to the kings. After one particularly fierce battle, Rameses II was said to have informed his officers that his horses would be dining with him since his horses acted nobler and more courageous than his officers did in battle.

Acquiring and keeping horses in ancient Egypt was a difficult task since it was an environment where horses were not meant to thrive. The harsh climate meant that special stabling needed to be designed and built so the horses did not become stressed from the hot and dry desert. Pharaohs were able to provide the stables and means to take care of their horses, and a breeding program was put into place to increase the number of Egyptian horses, which would strengthen their kingdom. Horses were not native to Egypt, but the kings of Egypt quickly realized their immense value. Ancient Egyptian pharaohs kept horses as symbols of their wealth and power, and their favorite horses were often mummified with them in their tombs.

~March 23~
Mini-Me

It is surprising to think that the Miniature horse has roots that go back to the 17th century. Back then, the Miniature horse was looked at as an oddity by nobility and not a legitimate breed. But quickly people began to realize they could use them for many unique work jobs. Over the centuries, these little equines have been used as pit ponies, therapy horses, cart ponies, adorable mounts for small children, and even royal gifts.

The Miniature horse's origins follow the Shetland pony, but soon they were being bred with Hackney ponies to refine their movement and build, and also small Pinto horses for unique color patterns. Miniature horses are small and mighty with lots of personality to boot, and can only stand as tall as 34 inches for class A, and 38 inches for class B. Any taller and they would be considered a pony. The first mention of a little horse being brought to the United States was in 1888, and from there the numbers grew as they could be used for many new jobs. Fame came for these little equines when in 1962, Julio Cesar Falabella, whose ranch is near Buenos Aires, Argentina, sold some Miniature horses to President Kennedy's family. Since then, kings, nobility, celebrities, and common folk have also purchased these amazing little horses for their families to enjoy.

When I think of my daughter's Miniature horse, all I can do is smile. He is the mini-me of our full-size Paint horse, and he is adorable. He is now in his late-twenties and retired from horse shows. He is a little king in his paddock and he knows it! God had a sense of humor when he created the Miniature horse, and what joy these amazing little equines had given to so many over the centuries.

Finally, be strong in the Lord and in the strength of his might.
Ephesians 6:10

~March 24~
Bucephalus

Alexander the Great is well-known as a great conqueror, but his most cherished horse meant more to him than all his victories. That horse was Bucephalus, a stunningly beautiful black stallion that carried him on all his conquests.

When Alexander was only 12 years old, he won a bet with his father that would change his life forever. Alexander's father had passed on buying a horse that was beautiful but very difficult to handle. No one had been able to tame the horse, and the horse was considered aggressive, rearing up at anyone who came near him. The young boy fell in love with the beautiful horse with the white star on his forehead and spent hours talking gently to the horse and watching for anything that seemed to distress him. Realizing that Bucephalus became anxious by the sight of his shadow, he would calmly turn the horse's head toward the sun, and then he could bridle him. The horse stayed very calm and quiet around Alexander, and his father witnessed the change in the animal and gave his son Bucephalus.

Bucephalus was with Alexander the Great in every war from the first to the last, and Alexander's horsemanship skills were far beyond anyone else's. What made Alexander's riding skills all the more impressive was that he rode the horse bareback. The Greeks didn't ride with saddles, and men had to be excellent horseman or it could lead to their death during battles. Alexander rode Bucephalus with ease and they took care of each other. Alexander loved Bucephalus so much that when the horse died in 326 BC, he named a city after his beloved horse: The city of Bucephala.

How should a man be capable of grooming his own horse, or of furbishing his own spear and helmet, if he allows himself to become unaccustomed to tending even his own person, which is his most treasured belonging?
~Alexander the Great

~March 25~
Ice Harvesting

In the days before mechanical refrigeration, ice boxes were used to keep food and milk cold in most homes. The ice had to be harvested off the lakes each winter and was referred to as the "ice crop." When January came around, the ice was usually in perfect condition to harvest. Ice was in high demand during the 19th and early 20th centuries, and the lakes, rivers, and ponds in the Midwest offered the perfect environment to cut and harvest the ice. The meat packing and brewing industries needed a lot of ice for their businesses and were willing to pay good money for it.

Once the ice was hard enough (usually 12 inches thick), it was "ripe" and ready to cut and take off. This was all done by real horsepower and was a very dangerous job for the horses and men. The first step in harvesting the ice was to mark the ice with a specially designed horse-drawn "ice marker." Next they cut nearly through the ice using a horse-drawn "ice plow." From there, the ice was cut by hand and stacked either on wagons, or if there was a waterway, it was sent down stream. Companies like Springfield Ice (formed in 1858) maintained ice houses on the shores of Lake Massasoit. Horse stables were built along the shoreline to house 60 to 80 horses during the wintertime. The horses were used for ice harvesting up until the early 1930's.

The teams of horses wore special shoes so they wouldn't slip and fall on the ice, but unfortunately, horses fell through the ice at times. One of the biggest mistakes that led to horses falling through was that the ice wasn't thick enough in certain areas to carry the weight of the horses. According to the recorded history of the ice industry, horses wore ropes around their necks so that if a horse fell in, the driver could pull the rope tight, cutting off air to help keep the horse from struggling in the water. Once the horse had calmed down, other horses would pull the horse and driver out.

~March 26~
The Newspaper

In the 1800's, it was common for larger cities to have a newspaper. Horse accidents always made the paper, and if your horse was the problem, everyone soon found out! Here are a few very colorful samples from past newspapers that are written exactly how they were printed at the time.

April 1882 - A lively runaway occurred on Chestnut Street early yesterday morning. The team of fine gray horses owned by Mr. Wm. Finke, and attached to his brewery delivery wagon, came tearing down the street going directly toward the White River Bridge. At the corner one horse made up his mind to turn to the right, while the other was as equally determined to keep on straight ahead. This sudden collision detached the horses from the wagon, broke the harness badly, and threw the wagon upside-down damaging it but slightly. The horses were okay.

August 1884 - Mr. E. G. Henderson's fine team attached to his double carriage, took a home run for dear life on Monday evening of last week and were only captured after a ten mile chase. The team started from the street in front of Denniston's drug store about 9 o'clock in the evening, and it was very late that night or very early Tuesday morning when they were found. Strange to say, little or no damage resulted from the runaway, either to the horses or carriage. The harness was broken in several places, but two or three dollars would repair all damages.

May 1885 - A lively runaway occurred on our streets last Friday morning. A horse attached to a top-buggy broke away from a hitching post in front of Jacob Gill's store and started down Chestnut Street. He turned at the corner of the cheese factory and ran for dear life towards Jefferson Street. Near Mr. Smith's residence the buggy was overturned and the frightened steed caught by John Storey who always happens to be around whenever a runaway occurs. John righted the buggy and drove the horse back to Chestnut Street where the owners (two ladies) anxiously waited to see what damage had been done. Fortunately the buggy was not damaged and the horse was only slightly bruised on one hind leg. It was hard to tell which was the most frightened, the ladies or the horse.

~March 27~
The Cattle Drive

The cowboy, his trusted horse, and the cattle drive often conjure up beautiful visions of being out on the trail with your horse on a warm sunny day. The reality was that the cowboy crew worked very hard in all kinds of weather, got extremely dirty, and made very little money moving cattle thousands of miles from Texas to other states. But for many of the cowboys, it was a good job and they loved being out in the open, and the other cowboys became family.

The Spanish conquistadors introduced cattle to the Texas territory in the mid-1700's and the cattle drive slowly gained momentum a century later. It took a lot of organization to move cattle thousands of miles, which meant you needed horses and a lot of them. The horse was the most essential part of the cattle drive (except for the Chuck Wagon!), and without the stamina and speed of the horse, the job would have been impossible. The cowboys rode the horses to keep the cattle moving in the right direction. Since the land was vast with no fences, stray cattle would take off and the horse and cowboy were quickly on its tail, turning him around and bringing him back to the herd. If a cow needed doctoring, then the cowboy would go after the cow, rope it, and do what needed to be done, all while his horse stood there holding the rope tight from the saddle horn to the animal. The horse made the cowboy's job much easier and they became inseparable.

The "Wrangler" was in charge of all the horses. An average cattle drive would require some hundred horses to keep the cowboys mounted and the cows moving. The wrangler drove the horses alongside the cattle and was responsible for taking care of any sick or injured horses. The horses were what made the cattle drive successful back then, and most cattle ranchers today still prefer horses over motorized vehicles for checking on their herds. The horse still is an invaluable part of the cattle industry today.

~March 28~
Ban'ei

Horse races are usually all about speed, but on the Japanese island of Hokkaidō, you will find the world's slowest horse race. Draft horse racing, which is called Ban'ei, meaning "pull-race" in Japanese, is a race in which a draft horse pulls a heavy sled over man-made hills for a total of about 656 feet. The weight of the sled varies based on the age and track record of each horse. The Japanese Ban'ei horse (also known as Banba) is a blend of Percheron, Belgian & Breton blood, uniquely bred in Japan for this type of horse racing. These workhorses are decedents of crossbreds imported from France and Belgium towards the end of the 19th century. These massive equines helped farmers work their land and are now considered a Japanese breed. Ban'ei horse racing can be traced back as early as 1887. During the mid-twentieth century, it became very popular in Japan.

There were once four racetracks in Japan for draft horse racing. Today, the Obihiro racetrack is the only one in operation, and most of the horses are bred nearby in Hokkaidō. The dirt track has ropes that separate lanes on the course. Depending on their class, the horses are expected to pull anywhere from 990 pounds to 1 ton on their sleds. The horses must climb two obstacles and two hills throughout the track. After the first climb, the horses are often given a short break before tackling the next. Jockeys play a role as well, but instead of riding, they stand on the sled and urge the horses on. They don't carry whips but only heavy reins to encourage the horses. Percheron & Brenton stallions are imported yearly to enhance the bloodlines and breed stronger horses. The horses that are successful will go on to become breeding stallions, and the less successful horses will be used for meat. Once used to pull logs and plow rice fields, now these giant Ban'ei horses show their strength only on the racetrack.

~March 29~
The Boat Ride

In today's modern world, horses are transported by horse trailers, ships, and airplanes with the most modern equipment possible to ensure their safety. We have gotten good at making sure the horses feel comfortable and are safe under very unnatural conditions. As I started reading about transporting horses by ships, I couldn't help but be shaken by the extent of what man has put horses through for greater causes.

In order for kingdoms to move a large number of horses across land that was divided by water, the only option was sailing transports. In 1174, the Italo-Norman forces attacked Alexandria with 1,500 horses that were transported on 36 Tarides. These Tarides were very crude transport ships used for hauling horses, food, and water. These early transport vessels could carry 20-30 horses at a time. Once on the ship, the horses were stalled in groups of three and their bodies supported by canvas slings. Long gangways thirty feet long by five feet wide were on many ships, making it extremely dangerous for walking the horses on and off the boat. If you had a nervous horse, it was a long walk, and often horses would spook, fall off the side and become injured or worse.

Many centuries later, ships were built larger to carry hundreds of horses for military transport. New designs were made in the vessels so that a side door built lower to the water would open, allowing the horses to go down a short ramp and jump into the water to exit the ship. The horses were often kept below deck with poor ventilation in very tight areas, creating dangerous situations if a horse panicked and became unmanageable. Transporting by ships was extremely stressful on many horses, resulting in a high death rate. Throughout the centuries, man has worked to improve boat transportation for horses, but the horse paid a high price along the way with sickness, injury, or death upon the ships.

~March 30~
The Trolley Car

Horse-pulled trolley cars became a major part of the horse-driven infrastructure in most large cities at the turn of the 19th century. In every large city you could find a trolley system that could take you wherever you needed to go, and those trolleys were powered by horsepower. Real horsepower!

The trolleys were extremely heavy, and it was hard work for the teams of draft horses. The horses would get tired, hungry, and thirsty and many of them dropped dead of exhaustion from the work load. The average lifespan of a trolley horse was only about two years. It took lots of horses to power a two-horse trolley car in a 24-hour period. A horse could only physically work four or five hours a day (even though many horses were forced to work longer), so a trolley company typically stabled ten or more horses for each car in operation. Those horses needed to be housed, groomed, fed, and cared for each day. All these things together created huge expenses for the trolley company owners, who often cut corners at the horse's expense.

With the coming of electricity to cities, the trolley car soon became hooked up to cable and electric lines above the cars and turned out to be much more efficient, especially when going up and down hills all day. The teams of trolley horses lost their jobs as each city modernized its transportation system, but in the end, it was a blessing for the horses. The horse-pulled trolley was a short-lived wonder that only lasted about forty years, but it revolutionized how people would get around in large cities. To that, we owe so much to the horses that worked the trolleys.

For by reason of long domestication, intelligent care and training, the horse has become more tractable and intelligent than he was in the time of Job. While neither men nor horses can inherit an education, they may inherit what is better – the power to acquire it easily and rapidly. ~Isaac Phillips Roberts

~March 31~
Mounted Drill Team

The art of riding in formation is deeply rooted in the military, both for ceremonial purposes and training for battle. Maneuvers used today by drill teams originated on the battlefield where effectively moving the cavalry around required order and purpose. An order was developed through riding drills, which helped the soldiers learn to ride in unison and become very skillful on their horses. As a result, each cavalry unit became much better prepared. In the 1930's drill team competition became very popular among military groups, and soon, they were competing against other cavalry units throughout America and other countries.

John Clarke, an officer in the 9th U.S. Cavalry, was instrumental in training and creating the routines for the U.S. Army drill teams. They successfully competed against many of the world's best drill teams, including members of the Royal Canadian Mounted Police, who were known for their famous "Musical Ride."

Mounted drill teams work together to create a sense of teamwork among members with a common mission. What makes drills teams so unique is the camaraderie and team connection you get by performing together instead of competing individually in a horse show. Based on the fundamentals of Dressage (training) and military formations, the equestrian drill is a well-established tradition worldwide.

Today's drill teams wear colorful matching costumes and perform to a variety of music, which gives the spectators an outstanding visual experience. What makes the equestrian drill team so special are, of course, the horses. Watching the horses move in perfect unison, crisscrossing each other and creating beautiful maneuvers and routines, is amazing. Above all else, it takes an incredibly well-trained horse who will listen to his rider with so much going on all around him.

~April 1~
The Sacrifice

The Vedic age (1500-500 BC) in Northern India was a time in history when the horse played a deeply spiritual role in the religion of the Vedic Indo-Aryans. The Ashvamedha ceremony, or the "horse sacrifice," was one of the most important royal rituals of the Vedic period and was often performed by the king. The horse sacrifice was used to prove the king's sovereignty to his people. During this ritual, a white stallion was chosen and declared sacred. The stallion was then set free to wander throughout the king's land for one full year. The horse was always followed and watched by the king's soldiers, priests, and magicians to ensure nothing happened to the horse during that year. While the horse was wandering, he might enter the territory of another ruler and a clash between opposing militaries would take place for the possession of that land. Under the law, whatever land was touched by the sacrificial white stallion was believed to fall under the sovereignty of the king who was performing the Ashvamedha. The people would honor the king with festivities throughout the year until the white stallion was returned. Once returned, the horse would be sacrificed by the king during a time of celebration.

Recent excavations have unearthed elements of horse sacrifice used for religious rituals or to honor kings when they died. In the earliest Chinese dynasties, there was horse sacrifice to honor the emperors. In Ancient Rome, they would offer up what they called the "October Horse" sacrifice. This took place at the end of the agricultural and military campaigning season during a celebration festival. The festival included 2-horse chariot races in which the winning chariot's lead horse would be speared. Once dead, its head and tail were cut off and used in sacred rituals. It's hard even to fathom what the horse endured, but it was a much different world back then, and the horse's role would not include an easy existence.

~April 2~
Police Horse Training

Before a horse has been christened a "Police Horse," it must undergo rigorous training. Basically they need to become bombproof, and only certain horses graduate ready to work as a police horse. This means when a plastic bag flies through the air, the police horse cannot take off as if a giant monster is after him! These well-trained horses need to stay calm when the sirens are blaring, and the tension becomes high for the officers and, above all else, he needs to listen to his rider at all times.

The training is extensive, and patience is vital for the horse to be successful. Police horses are going to encounter crowds of people who can become irate and physical, with the possibility of gunshots or flying objects like bricks or cans coming out of nowhere. Some horses naturally have a quieter demeanor, while others have to learn to stay calm, and each horse may learn a little differently. Through the training process, police horses develop the skills necessary to patrol the streets day or night. They are taken through many different obstacles that prepare them for real experiences. Part of the training consists of people banging on drums, waving flags, shouting, and screaming. Tennis balls and other soft objects are thrown at the horses to desensitize them. During training, the horses wear full riot gear, including boots and kneepads. Visas are attached to their bridles to protect their eyes and a nose guard to protect the front of their face. The horse's training can be up to two years and the goal is to go slow so the horse can mentally take it all in, gain confidence and learn in a safe environment.

Police horses are taken extremely well care of, and the officers who ride them realize how important the bond needs to be between horse and man. They trust each other with their life daily, and any mounted police officer will tell you that his horse's needs come before anything else.

~April 3~
The Makeover

The Mustang horse doesn't just represent the Wild West or the Cowboys and Native Indians of a world gone by. This American feral horse (we like to call them wild Mustangs, but they are actually feral since they derived from domesticated breeds of horses) represents so much more. This horse is a symbol of freedom for Americans. There is something unbelievably beautiful about driving across the Midwest and looking off into the distance and spotting a herd of wild horses. It can easily take your breath away.

Unfortunately, these Mustangs are in the mix of controversy surrounding their growing numbers and the lack of land to sustain them. During the last several decades, many organizations have worked hard to help preserve the Mustang horse and their environment. Still, it was realized that something else needed to be done to help bring better awareness of these amazing horses to the public. That is when the Mustang Makeover came into flight and started to showcase what these incredible horses could do if someone were willing to go slow and take the time needed to earn their trust.

The Mustang Heritage Foundation was founded in 2001 to help adopt out some of the Mustangs that had been in holding areas. Then in 2007, the Extreme Mustang Makeover took root as a competition to showcase what these horses could do. As the idea turned into a friendly competition, it grew immediately, and horse trainers from all over the United States were taking part in the Mustang Makeover Challenge that ultimately would help find good homes for these horses. Since its conception, the Mustang Heritage Foundation has placed more than 5,000 gentled and trained Mustangs into good homes. Keeping the Mustang numbers at a level that will ensure their survival is truly a balancing act for the people who love these horses and want them to flourish.

~April 4~
Warrior

The colt was born in 1908 and was named Warrior, which would prove to fit him well. He was a solid bay Thoroughbred owned by Jack Seely, who lived near the English Channel. The young colt grew up and was trained by Seely, but World War One broke out and soon Warrior and Seely were drafted for war. Seely had an incredibly strong bond with Warrior, and he rode him throughout the war.

Warrior miraculously survived all four years of the war through many battles in France, with horses dropping all around him from bullets and bombs. Many of the soldiers who knew Warrior would say, "The bullet hadn't been made that could kill Warrior," and it would prove true. On one occasion Warrior's nose was touching another horse when the other horse suddenly dropped dead from a gunshot. Twice, Warrior's stable was blown up moments after he was led out. During the Battle of Amiens, Warrior was stabled in the drawing room of an abandoned French villa, and it too was shelled. Seely looked at the bombed villa and knew his horse had been killed, but to his amazement, he saw Warrior's head poking out of the few bricks still standing, with the joist of the ceiling on his back. It was nothing short of a miracle. As the war continued, nothing seemed to bother Warrior as it did the other horses. Many horses became shell-shocked and hard to handle or ride from all the noise and fighting.

After the war, Warrior went home and lived until he was 33 years old, and his owner and war companion, General Jack Seely, road him until the horse's passing. Years later, Seely's grandson would say, "Warrior was the ultimate symbol of unquestioning, upstanding courage." Warrior's story is probably one of the greatest war stories of all, and he will be forever remembered along with so many other brave warhorses.

~April 5~
Mounted Orienteering

The origins of Orienteering can be traced back to the 19th century in Sweden. The term, "Orienteering," originated in Sweden in 1886 and meant "the crossing of unknown land with the aid of a map and a compass." Orienteering on horseback was an essential function of the cavalry and today remains an important training tool for mounted search and rescue units in many parts of the world.

Competitive Mounted Orienteering (CMO) was first envisioned as an equestrian sport in 1981 by Cliff Pladsen in Olgivie, Minnesota. He wanted a game to play with his family while trail riding to improve their map and compass skills. From there, it grew into a sport with active chapters and members in many states across the country.

Mounted Orienteering competition is essentially a "hide and seek of objects" on horseback, where you search to find treasure or other objects that have been hidden. You can only use a compass and an old-fashioned paper trail map with printed instructions on the back. You navigate by taking compass readings from the landmarks, and GPS, cell phone navigation or other electronics are not allowed! On the back of each map are listed the landmark descriptions to help a rider determine the location of the stations and narrowing the search area where the compass coordinates intersect.

Any breed of horse can participate, but some characteristics are desirable in a good CMO horse. Having a good trail horse is a must since you will be riding in many unknown areas, and it helps if your horse doesn't mind being separated from others as you get your compass readings and search for the leads. If you have a competitive spirit and want to win, then having a horse that likes to run is also a plus. It's like going on a long trail ride and looking for buried treasure!

~April 6~
Airborne

Transporting horses by airplane is a relatively new idea and has made horse competition worldwide much easier to attend, with the ability to fly horses to other countries to compete. In 1956, the U.S. Equestrian Team flew its horses to the Stockholm Olympics in Europe for the first time. Transporting horses by airplane was a huge benefit because it lessened the time in transit, but the early days created some serious questions about the safety of the horses.

The first horse transport airplanes were very loud, dark, and claustrophobic. The "horse containers" used at the time were plywood-sided boxes with an opening at the top, and they really didn't do a good job of containing the horses. Horses were led up a ramp into the airplane and into the plywood box. On top of it, the plane's ceiling was so low overhead that some horses would hit their heads on it. This could trigger a panic response from a horse already stressed by his strange surroundings.

In 1964, the U.S. Olympic Equestrian Team was in route at 25,000 feet between JFK and O'Hare airports when one of the horses had a panic attack and attempted to jump out of his crate. Quickly the staff tried to tranquilize and restrain him but failed, and the horse was humanely destroyed in flight. The decision to put the horse down had to be made quickly because he had broken through his container and cracked one of the interior windows. Any more damage could lead to the depressurization of the cabin. Once the plane landed at O'Hare, the rest of the team was able to complete their trip to Tokyo, sadly, with one less horse and rider.

Equine air transport has significantly improved throughout the years regarding the shipping containers used for the horses. There have also been major improvements, both in the aircraft itself and in the system for loading the horse into the airplane, which has made the flight much less stressful for the animals.

~April 7~
The English Saddle

During the 18th century, the typical saddles used in Europe were based on a model used for bullfighting, ranch work, long-distance travel, and the cavalry. The high pommel and cantle of those early saddles helped to provide the rider with support. The early style saddles of that era are still used today by the Spanish Riding School in Vienna and in Iberia and Eastern Europe.

Fox hunting grew in popularity in England when the deer population dwindled. To hunt for food, the rider now had to tackle fences, bushes, and ditches straight on if they wanted to keep up with the hounds and make a kill. The saddles of the day were hard to ride in with this new way of hunting. The cantle would get in the way of the riders as they tried to lean back over the fence (a common style of jumping until the "forward seat" was introduced), and the high pommel created pain as the rider went over jumps.

The new saddle design developed for fox hunting had a very low pommel and cantle with a flat seat, and there was no padding for the rider's legs. This created a new type of rider as he had to have a much better seat and balance while riding or end up on the ground. The English hunting saddle is the forerunner of all English riding saddles. Soon equestrians were jumping their horses for sport and competition, racing and polo. The term "English saddle" accommodates several types of saddles including those used for show jumping as well as hunt seat, dressage, saddle-seat, horse racing, and polo.

For the non-horsey type person, the most distinguishing difference between the English and Western saddle is the lack of a horn. That is usually what people will look for first, along with the style of dress or clothing. English saddles have influenced some styles of the Western saddle, removing the horn in the design for endurance riding and rodeo competition on saddle bronc horses.

~April 8~
Polo

Polo might be the oldest team sport that has involved horses, but the origins of the game are not entirely known. It was probably played by Nomadic warriors over two thousand years ago, and it was a way of strengthening and training the military while still having a friendly game of competition. The first recorded tournament was in 600 BC between the Turkomans and the Persians.

Today the game of polo is usually associated with the rich and famous and, in reality, things have not changed much from thousands of years ago. In Persia in 600 BC, polo was only played by the nobility and the wealthy, and competition was common between kings and princes. Polo has always been deeply connected to the British and is still a very important part of their culture and history. It took a person of wealthy means to play polo in competition because they needed to have at least two good horses, which most common people couldn't afford. In the middle ages, it was played as a miniature battle with rules made up along the way. The first official written rules were not created until the 19th century by Irishman Captain John Watson of the British Cavalry.

Small hunter-type ponies were once the preferred choice of horse, but they gave way to larger, faster ponies and small Thoroughbreds. For a time, the English tried to limit a pony's height to 14 hands, but in 1895 raised it to 14.2 hands. Then in 1919, they took off all restrictions on height. Today, most polo ponies stand around 15.1 hands tall, although you will see horses that stand well over 16 hands. In the United States, Thoroughbreds are bred with Quarter Horses in hopes of finding the best qualities of each breed for the sport. Great polo ponies are fast with great stamina, and are very responsive with a calm disposition that helps them to focus on their rider's cues during a competition.

~April 9~
Mongol Derby

During the 13th century, Genghis Khan set up the world's first long-distance postal messenger system. Using a massive network of horse stations called "morin urtuus" in Mongolian, his messengers and their horses could gallop from Kharkhorin to the Caspian Sea in a number of days. It was a long route where horses would be switched out for fresh ones after so many miles, so the messenger could keep going.

For ten days each August, the Mongol Derby recreates this legendary mail system by building a network of horse stations at 24-mile intervals along the entire 600-mile/10-day course. The Mongol Derby is considered the longest and toughest horse race in the world. Horse welfare comes first at the Derby, and what makes the Mongol race so unique are the horses. Only Mongolian horses are ridden in the race, and many of them are semi-wild. The horses live year-round in free-roaming herds when not working. Mongolian horses might only stand between 12 and 14 hands tall, but they are incredibly strong and have great stamina. They are also extremely hardy when it comes to the weather, temperatures, and food.

Due to the size of the horses, a weight restriction is put on competitors for the horse's safety. Every year before the race, 1,500 Mongolian horses are vetted and trained for the Mongol Derby. Each horse is checked by a team of veterinarians before they are cleared to race. They are then vetted again at each station during the competition. Riders will be penalized or pulled from racing if they find a horse has been mistreated. Once cleared, the riders switch horses to move on to the next leg of the race. The competitors will ride many different Mongolian horses during the 10-day competition through open land, rivers, and mountainous areas. The ride is grueling, but it is said that the beauty of the land, the Mongolian people, and the horses are truly unforgettable.

~April 10~
Time To Retire

The Lancaster City Police Department in Pennsylvania knew they would have a hard time filling the shoes of an 18-year veteran on the police force. Duke, a 22-year-old Percheron draft horse, finally walked his last beat. His saddle was hung up for the last time as he was retiring to green pastures and well-deserved relaxing days. Over the years, the huge 2,100-pound grey Percheron attended countless events in the city of Lancaster and has worked protection detail for numerous politicians and world leaders. In 2009, Duke was trailered to Pittsburgh to work as a police horse during the G20 summit. When Pope Francis visited Philadelphia in 2015, Duke was right there in the middle of it all.

Mounted Patrol Units are often seen in parades or special events, but these horses do so much more than that. They train with officers and are ready to be called out to work at a moment's notice, any time day or night. Duke was known for his quiet spirit, and was always calm even in tense situations.

Duke worked for the first three years of his life as an Amish plow horse in Canada and then joined the Lancaster Mounted Police Unit in 2002. After a full year of training to become a police horse, Duke started his new job in 2003. Duke has served as a trainer for many new equine members of the Mounted Police, including the unit's two newest horses, King and Jake, who will replace Duke after his last day with the force. Duke has also trained countless mounted officers, and Duke was known to be a "Pushbutton horse for the experienced officers, but would definitely test the limits of what he could get away with while training new mounted officers."

It's now Duke's time to rest and relax after a job well done for many years. He is retiring as the longest-serving police horse in the department's history.

~April 11~
Stunt Doubles

The number of movies that horses have played parts in is insurmountable. Since the first motion picture ever made, horses have been in films either as the stunt double, part of the background scene, or the equine star. Retired movie stunt rider and double Martha Crawford-Cantarini once said, "As we strive to learn the best ways to motivate our horses, they motivate us to be the best that we can be. Horses provided the action and the unforgettable identity of the Western. Their ability to jump, to fall, and to run, contributed hugely to a star's believability and status."

Horse stunt doubles are the unsung heroes of the movie industry. They are usually very quiet, gentle, and easy to train. Patience is something these horses need to have, and they have it in abundance. They often will have an actor on their back that is green at riding but needs to perform a specific scene or action shot, in which, the main horse is not capable or too high strung to perform the task. And they often have to repeat the same scene several times, which takes a huge amount of patience. These brave horses have had to rear on cue, gallop into buildings, stand quietly while gunshots are being fired in gunfights, chase buffalo, and run out of burning barns and buildings, all while taking care of the actor who is on their back. Stunt double horses have endured hours of having their faces and bodies painted to match the equine star's exact markings. It's all part of the magic and horses have helped make the movie industry what it is today. Without horses, there would not have been the classics such as National Velvet, Ben-Hur, Son of Paleface, The Black Stallion, Seabiscuit, Secretariat, and War Horse. The same is true for television shows like The Lone Ranger, Wagon Train, Gunsmoke, Bonanza, or Little House on the Prairie. Horses indeed are the stars of the big screen, and the horse stunt doubles are the quiet heroes that make these movies possible.

~April 12~
The Samurai

The early Japanese people regarded the horse as the keeper of magical powers. Being highly skilled riders along with mastering weaponry was important, and a huge part of establishing their powerful dynasty. The Japanese used their horses for warfare rather than for transportation, agriculture, or food and these horses were extremely valuable to the kingdoms. The warriors that rode these horses were called Samurai. They were military nobility and officers of medieval and early-modern Japan from the late 12th century.

The Samurai rode Kisouma native horses that were very sturdy and resembled stocky ponies. They had a stubby face, short legs, and they had long-haired coats. But they were extremely fast and very surefooted. The Samurai warrior mounted their horses, not from the left like modern equestrians, but from the right side of their steeds. Depending on the geographical area, some Samurai fought on horseback, while others rode to the battle and dismounted to fight their enemies. But eventually, all Samurai fought while on the horse. The Samurai used a fighting technique in which they would charge their horse straight at their enemy, which often would push the other horse off balance or injure the horse. Because of this warfare tactic many horses were seriously hurt. Often the horses were the first attacked. If a warrior could bring down the horse, then the Samurai would also come down. Learning to fight on horseback became a part of military training, and the horses became the strength behind the Samurai warriors.

There are only about 120 pure Kisouma horses remaining in Japan today. These sturdy horses were used by Japan's military in the 1930's and 1940's and many of the animals were left behind in China and Korea at the end of the war. Today there are breeding programs in Japan to bring this great little horse back in larger numbers and to preserve the breed.

~April 13~
The Thoroughbred

The Thoroughbred horse has impacted the sports world in a huge way. What makes this horse even more remarkable is its lineage. Thoroughbreds have long been associated with flat racing (racing horses on a flat surface with no obstacles), which has been called the Sport of Kings. All registered Thoroughbreds can be traced back in their lineage, thanks to deliberate breeding practices and impeccable record keeping beginning centuries ago. The Thoroughbred goes back to all or one of three original horses in their lineage: the Godolphin Arabian, the Darley Arabian, and the Byerly Turk. These three stallions were bred to forty-three royal mares during the reign of King James I and King Charles I. Record-keeping was meticulously done for every foal born into this new breed of horse—the English Thoroughbred.

This tall fine boned Thoroughbred stallion named Bulle Rock was said to be the first Thoroughbred brought to the new Americas in 1730. Bulle Rock was the son of the Darley Arabian. This began the 45-year import of 186 Thoroughbreds into the colonies as the foundation of the modern American Thoroughbred. This new generation of horses would be the foundation for all modern racing Thoroughbreds up through today.

To be eligible for the Jockey Club registry and considered a "true" Thoroughbred, the foal must be a "live cover," meaning a natural conception between the stallion and the mare and thus no artificial insemination. Their Arabian blood contributes to their long, lean face, but they are not quite as "dishy" as a pureblood Arabian. When it comes to height, they usually stand somewhere between 15.3 and 17 hands tall, but there have been exceptions. The Thoroughbred horse is truly a remarkable animal.

The Thoroughbred gallops with his lungs, perseveres with his heart, and wins with his character. ~Fredrico Tesio

~April 14~
The Icelandic Horse

The Icelandic horses were the original breed of the Vikings. They were taken to Iceland from Norway during the 9th and 10th centuries to help settle their new surroundings. One would automatically think Vikings used these horses for battle, but historical accounts tell a different story.

Vikings were seafaring people who preferred to conquer in a fast and unsuspecting manner on foot, instead of having the extra labor of feeding and caring for the horses they rode. The Icelandic horses were small, and if the Vikings had to travel a long distance, they would only use them to travel part way, then dismount and walk by foot the rest of the way to the battle. Since Vikings were seamen who often traveled by ship, the number of horses they would need to take on board the vessel to produce a strong and large cavalry would prove nearly impossible. The Vikings did slowly bring over more Icelandic horses to help with traveling, carrying people, and delivering materials and needed goods, and they made mail delivery much easier.

The Vikings, without realizing it, started the worldwide distribution of the gaited horse. The Icelandic horses they brought to their new land were very smooth to ride and had a unique fourth gait that made them easy to travel on for long periods. After a time, these gaited Icelandic horses spread throughout Europe and Asia. The Vikings had a very unique relationship with animals, and there have been graves uncovered with horses buried with their Viking owners. Whether it was a spiritual ritual or done purely for respect of both man and his horse, we may never know, but it sure gives us something to think about.

There are no more sagacious animals than the Icelandic horse. He is stopped by neither snow, nor storm, nor impassable roads, nor rocks, nor glaciers. He is courageous, sober, and surefooted. ~Jules Verne

~April 15~
Public Health Hazard

It's hard even to imagine horses being a public health hazard, but at the turn of the 19th century, things were much different. Horses powered everything in the cities, and with the growing number of people and horses cramped tight into city streets between rising buildings, there wasn't much room for anything else. Very quickly, large amounts of horse manure began piling up in the streets and there was no place to put it. On top of it, the large number of horses that dropped dead weekly on the streets, and left to decay right where they died, now posed serious health issues. Flies and urine also became a huge problem. Soon there was a desperate need for help in dealing with the public health hazards of the day, and the horses were front and center of all of it.

The horses working in the city kept the city's infrastructure moving forward. Goods needed to be moved daily, and it was backbreaking work for the horses pulling heavy wagons filled with everything that keeps a city alive. Big teams of draft horses pulled the trolley cars, and transportation was essential for the businesses to survive. In the city of New York, horses were poorly taken care of and lived in big garages in New York's "horse districts." Despite the presence of horses working and living in the city, most cities did not have any type of cleaning regiment to keep the city streets free of manure and dead horse carcasses. It is estimated that just in New York alone, up to 200,000 horses were in the city on any given day!

Eventually, street cleaning proposals were put in place, and the manure was cleaned off the streets and sent out to the countryside to be dumped in farm fields. Then, motor vehicles grew in numbers, and the use of horses slowly became less over many decades. City after city started keeping their streets cleaner, and the care of the horses improved over the decades for the equines still living and working in the cities.

~April 16~
The Four Horsemen

We all have watched movies where the prince rode in on a white horse to save the princess, while the villain rode away on a fiery black horse. The symbolism of the color of horses today may seem like fairy tales, but in medieval society, the color of a horse was taken very seriously. And yes, it is true; in many historical writings, kings often preferred white horses over black or spotted horses, for many different reasons. The connection between the horse and their "coats of many colors" can be found in medieval artwork displayed in the form of paintings, rugs, and literature. The Bible and the Four Horsemen of the Apocalypse is right in the middle of all of it. Religion was deeply woven into medieval society, and when you look at the artwork and the Four Horsemen of the Apocalypse, they seem to parallel in many ways.

The four horses in the book of Revelation are described as this; one of the horsemen, the Conqueror, rides a white horse. Later in the Apocalypse, the one who is Faithful and True comes on a white horse. A red horse carries the Rider of War, an appropriate image given the bloodshed of warfare. On the back of the black horse is Famine, and a pale horse is ridden by Death.

During the medieval period, these verses in Revelation were very important and extremely relatable to the people of those early centuries, because the horse was used in warfare to conquer or else be conquered. This meant survival and feast or the alternative, which was famine and death. Today, with our modern conveniences, fast technology, and longer periods of peace between nations, it is much harder for us to connect the two, but it is definitely interesting and worth thinking about.

I looked up and saw a white horse standing there. Its rider carried a bow, and a crown was placed on his head. He rode out to win many battles and gain the victory. Revelation 6:2

~April 17~
Horse-Pulling

The sport of horse-pulling started back when farmers were still using heavy draft horses for all their farm work. Their horses were tilling the fields, planting crops, and feeding the cows, plus so much more. What started as neighboring farmers getting together and bragging about their horses, ended up in friendly horse-pulling competitions between each other and the sport grew from there. Once the horse was replaced by the motorized tractor, the horse was still doing little jobs on the farm and the farmers still liked a good competition. Many farmers loved their big draft horses and wanted to keep them active, so horse-pulling became a great way to showcase these massive and very athletic equines. Soon, horse-pulling competitions could be found at county fairs all across the United States and in other countries as well.

Horse-pulling competitions are set up with either one or two horses in harnesses, hitched to a stone-boat or weighted sled. The beginning weight load is around 1500 lbs. As each team pulls the weight, more weight is added, and teams are eliminated when they are not able to pull the added weight. The last team pulling the heaviest weight added is declared the winner. Horses have pulled top weights up to 13,500 pounds! There are different weight classes and stringent rules to avoid animal cruelty, and the horses are watched carefully. There are both light and heavy horse classes and you will see many draft breeds at pulling competitions, but the Belgian horse is often the choice of competitors. Pony-pulling is also gaining momentum, and even though the ponies are small, they are mighty strong!

There is something beautiful about watching two draft horses showing the world what they are made of. These magnificent athletes are true symbols of how this country was built and gives us a glimpse into our past.

~April 18~
Hunting On Horseback

Hunting from the back of a horse has been done since the time that the horse was tamed, and man learned how to balance on his back. Horses became the tool that changed how man hunted and carried the deer or other dead animal back to his tribe. Horses made it easy to travel long distances to find food and then make the long journey home. Before that, man would be on foot hunting and then have to drag it back home with the help of his friends.

Today, hunting on horseback is mainly for sport and the enjoyment of being in the great outdoors. For men and women who love to hunt, riding a horse into the backcountry is the perfect getaway. The peace and tranquil beauty of the surroundings makes the trip more like a vacation. What many people don't realize is that you still need a good horse for a hunting trip on horseback, so that when you shoot your rifle, your horse doesn't take off. Otherwise you will be hoofing it back to the truck and horse trailer!

Temperament is an important trait in a good hunting horse. Horses used for hunting take loud noises like gunshots in stride. They have great stamina for the varying terrain and are very patient with their often green riders, especially when the commands they are given might be a bit confusing. A very confident horse makes the journey so much easier. After all, if your horse is spooking at every little bird that flies out of the grass or bushes, by the end of the trip, you both will be exhausted. If you are riding miles into the backcountry, then having a surefooted horse that can easily walk over logs and through creeks and rivers is of the greatest importance.

Hunting on horseback today gives the hunter a taste of what life was like just a few short centuries ago, when life was much harder but simpler. For many hunters, it gives them a whole new respect for their equine partners who are doing most of the work!

~April 19~
Falconry On Horseback

He sat upon his retired racehorse called, Caymens, while holding a Golden Eagle and he gently asked his horse, "are you feeling brave?" The Golden Eagle could definitely do some significant damage to both the horse and rider, and if Caymen freaked out and took off, then most likely, someone would be on the ground looking at the long walk ahead of him. The trust this horse had in his rider was nothing short of incredible. Falconry on horseback has been around for centuries, and it takes a special horse that can keep his wits about him while his rider handles a large Bird of Prey.

Today, we wouldn't think of using a Bird of Prey and our horse to go out and catch dinner. But back in the 13th century, it made finding and catching food so much easier than throwing a spear at the rabbit by horseback. Both the horse and the falcon enabled the hunter to cover many more miles looking for food, and both animals were good at what they were designed to do. Remember, this was long ago before shotguns. The horse was a constant in everyday life, and if you were planning on going hunting with your falcon, then you rode your horse to get to your destination. The two became inseparable for sport or to put food on the table.

In France, the revolution had pushed falconry into dormancy until the mid-19th century. Neighboring regions, such as Flanders in the northern part of Belgium, continued practicing falconry. Then in the Netherlands, the Loo royal hunting party, in which all the hunting members were on horseback, was immortalized by the famous artist Sonderland by means of drawings and sketches. Those drawings helped bring back falconry on horseback. Today, due to the effort of many passionate people, falconry on horseback is finding its followers who love the idea of the bird of prey, the horse, and man working together as a team.

~April 20~
Horse Car On Rails

The origin of the railroad was actually birthed out of the "John Mason Horse Car," which was pulled by horses on rails. Trains began as horse-drawn carts and wagons that carried heavy loads. The problem with the carts and wagons was that the ground was uneven and rutted up, and the wet springtime mud made things even worse. It became nearly impossible for the horses to cover any distance with such poor road conditions. On top of it, wagons were constantly breaking wheels. Then someone came up with the idea of laying down flat wooden rails and then placing rims on the wagon wheels that would keep the wagons on the rails. Rails reduced friction, and the horses could cover more miles without exhaustion, reaching their destination faster. However, the wooden rails quickly wore out. Soon, someone had the idea to nail strips of iron on top of the wooden rails and the railroad was born.

On November 27, 1832, the first horse-drawn railcar called the "John Mason," rolled down the New York and Harlem Railroad's Fourth Avenue line. The idea of the horse car and the railroad was born. Anyone having horses and wagons with flanged (rimmed) wheels could use the railway for a small fee. Pretty soon, these railroads were being built for both public transportation and to move goods from one place to another during a time when the cities were booming.

The creation of the railroads for horse-drawn wagons and horse cars became a huge success. At the height of its success in the 1880's, there were approximately 18,000 horse cars in the United States, and that number didn't include the number of privately owned horse-drawn wagons that used the rails during that time. As new technology developed, the horse cars and wagons declined in numbers with the invention of the steam engine, and soon trains took over the tracks which today we still call railroads.

~April 21~
The Mule

What is a mule exactly? Is it a horse or donkey or what? Those are common questions that many people ask, but the mule is truly a very smart equine that happens to have a horse for its mother. A mule is a hybrid equine that is created when you breed a female horse to a male donkey. A hybrid results in "hybrid vigor," which means that the animal created is healthier and, in many cases, larger than either parent. Mules are extremely smart and have served man well during wartime and peacetime. They are indeed the unsung heroes that have given their all for man's endeavors, and often have survived horrible situations due to their hardiness. Mules are 99.9 percent sterile because they have an odd number of chromosomes. The horse has 64, and the donkey has 62, and the mule ends up with 63. That amount makes it almost impossible for the mule to procreate.

In the Bible and ancient texts, there are many mentions of kings and generals riding mules. Since mules were taller than other indigenous horses due to their breeding, the kings and military generals could see all that they command above the other mounted troops. Later on during the 1800's, the mule again became very popular and the preferred choice of equine because they were extremely hardy. Often men chose to ride a mule when traveling long distances through harsh terrain because the mule handled everything better. They weren't as temperamental as the horse when it came to food or environment, and their hooves were stronger. God created an amazing animal when he created the mule.

"There is no more useful or willing animal than the mule. And perhaps there is no other animal so much abused, or so little cared for. Popular opinion of his nature has not been favorable; and he has had to plod and work through life against the prejudices of the ignorant." ~Muleskinner Harvey Riley, in his 1867 book, The Mule

~April 22~
Stroller

Stroller was Marion's pony, and she would learn to jump on the very sweet 14.2 hand little steed. Marion's father purchased the pony when she was 13 years old, and Stroller was 10. Stroller was a Thoroughbred/Connemara Cross, and her father thought he would make a nice junior jumper pony for his daughter. Right away, the two were a fearless match and a force to be reckoned with around the British junior show circuit.

As Marion got older, her father purchased a larger horse for her to compete on, but Marion was deeply attached to Stroller and begged her father not to sell him, and he finally gave in. Marion did well on the larger horse, but still competed on Stroller. Soon she was winning everything on the pony, leaving her horse behind. Marion and Stroller won the Queen Elizabeth II Cup at the Royal International Horse Show. They then tackled the Hickstead Derby, one of the most grueling show jumping courses in the world and came in second place. In 1965, Marion rode Stroller to a gold medal in the Ladies World Championship, and two years later came back and took first place at the Hickstead Derby. Marion and Stroller had the nation's attention, and in 1968, they represented Great Britain as part of the Olympic show jumping team and as an individual at the Olympics in Mexico City. After two grueling rounds and a jump-off, Marion and Stroller took home the silver medal, and that little pony would go down in the history books! Stroller got his well-deserved retirement the following year, which he enjoyed for a glorious 15 years before his death at the grand old age of 36.

"How tall does my horse need to be if I want to be competitive as a show jumper?" If you are ever asked this question, just remember Marion and Stroller and the silver medal won at the Olympics. Size doesn't matter, but the heart does.

~April 23~
Mister Ed

I was just a young girl when the show came on television in the 1960's. I couldn't believe my eyes! It was a horse that could talk! The show was called Mister Ed, and it was about the life and mischief of a horse called Mister Ed, who could talk, and his owner, Wilbur Post. The show was an overnight success, and it was every little girls dream to own a horse like Mister Ed.

Behind the character of Mister Ed was a beautiful golden Palomino horse whose name was Bamboo Harvester. The epic equine's celebrity story began in California. Bamboo Harvester was born in 1949 from a long line of purebred show horses whose sire was named Harvester. Bamboo Harvester wasn't the first horse picked for the show, but after filming the pilot, the chestnut gelding that was originally chosen for the part had a bit of a breakdown and was replaced with Bamboo Harvester at the last minute. A star was born, and Mister Ed became the most famous horse in America for a number of years.

Even though Mister Ed couldn't actually talk, the palomino horse had a lot to say. It was a mystery for many years how they were able to make the horse look like he was talking. They used an invisible string to pull up the flap around his lips that made him appear to be talking as his lips moved. The strings were run through his halter so they wouldn't be seen in front of his face. It worked perfectly. Bamboo Harvester would let everyone know when he was tired of filming—he would simply just walk off the set! When he was hungry, the filming stopped so he could have a snack. He loved sweet tea and, of course, plenty of hay. Bamboo Harvester won several Patsy Awards (awards given to animal entertainers). The success with Bamboo Harvester is much credited to his trainer, who never whipped the horse, but instead, used gentle training and cues to help the horse with each part.

~April 24~
Military Maneuvers

When we think of the warhorse, we often envision the horses we have seen in the movies; larger than life, robust with the greatest of stamina, and can run faster than their enemy. And, of course, the star equine of any particular movie is always beautiful.

Finally, over the last few decades, we are now starting to hear about the real warhorses and what their training and life was really like on the battlefield. These warhorses were trained to do many incredible maneuvers for the cavalry units, beginning with the Civil War when heavy artillery became part of warfare. Their training was rigorous, and not only did a horse learn to carry his soldier (who often was learning to ride), he would also carry his guns and ammo, water, and other military gear. The total weight was often heavy, which meant that the horse needed to be strong.

Horses in military training were taught to stand quiet during the sound of gunfire, and for some horses it was easy, but for others, it was very challenging and stressful. Horses would learn to lie down and be still when commanded and become a physical barrier for their soldier. They were trained to walk over many different surfaces, including planks of wood or rocky areas, and walk through narrow ravines or trenches where military vehicles could not go. Since horses have a fantastic sense of smell, the only thing that couldn't be replicated in training was the stench of blood and smoke-filled air. These brave horses also had to endure the horrific sounds they would hear from their fellow equines that had been shot or injured. This would prove to be horrific for the horses and the soldiers who cared for these animals. No one could fully prepare the horses for the battles they would experience.

His horses will be so many that they will cover you with dust. Your walls will tremble at the noise of the warhorses, wagons and chariots when he enters your gates as men enter a city whose walls have been broken through. Ezekiel 26:10

~April 25~
Jesse

The United States Forest Service was created in 1905. At that time, thousands of mules and horses were drafted into service and there were more equines employed by the U.S Forest Service than people. The horses and mules proved invaluable and were used for everything from carrying equipment for building trails to wildfire assistance, plus so much more.

Since 1905, not much has changed for the work jobs that the horses and mules do in the U.S. Forest Service. They are often seen packing equipment for workers in the high country for maintenance on all the trails. If you are a fan of hiking, mountain biking, cross-country skiing, or backpacking in any of the National Parks and Forests, then you could thank a horse or mule because the trails are all maintained with help from these hard-working equines.

One particular mule worked for the Forest Service in the High Unitas of Utah. Jesse was seven years old when she was purchased for the Forest Service in 1999, and she proved her weight in gold over the next two decades. She packed both on her own and as part of tandem teams, and due to her reliable and steady personality, she was often sought after to pack sensitive things like saws and explosives. She has carried people stranded or under the threat of wildfires, carried supplies and food to working trail crews, and carried lumber for bridges, and that is only the beginning.

Jesse had always worked willingly and without complaint and was as dependable as they come. Jesse's personality made her a great teacher of the younger mules that have been purchased over the years for the Forest Service. In Jesse's 21 years of service, she had packed almost 18,000 pounds of equipment and supplies. She is in her thirties now and is getting a well-deserved retirement.

~April 26~
Those Beautiful Eyes

There is something about the eyes of a horse that seems to look deep into our soul. You can look into their big eyes, and they will tell you exactly what is going on with them at that moment. Their eyes will tell you if they are scared, excited, calm, or relaxed, and they only speak the truth in their eyes. If you look into a horse's eyes, you will see if a horse has a mean streak or is just misunderstood for having been abused often. Sadly, most people don't look deep enough to see what is really going on.

The horse with a "soft eye" often tells us he is calm and has a gentle spirit, whereas the horse that shows the "whites of his eyes" is signaling that he is possibly nervous or frightened. The equine eye is roughly two inches in size and is the largest of any land mammal, and nine times larger than a human's eye. It is no wonder that we love to stare at their eyes.

Horses have a surprising blind spot. They cannot see from their eye level to the ground directly in front of their nose and about six feet out. This means they cannot see the grass they graze on, the treats you feed them, or the bit you put in their mouth. That is why the horse depends heavily on his whiskers to feel what is near him and his nose to smell the treats you are trying to feed him. He often needs to smell it before he puts it in his mouth unless he is a chow hound that eats everything no matter what it is!

The eyes of a horse have calmed the frightened soldier and brought a man to his knees in tears as he sees the pain his horse is suffering. A horse's eyes bring us the greatest joys and deepest sorrows throughout their life with us, and we wouldn't trade it for the world.

"For their eyes are the window to their soul if you are quiet enough to watch and observe." ~Author unknown

~April 27~
Horse Powered Wine

If you love to drink wine, then you will be pleased to know that many vineyards are going back to using horses for much of the harvesting of the grapes, along with other jobs. Up until the motorized trucks and tractors were invented, horses did it all. They pulled the wagons filled with grapes or the cultivators that covered the vine crowns with soil to keep them warm when the temperatures dropped. Some of today's vineyards in Europe and America are going back to some of the traditional wine making, and they are bringing in the big boys—draft horses. The vineyard owners are using draft horses to tend the vines, which includes jobs such as pulling cultivators and plowing down the aisles each spring to aerate the ground and cut down the weeds. Many owners are now saying it is better for the soil and the environment, plus it creates a quieter and more peaceful working atmosphere.

Christophe Baron, who operates Cayuse Vineyards, is using horses (Belgians and Percherons) at his biodynamic vineyard and says he is producing higher-quality wines. Other businesses are following and have also noticed that soil compaction is far less than with traditional heavy motorized tractors. The work is harder and slower, with longer hours put in each day, because the horse's care is top priority and they need to be fed, groomed, and taken care of daily. But for many, they are finding it worth the extra work and time. There is also a desire among some vineyard owners to keep the tradition of horse viticulture alive, and they are finding that their customers love the idea of using horses in the vineyards. Vineyard manager Joel Sokoloff said, "There's something irreplaceable and really authentic about using horses. We do it because it's a choice to farm in a much more artisanal and ancestral way." So the next time you are having a glass of wine, you might be drinking fermented and aged grapes from a vineyard using real horsepower!

~April 28~
Rescuing Each Other

The mare was an ex-racehorse that had been abused and neglected for a very long time. When the horse first arrived at Devon farm, the vets thought she had no will to live. Her hind legs were terribly swollen, her coat was in poor condition, and her mane and tail were badly matted. Her eyes were hollow and sunken in, and she showed no life in her expression. She wouldn't approach any of the regular stable hands that would feed her daily, and she often stood off by herself.

The little girl sat quietly in the car as her parents drove to Devon farm. The teenager hadn't spoken a word in over two years. She had sunken into a very deep and quiet place that no one could reach. The only thing that she seemed to enjoy was reading books about horses. When they reached the farm, they were greeted by the owner with a warm smile. The owner quickly invited the girl to come meet a special horse that had just come to the farm a few weeks earlier. When the little girl saw the mare, it was as if a connection had been born. The horse quietly walked over to the girl and lowered her head down to her level.

The following weekend the parents drove their daughter back out to Devon farm, and this time, the owner asked the little girl if she would help her change the bandages on the infected cuts that the mare was still recovering from. It quickly became clear that these two had some kind of special connection. The frightened horse would normally back away from people, but instead, she lowered her head and stepped forward to let the girl stroke her nose. It was the start of a beautiful relationship that would transform both horse and child. Soon the little girl was talking and the mare would nicker loudly when she saw the girl walking toward her. The lives of both a troubled horse and a little girl were changed forever.

~April 29~
The Aussie Police Horse

Horses were highly sought after in early colonial Australia. In the 1790's, policing the convicts and bushrangers (criminals living in the bush in Australia) was done on foot by night watchmen, constables, and the colonial military. By 1801 the Governor King formed the "Body Guard of Light Horse" regiment for dispatching his messages to the interior (department on which to help keep peace and order) and also as a personal escort. At the height of Aboriginal resistance in the Sydney Wars, the number of horses being used for military and protection had grown. The horse became a crucial element in occupying Aboriginal land and controlling the workforce made up of convicts.

In 1825, the first Horse Patrol was created, which soon was renamed the Mounted Police. The Mounted Police and military were critical during a very violent time in Australia's history between 1822 and 1824. By the 1830's, the horse patrol had proved invaluable as a highly mobile military unit in combating Aboriginal resistance, as well as the bushrangers. By 1850, the Mounted Police disbanded and became the Native Mounted Police, made up of Aboriginal men working alongside British officers. Men on horseback would now ride to the most remote bush areas to help control uprisings.

The use of horses for crowd control and policing in Australia has a long turbulent history with its roots in warfare. One of the major tragedies of this period was the large number of horses that were seriously injured or killed during the numerous battles and uprisings within the country. The horses would have to go where their riders took them, and the frontlines proved extremely hard on the animals. A lot has changed for the police horses of today, and Australian officers make sure the horses in their units are well taken care while working or when they are back at the barn.

~April 30~
Ship Ahoy!

The port town of Wells-Next-The-Sea on the North Norfolk coast of England has a long colorful history of using draft horses to pull the large lifeboats out into the water and then pulling them back onto land. The horses were called "Lifeboat horses," and they played a crucial role in history by saving lives.

When the call came in that a ship and crew were in distress, speed was of the essence to get the horses hitched up to the massive lifeboat and then pulled out to sea to be launched. A person called a "runner" would yell out, "Ship Ahoy!" to let the lifeboat crew know they were needed. This cry also summoned farmers to bring their horses, as well as men, to come help in launching the lifeboats. The teams of horses pulled the boat carriage down to the water while the crew pulled on ropes behind the boat to act as a break. Then six more horses were hitched on, with a single horse leading to take the lifeboat into the sea. To keep the horses safe in the deep water, they were shackled onto the back wheels of the carriage. The horses would stop in the water when it reached their chests. The most difficult work was pulling the lifeboat back up to the Lifeboat House after the work was done, and for this, two more horses were added, making ten horses in all! Lifeboat-launching with horses was dangerous, and many farmers became reluctant to loan their horses out to the lifeboat station because of the numerous injuries. At some port stations, it became impossible to hire local horses, and they had to be brought in from a distance which often delayed the rescue. February 11, 1936, marked the end of the iconic lifeboat horses. They would no longer be used for pulling lifeboats through city streets and across the sand to help save lives. It was a heartbreaking day for many people.

"Thus passes away one of the most familiar and spectacular features of lifeboat work, a feature at one time as familiar as the horses of the old fire-brigades."

~May 1~
The Trainer

There have been notable people throughout history who were considered by others to be great horse trainers. Without some of these very wise people who believed in having a relationship with the horse instead of using brute force to make the animal obey, horses may have had a much harder life even today.

The philosophy of training the horse had a much different look in past centuries. Horses were not used for pleasure, but instead for military, hunting, work, and racing. Each held a purpose and the weakest, slowest learning, or difficult equines were not tolerated at all. It was almost life or death when it came to training horses and if the horse didn't comply, his fate might be bleak. The horse's training was often severe, with the idea of breaking the horse's spirit and gaining compliance quickly.

Early training methods differed depending on the region and culture. Many cultures respected the horse, and even though their training techniques would be considered very primitive compared to today's training methods, people like the Mongolians learned early on that gentling the horse reaped many more benefits, and encouraged the horse to want to please his master. This proved to be a much better way to train horses than severe equipment that would cause pain and even blood.

Athenian cavalryman, Xenophon, also understood that the horse needed to be cared for, along with gentle training and fair corrections that didn't harm the animal. His writings paved the way for better horsemanship thousands of years later.

Many horse trainers have learned so much from the mistakes of the past, and that is why it is important never to forget where man has come from regarding his relationship with the horse. Only then can we ensure that we don't repeat the same mistakes again for these amazing creatures God has entrusted us to care for.

~May 2~
A Time To Honor

Fire horses became a beloved part of most fire departments in the 1800's and early 1900's. They gained the love and respect from the firemen who watched these brave horses handle the most ferocious fires, sometimes for hours on end. As the fire horse was being replaced by the motorized fire engine, everybody knew that a special time in history was coming to an end. It was now time to honor a few of the great fire horses.

It was February 21, 1933, and the local newspapers reported the death of Rochester's last fire horse, a white Percheron named Chubby, who died at the age of 33. Chubby had a long career as a fire horse before he retired in 1926. Due to his many years working as a fire horse and his beautiful appearance, Chubby was the best-known of the city fire horses. He was said to be "one of the strongest, most willing, and good-natured horses ever in the fire department."

Jim, the fire horse, had responded to eight calls during the day and was willing to respond to the ninth, but tragedy happened on the way to the last fire when Jim went down, and it was discovered that his leg was broken. Jim was only seven and a half years old and had only served the fire department for two years, but in that short time had proved himself to be an exceptional fire horse.

Fire horse Fred served for 17 years pulling the company's hose wagon. He was known throughout the area as a champion hose wagon racer. Fred was on call during a notorious town fire where 100 homes had to be dynamited in order to create a firebreak and save the rest of the town. He is remembered for his incredible bravery when most horses would have taken off with the water hose attached and ran away from the explosions. Fred was so loved that the firefighters had his head stuffed and mounted when he died at the age of 25. His head is now displayed at a local museum.

~May 3~
The Religious Ceremony

Man has attempted to find the answers to life through religious practices for thousands of years. And for most of those centuries, religious practices often involved the horse. Once the horse was domesticated and could be ridden, it became an animal above all other animals that was revered and worshipped by many cultures. The horse had an unexpected but very strong influence on how people developed religious rituals in different cultures.

In China, the horse is considered a good omen and represents heaven and fire. In Japan, the goddess, Bato Kannon—also known as the Merciful Great Mother, is seen in the form of a beautiful white horse. In Buddhism, the horse symbolizes the qualities of being indestructible and permanent. In Caucasus, a region between the Black Sea and the Caspian Sea, the horse was a central part of the funeral and memorial ceremony where the horse is dedicated to the deceased. During the ritual, the horse is circled around the body while a bridle is put in the hand of the deceased. The horse's ear is then cut or hair is cut and taken from the horse. During these ancient Shamanic religious rituals, the horse was worshipped as a carrier of souls from death to life.

In ancient practices, witches would ride their horses all night to go to the Witches' Sabbath. They would run the horses until they were hot and foaming all over their bodies. It became known as "witch racing." Many horse owners would put trinkets and amulets around their horse's neck for protection against evil spirits. It was believed that the devil and the witch could turn into horses when a witch hunt was taking place.

During ancient Vedic (Hinduism) rituals, horses were sacrificed, signifying the complete circle of creation. The ritual was intended to cleanse people from sin and to offer fertility. Traces of these ritual practices can be found among the Germans, Iranians, and Greeks.

~May 4~
Ancient Rome

Rome was one of the greatest empires in ancient history, and much of its incredible wealth was shown off to the world through their great horses. Rome's overabundance of gold and silver from battle victories, allowed them to breed the finest horses and build the best stables for the nobility and wealthy, but was unattainable for the common man. There was literally no expense spared when it came to buying and breeding the best warhorses and chariot horses.

A Roman poet described the ideal horse as follows: "High neck, short belly, elongated head, full back and chest of the muscles that cannot be hidden." Often the spotted and sorrel horses were worth more money than the dun-colored horses. When it came to buying and selling horses, the Romans started the practice of covering the horse's head and body with a sheet, except for the legs and hooves of the horse. This was to give the buyer a chance to look at the horse objectively without being blinded by its beauty. Boy, think of all the horses today that have been purchased just on looks alone, only to find out later that the horse has horrible feet or legs. It happens even today!

The Romans kept their horses clean, and they used tools like course palm-leather gloves, horsehair brushes, and wooden scrapers when they bathed them. Their manes and tails were washed with scented oils, and the manes were always brushed to the right side. It was a common practice to put oil on the horse's lips to keep them soft, especially in the dry, hot temperatures. It was also believed that if you rubbed the horse's legs while they were eating, it would help form a relationship between you and the horse. The Romans were very eccentric, and when it was time to breed a mare, they would bring the stallion and the mare to the "breeding room," where paintings of famous stallions hung on the walls, along with musicians playing music to set the mood! Now you've heard it all!

~May 5~
Feeding Horses

Nutrition and feeding horses has come a long way from centuries ago. If we study and learn from the past, we will gain a better understanding of the horse's nutritional needs for the future. Throughout history, when it came to feeding horses, man had to rely on foods that were readily available depending on the area and climate. While we may think of horses in past centuries as living in rural areas with plenty of grass to graze upon, the truth is that they worked extremely hard, often every day of the week, and had minimal or no access to pasture grazing in most cities.

During the Bronze Age (1600-1100 BC), chariot horses were often fed wheat cakes and even wine as a substitute when water was not accessible. During the medieval period, horse bread was fed to horses and easy to transport. Horse bread was made from legumes, bran, oats, maize, and seeds such as ground acorns. Foods fed to horses in the 19th century were usually rooted vegetables that were first boiled or steamed, with the exception of carrots. Horses were fed turnips, potatoes, parsnips, sugar beets, mangel-wurzel (beets), carrots and yams. These rooted vegetables were fed during the winter months when there wasn't much else to feed the horses. During World War I, horse fodder (high-quality forage in a dry matter base) was in high demand for the warhorses. It was easy to transport during wartime and the shelf life was long.

Throughout history, there have also been some serious nutritional mistakes made when it comes to feeding horses. Historical writings have shown us that horses died after being fed meat and poultry along with poisonous flowers, among other things. The evolution of horse nutrition has undergone many changes depending on the culture, landscape, peacetime, or war. Still, the horse has somehow managed to survive despite all our feeding blunders. And for that, we are forever thankful.

~May 6~
Diphtheria

In 1901, horse owners would make a few extra dollars by selling their horse's blood to local firms that made the diphtheria antitoxin. Scientists found that they could inject the weakened diphtheria toxin into a horse and wait for the horse to produce the antibodies. They would then bleed the horse and collect the serum. Now very rare, thanks to the childhood vaccination, diphtheria was a serious infectious disease at the turn of the 20th century.

Jim was an ordinary milk-delivery horse who clattered down the city streets of St. Louis every morning, delivering fresh milk to many families. Jim's celebrity status stemmed from a tragedy in St. Louis in 1901. At that time, the standard treatment for children with diphtheria was an antitoxin serum made from the blood of horses. When Jim wasn't pulling a milk wagon, he would often have his blood drawn, and he had produced over 30 quarts of antitoxin in three years. Sadly, during one of the treatments, Jim contracted tetanus and had to be destroyed. The serum from Jim's tainted blood was accidentally bottled and used to treat diphtheria patients, causing the death of 13 children.

The serum had been manufactured in local establishments with no safety protocols or testing in place to ensure the purity of the vaccines. The death of Jim the milk-delivery horse, and the 13 children ignited a public outcry to push for better medical safe guards for vaccinations and other medical products. Jim had an extraordinary impact on public health and is a huge part of medical history. In fact, some say this gentle milk delivery horse was instrumental in the passage of the law that eventually gave the Food and Drug Administration its regulatory authority over vaccines and other biological products.

A horse is willing to give everything, even his lifeblood for the good of mankind.

~May 7~
Pony Express

Back in the 1850's, mail delivery from the east coast to California by stagecoach was extremely unreliable, slow, and often delayed by months with winter's arrival. Such delays were felt by the Californians that were missing their loved ones on the east coast. There had to be a better and faster way to get the mail delivered. Then, the Pony Express was born.

It was a joint effort between several men who came up with the Pony Express idea. They would purchase 400 horses, build 200 stations across the country, hire men to staff the stations, stock them with provisions and, of course, hire the riders themselves. The relay stations would be 10 miles apart, and every third station was a home station where extra horses, firearms, men, and provisions were kept. Here the mail would be handed over to a new rider. Very quickly they realized they needed to reduce the miles between mount changes from 30 to around 12 miles to keep the horses fresh. The route would start in Missouri and end in California and was 1,966 miles long. About 80 young men (orphaned boys were preferred because of the danger involved) rode for the pony express, and the horses averaged around 14.2 hands tall. The horses needed to be fast, which meant the riders, tack, provisions, and mail needed to be light. It was very dangerous for both the horses and the riders, and they would travel no matter the weather. The best horses were purchased for this endeavor, and most of the horses came from the military out west, which had access to the strongest and fastest horses available. These "western horses" were sure-footed, strong, and fast. The cold winters or summer heat didn't stop them, and they accomplished what wasn't thought possible. The Pony Express only lasted from April 3, 1860 to October 26, 1861, when the telegraph connected the east to the west, but we will never forget those little horses that changed history.

~May 8~
Jack & Jack

The fire horse team of Jack and Jack were famous around the city of Des Moines. The horses were often identified as "Old Jack" for Jack senior and "Young Jack" for the younger horse. Together, this fire horse team had a great reputation as the dynamic duo. Old Jack retired at 23 years of age from the fire department, but he had first become a fire horse at the young age of six. He had gotten the undeserved nickname of "man killer" due to an incident where his original owner had fallen over the front of his wagon right beneath Jack's hooves. Old Jack spooked and kicked the man's head. Young Jack had been a carriage horse and was purchased for $175 by the fire department. The two became such an incredible team that they won a race in the 1903 Iowa State Firemen's Tournament and many races after that, earning them the title of "World Champions."

Firefighting was a hazardous occupation, but equally dangerous was driving a team of horses to a raging fire as fast as they could pull a heavy wagon. These fire horses would run at a full gallop through city streets crowded with other horses and wagons, streetcars, and people everywhere. On one occasion, Jack and Jack were racing to a fire when the team collided with a streetcar. The accident resulted in the deaths of two firefighters, but somehow the two horses miraculously came out of the crash uninjured. The team continued to work for many years together, often making numerous runs a day.

Upon their retirement from the department, a councilman noted, "Usually worn-out horses are turned over to the Street Department, but if I were to attempt to do that with Jack and Jack, the Fire Department would mob me." Jack and Jack were heroes and spent the rest of their lives on a farm grazing in huge pastures belonging to a firefighter's brother.

~May 9~
Chetak

In 1540 AD, Maharana Pratap became the ruler of the Mewar Kingdom (western India region) after his father had passed away. During that era, there were three familiar breeds of warhorses: the Sindhi, Kathiyawari, & Marwari breeds. Chetak belonged to the Marwari breed of horse, and it is thought that he stood somewhere between 14.2 to 15 hands tall. It is written that Chetak was beautiful beyond many other horses of that time. He was a very light color, but what made his coat so unique was the blue hue it gave off when it glistened in the sun. He had curled ears at the tips with a long peacock neck, a broad chest, and his eyes were the deepest blue. Chetak was said to be a very sweet horse but was also known to be aggressive and very difficult to handle. Several riders tried taming and breaking Chetak, but all failed. Only one man could tame and ride Chetak. That man was Maharana Pretap.

The Battle of Haldighati was fought on June 18, 1576, between the Mewar and Mughal dynasties. Chetak carried his king, Maharana Pretap, into battle against the Man Singh I of Amber, who was riding a massive elephant used in warfare. Chetak aggressively went straight for the elephant and reared up so that both front legs were on the elephant's head. In the process, Chetak injured both his front legs but continued to carry his king during the battle until Pretap became severely wounded himself. Chetak quickly carried him far away from the battlefield. Chetak had to jump a 25-foot ravine, which saved his king but led to Chetak's death from the injuries he sustained. A memorial was later built at the same spot where Chetak took his last breath to honor the loyalty and bravery of such a great warhorse.

I saw heaven standing open and there before me was a white horse, whose rider is called Faithful and True. With justice he judges and wages war. Revelation 19:11

~May 10~
Figure

In 1789, a little bay colt was foaled that would one day have a widespread and very profound role in American history. This little foal was owned by Justin Morgan, and at the time, he didn't even realize how this horse would become a "once in a lifetime" stallion that we now know and love as the Morgan Horse breed.

Justin Morgan named the colt, Figure, and he went on to become known as the Justin Morgan horse. During that time, the people who followed the young stallion simply called him "The Justin," and he spent the majority of his life in and around the state of Vermont. When Figure came of age, he was entered in a few races and easily beat his equine competitors. He was raced against horses in Brookfield, Vermont, in 1796 and defeated both purebred racehorses with ease. Soon the stretch of road they raced on was known as the "Morgan Mile," and to this day, it is still called by that name. His most admirable quality was his ability to reproduce horses that reflected all his greatest assets. His offspring were easily recognizable and were respected for their stamina, willingness to please, and easy-keeping qualities, which weren't often found in other breeds of horses at the time.

Figure's descendants excelled at farm work and as stagecoach horses. They also became top competitors in the early harness racing that was popular at the time. The first Vermont cavalry was mounted entirely on Morgan horses during the Civil War. It is thought that Figure stood at around 14 hands tall but had a very muscular build. He was used for breeding for a long time, and his wonderful traits carried through to his babies for many more generations. Figure died in 1821 at the age of 32, but he left an incredible legacy behind that we still admire today in the Morgan horse.

~May 11~
Reining

There is something drop-dead beautiful about watching a reining horse in action, doing what he was bred to do. These amazing horses can really put on the speed, power, and agility when working, but things were much different for the ranch horses of long ago.

The history of the reining horse developed centuries ago in Mexico and Southwest America as a way to work the huge ranches. Vaqueros (a Spanish word for a herder of cattle) spent many days on the open range tending to cattle. Before fences or barns, the cowboys had to figure out a way to control their herds. The horse was a necessity for its speed and safety of the cowboy. If a cowboy was on the ground and a bull started running towards him, he could jump on his horse and outrun the bull. A good ranch horse was versatile and adapted to his situation when moving cattle. He needed to be blistering fast to chase down cows and be able to cut back just as quickly for runaways that changed direction. He could get up to top speed with the slightest touch of a spur and come to a halt with amazing ease. These horses learned to spin in any direction to keep with the cattle. Vaqueros needed a free hand to handle their rope, so they rode with only one hand on a loose rein.

Cowboys were proud of their hardworking horses, and they started to participate in informal competitions to show off their horse's talent. It was a way to practice while at the same time demonstrating their horse's athletic ability. Sadly, by the 1940's, many of these cow horses were being phased out. Then in 1966, the National Reining Horse Association was formed and reining bloomed again. Some of the earliest reining contests involved tying a thread between the bit and the reins. The object was to see whose horse could perform the best without breaking the thread. New reining maneuvers have been added over the decades to enhance the sport, and these horses just keep getting better!

~May 12~
Trading For Power

Horse-trading and politics actually have a unique relationship that began hundreds of years ago. In today's modern political world, if a particular party cannot gain power after an election, they often will work in special areas of interest and negotiate special deals to achieve their goals and get the votes they need. This practice is called horse-trading. But what makes it all so fascinating is where the term "horse-trading" originated, and how it was woven into politics and the quest for power among countries.

Before modern warfare of the 19th and 20th centuries, horses were the most important part of any military. In the late 13th and 14th centuries, India was a breeding ground for conflicts with other countries, but they lacked good warhorses for battle. The reality was that the country with the best horses won the battles and became the ultimate conqueror. Very early on, India got its best horses from Arab nations because the Arab traders were the only ones who knew the route to India, and thus, could bring them strong and fast horses. Other countries were vying for India's money from the sale of good warhorses, and soon Portugal became very competitive in selling horses to India as well.

The rulers of that time had special chieftains who took care of the warhorses. It was a special privilege to be the king's chieftain, and the number of horses a chieftain was in charge of had direct influence and status with the king. During times of battle and warfare, it was common for kings to buy out chieftains from other tribes or countries with money to increase their military's horse supply. The word "horse-trading" meant at that time, "buying an opposite party's strength to win a confrontation." In other words, buying the horses! Modern machinery in the 20th century made warhorses obsolete, but the term "horse-trading" is still used in certain political negotiations today.

~May 13~
Ancient Greek Life

The proof that horses were significant in Greek life can be found in their various art forms that have recently been uncovered in the last few decades at different archeological sites. The horse was more than just an animal to use for work or warfare to the Greeks. They worshipped the horse and believed that horses were created by Poseidon, "god of the sea," and on special occasions horses were sacrificed to their god by drowning them.

Horses were used in warfare as early as the late Bronze Age in Greece (around 1200 BC), first to pull chariots and later for cavalry. The poet, Homer, mentions that the best horses were fed wheat instead of the typical barley and even given wine to drink. Most people did not own horses because they were too expensive. It was usually only the nobility and cavalry that rode. Horses that were ridden for battle in ancient Greece would be outfitted with beautifully made bronze armor to help protect them.

Chariot races were popular events in ancient Greece, originating as part of the ceremonies that took place during the "funeral" games. The racing of four-horse chariots became an event at the Olympic Games beginning in 680 BC. Greek athletic competitions also took place and included horseback acrobatics and military equestrian sports, such as throwing javelins from horseback.

During that time period, there were three handbooks written with instructions to horse owners on the correct treatment of their animals. The oldest handbook still surviving today is, *On the Art of Horsemanship* by the Greek writer and philosopher Xenophon (430-354 BC), which details the proper care and training of horses.

No matter the amount of training, it must have been very uncomfortable to ride a horse in ancient Greece, since most warriors rode without a saddle or stirrups. I would imagine it was equally uncomfortable for the horse as well.

~May 14~
The Quest For Wood

By the mid-1800's, the insatiable need for wood increased dramatically in the United States. Farmers who planted and worked their fields during the summer months, would leave the homestead and head to the big woods in the north to meet up with other lumberjacks to down trees all winter long. In order to supply the millions of feet of lumber demanded by the general public, it was estimated that 10,000 draft horses were used each winter to move the logs to railway spurs or river openings where they could float the logs downstream. They needed strong horsepower and lots of it.

Since most logging was done in the wintertime, snow became either a friend or foe to the loggers and horses, depending on the depth. The teams of horses pulled sleds that were often loaded with logs, stacked 20 feet high by 20 feet wide. The weight of the sleds and chains were around five tons alone, without the wood. There were also chains hooked up to the runners on the base of the sleds to keep it from becoming a "runaway." Once the snow became hard-packed, it made it much easier for the horses to pull the logs, which could weigh 50 tons or more! There was nothing more dangerous than two spooked draft horses out of control while pulling massive logs through snow and uneven ground. Most loggers understood this quite well and had a healthy respect for the logging horses.

Caring for the horses was a major part of lumber camp life, as horses were the power sources that kept the logging operations running. The men who drove the sleds and wagons were called Teamsters. Each teamster brushed, fed, and watered his own team. Many of the teamsters bonded with their horses and they knew that the horses' care came first, before anyone else's. The logging horses throughout the last two centuries have played an amazing part in the modernization of America, as well as other countries.

~May 15~
Horse Of A Different Color

If you talk to five different horse owners, you will find out quickly that each person has a favorite color of horse they are partial to. Some people love white horses, while others are crazy about black horses. The one thing in common is that we all love horses and part of the joy they bring us is just admiring their coats of many colors. Cultures and religion have always played a role in how people looked at the colors of the horse, and many societies were highly influenced by what was in style or popular at the time. Color preferences in horses have changed throughout the centuries, especially during times of war and even disease.

Since the horse's domestication around 3500 BC, special preferences, such as size, confirmation, and even coat color requirements of royalty and military, have strongly affected and influenced specific breeding trends for horses throughout the ages. During the Middle Ages, the attractiveness of spotted horses decreased, and solid coat colors, especially the chestnut-colored horse, became dominant. This color type was preferred by royalty and possibly influenced by the last book of the New Testament, the "Apocalypse of St. John" (81-96 AD). It described four riders on different colored horses. The rider of victory was sitting on a white or white spotted horse, whereas the riders of famine (black), death (bay), and war (chestnut) rode on solid colored horses. Then the symbolism of horse colors changed after several mass epidemics. The "bad" rider of plagues was now sitting on a white or white-spotted horse, and for this reason alone, these light colored horses were now looked down upon. Since the church was highly influential and one with the government, they often dictated the trends of the culture, and that included the horses that were being bred. Color was important to these early societies, and it played an important role in their breeding programs.

~May 16~
The Carousel

Many children have watched a beautiful colored Carousel go round and round as they waited patiently to hop on their favorite painted horse or animal when it was their turn. I can remember picking the horse that I thought was the most beautiful and racing to beat the other children who had the same idea! Sometimes I won, but usually, I didn't. What I didn't realize is how the horse played a huge part in the creation of the carousel, and its origin is quite surprising.

In the 12th century, horsemen played a game on horseback that was taken very seriously. The Italian and Spanish Crusaders who watched this high-level competition described it as a "little war" or garosell and carosella. The Crusaders then brought the game back to Europe, where it became a popular way to show off your equestran skills without the use of a real horse. The French called it a "carrousel." Then in the 15th century, the Turkish cavalry rode on a moving carousel to practice their riding skills. The riders had to knock off the hat of the man holding a stick along the outside of the carousel, which proved to be quite dangerous for both.

By the 17th century, it evolved into a military practice where the riders tried to pick up small brass rings with the points of their lance, that were hanging on posts outside the carousel. The men sat on wooden horses attached to a central pole which was turned by horses in a pit below. This birthed the carousel that we know today with the revolving wooden horses.

Hundreds of years later, the carousel became a type of entertainment for people all over the world but was still powered by horses until around 1860, when steam-power replaced the horses in the pit. Carousels still remain a favorite at amusement parks and fairs today, but the history of the carousel and the horses that powered them makes it all the more special.

~May 17~
Humble Beginnings

The world-famous Clydesdale horses that we see in Super Bowl commercials pulling the Budweiser wagon, are truly an iconic symbol of America's ingenuity. But what most people don't know is that these beautiful horses came from very humble beginnings.

At the turn of the 20th century, draft horses were used for pulling the heavy brewery wagons that would deliver barrels of beer to many places in the cities. It was very hard physical work for the horses, who worked long hours, often six days a week. The original Clydesdales came from Manitoba, Canada, and started out as the property of McDonough & Shea's Brewery. In 1933, Patrick Shea sold a team of six Clydesdale horses to August A. Busch, who then gave them to his father, August A. Busch Sr. of the Anheuser-Busch Company in celebration of the end of Prohibition. From 1920-1933, it was illegal to sell alcohol in the United States.

The Anheuser-Busch company quickly realized they had a great marketing gimmick with the Clydesdale horses. They decided to make their way to New York, where the team pulled the now famous wagon down the city streets all the way to the front of the Empire State Building. They drew large crowds and delivered a case of Budweiser to former governor and anti-Prohibition activist Alfred E. Smith. It proved so successful that they drove the team to other cities and made their way to Washington D.C. to deliver a case of beer to President Franklin D. Roosevelt. The hitch team would grow from six horses to eight in 1950 and would continue to be the symbol of the Budweiser beer company. As television and football grew in popularity, the famous horses soon found themselves making commercials that tugged at the heartstrings of all Americans. You don't even have to like beer to fall in love with the Budweiser commercials and the magnificent Clydesdales. Once you watch one, you will never forget it, or the horses.

~May 18~
The Best Horses

The Native Americans quickly became expert warriors and hunters on the back of the horse. Friendly competition between the Plains Indians for the best hunting and warhorses eventually turned tribes against each other. Owning better horses and more of them meant you could expand your hunting territory, which would bring more wealth to the tribe.

Soon, raiding and capturing horses from other tribes became a part of warfare, and it was also a way for a young man to earn his rite of passage and gain honor as a warrior. If you could steal another tribe's finest horses, then it would cripple their strength and give your tribe the upper hand. Some warriors would walk for miles to a rival tribe and scout out their prized horses. Then they would wait for nightfall to make their move. Some men were so concerned about their best horse, they would tie a rope around the horse's neck, and it would then be tied to the man's wrist under the teepee while he slept. He could tug anytime on the rope to see if his horse was still on the other end.

If the brave and daring warrior was lucky enough to make it out of the enemy tribe alive, many didn't; the final act was to give away the stolen prized horse to a widow or someone in need in his own tribe. This act was a way of showing off their bravery and generous heart at the same time. Horse-trading soon became a large part of many Native American tribes, as well as breeding their finest horses in order to bring up stronger and faster horses for their warriors and hunters. The Native Indians understood the horse better than many during that time and became excellent breeders of fine horses.

"If you talk to the horse, they will talk to you—if only you are willing to listen." ~Author Unknown

~May 19~
Opening The American West

During the 19th century, millions of people headed out west, lured first by the promise of inexpensive or free land and later by gold and silver. The heavy draft horse was imported for working the farms in the Midwest but soon was being bred in large numbers with the offspring being sold for new jobs, including much larger farms as the nation moved towards the pacific.

The railroads were also headed west and employed thousands of horses and mules. These equines worked side by side to carry railroad ties and supplies to the rail heads (the farthest point on a railroad to which rails have been laid). When the job was complete, the amount of dirt and rock these horses had hauled from the blasts and excavation of mountain tunnels would be staggering. Many new western stagecoach lines were in operation using a hitch of six horses to transport mail and passengers over dangerous rough roads. By the end of the century, new large farms comparable to those in the Midwest were growing food on the western prairies. These new farms relied on more draft horses to power their equipment. Times were changing quickly in America, and the draft horse was right at the forefront of it all.

In 1790, the average American farm was around 100 acres. By 1910, it was common to see 500-acre wheat fields. While oxen and light horses had been adequate for tilling the fields of Europe and the eastern United States, a stronger horse was needed to work the virgin soil on the western plains. This created a greater demand for larger farm equipment and larger draft horses to power them. By 1900, there were over 27,000 purebred Belgians, Clydesdales, Percherons, Shires, and Suffolk Punches in the United States, and if they were not working, they were being bred to keep the heavy horses coming. The supply and demand of the draft horse during this time was astonishing and played a big part in opening the West.

~May 20~
The Flood

The Netherlands had just been hit by a violent storm and the rain came down so hard and fast, that the open lands were quickly swallowed up by water. It was 2006, and the world awoke to hear about the numerous horses that were stranded on a small lowland "island" created overnight due to high water. The raging storm had pushed the seawater into far-reaching areas outside the dikes of Marrum. As the world became aware of the situation, nineteen horses had passed away from the harsh weather, lack of food, and stress. The rest of the nearly hundred horses huddled close together on the small island with no room to spare.

News of the trapped horses spread but the rescue efforts were failing. Local people had taken their small boats and tried to lure the horses into the water, but the horses would not move. Three days had passed, and time was running out. Another storm was approaching, meaning the horses would probably not survive. That's when a post appeared on the Friesian Horse Forum that read, "Horses and riders sought…Only experienced riders with horses without fear of water." Seven women responded to the post and quickly they met to talk about their plan to save the stranded horses. They decided that if they rode their own horses out into the water and swam to the island, there was a possibility that the horses would follow them back to safety. It was a huge chance, but at this point, anything was worth a try. As the women on horseback started towards the stranded horses, the horses on the island began to take notice. The women got very close to them and as they turned their horses around in the water to head towards higher ground, the most amazing thing happened. One by one the horses cautiously stepped into the water and followed the women. They never stopped swimming until they made it to higher ground. All the horses survived, and on that day the world witnessed a miracle.

~May 21~
Skepticism Of The Automobile

It's hard to imagine a time when people laughed at the automobile and thought it could never replace the horse, especially in our modern era of fast cars that come with hundreds of horses under the hood! But if you look back at history, there was actually a time when people didn't want change and preferred to use real horsepower instead of a horseless carriage.

The greatest obstacle to the development of the automobile was the lack of public interest. Horses had been used since they were domesticated and trained thousands of years earlier, and man had become very comfortable with the horse and all the different jobs they were used for. The old saying, "why fix something that's not broken," was the sentiment back then for many people.

In the 19th century, there was lots of discussion "think tanks" in circulation around the horseless carriage of the time. Horses were dependable and all they needed was grass and oats. What would be used for fuel for these new vehicles, and how would it be stored? A horse could eat along the way when being ridden or hitched, but when a vehicle was low on fuel, you would need to find a station fast before you ran out and found yourself being towed by a team of horses! This would take thousands of fuel stations and the cost was mindboggling. If the automobile breaks down, who was going to fix it? More importantly, a team of horses would have to be hitched up, to pull the broken vehicle to the repair shop! What about the horse rails that had been built? The new vehicles couldn't drive on the rails, and this meant new roads needed to be built everywhere that didn't have ruts. The other argument was that the new horseless carriage was a rich man's toy, and most ordinary people could never afford such a vehicle. The questions were numerous, but in the end, the vehicle became the preferred choice and it would change the life of the workhorse forever.

~May 22~
The Stagecoach Horses

The invention of the Stagecoach by Jonathan Wardwell in 1718 had an incredible impact on transportation and mail delivery. The horse-drawn stagecoach would lay the groundwork for future transportation systems and the stagecoach would endure for almost 200 years. Following Wardwell's example of long distance travel throughout the East using stagecoaches, many other builders began designing and building stagecoaches in large numbers.

The horses that pulled the long-distance stagecoaches worked extremely hard, but it was said that they were treated very well. The companies that owned the horses and coaches knew that the stagecoaches couldn't run without the horses, and their care was often a top priority. For the longer trips and for mail delivery, there would be stations set up along the way so that the tired horses could be traded out for fresh teams of horses to keep the stagecoaches moving at a fast pace. During this period, a stagecoach horse in England lasted only about three years but American stagecoach horses lasted much longer. One horse working in California pulled a stagecoach for 15 years and it was said that he traveled a quarter of a million miles!

A writer in the early 1800's gave a description of stagecoach horses: *"Every horse had a name. It was 'Git up, Joe, Git up boys or gals, you are shirky, Bill; you want touching up, Ben; if you don't do better, Ben, I'll swap you for a mule! ... Some drivers would fret a team to death while others would get over the road and you would never hear hardly a loud word to the team."*

By the middle of the 19th century, the stagecoaches were largely replaced by the railroad. The stagecoach, however, remained important for transportation in rural areas until the 20th century. In the end, the automobile became the king of the road, and this led to the end of the stagecoach in the early 1900's.

~May 23~
South Of The Sahara

Far south in Africa, past the Sahara desert, you will come to a region that is rich in history in regards to the horse, and its domestication and influence on the people of that area. The horses seem to be descendants of a few breeds, but the most common are the Afro-Turkic/Oriental breeds of horses, also known as the Barbs. The horses are short, slender-bodied, with fine hair and thin skin and their legs are very small-boned. Several groups of people kept detailed breeding records of their horses for the purpose of building up their military with stronger warhorses over the centuries. The horses were a crucial element in the military during the region's unrest and the numerous battles of that time.

During the 19th century, the Nigerians began trading horses to other tribes to gain larger horses for breeding and warfare, and to help them become more aggressive in battle. The Baguirmi Kingdom became powerful with the use of these war ponies equipped with quilted armor made of leather and chainmail, consisting of small metal rings linked together in a pattern to form a mesh. Horses were deeply embedded in the Nigerian culture, and the best horses were used as "bride wealth" payments between two families to prove a person's wealth and to ensure the marriage would take place as promised.

During the 1800's, there were reports of certain tribes that would deliberately cut the back of a horse and then let the blood clot up. This would eventually create scar tissue, which would then create a type of permanent "roughed-up pad" on the horse's back to help the riders stay on! There were also many accounts of the bond people had with their horses, and not all of them used these barbaric practices. Many believed the horses were their lifeblood, and they tried to take very good care of them under the harshest living conditions and social practices of the day.

~May 24~
The Space Shuttle

If you are wondering what the Space Shuttle has to do with horses, you are about to find out. Horses have even played a role in space exploration and the origins of this are simply fascinating and it all began centuries ago.

Imperial Rome built the first long-distance roads solely for the benefit of its military. Those same Roman roads have been used ever since. The Roman chariots created the original ruts and those ruts became deep and rock hard over the centuries. This became problematic and required everyone else to match their wheel size for wagons and carriages in order to keep their wheels from breaking. The Roman chariots were built just wide enough to accommodate the back-end of two horses. That same spacing between wheels spread throughout Europe and then made its way to America.

Now fast forward to the 20th century. The Space Shuttle has two big booster rockets attached to each side of the main fuel tank. These are the solid rocket boosters, also called SRBs. The engineers who designed the SRBs wanted to make them larger in the original design, but the SRBs had to be shipped by railroad, from the factory in Utah to the launch site. The first railroad tracks were built with the same gauge (distance between rails) as the ruts from the Roman Chariots! Since the tracks are only as wide as two horses rear-ends, this made going through tunnels challenging when designing the big booster rockets for the Space Shuttle. That is why the rockets are the size they are today.

So a major design feature of the Space Shuttle and the future of space exploration was originally decided by the width of a horse's butt! And yet another reason to thank a horse today for the advancement of mankind into space and space travel.

~May 25~
Carriage Driving

Horses have been pulling wagons, carriages, and carts for thousands of years, but the carriage soon became a symbol of wealth and social standing. By the 16th century, European nobility found driving horses and coaches the quickest and easiest way to travel. If the passengers had the financial means to travel in such a way, they could enjoy a relaxing conversation with the other passengers and reach their destination without having to walk or ride. To simply call for a coach, even for very short distances, was sending a very clear message to others in their social circles that they had the means to travel in luxury. In short, the horse and carriage became a status symbol.

The carriage designs used for transportation by royalty, aristocrats, and the wealthy, were becoming extremely showy with elaborately decorated carvings and lavish detailing that were adorned with precious metals and even jewels. These beautiful or sometimes very gaudy carriages were purposely designed to make them stand out for others to notice. They were often pulled by two or four matching horses, depending on the size and weight of the carriage. On the other end of the spectrum, carriages used by commoners and peasants were known to have their wagons covered in plain leather and nothing more. The carriage became a status symbol, separating the rich and royalty from the lower classes.

What was once a very heavy carriage had been redesigned many times throughout the centuries to create a lighter design that had shock absorbers and other modern conveniences. It would make travel much easier on long trips for both the horses and people. By the 19th century, many carriage types were being used every day. It is even noted that ideas were taken from the construction and design of the carriage to help create the first automobiles being built during the early part of the 20th century.

~May 26~
The Insane Disguise

The battlefield and the warhorse have been bound together for thousands of years, but during World War I, not only did the horses serve while alive, they were the inspiration for sneaky warfare even after they had been killed by enemy fire. Trench warfare became a standard part of fighting, and not only were the men deep inside the trenches, so were the horses. Often when the horses came out of the trenches up to ground level, they became easy targets from bullets and artillery fire.

As you could imagine, dead horses were everywhere during World War I. At first, the French realized they could hide behind the dead horse carcasses and be somewhat protected. Then one specific day, a horse had taken off without his rider heading right into "no man's land," which was a stretch of scorched ground and barbed wire, with explosives everywhere. This no man's land was the divider between the French and the enemy. The horse that had taken off was shot numerous times and died. Then the French soldiers came up with an idea from this particular dead horse. They would make hollow, papier-mâché horses large enough for a man to crawl inside and aim his gun through. Soon papier-mâché horses were being made that looked like dead horses lying on their side with their legs stretched out stiff. Once nightfall came, the French soldiers would sneak out and drag away some of the dead horses and replace them with the papier-mâché horses. They would climb inside the fake horse, stick their guns out a small opening and wait for daylight. The soldier would then have to stay inside the horse all day until nightfall. At first, the insane disguise actually worked, until one day, a French soldier was spotted trying to get out of a papier-mâché horse. The cover was blown, and soon enemy fire played havoc on both real horses and fake ones. The French soldiers very quickly realized that the papier-mâché horses wouldn't stop bullets!

~May 27~
The Police Horse

The London Bow Street Horse Patrol was established in 1758 and is considered the oldest equestrian police force. The beautifully stoic horses and their riders would patrol the country roads around London, and it became a deterrent for people who were thinking of breaking the law. After all, if you were going to try and outrun a horse, you would quickly learn a hard lesson about their speed. In the late 1830's following political unrest and rioting, it was decided to increase the number of police horses and move them to inner London to assist in keeping public order. Soon police on horseback became a common sight. The idea of mounted police quickly caught on and spread to other large cities in Britain and across Europe.

Mounted police in Japan perform traffic duty every day on the congested streets of Tokyo and have used horses to fight crime for many decades. The horses are well-trained before they walk the streets, and the people and noise usually doesn't bother them.

The Barcelona Municipal Police in Spain, founded in 1856, would ride Andalusian stallions rather than geldings or mares. They had a very unique way of dealing with rioting crowds—hind-end first!!

The Canadian Mounties are one of the most well-known mounted police units worldwide. The Mounties ride solid black Thoroughbred horses or Thoroughbred-Cross breeds. In 1989, Hanoverian stallions and mares were introduced into the breeding program to help enhance some of the required characteristics of their police horses.

The first equestrian police unit was started in the United States with one horse that was rented from a local stable in 1934. As the horse proved to be an asset to law enforcement, the number of police horses grew in most major cities and venues across America.

~May 28~
Forest Service Mustang

Horses are used all over the United States as working animals for the Forest Service. What is unique about the Blackrock Ranger Station in the Bridger-Teton National Forest (located in Wyoming) is how they acquire their horses. The Bureau of Land Management rounds up some of the weanling and yearling Mustang horses each year and gives them to the Forest Service. The horses are then trained to ride and work in the wilderness, which makes it a win/win for both the Mustangs and the Forest Service. The great thing is these horses are not taken out of their natural environment. They will still live and work in the most remote areas of the country instead of being shipped off to holding pens near larger cities.

The Teton Wilderness area consists of 600,000 acres of streams and river crossings, mountainous terrain and beautiful forest landscape. The Mustangs are excellent horses for the type of terrain since they are extremely surefooted equines and it comes natural to them.

The young horses are trained to be well-behaved and the process is slow but the results are worthwhile. The horses learn to carry a rider, pack tools or equipment or whatever else is needed. Even though the work is hard, the horses seem comfortable in their surroundings. The rangers who work with the horses have said that they are more impressed with the Mustang horses and now prefer them over other domestic horses. They tend to be hardier with stronger hooves and handle the fluctuation of weather and temperatures well. Once the young Mustangs mature and are ready for work, they are often very willing to please and are naturally "street smart" when handling wilderness conditions, which is important. There is a strong bond between the Forest Service trainers, rangers and these Mustangs and they take very good care of each other.

~May 29~
Vanning

During the 18th century, the idea of transporting horses to save on their feet and legs took shape by way of "Vanning." The introduction of shipping horses long distances, by being loaded into a large box/van and pulled by other horses, almost sounded crazy, but it worked. It seemed very unnatural to many and was an extremely slow way to travel, but it was very effective.

The first equine vanning dates back to 1771 when a horse-drawn van was designed and built to spare the bad feet of famed British racehorse Eclipse, who needed to make long journeys in order to race. Eclipse could not travel under his own feet because of the poor condition of his hooves, which would often become sore to the point of lameness. The horse-drawn van, in which, Eclipse made his first ride to breed a mare, also made it into history as the first horse trailer ever to be used.

In 1816, the racehorse Sovereign was carefully loaded and transported to his next race in an adapted horse-drawn van by his trainer John Doe. Then Doe convinced the horse's owner to transport another one of his racehorses named Elis, using the horse-drawn van to a much farther track. The Thoroughbred came off the van well-rested and won the race at such high odds that the new vanning mode of transport soon caught on, despite the reservations by many at the beginning. By 1836, horses were being vanned regularly, and it had become a common practice among wealthy horsemen, especially racehorse owners who wanted to minimize strain upon their highly valued Thoroughbreds. It must have been a nice way to travel for the horses, since the roads were slow and quiet, and both the horses in the van and the horses pulling the van took many rest stops together and, of course, to eat along the way.

"It takes teamwork to be successful, especially when it comes to horses."

~May 30~
The White Horse

Horses were significant to the Japanese culture and their religion. Even today, at certain shrines, a sacred white horse is stabled. The old Japanese tradition began with the donations made by one of the first Emperors of Japan to the Kibune Shrine in Kyoto. During a rainy year, the Emperor's offering to a Shinto Shrine consisted of a white horse as a prayer to stop the rain. If it was a year of drought, the Emperor would then donate a black horse with prayers to bring the rain. Horses were sacred symbols that were also associated with fertility. White horses were symbolic of the sun and often used in ritual sacrifice. Horses were also associated with death and funeral symbolism.

Before the defeat of Japan by Allied forces in 1945, Emperor Hirohito, the commander of the Japanese Armed Forces, was frequently pictured in military uniform atop his white horse. Hirohito would only ride white horses, and they were a part of his carefully cultivated image. Japanese tradition viewed the royal family as direct descendants of the Sun god. Emperor Hirohito's two favorite mounts were two white Arabian stallions named Hatsu Shimo (First Frost) and Sirayuki (White Snow). They were bred in the special Imperial stables. Hatsuyuki (First Snow) was another white horse that the Emperor preferred to ride because he was much gentler and calm. When Hatsuyuki died in 1957 at the age of 23, he was immortalized as a sacred horse at the great Isa Shrine, Japan's leading Shinto Shrine.

The friendship between New Zealand and Japan has always included a white horse, symbolic of their close relationship. New Zealand has gifted five white horses to the Nikko Toshogu Shrine in Japan since the 1964 Tokyo Olympics. In Japan, the white horse still symbolizes so much that is good and runs deep within the Japanese culture centuries later.

~May 31~
The Saddle

Horses have had to endure many of man's inventions, including the saddle. Early saddles were often very uncomfortable and poor fitting for the horse. They would leave rub marks, raw open sores, and create sore muscles that left the animal in pain often. As man started to learn more about how the saddle should fit properly on the horse, many improvements followed.

The Nomadic people were the first to design a saddle (around 500 BC) with a frame, and made it more solid by adding many details such as the girth, a pommel and cantle, leather thongs, a crupper, a breastplate, and a shabrack (saddlecloth). The Han dynasty of China (around 200 BC) was the first to design a saddle with material covering the wood frame. The Romans were the first to create the four-horn saddle made with wood. This four-horn saddle design greatly improved comfort for the horse because it distributed the rider's weight evenly, instead of having the rider's seat bones digging into the horse's back.

The Middle Ages brought much advancement to the saddle. The need for comfort for the knights during battles with all the excess weight of armor and weaponry, made the regular saddles useless. A higher cantle and pommel allowed the rider to be more secure in the seat, and a stronger wood frame made it possible to carry the heavier weight. This new design was much harder on the smaller horse with all the extra weight, and soon, larger horses were being bred. New saddle designs were being tried out on larger draft-type horses to carry the heavy weight of the knight, his armor, and the horse's barding (body armor), which was also very heavy.

Eventually, the three-point saddle was created for dressage, and saddles were modified for fox hunting and jumping. Today more than ever, the focus is on the horse with better designs to give optimal movement and comfort to the horse at all times.

~June 1~
Jappaloup De Luze

He was initially overlooked as a show jumper because he was only 15 hands tall. The horse was a Thoroughbred-Cross and didn't fit the perfect idea of a show jumper. In fact, his rider Pierre Durand refused to ride the gelding at first because he was too small. His name is Jappaloup De Luze, and he became the little horse that could jump anything.

Besides being too small, Jappaloup had earned the reputation of being difficult to compete on. His claim to fame had been tossing Durand off in the arena at the 1984 Olympics in Los Angeles, and then happily galloped out of the arena. That doesn't happen in the Olympics, or at least it's not supposed to. Durand had to walk out of the arena on foot, and was completely embarrassed. Things were about to change for the little horse and his rider.

Durand decided to change how he looked at Jappaloup and rethink his training for the challenging horse. Soon it became so much more than just a competition to Durand. It now was about the trust and relationship with Jappaloup, and as the trust grew, they started winning competitions. As a team, they jumped everything and cleared the rails with ease, and qualified for the Seoul Olympics in 1988. Jappeloup and Pierre Durand went on to become legendary in the world of show jumping, overcoming the odds with determination, and winning a gold medal in the 1988 Olympic Games. This underdog team would go on to inspire dreams for many equestrians. Jappeloup's retirement ceremony was held at the Eiffel Tower in Paris, which gives you some idea of how much the French loved their little horse.

Champions do not become champions when they win the event, but in the hours, weeks, month, and years they spend preparing for it. The victorious performance itself is merely the demonstration of their champion character.
~T.A. Armstrong

~June 2~
Time For A Change

In the 1870's there were an estimated 200,000 pit ponies working deep in the mines in Great Britain. Life for these horses was extremely harsh, often working up to 16 hours a day. At a time when animal health and care was not a concern for most people, these horses would often go without food or water until the end of the day's work. Many pit ponies became blind due to falling rocks or sharp objects hitting them, and often horses became sick due to infections from cuts that were not looked after. Pit ponies often developed lung problems from the coal dust, just as the miners did. There were massive reports of abuse, injuries, and sickness for the horses working in the mines, but most people looked the other way.

The Royal Society for the Prevention of Cruelty to Animals (RSPCA) began a campaign to help the pit ponies in 1876. They urged the government to consider the suffering of the horses that worked deep underground in the coal mines. The first protection for the horses came from the Coal Mines Regulations Act of 1887. Mine inspectors would now monitor how the pit ponies were treated underground, but sadly, it was only to the extent that the tunnel roadways be made large enough to allow horses to walk without rubbing their hips and sides against the tunnel walls. The Coal Mines Act of 1911 was much more effective, and now inspectors would oversee how the pit ponies were being treated regarding their care, working hours, veterinary checks, and adequately sized stalls with clean bedding. Also, horses could no longer work in the mines until they reached the age of four. Further acts of 1949 and 1956 enforced protective care even more. These were welcome improvements for the pit ponies, and many of the miners who worked with these horses were glad changes were finally being made for the health and care of these hard-working equines.

~June 3~
The Buffalo Hunt

Nothing transformed the Native American's way of life like the horse. Before using horses, Native Indians pursued large herds on foot, but it was dangerous and very difficult. These men had to travel by foot and cover a lot of area to hunt the buffalo, and often the buffalo ran in a different direction and they were too fast for the hunters. One technique was to startle and chase the buffalo toward a cliff or drop-off called a "buffalo jump." Once wounded, the buffalo was easier to kill.

When horses were introduced and the Native Indians became skillful riders, everything changed. For the Plains Indians, the newfound speed of the horse enabled them to hunt buffalo easier, have more high-quality meat, hides for the Teepees, clothing, and much more. The Native Indians could now use the horse to pull a sled called a "travois," which enabled entire tribes to follow the buffalo during their seasonal hunt.

The American Indians mastered the art of the hunt on horseback. They would often use the "straightway chase," in which each hunter singled out an animal in the herd, rode alongside it at a fast gallop, and killed it at close range. When hunting buffalo on horseback, the hunters still preferred the bow and arrow even after firearms became common. The bow was preferred for two reasons: First, it was difficult to reload a muzzle-loading gun at a gallop, and second, the hunter could easily claim the dead buffalo by identifying his arrows.

It took an exceptional horse to hunt buffalo. The horse needed to be fast and not afraid to get up close to the buffalo. These horses were extremely valuable to the tribes, and often men tied their best horses up close to their teepee to keep them from being stolen at night from enemy tribes. A warrior might have up to ten horses, but only one brave "Buffalo Horse."

~June 4~
Horses In The Bible

The Bible shows us a glimpse of the importance of horses and their roles throughout its pages. History shows us that horses were ridden by kings, princes, and warriors. The use of the horse was intended for warfare, and it symbolized just that. Horses were a sign of a strong military, and often the country that had the strongest horses became the victors in battle.

Two thousand years ago, men of peace typically did not ride horses but instead rode camels, donkeys, mules, or drove a cart pulled by a team of oxen. These other animals were definitely not a symbol of a mighty conqueror. After all, it's hard to look like a conqueror on the back of a small donkey.

Horses were, however, very important in ancient times, and "Chariot cities" were built to stable and care for large numbers of horses. There were skilled horseman, charioteers, and chariot makers. Men were trained to be leather and saddle makers and custom bit makers. Farriers and veterinarians (as we call them today) were also very important for the horse's physical needs. Almost everything we have today for horses was available back then, except a truck and horse trailer! It may all seem so primitive to what we know today, but the care of these horses, was equally or possibly, more important to man than what is often witnessed today. Horses were never taken for granted because they were too valuable.

There is something in the beauty and strength of the horse that has always humbled man. The equine was never meant to be worshipped, but instead a gift from God for us to take care of as they have taken care of us throughout the centuries.

But those who hope in the Lord will renew their strength. They will soar on the wings like eagles; they will run and not grow weary, they will walk and not be faint. Isaiah 40:31

~June 5~
Traveller

When the tiny foal was born in 1857, no one knew that this young colt would become the most famous warhorse of the Civil War. Years later, when it looked like war was imminent, this beautiful and very proud horse caught the eye of one particular General. That man was Robert E. Lee. At the time, the horse was owned and in service of another confederate officer of the 3rd infantry. When Lee first saw the nice horse, he was utterly smitten and called him "my colt," and made a promise to himself that he would purchase the horse no matter the cost. General Lee did purchase the horse from the officer for $190.00 dollars, and quickly changed his name to Traveller because of his ability to walk at a very fast pace. The bond between Lee and his horse happened quickly and was something to behold. General Lee had several mounts but rode Traveller the most, and the two were almost inseparable. It was witnessed a time or two where the General was seen after a long bloody battle, hugging Traveller as if to hold himself up and never let go. Traveller would stand quiet and patient as the General hung on to his neck.

After the war, Lee kept Traveller and promised to take care of him until his last breath. Lee became President of Washington College in Virginia, and while Lee worked on campus, Traveller would graze freely all day long. Admirers would stop by to see the beautiful horse, and many times Lee would catch them plucking hair from Traveller's mane or tail for a keepsake. When General Lee died, Traveller walked behind the casket in the funeral procession. Traveller was cared for up until he had to be euthanized a year later after he had stepped on a nail and contracted tetanus. He was buried near Lee Chapel in Lexington, and he will always be known for his bravery, stamina, and gentle soul.

~June 6~
The Only Wild Horse Left

There's a Mongolian phrase that says, "A Mongol without a horse is like a bird without wings," and this sums up how important horses were, and still are today, with the Mongolian people and culture. The Mongolian wild horse is commonly known as the Asian wild horse, Takhi, but most recognizably known as the Przewalski's Horse.

The first record of these wild horses is found in rock engravings and paintings that were discovered in caves across Spain and France dating back thousands of years. Bodowa, a Tibetan monk, was the first to mention the horses in his writings, and Genghis Kahn talks about seeing these sturdy horses during his Mongolian conquests. These wild horses are still very important to the Mongolian culture, and according to Mongolian legend, the horse is believed to carry the gods in their travels. These sacred horses were named Takhi, meaning "spirit" (or worthy of worship) in Mongolian. These wild horses are smaller than other equines, but they are very strong and have incredible endurance. They are identified by their large head, stocky build, and short legs. It was discovered that the Przewalski's Horse has 66 chromosomes, and domesticated horses have 64 chromosomes, and if they interbreed, the offspring often have 65 chromosomes. The hybrid offspring share some of the same physical traits of the Przewalski's Horse (including their stiff mane and coloring), and chromosomal testing is required to identify them. These horses live in either a harem or bachelor herd and are very social equines. To protect their babies, the mares will form a circle around their offspring while the stallion patrols the outside perimeter, prepared to charge at any threat. Throughout the night, one horse will usually stand guard watching for predators while the rest of the horses rest. The Przewalski's Horse is recognized as the only wild horse left in the world.

~June 7~
To All The Old Cow Horses

The poem is dedicated to all the old cow horses that gave everything they had in their youth and now can enjoy their deserved rest and retirement.

RETIRED

He's in the past're left behind, a hoss that's had his day,
What might be goin' through his mind is might hard to say.
Yes, time and age has made a change, he can't do work that hard,
Nor carry men who ride the range or take their turn on guard.

He knows about the rope corral, at morning, night and noon,
He knows the wranglers voice and call; the nighthawks droning tune.
He knows the way a circle's thrown and how to point a drive,
And now they leave him here alone, to old but still alive.

He dimly recollects with pride the way he used to buck,
The hand that topped him had to ride or he was out of luck.
He dreams of summer and of spring, and then those days of grief,
The snow and mud and everything, the late fall work for beef.

It seems he sort of understands the reason he must stay,
Just like a lot of old cowhands who's hair is thin and gray.
His work upon the range is through, he's not so quick and strong;
In fact there's nothing he can do, so he can't get along.

Poem by Bruce Kiskaddon – 1945
The Los Angeles Union Stock Yards

~June 8~
Sharing The Roads

Before the car, the horse ruled the roadway. People rode their horses and drove wagons and carriages everywhere, but the city streets were the most challenging because they were heavily congested with every type of wagon or cart you could imagine. Back in the day before motorized vehicles, the horse was the only means of transportation besides the train, once it was invented.

Then in the late 1800's, the motorized vehicle came on the scene and life was about to change in ways man and horse could never imagine. When the first automobiles hit the roads, most people had never seen a car, and the horses did not handle the noisy machines very well. It was a time of men learning to drive the new horseless carriage, and the poor horse was just trying to figure out what the heck it was! Soon the city streets were congested with both horses and vehicles, and the horses were on the losing end. The first vehicles were extremely loud, and for many horses this became very problematic. Horses would take off in fear, dragging carriages and wagons behind them, and running into vehicles or other wagons. This led to many injuries and deaths for both horses and people. It was a very hard time for the horse and a lot of growing pains for the future of the motorized world.

Because of the large number of accidents between the horse and the motorized vehicle, Uriah Smith, a preacher and inventor, came up with an idea that would make the horseless carriage less scary to the horses on the roads. In 1899, Smith introduced the Horsey Horseless. It was a huge wooden horse head that could be strapped to the front of a motor vehicle. Smith said, "The live horse would be thinking of another horse, and before he could discover his error and see that he had been fooled, the strange carriage would have passed, and it would then be too late to grow frantic and fractious." So there you have it, the birth of learning to share the roadway!

~June 9~
Horse Camping

In today's busy world, many equestrians are finding out that horse camping is a relaxing way to see the country. What was once a normal way of travel in the 19th century has now become a way to unwind and experience the great outdoors from the back of a horse. There are many types of horse camping, from public parks where you can put your horse in a rented round pen or stall while you sleep in your motorhome, to the hard-core horse campers that travel miles deep into the high country while leading behind them a couple of pack horses or mules with everything they need for the weeks they are gone.

The wonderful thing about horse camping is that the entire family can do it, and it comes with so many beautiful lessons. It is a way to bond with your horse like never before because you both are in a new place and everything is different. He is trusting in you to take care of him, and you are trusting in him to do the same for you as you ride. It's time in the saddle and time back at the campsite that really grows a rider and his horse to a new level. For the people who horse camp and travel all over the country, their horses go from being good trail horses to great trail horses that gain confidence with each new adventure. And it does the same thing for the riders.

Horse camping may be a leisurely activity today, but it still teaches the horse as much today as it did for the horses that were used by people of yesteryear. It also is a great way to get away from the mundane and repetitive riding that is done in an arena. After all, it can become very boring for the horse, and since they are a living, breathing animal, they could use some new scenic views in their life. It just might be worth checking into for the horse that seems to need a break or has become arena sour. Sometimes, all we need is some new scenery to refresh our horse and us.

~June 10~
In Times Of Desperation

Historically, horses have become a food source for humans when other foods were scarce. It was a way for man to survive when other food sources had disappeared. Before the horse was domesticated and trained, it was common for these animals to be hunted for food. As man realized that he could train and even bond with this beast of burden, the tide started to slowly change over the centuries about how humans viewed the equine. Some cultures started putting a taboo on horse meat, as it was soon looked down upon to eat the equine companion who had faithfully served.

Horse meat has often been the last option in times of war and poverty. One of the consequences of war has always been food shortages, and time and time again, horse meat is what kept the masses alive. During the revolution in France and the fall of the aristocracy, its military, affluent people, and commoners had depleted all their food sources. It was a time of desperation, and the beautiful horses formerly maintained by the nobles and wealthy as a sign of prestige, ended up being killed and used for food to feed the starving people. The surgeon-in-chief of Napoleon's Grand Army strongly urged the starving troops to eat the meat of horses to stay alive. It was said that the meat of young Arabian horses relieved an epidemic of scurvy that would have killed many people.

After years of fighting in the Civil War, food became scarce and the horses that could no longer work were put down and used for food. Despite the taboo of eating horse meat during WWI and WWII, horse meat was eaten in Britain and other countries during the many postwar food shortages. People did what they needed to do in order to survive and the horse paid a price in man's survival. The horse not only served man physically, but in the end was used as a lifesaver so that humans could live. The horse gave all he had and we will never forget his ultimate sacrifice.

~June 11~
The First Speed Limits

The first law governing the speed of automobiles was passed in the state of Connecticut. This was huge for the horses that vastly outnumbered the motorized vehicles that were now sharing the roads. The loud horseless carriage and the horse did not mix well, and runaway horses and accidents soon became a common occurrence. Horses and people were being injured, and many horses died from their injuries. New problems and questions were coming from all ends with the invention of the motorized vehicle. Who was going to replace the horse that was killed or needed to be euthanized from injuries? Who was going to pay for the vet bills or medical bills? What about the wagons or carriages that needed to be fixed from the accident? The problems were mounting and needed to be addressed. There were no laws set on appropriate speeds for the motorized vehicles, but speed limit laws had been passed earlier in American history in Boston and New York. These laws made it unlawful to gallop a horse through the city streets. It was time for some new laws.

The first laws were passed in 1901. Vehicles were not to exceed 12 miles per hour within the city and 15 miles per hour on rural roads. This proved difficult to enforce because the speed measuring devices were not very accurate. Since riding horses and horse-drawn carriages still greatly outnumbered the vehicle, the law also governed the interaction between the two. Upon approaching any horse, the automobile had to slow down. If a horse appeared frightened, the automobile was required to come to a complete stop. Well as you can imagine, there were people who followed the new laws and others that ignored them. This became a time of learning for everyone, and creating new laws and protocols for sharing the roadways soon became a top priority to keep everyone safe, including the horses!

~June 12~
Sport Of Kings

Horse racing has its roots found in the early Roman era. Chariot racing was the norm, but racing on horseback was gaining interest. From 1096-1270 AD, the Crusaders rode Turkish cavalry horses that dominated the English warhorses of that time. After many battles, England's horse population was decimated. Then a long list of kings, all named Henry, worked hard to rebuild their kingdom's cavalry. Beginning around 1140 AD, Arabian stallions were imported to England to improve the country's warhorses, but these kings imported horses for another reason—horse racing.

King Henry VIII imported horses from Italy, Spain, and Africa and built his own "racing stable," claiming it was needed to breed faster warhorses. Henry's horses raced against horses owned by other nobility, which soon became known as the Sport of Kings. Henry used tax revenues from the people to maintain his stables, arguing that, by breeding champions to champions, he could improve the quality of the cavalry. He could use the guise of the cavalry to promote his true passion, which was horse racing. Henry's daughter Elizabeth I, significantly improved her father's racing stable during her long reign. She only bred the fastest stallions and soon the finest of her horses were being sold throughout Europe as horse racing grew in popularity.

Settlers from Britain brought horses and horse racing with them to the New World. The original racetrack was built on Long Island in 1665. Although the sport became popular, organized horse racing didn't turn up until after the Civil War in 1868. Because the sport grew at such a fast rate without any governing authority, it led to massive corruption at many racetracks. In 1894, leading track and stable owners in the country met to form the American Jockey Club, setting up rules to curb the corruption in breeding and racing. Some still call horse racing the Sport of Kings even today!

~June 13~
The American Indian Horse

By 1710, the Plains Indians had become skilled horsemen. The Kiowa and Comanche Indians became known as some of the finest horsemen and mounted warriors in the history of the world. Some tribes established well-thought out breeding programs within the horse herds in an effort to produce stronger and faster horses and improve the quality of the breeds. At one time many individual tribes had certain types of horses they preferred, but when the tribes were decimated, their horses were taken by the cavalry and many were destroyed. Many horses did manage to escape, and they bred and thrived out in the wild.

In order to preserve these horses, the American Indian Horse Registry researched the conformation and traits of these horses. It combined the remaining tribal lines of horses into one all-encompassing breed called The American Indian Horse. There are still breeders today who select horses only from particular tribal lines. One of the most famous of the very early American Indian horses was the Chickasaw horse originating from the Southeast. The genes of these extraordinarily tough little horses were passed on to the Florida Cracker and to the earliest Quarter-Pathers, which are the ancestors of our modern-day Quarter Horses. These solid and fast Chickasaw horses still exist today.

The American Indian horse carries strong Spanish traits, and each of the tribes developed particular qualities in their horses that they preferred. You could often see those traits and qualities in the babies, and those traits have carried on through today. The American Indian Horse Registry was established in 1961, and there approx. 3,605 horses registered, with somewhere between 75 new registered foals each year.

What is a man without the beasts? If all the beasts were gone, man would die from a great loneliness of the spirit. ~Chief Seattle, Duwamish Chief

~June 14~
The Western White House

Up until motorized vehicles were invented, American Presidents rode or drove horses to get to their destination. In fact, the White House had a horse stable right next door, and the standing President had access to horses anytime he needed them. During the last few decades, very few sitting Presidents have been known for riding horses, only because they didn't need a horse to travel. So when you come across a President who loves to ride horses for enjoyment, it is definitely worth sharing.

Ronald Reagan loved horses long before he became the 40th President of the United States. In 1974, Reagan purchased a ranch in the Santa Ynez mountain range, and when Reagan became the President of the United States, it was soon dubbed "The Western White House." President Reagan and his wife Nancy loved horses, and they tried to visit their ranch as often as they could, especially after he became President. Reagan wasn't afraid to get his hands dirty in the barn, and he loved to groom his horses and muck out the stalls. Reagan was the first President to need Secret Service that could ride a horse. Reagan was an excellent horseman and when he became President, he needed protection even when he went out for a ride. Reagan's Secret Service needed to be able to keep up with him even in the saddle, and he helped more than a few agents out of the brush and back in the saddle during some of their rides.

One of President Reagan's favorite horses was named El Alamein. El Alamein was a grey Anglo Arab that the President received as a gift in 1980 by the President of Mexico. Nancy Reagan also had a favorite horse named No Strings. The Reagan's other horses included Baby and Little Man, as well as many others over the course of the Reagan's life. President Reagan was still riding at the age of 78, and even as he started to slow down physically, he still enjoyed being around his horses as much as possible.

~June 15~
Miracle Twins

Identical twins in the horse world are considered extremely rare. In fact, there are only a handful of recorded twin births where the twins have both survived and thrived into adulthood. So when twin horses are born that are doing well, it is a celebration!

The beautiful twin foals Masta Blasta and Shockwave were born at a British Stable in June of 2018. The foals are genetically identical all the way down to their matching buckskin color and the spots on their butt. It is said that the chances of this happening are more than 10,000 to 1. The foals were little miracles from the moment they were born and started drinking momma's milk quickly, which was a huge relief to everyone.

Tania Mackee, who runs Gassons Farm Stud, where the twins were born said, "Horses are only really designed to have a single foal during pregnancy. For this to happen is defying Mother Nature." What made this birth of the foals so rare is that they were born from a single egg division and survived full term. A horse's placenta is normally not potent enough to transport oxygen for two babies. The most common outcome is that the weaker twin will be stillborn or only survive for a very short time after birth. Sometimes the stronger of the twins will also struggle.

What made this birth such a big surprise was that no one, not even the equine vets, suspected twins. The mare had a normal routine scan and everything looked good with one fetus. No one knew it was a split cell pregnancy and what a miracle when they arrived! The mother did great during pregnancy, and after the delivery, both foals latched on to her udders quickly. Sometimes the most beautiful gifts come in doubles, and these twins have been a special gift to horse lovers all over the world.

Surely your goodness and unfailing love will pursue me all the days of my life, and I will live in the house of the Lord forever. Psalm 23:6

~June 16~
Horse Crazy Celebrities

Sometimes the horses we watch in movies and on television become stars, and often they make horse lovers out of their human co-stars. I thought it would be fun to share a few names of famous people who are absolutely crazy about horses.

Julia Roberts is an actress who loves horses and did some barrel racing when she was young. A few years ago, she traveled to Mongolia to film a documentary titled, Wild Horses of Mongolia. She lived several weeks with the Mongolian people, and learned about their lifestyle and their deep relationship with the wild horses.

Viggo Mortensen is an actor who is best known for playing Frank Hopkins in Hidalgo, but he is also very passionate about horses. Mortensen has purchased a couple of his equine co-stars after filming was done because he had bonded so close to each horse. He is also a huge advocate for wild Mustang welfare and even published a book of horse photographs entitled, The Horse Is Good.

Shania Twain is a country music star, and she is horse crazy. She loves horses so much that she decided to include them in her live show at Caesar's Palace in Las Vegas! Shania enters the stage singing while sitting on a beautiful gray horse, and the bond and trust between Shania and her horse are quite evident.

William Shatner is an actor who first fell in love with horses as a young boy. Then as an adult, he learned to ride on a horse while making the movie Alexander the Great, and he was hooked ever since. He still rides today in his 90's!

Robert Redford is a well-known actor who had always loved horses and been involved with them on a deeper level. He has produced and starred in movies such as The Horse Whisperer, and has helped bring awareness to natural horsemanship, along with learning ways to better understand the horse.

~June 17~
Doma Menorquina

Doma Menorquina is a unique style of riding that holds deep traditions from the island of Menorca. Menorca is one of the Balearic Islands in the Mediterranean Sea. The culture and people of the island are closely associated with the Menorquín horse, and the breed is native to Menorca. These flashy horses are known for their strong and agile body along with a slim and elegant frame. The horses are associated with a particular riding style called the Doma Menorquina (Spanish for Menorcan dressage). The Menorquín breed has very smooth gaits with suspended and elevated movements. The men only ride stallions, and the horses begin training around three or four years old. As they mature, the movements they are taught become much more challenging.

Horses and riders are at the center of the fiesta celebrations in a tradition that goes back to 14th century. Around 150 riders participate in the festival of Mare de Déu de Gràcia and pass through the crowds while performing complex moves on the horses. The louder the applause, the more difficult the horse's movements become. The Menorquín horse is almost worshipped by the people, and touching the horses is believed to bring good luck. People will crowd the horses to touch them as they move through the city streets.

Three types of riding skills are held at the festival. The Ensortilla is the skill in which the rider is armed with a lance and attempts to take a small ring suspended from a cord. The Rompre Ses Carotes is a jousting contest in which one rider attempts to break a hand-painted wooden shield held by the other rider. But the most dangerous skill is called the Córrer Abraçats, "running embraced," in which two horses gallop with their riders arm-in-arm as fast as they can run through a course. There are less than 4,000 of these magnificent Spanish horses alive today.

~June 18~
Women And Horses

It's hard to believe that just a few hundred years ago women were not allowed to ride a horse in much of the world. In fact, in many countries, it was viewed as "unladylike," and it was beneath a "well-bred" woman to sit on a horse. It was only a century ago that women were not allowed to compete in the equestrian competition at the Olympic Games. The first woman to ride a horse in Olympic competition was Lisa Hartel. In 1952 she competed for the country of Denmark as the first female equestrian Olympian and won a silver medal at the Helsinki Olympic Games. Thank goodness for the women before us who chose to go against the rules of society and hop on a horse!

Women bring something very unique and special to the horses they care for, and the bond between a woman and her horse runs deep. There is something heartwarming about watching a young girl ride a horse for the first time, and it takes us back to when we were young and rode our first pony. It's something we never forget. And many of us know that once the horse bug bites a female, she will be hooked for the rest of her life. If you are horse obsessed, then you will find any way possible to be close to these amazing animals, and you will sacrifice the finest jewelry or vacations just to call a horse your own. It is a crazy kind of love that is understood between women in every culture and language all across the globe.

Women today are such a major part of the horse world that it is hard to even imagine a different way of life. Today we celebrate the women who came before us and who dared to go where no women had gone before with horses. We've come a long way baby!

Have I not commanded you? Be strong and courageous! Do not be afraid or discouraged. For the Lord your God is with you wherever you go. Joshua 1:9

~June 19~
The Meat Eater

Nothing is more peaceful or soothing than watching a horse munch on his hay. It's hard to even imagine that at one time horses may have been meat-eaters, or at least ate meat out of desperation and severe hunger. But the truth is there have been many recorded accounts throughout history where horses ate whatever was available including meat, in order to survive.

A century and a half ago, when exploration of the South Pole was still important, it was common for explorers to use hearty Siberian horses to help travel to the pole. It was also common practice to teach these horses to eat meat and animal fat so that when there was no grass or forage for months at a time, they would still have food to sustain them. During these great explorations, a very famous explorer Sir Ernest Shackleton had a Manchurian pony named Socks. It was journaled that Socks shared meat-based meals with Shackleton in 1908 while on their way to the South Pole. No other horses had come as close to the South Pole as Socks, but that meant he needed protein and fat to sustain him, so he ate meat.

A team of German Explorers in 1938 filmed Tibetan horses eating a mixture of sheep's blood mixed with Tsampa, which is dough made of roasted flour. The practice of feeding meat to the horses in Tibet continued until the 1970's. In Iceland, salted fish was often fed to horses as a form of protein and mineral/salt supplement. The Kingdom of Bhutan, located in the Himalayan region, was noted for feeding the king's horses a special meal of Tiger fat and Yak meat. There have also been notable writings where horses have eaten raw meat willingly in Arabia, New Zealand, and the United States. It's hard to know if the horses were desperate for food since history doesn't tell us all the details, but it does show that horses will adapt to their surroundings when forced.

~June 20~
La Voltige

Watching a person or team perform a gymnastics routine on the back of a horse while the horse slowly canters in a circle is beyond beautiful. You have probably watched this type of competition on television or at horse shows, and for most people, it is one of the most graceful equestrian sports you can witness. We call it Vaulting, and its history stems back hundreds of years.

It is believed that Vaulting possibly originated in ancient Crete, where bull-leaping was a common sport at the time. Yes, you read this right! Bull-leaping was a sport for the military, and the idea of Vaulting is said to have been birthed out of bull-leaping, which traces back to the Roman games. Vaulting or La Voltige became popular across Italy and France during the Renaissance period of the 17th century. Noblemen showed off their agility on horseback and enjoyed it as much as they did fencing and wrestling. It also became an essential part of military training for the men going into battle. It helped them gain balance on the back of a horse while holding a sword or shield.

Vaulting is an equestrian sport that requires a very quiet, patient, and strong horse. These horses need to have a strong back and strong leg muscles that can withstand cantering continuously in a circle for periods of time. The horse must be graceful and able to make smooth transitions which are so important in this sport. Draft or draft-crosses are used often along with Warmbloods since they tend to be mild-mannered, and they are built with a broad strong back, which makes them ideal for this magnificent sport.

"We have almost forgotten how strange a thing it is, that so huge and powerful and intelligent an animal as a horse should allow another, and far more feeble animal, to ride upon its back." ~Peter Gray.

~June 21~
"Blue" Lakota Warhorse

Joseph No Two Horns was a cousin of Sitting Bull. His Lakota name was He Nupa Wanica, and he was a Hunkpapa warrior. No Two Horn's favorite horse was a fierce blue stallion he rode in all his battles. During the battle of Little Bighorn, No Two Horn's courageous Blue Lakota warhorse was shot and badly wounded seven times but found the strength to carry No Two Horns safely off the battlefield before collapsing and dying. No Two Horns was 24 years old at the time, and it is said that he never got over the loss of his beautiful and brave blue stallion. Later on, he became a gifted artist and his chief subject was his mighty blue stallion.

Horses played a vital part in warfare for the plains Indians. Wild and bold-colored horses were highly valued by the Lakota warriors, and embodied powerful medicine and protection in battle. Blue roan horses were known for their extraordinary mix of black, grey, and white hairs that have a blue hue, and were considered sacred horses. These colors represented black (war), blue grey (storms), and white (light), and it was believed these colors shielded the horse and rider from danger.

No Two Horn's blue roan stallion had striking white coloring that melted into his blue coat. The stallion also had a white blaze over most of his face and four white socks up to his hocks. It was said that the stallion was fast, smart, and most of all, courageous in battle. No Two Horns said his horse had an incredibly strong heart, and his portrayals of his blue stallion through his artwork can be seen in museums across the country, including the Smithsonian.

"Swiftly running friend of man, I ask you to enter this moment. I seek the strength that allows you to leap obstacles in your path. I seek the stamina that allows you to travel great distances. I seek the nobility of your spirit that allows you to carry the heaviest of burdens." ~Author Unknown

~June 22~
Horse Galloping Ceremony

In the country of Ethiopia, in the region of Oromia, there is a culture of people who still practice the same rituals of manhood, religious ceremonies, funerals, and weddings as they have done for many centuries. In this remote and undisturbed area of the world, the people come together several times a year to celebrate what they call the Horse Galloping Ceremony.

The Oromo people are the biggest ethnic group in Ethiopia. They speak the Oromo dialect, which is different than the country's official Amharic language. Each year the men and boys gather with bamboo sticks and wait for the horses to arrive. One by one the horses are led to the specific area where the ceremony will take place. The horses wear special ceremonial decorations in their manes and tails and on their saddles and bridles. Each bridle has uniquely woven designs that might seem relatively primitive compared to the modern-day bridles we use today. The Horse Galloping Ceremony involves boys as young as eight or nine years old when they are just being taught how to ride. The ages go all the way up to grown men who will share in the equestrian rituals. The young boys team up in groups of two or four, and they each get on a horse. The ceremony begins as they pretend to fight with their bamboo sticks while on horseback and sing ceremonial songs while standing in a circle. It is said to be all symbolic, but as the ceremony continues, the riders become more aggressive. The riders use their horses to show their strength and courage, but as the riding progresses, the horses are often pushed to their limits by force and made to do tricks and maneuvers that are physically very hard on the animals. To the outside world, it can leave a person feeling uncomfortable with what they have witnessed. For the people of Oromia, this is normal and acceptable horsemanship and they do not seem to worry about the horses at all.

~June 23~
Real Horsepower!

The large fields between the United States and Canadian border were used for farming crops. It was 1939, and the land was still worked by teams of draft horses pulling farm equipment. World War II broke out and Britain was in need of help from the United States. With the rise of Nazism, almost half of Europe was under the control of Hitler, and since Britain was an island country, it relied heavily on outside help against Germany. The United States at that time was part of the Neutrality Act, which ensured the U.S. would not get involved in foreign conflicts. Britain had ordered warplanes from the United States, but due to the Neutrality Act, the United States could not deliver the planes by air. Behind closed doors in top secret meetings, both countries devised a plan to help Britain get more warplanes. They came up with the most unusual idea that would involve the U.S/Canada border and draft horses.

An area of farmland on both the United States and Canadian sides would work as temporary airstrips. The U.S. would fly the airplanes to a farm field in North Dakota. From there, they would empty the fuel tanks and hook teams of horses up to the planes and pull them over to the Canadian side, where the airstrip was located. Once the planes were on the Canadian side, they could unhook the horses, fuel up the aircraft and then fly off to the closest military base to get the planes ready for war. Since civilians were used to move the airplanes between countries, and they did not fly across the border, the Neutrality Act did not apply. Farmers brought their teams of horses to help pull the planes across and were paid for the use of their horses at $3 to $5 dollars per take-off.

When Japan attacked Pearl Harbor, the United States broke the Neutrality Act and joined the Allied Forces. It is not clear how many planes were pulled over the border by horses, but it is said to possibly be a couple of hundred. Now that is real horsepower!

~June 24~
Equine Reenactors

Today we are lucky enough to watch reenactments from past battles and other events so that we never forget our history. These reenactments are special because the men and women try to authentically show us what the soldiers and horses went through during wartime. Now we know that the equine reenactors are taken much better care of than their warhorse decedents, but there is still a lot of work that goes into reenacting a battle scene using horses and riders.

Two hundred years ago, the horses were probably ridden every day through every terrain imaginable. They also became very familiar with the sound of gunfire since it was used as a standard tool for hunting or in times of warfare. Those horses were probably exhausted from the miles they traveled daily, and food was usually in short supply for the horses during wartime. The truth is that most horses during battles probably became numb to everything going on around them, and they were just trying to survive the only way they could under the constraints of men.

The horses used in reenactments have to get accustomed to so much. When reenactors are looking for horses (if they don't have their own) to be a part of the event, they need a quiet horse that can handle loud noises like gunshots, canons firing, and the beating of drums. They will be asked to gallop alongside a bunch of other horses headed directly at the "enemy," then other times, horses and riders will be running in different directions. Reenactments can seem like mass chaos during the battle scenes, but it's supposed to because that is what it was like during actual warfare. So when a reenactment is taking place, it takes a very special horse that will stay relaxed and go through the paces without much effort. After all, it wouldn't look good if the equine actor took off and ran the opposite way during the final battle scene!

~June 25~
This Armor Is Heavy!

During the medieval period, the horse was an essential part of warfare. We often romanticize about the knight riding on his steed in full armor ready for battle, and many people have a vision of a huge and very muscular horse that never tires and helps save the damsel in distress! The truth is, often, these warhorses were small, at around 14.2 hands to 15 hands, but stocky. Very few knights or military had larger horses during the early part of the medieval period. The barding (body armor) that the horses wore for jousting or battle was very heavy and often covered most of the horse's body. The heavy armor physically exhausted the horses, and later, it was finally realized that less body armor was better for the animals.

- The Chanfron was created to protect the horse's face in warfare and jousting. Sometimes this included hinged cheek plates. Often a spike was added between the ears for decoration and to intimidate the enemy.
- The Criniere was a set of segmented plates that protected the horse's neck and would often wrap around the entire neck.
- The Croupiere protected the horse's hind quarters. It was made from leather or plate armor.
- The Flanchards were used to protect the flank. It was attached to each side of the saddle, then around either the rear or the front of the horse and back to the saddle again.
- The Peytral was designed to protect the chest of the horse.

During the battle, a horse would have been expected to carry his mount in full armor, weapons, the horse's body armor and anything else the knight needed. This was often debilitating for both the rider and horse, and it proved to hinder the knight during warfare.

~June 26~
Chinese Horse Proverb

The horse has always been an important symbol in Chinese culture and was often used as the main subject for their teachings, which were expressed through their many Chinese proverbs. The Chinese used the horse for warfare, agriculture, religion, and even the afterlife. These short sayings or stories each taught some greater truth for everyday life according to the Chines culture.

One of the most famous Chinese horse proverbs is "塞翁失馬 Sāi Wēng lost his horse."

Sāi Wēng lived on the border and he raised horses for a living. One day he lost one of his prized horses. After hearing of the misfortune, his neighbor felt sorry for him and came to comfort him. But Sāi Wēng simply asked, "How could we know it is not a good thing for me?" After a while the lost horse returned and with another beautiful horse. The neighbor came over again and congratulated Sāi Wēng on his good fortune. But Sāi Wēng simply asked, "How could we know it is not a bad thing for me?" One day his son went out for a ride with the new horse. He was violently thrown from the horse and broke his leg. The neighbors once again expressed their condolences to Sāi Wēng, but Sāi Wēng simply said, "How could we know it is not a good thing for me?" One year later, the Emperor's army arrived at the village to recruit all able-bodied men to fight in the war. Because of his injury, Sāi Wēng's son could not go off to war and was spared from certain death.

Do not be anxious about anything, but in every situation by prayer and petition, with thanksgiving, present your requests to God. And the peace of God which transcends all understanding will guard your hearts and your minds in Christ Jesus. Philippians 4:6-7

~June 27~
Modern Day Packhorses

There is something special about heading out into the wilderness with nothing but a couple of packhorses, the gear you need for the week, and the friends you are going to enjoy the week with. Many people experience this type of vacation every year all over the world, and for most of them, just being out in the backcountry where life is simple is worth every penny. The one thing you may not realize is that the horses taking you safely to your destination are not your average horses at all!

Packhorses are highly trained, and each is uniquely picked for this type of work. They need to have a very calm demeanor that doesn't get bothered by much at all, and they also need to be strong and sure-footed. They should have a good mind and temperament and even a great sense of self-preservation. Walking on cliff's edges, through knee-deep water and steep terrain is no big deal for these horses, and they are not going to spook at the slightest little sound. On top of it, they need to be an extremely patient horse because they are often carrying a person on their back for long hours that has zero riding experience. Talk about a saint!

The horses that are trained for this kind of work have experienced everything you could imagine, and keeping calm under pressure is their strong suit. Packhorses are not glamourous or win blue ribbons, but they are worth a million dollars. Ask anyone who has ever gone into the backcountry with a packhorse, and by the end of the trip, they have fallen deeply in love with their equine companion. It's an unexpected bond that surprises most and is never forgotten. Packhorses are amazing animals that take us to the most beautiful places on earth and help us to see God's creation in ways we never imagined.

A horse will carry his load without complaint or comparison, but a man will carry his load and think it is the heaviest among others.

~June 28~
Harness Racing

As early as 1554 in Valkenburg, Holland, as many as 3,000 horses would be entered in large trotting matches each year at the Horse Fair. Two centuries later, Holland's most famous trotting event, "The Golden Whip," was first run in 1777 at Soestdijk. During this time, a gentleman by the name of Count Orlov had been breeding horses and bringing up a strong trotting bloodline from his stallion Barss. This magnificent stallion became the foundation for many strong Russian trotters known as the Orlov trotters. England's Norfol Trotter became a strong trotting breed around 1750 and was purely a road horse, but its popularity led to many road races because of the speed and distance in which these horses could trot continuously. In North America, road racing became contagious and by the early 1800's trotting tracks for racing and entertainment began popping up in many areas throughout the country.

The creation of the Standardbred horse and the breed's impact on the world rested upon one Thoroughbred stallion named Messenger, out of England. Messenger was shipped to America, and he became both a major sire to the American Thoroughbred through his undefeated grandson American Eclipse, but was also infallible in harness racing, which started an incredible lineage of trotting racers. Harness racing was growing fast worldwide at the turn of the 20th century. The breeding of stronger, faster horses became very competitive, with no expense spared and today the Standardbred is still the breed of choice.

Just because I have an extra gate doesn't make me different or untrainable, it makes me special and one of a kind. From the race-track to the show ring, for the beginner mount or pleasure rider, anything is possible if given the chance. To those who have owned me and know how great I am—I am the Standardbred.
~Author unknown

~June 29~
Left Or Right Handed

The early design of the automobile and the side the steering wheel was placed on has roots in the horse-drawn carriages of centuries ago. Up until this last century, most people were right-handed. In fact, if a child showed a tendency to use their left hand, they were often reprimanded and forced to use their right hand, as it was looked down upon to be left-handed.

In early history, the charioteer would drive his chariot and team of horses from the right side, placing the reins in his left hand so his weapon could be ready in his more dominant right hand to defend at a moment's notice. From chariots to horse-drawn carriages, nothing really has changed in how the driver drove the team of horses. The carriage drivers still drove on the right side so they could have their right hand (dominant hand) ready to pull out a gun if needed. The earliest automobiles were designed directly from carriage driving with the steering wheel placed on the right side. Then in 1908, Henry Ford moved the steering wheel to the left side of the automobile, putting the controls in the center. This made things easier for the right-handed driver since you no longer needed your sword or gun to protect yourself while traveling.

Since most people were right-handed, riding horses took on some of the same left and right practices. The reins would be held in the left hand so a person could hold their weapon in their right hand. Today, we mount the horse from his left side because of how the military used their left and right hands. The soldier's weapon would fit into a sheath on the left hip, so he could pull it out easily with his right hand while his left hand was still holding the reins. The placement of the sheath required that the soldier mount their horse from the left side to avoid hitting his leg on the sheath when throwing his leg over the horse's back. So, if you were left-handed, you were out of luck!

~June 30~
Cincinnati

Cincinnati was born from a distinguished line of Thoroughbred racehorses. His sire, Lexington, held the record as the country's fastest four-mile Thoroughbred during a time of turbulence in America. Cincinnati was given to Ulysses S. Grant as a gift shortly after the battle of Chattanooga, sometime in 1863. A gentleman who knew of Grant's expert horsemanship contacted Grant and told him that he wanted to meet with him. When Ulysses showed up at the hotel, the man told him that he could no longer ride and wanted to give him his favorite horse with one condition. That condition was that the horse would always be well cared for, never be harshly treated, or fall into the hands of someone who would treat him bad. Ulysses S. Grant fell in love with the Chestnut horse right away and gave the gentleman his promise.

Cincinnati stood 17 hands tall and was exceptionally strong. He was an extremely calm horse that hardly blinked an eye at anything going on around him. Very quickly, Grant and Cincinnati bonded and became a strong team on the battlefield. Grant had many great horses to ride during the Civil War, but he chose Cincinnati often. You could not deny the impression they made when they rode up to a camp or stood in front of the soldiers, giving them the next orders. Just their presence gave encouragement and mental strength to the men fighting on the ground.

After the war, Grant was offered $10,000 for Cincinnati (which was an incredible amount of money in those days), but he turned it down. He would never part from his beloved horse. Cincinnati grew old and was retired to a close friend's farm in Maryland where he lived out his days with the best care a horse could be given.

Ah, you know my weaknesses – my children and my horses.
~Ulysses S. Grant

~July 1~
Belle And Sundance

It was a race against time. The temperatures were a brutal -40 degrees and the two horses were left to die in the backcountry of Mount Renshaw, British Columbia, in six feet of snow. To make matters worse, they were trapped and couldn't move to find food and were losing weight and becoming weaker every day. Belle a 3-year-old mare, and Sundance, a 15-year-old gelding, had been abandoned by their owner, when by chance they were discovered by two snowmobilers traveling through the high country. As the snowmobilers got closer to the horses, they could see that they were emaciated, frostbitten, and close to death.

The snowmobilers returned to town and quickly shared what they had seen. It wasn't long before people gathered to create a plan to rescue the horses, and it would involve the volunteer efforts of an entire town. First, they needed to get some hay to the horses and see what kind of condition they were actually in. Would they eat the hay or need to be put down, was the question on everyone's mind. Once a few people reached the horses and looked into their eyes, they saw a glimmer of life and hope in the animals. They fed the horses and decided to give them a fighting chance. What needed to be done first was the excavation of a trench 6 feet deep and over 3,280 feet long. Then they would have nearly a 20-mile descent. The rescuers used snowmobiles and had to travel an hour just to reach the horses. They loaded hay on their snowmobiles to feed the horses, and melted snow so they could drink water. Nearly 25 people would work many hours each day digging a trench wide enough so that finally, a week later, the horses were able to walk out to freedom. After being set free, the horses were taken to Prince George Equine Rescue. The two horses were nursed back to health and eventually adopted by new owners. The man who abandoned the horses was arrested and charged with animal cruelty.

~July 2~
The Movies

In the 1920's the motion picture industry was taking off, and horses were a huge part of it all. Unfortunately during those early decades, horses were often viewed as disposable. Laws had been passed to stop horse cruelty as early as the late 1800's, but in those early days, the movie industry was able to get away with pretty much anything they wanted to do. People just looked the other way.

In the 1926 epic movie Ben Hur, as many as 100 horses died in the filming. With the arrival of sound on film, the movie industry quickly started making westerns in the 20's and 30's. The western movies brought big money to the studios. Since horses were still being used in everyday life as working animals, there were plenty of horses available for films, and it became easy to toss them aside afterwards. The popular western movies proved to be extremely hard on the horse. The early westerns showed lots of horses and riders falling because the public loved it. Tripwires were set up make horses fall, and horses were forced to jump through glass or leap over wagons and the scarier the action on film, the more money it brought in. This was all at the expense of the horse, and injury or death was just a part of the industry at that time. In the 1930's, the western movie Jesse James came out, and two horses died in the making of that film. The director had put blinkers with painted eyes on the horses so they couldn't see where they were going to be running, and the horses were forced to run towards a 75-foot cliff. The stuntman made a lot of money, the shot was spectacular on the movie screen, and the horses were dead. It was a sad few decades for the horses that were forced to do things that often injured or killed them. Many people and animal welfare organizations started taking notice, and soon laws were passed to ensure the safety and well-being of all horses working in the motion picture industry. Things finally began to change for the better.

~July 3~
Old Wives Tales

Hundreds of old sayings about horses have been passed down from generation to generation. It is amazing how the horse has been such an influence on everything, including tales and superstitions. As you read the ones listed below, you can decide if you think they are true or just a bunch of horse manure!

- *One white hoof, buy the horse; two white feet, try a horse; three white feet, look well about him; four white feet, do without him.*
- *A horse with two whorls on his forehead will be more difficult.*
- *Inhaling a horse's breath is a cure for whooping cough.*
- *Seeing a grey horse on the way to church is considered lucky for the bride and groom.*
- *In England and Germany, dreaming of a white horse is considered a death omen.*
- *Eating hair from a horse's forelock is a cure for worms.*
- *A horse is only worth as much as how many times he can roll over.*
- *Copper pennies in a tank will prevent moody behavior in a mare!*
- *Horses standing with their backs to the hedge means it's going to rain.*
- *Take a hair from the mare's tail and tie a nail to it. Then you hold it above the mare's hips… and if it doesn't swing, she's not pregnant. If it swings in a circle, she's carrying a filly; if it swings straight, a colt.*
- *When you cut a horse, throw one testicle to the east and one to the west, and don't look where they fall, or he will be proud cut.*
- *Changing a horse's name is bad luck.*
- *If you lead a white horse through your house, it will banish all evil.*

"If you are fearful, a horse will back off. If you are calm and confident, it will come forward. For those who are often flattered or feared, the horse can be a welcome mirror of the best in human nature." ~ *Claire* Balding

~July 4~
Light Horse Troop

When we think about the 4th of July, we often forget about the horses that helped win the war. The truth is, George Washington and the cavalry often struggled but also claimed many victories using very ingenious ideas to weaken the British soldiers. And it all had to do with the horses.

Captain John Leary led the first cavalry unit used in the Revolutionary War. They were known as the Light Horse Troop of New York City, and they were a company of forty Light Dragoons that were put together. George Washington petitioned Congress, and on June 21, 1775, they were accepted as a Continental Unit. Light Dragoons were special units of mounted cavalry.

Winning the war wasn't just about winning the big battles, it was essential to conquer as many smaller battles as possible to weaken the British. The Light Horse Troops became well-known for their scouting missions to locate the enemy. They were much faster on horseback and could sneak in and out quickly. Because the British had bright red coats, the dragoons could see them from miles away and then plan accordingly. These men and their fast horses were a major asset to Washington's army.

Washington's cavalrymen used unusual tactics to weaken the British. On one colossal raid, the cavalry seized 300 tons of the British hay supply, which left the British army and their horses helpless. Without hay, the horses would never last, and the British would not be able to move weapons or supplies. The loss of hay crippled the British at that point. It is said that without the horses in the American Revolution, the patriots wouldn't have survived against the huge British Army. The horses provided the speed and strength to carry men into areas and back out without the British ever knowing.

"The harder the conflict, the greater the triumph." ~ *George Washington*

~July 5~
The Posse

It's easy to drum up a vision of the Wild West along with the sheriff and his posse riding out to get the bad guys, especially with so many western movies portraying this scenario. It is interesting that the word Posse stems all the way back to Medieval Latin with the meaning of "Body of men and power." The one part that is missing from the definition is the horse. After all, when we think of a posse, we think of the horses. Even in today's modern world, there are mounted posse units all over the country ready to help at a moment's notice.

Fast riding horses and horse-drawn wagons were the exclusive transportation for the sheriff and deputies before the automobile. Law enforcement depended heavily on good horses to help keep the town safe. Even after the first automobile was purchased for a sheriff's department, most town or country law enforcement maintained a group of mounted reserve deputies or volunteers which they called the posse. The sheriff's car may have been faster than a horse, but it couldn't go into the brush or up steep terrain as the horses could.

The mounted posse has been used for hundreds of years when a group of civilians were needed to help catch a lawbreaker or to help in search and rescue efforts. Often the sheriff and his deputies would be outnumbered when it came to gangs or lawbreakers, and if they needed to travel out of the city limits, the help from mounted riders was a plus. There was strength in numbers, and with more horses and riders, the chances of getting your man became much greater.

The sheriff, posse, and the horse go together like peanut butter and jelly, and the horse is credited with helping keep law-n-order for centuries.

~July 6~
The Good Death

Equine Euthanasia comes from the Greek meaning "good death" or "gentle and easy death." It was once said that "letting your animal go a day too soon is better than a day too late," which really means—don't let them suffer. That is good and very true advice. But I am just like most horse owners. It can be extremely hard to follow those words of wisdom, especially when it is time to say good-bye to a horse that you have loved and taken care of for many years. Euthanasia, though hard to discuss at times, is a very practical and responsible part of horse ownership. When it comes to ancient techniques used in euthanasia, not a lot was written. But with the help of the tools uncovered at burial sites from the past centuries, it tells us a little about the practice of euthanasia and the horse.

Thousands of years ago, gun powder and guns were not yet invented, so other means were used out of desperation to put the poor animal out of its misery. Stabbing the horse or cutting its throat was one way of killing the animal, but it was horrifying to watch while it was happening and could take a long time for the horse to eventually die. This was painful to watch and often the owner of the sick or injured horse had to wait it out while feeling utterly helpless. Later on, after gunpowder and the gun was invented, a person could put down a horse much faster and without pain, as long as they did it right and shot the horse in the correct spot on his head. During wartime this became a common practice with so many horses becoming seriously injured or sick.

Today we are fortunate to have modern equine medicine that has improved the end of life for the horses we love so much. It is still the most difficult thing a horse owner will ever have to do, but the goal is to make their end of life a "good death" and to die with dignity.

~July 7~
Making People Laugh

Poker Joe was named the funniest horse under saddle, and this intelligent equine proved he could keep a crowd laughing. In 1995, Tommie Turvey was looking for a new horse to train for an act he was creating, and he saw this beautiful Paint horse at an auction and purchased him right away. Tommy was attracted to the horse's white tail, black mane, and unique markings on his body. When he got the horse home, he quickly realized that Poker Joe was not easy to handle, and it would take a lot of patience to bring him around. Tommie worked with the Poker Joe every day and even slept next to him for a month to create a bond between him and the horse.

Poker Joe and Tommie started traveling and performing in front of crowds and the horse started to come alive with a personality that was larger than life. In 1999, Tommie created an act with Poker Joe, and that allowed the horse's personality to shine through. After working with Poker Joe for two years, "The Riding Instructor" was born. In the act, Tommie plays a snooty riding instructor who tries to teach his horse the fine art of dressage, but the horse has other ideas. It is hilarious and Poker Joe gets the best of the trainer in the end.

The act became a total success overnight, but what made the act between Tommie and his horse so special was the complete trust that Poker Joe had for Tommie. In the act, Poker Joe is on his back with legs straight up, and Tommie is standing over him. This takes trust beyond normal for a horse to allow himself to be put in such a vulnerable position. It is truly beautiful to watch Tommy and Poker Joe work together so well, and even though it is one of the funniest horse acts you will ever see, what makes it so much more special is the incredible bond these two have. Tommie Turvey has shown tens of thousands of people all over the country what total trust and love look like between a man and his horse.

~July 8~
Palomo

Simón Bolívar was a soldier in South America who was instrumental in the country's revolutions against the Spanish empire. Born into privilege, Bolívar was sent to Spain for his education but quickly decided to become politically involved in Europe. After France invaded Spain in 1808, he joined the resistance movement and played a key role in the fight for independence.

Palomo was Simón Bolívar's beloved horse, and together the two had a strong bond. The way the two came together was quite unusual. According to local lore, Simon Bolívar visited Santa Rosa in early 1814 on his way to Tunja. His mission was to report to Congress on the United Provinces of New Granada in Venezuela. Bolívar was approaching the town, but his horse was exhausted and had refused to move any further. Bolívar got off his horse and asked for a guide to take the tired animal and lead him into town. During the walk, Bolívar and the guide had a conversation in which the guide told Bolívar about his wife Casilda's dream. In her dream she saw herself giving a recently born colt to a famous General as a gift. He said to the guide, "Tell Casilda to keep the colt for me." Five years later, when General Bolívar returned to New Granada, he was given the colt promised by Casilda, Later on his way back to Venezuela, Bolívar stopped in Santa Rosa to visit Casilda and thank her personally for the horse. He named the horse Palomo (Cock-pigeon) after his grey-white color, and the horse accompanied him on most of his campaigns throughout the liberation.

Palomo died after a very long and arduous march while in the care of one of Bolívar's officers. Palomo was buried next to a hacienda chapel, and the horseshoes of the beautiful white horse are displayed at the Museum of Mulaló in what is now Columbia.

~July 9~
Equine Therapy

Horse therapy has been proven to be good for the mind, body, and soul. But when did humans first realize this? Winston Churchill said it perfectly, *"There is something about the outside of a horse that was good for the inside of a man,"* and the statement couldn't be truer.

We really don't know the exact date or even decade that therapeutic riding or horse therapy became a specialized field, but there are some ancient Greek writings that document the benefits of horseback riding around 460 BC. Hippocrates wrote a chapter on "Natural exercise" and explained how horseback riding is healthy.

Fast forward many centuries to 1569, and Merkurialis of Italy wrote publications about the physical benefits of horse riding, and Tissot of France followed with similar writings around 1780. Then almost a hundred years later, French Neurologist Charles Chassaignac added his research to the equine field by conducting a study demonstrating that therapeutic riding improved muscle tone, balance and even the mood of his patients .

During World War I, Olive Sands from the UK used horseback riding at the Oxford hospital to help rehabilitate soldiers who had been wounded during the war. From that point on, many British doctors started using therapeutic riding as a way to help all types of handicaps and disabilities. In 1952 Liz Hartel of Denmark won a silver medal at the Helsinki Olympic Games as an Equestrian Olympian. But what caught the attention of many physicians was that Helsinki had some paralysis from polio, and she used horseback riding to strengthen her core and leg muscles. Horseback riding helped her so much that she began competing against other equestrian athletes. That was a huge game changer, and today thousands of horses are helping people all over the world through horse therapy.

~July 10~
Love In A Tiny Body

The doctors, nurses, and patients at Chicago's Rush University Medical Center did a double-take when they heard the sound of tiny hooves coming down the hallway on the pediatric unit. Children hooked up to IV poles stepped into hallways to get a glimpse, and kids too sick to leave their rooms giggled with delight when the two little pint-size horses showed up for some bedside nuzzling with the sick kids at the hospital.

Mystery and Lunar are Miniature horses with big hearts who love to visit children in hospitals. The tiny horses are part of the therapy organization Mane in Heaven, where the horses travel to different places to comfort those in need. They also offer distraction therapy to children who are seriously sick and it takes their minds off the pain or illness they are experiencing. The therapy that the Miniature horse offers is in complete contrast to the high-tech hospital environment. There is nothing better to warm a heart and bring a smile to a patient than the touch of very soft ears and face, and big beautiful eyes to stare into. Some children will actually have tears of joy when they see one of the Miniature horses come into their hospital room.

Miniature horses are very small, standing around 34 to 38 inches tall, and most children have never seen a small horse before. It brings even more excitement to the floor when the staff and children see the size of these amazing horses in little bodies. They almost look like mythical animals or something out of a fantasy movie or book. Mane in Heaven's owner, Jodie Diegel, a former obstetrics nurse says, "The minis bring smiles, joy, love, and laughter, and that's the true healing in action."

A cheerful heart is good medicine.
Proverbs 17:22

~July 11~
War Paint

Native American Indians painted symbols on their horses for specific purposes. They painted their horses for battle, for the hunt of buffalo, and for medicine. They painted symbols for the spirits and to ask for safety on their missions. It was a very important part of their life, and the horse played a beautiful role in all of it. Each painted symbol had a meaning that ran deep within the tribes.

- *The horse's battle scars were always painted red, and the left handprint on the horse's right hip was the highest honor.*
- *Long zig-zag lines were often painted on the horse to symbolize lightning and to add power and speed to the horse.*
- *When a horse knocked down an enemy, left and right handprints were outlined on the horse's chest to show others what had taken place.*
- *Arrowheads on all four hooves indicated a surefooted and fast horse.*
- *A circle was painted around the horse's eye and nostrils to help the horse keep alert vision and a sharp smell when danger was near.*
- *When men were going on a dangerous mission, they would paint an upside-down handprint on their horses. It was the most valued symbol a warrior could place on his horse.*
- *To please the warrior's god of war, they would paint thunder stripes on the horse's front legs.*
- *The Sacred Buffalo symbol was to show the Great Spirit that the hunter was thankful for his past kills.*
- *Buffalo tracks were painted over the horse's hips, symbolizing hunts.*

The Native American woman would draw a "secret" prayer on her man's horse's hindquarters. This prayer was never explained prior to the hunt, and if her hunter came home victorious, she would then tell him the meaning of her symbols.

~July 12~
The Cutting Horse

The land was vast, and it seemed like it would go on forever. It was a time before fence posts and barbed wire. For the cowboy, moving cattle across the dry and dusty landscape was hard work, and it couldn't have been done without the help of their horses. If a cowboy needed to chase after runaway cattle or cut a cow from a herd, the easiest way to do it was by letting his horse do the work, and that is just what he did. The early cutting horses took to their job like a fish to water, and the cowboy never looked back. The cutting horse truly changed the landscape of the west, and a good cutting horse was worth its weight in gold.

To own a good cutting horse was the envy of every cowboy, and soon cowboys were having friendly competitions between each other to see who had the best horse. In 1898 at the Cowboy Reunion in Haskell, Texas, the first known cutting horse competition took place. Today the cutting horse industry has grown into a multi-million dollar business, and this sport is growing in many countries, with Australia and the United States at the forefront .

In a cutting contest, the horse and rider have two and a half minutes to work two or three cattle and keep them from returning to the herd. Once a cow has been chosen, it is separated from the other cattle, and the rider drops his reins and lets the horse take over from there. The goal is to work the cow and not let the animal get away from the horse. The agility and lighting speed of the cutting horse is truly amazing, and to watch a cutting horse go down on his front legs as he almost touches noses with the cow is quite impressive. A great cutting horse possesses a strong "cow sense" that makes him good at anticipating the cow's next move to return to its herd. The well-trained cutting horse knows his job and actually seems to enjoy it.

~July 13~
Amish

There is something peaceful about seeing farms with buggies in the yards and horses with foals in the pastures. The Amish community has not changed how they live to keep up with the 21st century. Instead they have chosen to keep their life as simple as possible, and that very much includes the horses they use for traveling and working their farms.

The Amish horse and buggy is something that most people are familiar with. These horses travel at a steady pace paying no attention to the vehicles zooming by. Driving by an Amish horse and buggy on the roadway amazes me and makes me nervous, only because I anticipate the horse spooking and taking off with the buggy. But the truth is, these horses are exceptionally trained and tune out the traffic and noise around them.

It is said that the Amish prefer the Standardbred or Saddlebred horses for pulling their buggies. Since the Standardbred has been trained to trot or pace while pulling something behind them, they make a wonderful cart horse. The Standardbred is also known for having a calm temperament which is vital since they are sharing the roads with cars, trucks, and motorcycles. The American Saddlebred is another breed that the Amish prefer for pulling their buggies. These horses possess a wonderful personality and incredible willingness to please their owner.

The Amish still use draft horses to work their land and pull the wagons. They keep a large number of draft horses on their farms to get the work done each year. The most common breeds of draft horses that are used on Amish farms are the Percherons and Belgians, but you will see other breeds as well. The horses are a major part of the Amish way of life, and they realize the importance of their horses and that they are a gift from God.

~July 14~
Medicine Hat Horse

The Native American Indians believed The Medicine Hat horse was good luck for the warriors. This uniquely marked horse was chosen among the other wild horses because of the "War Bonnet" these horses possessed at the top of their head. The War Bonnet is a distinctive facial or head coloring that looks like a cap or bonnet that is a different color from the rest of the face. These horses have a white face with a colored patch covering their ears and head, and they are easily recognizable. Some say that the sides of the horse's face, which are opposite in color, is another distinctive feature of the Medicine Hat Horse. Others will say that the horse's eyes have to be "painted" or "circled" or at least one eye must be blue, which is called a "heaven eye." All these special markings were prized in the Native American tribes and if a foal was born with these special markings, it would be a celebration within the tribe.

Some of the Plains tribes believed Medicine Hat horses had a magical ability to protect their riders from injury and death while in battle or hunting. They were thought of as supernatural protection for their warriors, and the warriors looked to these special horses to keep them safe and to warn them if danger was coming.

These horses were closely guarded at all times because if a tribe owned a Medicine Hat horse, it was common for other tribes to try and steal the horse away, and it was believed to bring good luck to the warrior and tribe who stole the horse. These horses were so revered that only tribal chiefs, medicine men, and great warriors who had earned that title were allowed to ride a Medicine Hat horse.

Many of today's Medicine Hat horses living out on the plains are tied to the Sioux tribe and Chief Sitting Bull, and they are direct descendants of Sitting Bull's war ponies from the late 1800's.

~July 15~
The Last Pit Pony

Sparky was the UK's last surviving pit pony. He was a small mixed-breed pony who had started working in the mines at the age of four. Sparky had several weeks of training before working in the mine, but once he was lowered down, he would stay there for many years. The mine he worked in was six miles offshore beneath the North Sea. During the day, he would drag steel girders and wooden supports along narrow pit paths, and at night he would eat and sleep in his pitch-black stall. At the peak of the mining industry in 1913, there were 70,000 ponies in the mines. Sparky became the sole survivor of a 250-year history of pit pony mining. His stables were four miles underground, and there were 20 stalls in total. It was a harsh existence, but due to the 1911 Act (to create safe working environments for animals), he was washed, groomed, fed, and kept in an area with electricity and water. Every day Sparky was checked by the farrier, and each year a veterinarian would give him a complete medical exam.

The hours a pit pony could work were laid down by law, and the maximum was 48 hours per week. Every summer Sparky and the other pit ponies would be hauled up in a sling out of the mines for the annual mining holiday. The pit ponies would get to see daylight for two weeks then the horses would be rounded up to go back down in the mines for another year. Unlike the miners who would go up and down the shafts in a cage, the ponies were lowered in a net or sling, which was very scary and uncomfortable for the horses.

Sparky retired in 1988 from the mines and was given a good life at the National Coal Mining Museum with his pit pony mate Carl, a Welsh Mountain pony. Sparky's retirement life consisted of staying out in a field overnight and spending his mornings in the stable eating oats and barley and meeting visitors. Sparky passed away at 35 years old. He had lived at the museum for 18 years.

~July 16~
The Hunter/Jumper

When we hear the words, "that horse would make a great hunter/jumper prospect," many of us will conjure up an image of a beautiful horse easily jumping a course with grace, confidence, and speed. The equestrian sport is actually made up of two different disciplines but is often referred to as show jumping. Most people don't realize that the sport has a rich history that laid the foundation for today's jumping competitions.

The Hunter-type horse originated hundreds of years ago when fox hunting became popular. At first, it was a means of hunting red fox or other small animals, but later it became a social pastime for the wealthy. It was associated with wealth and status, and of course, the horses used for hunting were the status symbol of choice. Up until King Henry I took the throne in the 12th century, commoners were not allowed to participate in the fox hunt. Only royal blood could ride in the pursuits of that day. Many of the traditions later carried over to North America, where in today's hunter competitions, proper attire and behavior are important for the rider, and the horse must also show great qualities like obedience, ease, and softness of movement, along with a proper jumping style that emulates the traditions of the past.

The Jumper-type horse is traced back to the 18th century and the Enclosure Acts in England. These Acts were put in place to establish boundaries between wealthy landowners. With boundaries came fences. Those who now wanted to fox hunt found it necessary to have a horse that could run across the countryside and jump any obstacle when asked. The early jumper competitions became popular and the emphasis was on speed and power, not technical skill. The earliest jumping competitions (late 1800's) were for military only, but over the years, the door was opened to all riders, including women.

~July 17~
A Very Special Horse

It takes an extraordinary horse to take care of the Para-Equestrian. Most people think that if you have a disability and sit on top of a horse without full use of your limbs, the horse knows naturally what to do. That's not the case, and not every horse makes a good mount for the para-equestrian. It takes a quiet, sensitive horse that is willing to learn special signals, depending on the rider's disability or limitation. The communication aids for the horse range from hand, leg and voice signals to using the shifting of a person's body in the saddle.

The bond between the horse and the para-equestrian is unlike any other, and it is critical in keeping the rider safe while riding and competing. The horses that are trained for the Para Olympics are trained first by a horse trainer who has full physical ability of their body to communicate with the horse using aides. Then depending on the disability of the para-equestrian, the trainer will introduce new cues and aides to train the horse so that they mimic how the para will be riding.

For example, if a rider has no feeling in their legs, then the cues will be coming from other areas since the rider will not be able to give leg or heel cues. Then when the training is done and the rider gets on, the horse understands quickly what his rider is asking, and there is very little confusion between the horse and the rider. It is said that these special para-equestrian horses have a sixth sense, and it seems to come naturally for them when adapting to special aides and cues to make up for the physical or sensory limitations the riders have.

It's a very slow process but so rewarding to observe a horse listening to his rider and moving so well, that you can't tell the rider is disabled. The time in the saddle for the para-equestrian is a little piece of heaven on earth, and the horses are their angels.

~July 18~
Shetland

When you mention the Shetland pony, someone usually has a good story to share about a pony they rode when they were a kid. The Shetland pony has a reputation for having a mind of his own, but they have taught many children how to ride and, dare I say, have taught many children important lessons about good horsemanship, sometimes the hard way!

It is believed that the Shetland pony originated on the Shetland Islands (Scotland's northernmost point) around 2,000 years ago. The ponies quickly adapted to the harsh climate and handled the weather better than many other animals. These small equines stand at around 42 inches tall and have large feet, which are perfect for traversing the wet and muddy landscape. Shetlands in the wintertime look bigger and fatter than they really are with their double-layered hair coat. Their thick coat keeps them entirely waterproof and warm. The Shetland has done so well in the cold climate that the little ponies would prefer to stay outside as much as possible, and they do quite well grazing the rough grasses that grow in the area. Shetlands are very social horses and also extremely smart—sometimes too smart for their own good. If a gate has been found open, the finger usually gets pointed at the Shetland!

Between the early 17th and late 19th centuries, Dutch fishermen set their boats looking for fish off the coast of Shetland and would often dock during the summer. Doctors who traveled with the Dutch fishing ships encouraged the fishermen to get exercise after being on the water for so long. The men found exercise and entertainment with the Shetland pony. The men would hop on the strong little ponies and race them across the fields. During one of these races, one of the fishermen couldn't stop his fast pony and they both went over the high cliff into the water and perished. To this day, the spot is still known as the "Dutchman's leap."

~July 19~
Chincoteague

The ponies were initially bred to work in the coal mines in Spain back in the 17th century. They were small with a great temperament, making them popular with the miners. There has been a lot of research done on how the hardy little ponies arrived on Assateague Island in the United States, and to this day, there are two views.

Legend has it that the ponies were shipped over on a Spanish Galleon in the 16th century bound for South America. The ship encountered a violent storm off the coast of Virginia which broke the ship apart. The ponies fell into the water and swam to Assateague Island where they still live today. Another legend is that in the 17th century, local farmers didn't want to put up fences and pay tariffs, so they swam the ponies to the island to avoid paying taxes. The ponies were left to survive on their own and they adapted to eating the grasses on the island, and the hardiest ponies survived and had offspring that are the ponies of today.

Either way, the Chincoteague ponies have always fascinated people who come from all over the world to watch them make their yearly swim in the Assateague channel, and then come ashore on Chincoteague Island. The ponies each have a health check and then some of the foals are auctioned off to help control the size of the herd. This protects the ponies and the native and sometimes meager grasses that they eat on the island. The ponies then make their swim back to the island to roam free again.

The Chincoteague pony swim began in 1925. The foals are born in spring or early summer, and once old enough, the horses are rounded up for the brief three-minute swim they will make. The swim takes place when the tide is "slack calm," so the young ponies are safe from strong currents. The Saltwater Cowboys (the volunteer fire department on horseback) make sure the ponies safely cross the channel each year.

~July 20~
Copenhagen

A mare named Lady Catherine was a warhorse for the brigade commander at the battle of Copenhagen in 1807. Unknown to the commander, Lady Catherine was pregnant during that battle with a foal that would grow up to be one of the greatest warhorses in history. When the strong colt was born, he was named Copenhagen after the battle.

Copenhagen's sire was a Thoroughbred and was a descendent of both the Godolphin and Darley Arabians. Copenhagen initially was set to be a racehorse, but didn't do well at the sport of kings. He was only 15.1 hands, but the Duke of Wellington saw the stallion and liked what he saw in endurance and strength, and the horse's ill-tempered personality didn't bother him at all. He may have been a difficult horse to handle, but he proved to be a brave and courageous warhorse. Wellington was very good at handling the stallion, and he took him on long hacks out in the countryside to build up his strength and give Copenhagen a mental workout that seemed to relax him .

When the Duke went to battle at Waterloo, it is said that Copenhagen carried him for 17 hours to his victory! The Duke and Copenhagen rode into many battles together and became victorious in all of them. After the Napoleonic Wars were over, Copenhagen returned to the Duke's farm and was still ridden on hacks, but this time, it was just for pleasure. Many people admired the horse, and the ladies wanted a strand of his hair to wear in their jewelry. Copenhagen was finally retired in 1828. He had become deaf and blind but was given the very best care until his death in 1836 at the age of 28.

Their horses are swifter than leopards, fiercer than wolves at dusk. Their cavalry gallops headlong; their horsemen come from afar. They fly like an eagle swooping to devour. Habakkuk 1:8

~July 21~
Tithes, Taxes And Rules

The warhorse was an essential part of the medieval European military. Heavily armored men on huge steeds, equally armored up, made for a very intimidating impression and often victorious outcome. But in order to supply each man and horse with the proper outfitting, it took a lot of money and only the wealthiest of kingdoms could afford this. Henry II was able to move his army more than 400 miles across the French landscape in just six weeks, overtaking many castles along the way. Such a speed of advance would not have been possible without horses. It is said that many countries fell because their soldiers could not travel as far or as fast as the kingdoms that had strong horses. The success of a kingdom was directly connected to how many good warhorses they owned.

Good horses were valued as much as land or the food grown on the property and by the 11th century, the best horses were being traded for land. Even the churches of the time accepted the payment of horses as a tithe! The tithes and taxes (they both were interchangeable) required to be paid to the church were commonly satisfied in whatever goods a person could grow on their land, and that included horses.

The Templar Knights (known as one of the most skilled fighting units of the Crusades) had the most stringent rules for the care of the horses in their army. The practices influenced by chivalry and monastic orders had over a hundred rules for proper care of their steeds and equipment. The only other written rules that outnumbered the monastic orders for appropriate horse care, were directed solely at prayer and worship. There you have it. Horses were right up there with religion and taxes!

In the steady gaze of the horse shines a silent eloquence that speaks of love and loyalty, strength and courage. It is the window that reveals to us how willing his spirit, how generous is his heart. ~Author unknown

~July 22~
Riding The Rails

The use of horses for transportation has been a way of life for thousands of years, and it was the only choice available until the railroad replaced horse-drawn transport with a much faster way to travel to your destination. Soon the horses themselves were being loaded onto trains and taken to different cities for many reasons. Horses were still being used in the cities and rural towns as a regular mode of transportation, and was the only option for places the train could not travel. It was at that point that man realized he could load the horses into railroad cars and ship them to their new work location much faster. There was only one huge problem. The horses did not like being shut inside a dark rattling box that moved beneath them.

The early trains of the mid-1800's were extremely loud, and often the rail cars that the horses were loaded into were crude, dark, and poorly built. The noises alone from the rattling made the horses extremely nervous, and many would panic inside the boxcars. By the time they reached their destination, many of the horses had such horrific injuries that they would need to be euthanized. Horses were scared to load into the railroad cars and often had to be forced with harsh persuasion. The former president of the Royal College of Veterinary Surgeons, J Wortley Axe, wrote in 1905, "The conditions on board often seemed intentionally designed to spook horses, with loud noises everywhere, and tethers too short to allow the animals to maintain their balance."

As the years progressed, rail travel for the horse slowly improved, but it was never a perfect way to transport the horses to their destination. The roughness of train travel meant the creation of leg wraps, shipping blankets, head bumpers, and other protective gear, and that quickly became a booming business. It would later evolve into the modern equine traveling gear we use today.

~July 23~
Old Billy

Billy was born in 1760, and Henry Harrison was only seventeen when he began to train the two-year-old as a plow horse. Later, Billy was purchased by Mersey and Irwell Navigation and became a "Barge horse," pulling barges on the canals. In the 1700's, horse-drawn barges were used to transport cargo throughout England by way of canals. Horses would be rigged up to the barge and travel along an adjacent path to pull the barge along the canal. Later, Billy also became a "Gin horse," which had nothing to do with liquor. The term gin was short for "engine." Gins were short wooden wheel devices on a spindle that were pulled around in a circular path by a horse tacked up in a harness, which was attached to a beam. As the horse walked, it powered the pulley wheels.

Old Billy had become a celebrity in his old age and worked until he was 59 years old when he was finally retired. He earned the right to a restful retirement and died peacefully in 1822. He had lived to be 62 years old! This was amazing at the time since horses were considered work animals, and veterinary care was still primitive in many ways. Old Billy's exact breeding was unknown, but it was said that he looked like a Shire/Cob-Cross. Billy was a common brown color, with a white blaze, but his gentle and willing personality is what people loved the most.

Rarely in history did a horse get recognition for the years of service to a business, but Billy did. Billy became a symbol for all the equines who served their humans well. All modern societies owe an enormous debt to the workhorses of the past.

The old horse is like an old friend. You have so many memories together and even a few secrets from your younger days of youth, but you are closer now than ever before. The only thing that matters to the senior horse is a kind word and loving touch. ~Author unknown

~July 24~
Horse Whims

The horse whim was a horse-powered circular wooden machine that powered a connection of wooden wheels connected to a shaft. The horse whim could be used for grinding food or to power boats on rivers and lakes. The horses would walk in circles harnessed up to the wheel and the forward motion would move the large, heavy wheel, which would set in motion the machine. This proved to work well for man but was extremely demanding on the horses. Walking in tight circles was hard on the horse's body and mind. Some horses would become dizzy and disorientated after hours of walking in circles.

The earliest horse whims were used to turn rotary mills in Greece around 300 BC. The Romans used horses for grain-grinding and olive-crushing mills around 100 BC. Centuries later, Prince Rupert, a cousin of King Charles II of England, designed and built the first horse-powered boat around 1680. By 1682 bigger boats were being built that used horse whims and were powered by four or eight horses. The Royal navy started using these boats to tow the larger ships into the Chatham Dockyard on the Medway River.

In 1820, William Bird tried to compete with horse-powered boats for long-distance travel. One of Bird's boats, the Genius of Georgia, was designed with a double-hull configuration. This boat had a gigantic horizontal wooden wheel that was placed between the hulls on the boat. It carried a crew of 24 horses harnessed two abreast when they walked on the flat wheel. By the 1840's the circular horizontal wheel was considered obsolete and replaced by the horse treadmill, which was much easier on the horses.

"Oh, to be the most powerful and still be the most sensitive and fragile of any flower. The work is never done, but a kind word and soft touch can add years onto my heart – said the horse." ~Author Unknown

~July 25~
Horsepower

Today's cars are measured in horsepower, which goes back to the horse and his incredible strength. The term "horsepower" was coined by Scottish inventor James Watt. He arrived at the term "horsepower" using math and, of course, by observing the horse using every muscle in his body to produce the power. Watt used the relationship between how much weight a horse could lift while pulling a rope running through a pulley that was connected to a heavy weight on the ground, and he set a standard height of 1 foot per second. Today, we say that horsepower is equal to a horse lifting 550 pounds of weight at a rate of 1 foot per second. Since horses vary in strength, that number is what Watt arrived at when needing to settle on a standard.

Then in 1776, James Watt redesigned the steam engine to improve performance, but he needed a way to show his new engine's capabilities to a market still driven literally by horses. He figured what better way to sell his improved steam engine than to put it up against the horse-driven machines such as the grain mills used in the breweries. Watt had his eye on a London brewery as his first customer for his steam engine. He knew the brewery operation well and had already determined that the horses lapped the mill's 24-foot diameter circle 144 times per hour. To prove his invention, they would have a competition between the brewer's strongest horse and Watt's steam engine. Watt's engine proved to be more powerful than the horse, and the brewer was sold on steam-powered engines for the brewery. Today, all motors, small and large, are configured in horsepower (HP), and even though the thought of horsepower under our car hoods may sound abstract in today's world, it really isn't at all. In fact, there is something really cool about having all those horses under your hood and how it ties us with the incredible horsepower of the past.

~July 26~
Sandy

During the First World War, 136,000 horses (called Walers) were sent from their homeland in Australia to the Australian Imperial Force and the British and Indian governments to help in the war effort. Waler was the name they used for all the warhorses that came from down under.

Only one horse out of 136,000 ever made it back to Australia after the war. His name was Sandy, and he was a 16-hand gentle bay that caught the eye of Major General Sir William Bridges. Sandy quickly became the Major's favorite horse to ride. During the war, Major William Bridges was killed, and his last dying wish was that Sandy be retired and sent back to Australia. He wanted Sandy to live out his days with the best care possible, as a thank you for the horse's service to the military. After the Major's passing, Sandy was put in the care of Captain Leslie Whitfield, transported to Egypt, and then to France in 1916. It wasn't until the following year that the Australian authorities were able to grant the Major his last dying wish and have Sandy return home to Australia. Sandy was in a three-month quarantine to make sure he was disease-free before he made the long journey home.

When Sandy finally made it home to Australia, he was turned out to graze at the Central Remount Depot at Maribyrnong. He had a peaceful life roaming large pastures all day long. Eventually due to increased blindness and failing health, Sandy had to be put down in 1923.

It is tragic to think that Sandy was the only horse out of 136,000 warhorses to make it home to Australia after the war. The soldiers who took care of these horses throughout the war were heartbroken at what they had seen these horses endure during the war. Sandy will forever be a symbol of all the horses that didn't make it back home.

~July 27~
Chariot Racing

There would have never been chariot races without the horses leading the charge. Chariot racing consisted of two-wheeled carts pulled by 2, 4, or 6-horse teams. Each race was seven laps long, which equaled about four miles in length. Even back in the time when the Romans held the Circus Maximus games every year, the trainers knew that to win, you needed horses that had great stamina, speed, and a sharp mind. They needed to be sensitive to the bit and cues their charioteer was sending them, after all, chariot racing was extremely dangerous and one mistake could be fatal for both the horses and charioteer.

The Spanish-bred Andalusian was considered the best breed for chariot racing, and they were called "the horse of kings." The Andalusian had been used as a warhorse long before chariot racing and was not only beautiful, but very strong in the hind quarters, which gave them the power to move out fast and still be able to make the sharp turns at fast speeds without too much trouble.

The training of a chariot horse would begin when the horse was around five years old, and their racing careers could last well into their teens. If they were successful, they would go on to become breeding stallions. The lead horse in a chariot team would often become as famous as the driver, especially as they won more races. Emperor Nero was so impressed with a chariot horse called Incitatus that he built the horse a magnificent stable out of marble with an ivory stall. Nero also had the finest purple cloth made into blankets and a jeweled collar designed for the horse's neck. Incitatus was also given his own team of slaves to care for him day or night. The chariot horses were prized, taken very well care of, and often worshipped and immortalized in artwork.

Behold, he advances like the clouds, his chariots come like a whirlwind, his horses are swifter than eagles. Woe to us, for we are ruined! Jeremiah 4:13

~July 28~
The Capture

Every Plains Indian warrior dreamed of capturing a prized horse from the enemy. Young warriors would risk their lives to sneak into an enemy tribe and leave with a warhorse. The warrior that came back with the stolen horse had permission to boast, and there would be a celebration among the young warrior's tribe. The art of capturing the enemy's horse was passed down through many generations, even into World War II. Joseph Medicine Crow shared the story of how his grandfather, White Man Runs Him, was a soldier in World War II and finally earned his boasting rights.

It was near the end of the war, and the Germans realized they were losing the war. One night, White Man Runs Him and his platoon were following a group of S.S officers that were on horseback. The platoon could hear the clip-clop of the horses' hooves ahead of them. The German officers were heading to a farm in a remote area where they planned to hide during the day. The commanding officer sat down with the platoon leaders to discuss the best way to handle the German officers. White Men Runs Him began to think about the horses that the Germans were riding and suggested that maybe he should get the horses out of the corral, otherwise some of the German officers might be able to escape on them. After thinking about it, the commanding officer gave him the okay, and soon he and another soldier snuck up toward the corral. White Men Runs Him crawled through the paddock fence, tied a loop in a rope he brought with him, and put it in a horse's mouth just like the old Crow warriors used to do. Then he hopped on the horse's back. The other soldier opened the gate and off they ran with about fifty horses following behind! White Man Runs Him had stolen the enemy's horses and the Germans surrendered at the farm to the Americans. It was a great day to celebrate the young warrior's capture of the horses during World War II.

~July 29~
Chemical Warfare

Horses have endured horrific and unimaginable things during wartime, no matter the century, but almost nothing compares to World War I and the creation of chemical warfare. No one could have imagined how it would affect the millions of horses that were used in that war, and no one could fathom at the time that a gas mask would need to be designed for the horses used in the war effort.

Germany became the first military to use chemical warfare with chlorine gas. It was used on their enemies for the first time on April 22, 1915. From that point forward, chemical warfare became a serious threat, and gas masks became standard issue. Horses were vital to the military, and it soon became of great importance to protect the horses as well. A gas mask was designed after the horse feed bag called the flannelette bag. The respirator used by the horses would be inside the flannelette bag with a connected canvas mouthpiece which would then need to be inserted into the horse's mouth. An elastic band ensured the respirator would remain close to the horse's face when in use. Protecting the horses was more difficult than protecting humans. At least humans understood what the danger was and the importance of properly securing the mask. The horses were frightened of the gas mask and needed to be restrained for the mask to be put on properly. Soldiers would spend a lot of time getting their horses used to the gas mask and eventually have them wear them for periods of time while being ridden or pulling artillery. The goal was to be able to put the gas mask on as quickly as possible while the horse stayed calm. The soldiers knew there wasn't time to mess around with a horse that was scared if they were in danger of a chemical attack. The horses learned to wear their gas mask and did their job like true heroes during an extremely dark time in history.

~July 30~
Tent-Pegging

The origins of Tent-Pegging or Naza Bazi on horseback can be traced back to Alexander the Great (326 BC). The Macedonian conqueror and his military couldn't defeat the Raja Porus of Purushottama, which was the ancient King of Paurava (modern day Pakistan), because the Raja's army was not only equipped with weaponry, but they had something far more dangerous and powerful. They used armored elephants trained to attack the enemy armies aggressively. Alexander the Great's horses and warriors could not stand up to the massive size of the elephants and their trained aggressive behavior. The soldiers found that the only way to incapacitate the armored elephants was to spear them in the toe. This battle tactic was called tent-pegging, and the warriors became very skillful at spearing before they went up against the elephants.

There is also the belief that tent-pegging was used by mounted soldiers during the same time period but the battle tactic was much different. During the early morning when the enemy would still be asleep, the soldiers would charge the enemy camps removing the pegs, which held the tents in place. This would cause mass confusion in the camps and give the attacking soldiers a clear advantage.

Tent-pegging has been a training method for cavalry units in many parts of the world, but today tent-pegging is an equestrian sport that is most popular in India and Pakistan. Tent-Pegging can be performed on any breed of horse as long as the horse is trained to gallop in a straight line with little direction from the reins, as the rider is busy in the saddle holding a lance and sword. The horse's height is critical in the sport of tent-pegging, specifically with the sword, since any mistakes can injure the horse or rider. The best height of a horse for this event is 14 hands to 14.2 hands tall. Thank goodness horses are not used in battle against elephants anymore!

~July 31~
The Disney Horses

The horses you see pulling carriages while clip-clopping down Main Street U.S.A., and the fancy horse-drawn carriages that Prince Charming and Cinderella ride in during the parades truly add so much magic and charm to Disneyland. The horses that end up with those gigs have a pretty nice life. So my one big question was…how does a horse get a great job at Disneyland? Well, with a bit of research, I found out.

Alan Cooper, an equine trainer at Circle D Stables, where the Disney horses live, said in an interview, "When casting a new horse for a role at Disneyland, what we're looking for is comfort. The handlers will observe things like interaction and personality when interviewing a new horse to work in the park, and they look for horses that will be comfortable when surrounded by lots of people and activity." The color of the horses is also important and special markings add even more to the entire picture of what Disney is trying to create with all their beautiful horses. The Disney horses come in many different breeds, from Clydesdales and Percherons to Quarter horses, Arabians, Appaloosas, Gyspy Vanners, and Shetland Ponies. The breeds of horses might all be different, but the most important element is that they have a quiet personality and love people. It is so important that they stay calm no matter what is going on in the theme park because with lots of children, you never know what may happen.

The training for a new Disney horse usually takes around six months to a year, depending on the horse. The training and foundation is vital in building trust and respect between horse and human, plus the horses learn voice commands. The trainers believe in going slow, and the end results are happier and more confident horses who truly love their jobs working at the happiest place on earth.

~August 1~
Mackinac Island

In today's busy and often loud world, an island in Lake Huron is a slice of heaven. It is called Mackinac Island, and what makes this tourist destination so special is the fact that no cars or motorized vehicles of any kind are allowed on the island. Everything is completely powered by horses and that is the way it has been for well over a hundred years. Everything is done by walking, riding bicycles, or horses and the only sound you hear is the clip-clop of the horses pulling wagons or carriages as they do their daily jobs.

Back in the 1890's, a few motorized vehicles had made their way to the island, but quickly the local people became upset with how loud the horseless carriages were, and the noisy machines constantly spooked the horses. By 1898, the townspeople decided that they were done with motorized vehicles and banned all of them! That decision in the late 1800's is what makes Mackinac Island so unique and special today. The island draws tens of thousands of tourists each summer, and the horses are a big part of why people make the island a vacation destination.

During the busy summer season there are around six hundred horses working on the island. They do everything from making deliveries of food and goods to the hotels and stores, to giving tourists a very scenic ride on horseback or by carriage. The ferries come in bringing everything needed to keep the homes and businesses running and people fed, and it is all unloaded onto horse-drawn wagons just like in yesteryear. The horses are taken excellent care of and live on the island all summer long. Then in the fall most of them will load onto a ferry and return to their winter home to rest for the long winter. Only a few horses stay on the island all year. There is something beautifully nostalgic about watching the horses do their daily jobs, and it gives us a small glimpse into the life of the working horses of the past.

~August 2~
Babieca

In 11th century Spain, the Carthusians (a famous order of monks) were known for breeding and training the finest Spanish horses throughout the Spanish Peninsula. A young boy by the name of Rodrigo Diaz de Bivar was brought up near the Carthusian monastery. When Rodrigo came of age, his godfather, who was a monk, gave the boy a gift to choose any of the monastery's finest Andalusian horses for his very own. The boy could not wait to enter the stable and pick a horse. As he stood there gazing at all the beautiful horses, his eyes froze as he saw this gangly little white-colored foal that seemed to be very frail. That little horse stole his heart and that was the horse he chose. His godfather was disappointed in his poor choice, but Rodrigo defended his decision and named the foal Babieca, meaning "My stupid one," for that was the name that had been shouted at him for being such a poor judge of horseflesh in the eyes of his godfather.

Babieca grew up to be a strong and imposing horse that was calm and surefooted under all circumstances. He would carry that young boy who grew up into a man into many battles. Rodrigo became so famous that the people started calling him El Cid Campeador, which in Arabic means My Lord, the Champion of Warriors. Babieca carried El Cid for 30 years and was revered by everyone as the magnificent horse that carried his warrior to victory and freedom for Spain. After El Cid died, Babieca was never ridden again and lived to be 40 years old. He was buried next to El Cid and his wife. Fool! Dolt! Babieca! That was the name of the most famous horse in the history of Spain.

"Sometimes, the most awkward and ugliest of colts grow up to be the most courageous, fiercest, and beautiful horses ever known to man. Only a wise man truly sees the beauty and strength before it blossoms." ~Author Unknown

~August 3~
The Parade

Horses are often the most anticipated part of any parade. Children and adults love to look at the horses dressed up in fancy saddles dripping with silver along with the colorful costumes the riders wear. There is something almost magical about a parade horse. The actual concept of the parade involving horses originated to acknowledge battle victories and to honor the soldiers, officers, and warhorses that fought in battle. And this is something that has been done for centuries.

The parade horse can be traced back to 1745. The British Monarchy's Horse Guard Parade was performed daily throughout the city streets by the Palace Guard, and this well-known ceremony is still important today for the British Monarchy. The origins of the parade horse in the west, dates back to the mid-1800's. That is when wealthy landowners in the southwest region of the United States (particularly near the Mexico border) spared no expense with their saddle horses. These proud ranch and hacienda owners saddled their very fancy and well-trained horses with beautifully hand-tooled saddles and bridles trimmed in the finest silver. They would travel to town on horses with a high-stepping walk or trot that made many people do a double-take.

Today's parades allow the rider to show off their beautiful costumes, tack, and of course, the high-stepping horses that take your breath away. They also give the audience a stunning visual experience of the cultures and traditions of yesteryear. Large parades will showcase many different types of breeds and disciplines as well as a time to remember the workhorses over the past centuries. It's not just about flash and silver anymore. Today's parade horses come from all backgrounds, and they are an important and hopefully permanent part of parades for many years to come. The truth is, a parade would be boring without the horses!

~August 4~
Never Forget

This poem was written and dedicated to the millions of warhorses that didn't come home and those very few that did.

From the peaceful land
to hellfire we were sent.

Bomb blast, shell fire and barbed wire
Explosions, fearful gas and groans.
Lay man and beast, wrenched and maimed
On foreign soil last breath exhaled.

Through horror, fear and pain
Knee deep mud, cold and rain
We heaved and pulled with little to sustain.

We don't feel like heroes, though heroes' tasks were done,
We knew it was our duty to get the battle won.

I am home again at last,
My legs are swollen and my body weak.
My skin and cuts are healing
But I will not forget.

So here in silence with lowered head
over the bones of fallen friend
I stand forever to honor
those who came not home.

The War Horse Memorial Poem – By Susan Leyland

~August 5~
Horses Act 1535

Historically, there have been horses in Wales for thousands of years. Writings have been found from the Middle Ages referencing a breed of horse that we now call the Welsh Cob. These horses were small but very strong and fast, and could jump as well as carry their riders for long distances. These little horses were the choice of mount until the introduction of the larger draught breeds centuries later.

In 1535, King Henry VIII needed warhorses to keep his kingdom strong. He believed horses that were of smaller size were completely worthless for battle and his kingdom. He also felt that the breeding of good horses was deteriorating, and he took it upon himself to do something about it. Henry VIII quickly passed the Breed of Horses Act which ordered the culling (the rejection or removal of individual horses that are considered inferior) and destruction of all stallions under 15 hands and mares under 13 hands tall. The sole purpose was to improve the breeding of horses. Henry also passed the Horses Act of 1540, which stated that no stallion or mare of smaller size was permitted to run out on common land and breed, and no two-year old colt under 11.2 hands was allowed to run out in any area with mares. He instructed annual round-ups and culling of smaller horses and gave orders to destroy them. These laws were short-lived and repealed in 1556 by Elizabeth I on the suggestion that the land, which was poor in soil, could not support the weight or food supply of the horses desired by Henry VIII.

How thoroughly King Henry's laws were carried out is hard to determine, but many of the mountain ponies escaped culling and continued to breed. To this day, wild horses have continued to thrive and are seen as an important part of the heritage, history, and landscape that make Wales so unique.

~August 6~
The Horse Stable

Who built the first horse stable? The truth is no one really knows the exact century or people who decided to keep horses in stables for the first time, but we do know some of the finest horse stables were built thousands of years ago.

The ancient city of Qantir-Piramesse in Egypt was unearthed in 1999 and the discovery of a huge complex of stables was found during the excavation. It seems the stables were built by Ramses II (1304-1237 BC) for all his warhorses and horses used for hunting and recreation. This massive stable is approximately 182,986 square feet, and it was found to house close to 500 horses. The interior consist of six rows of halls with floors that sloped along with countless divided stalls. Exercise arenas were also uncovered.

Other ancient stables have been unearthed throughout the European continent and other parts of the world. Horses and horse stables were a large part of the Roman Empire, and in 2009 the stables of the great Emperor Augustus were discovered during an excavation in Rome. The remains of this imperial stable are said to be built with marble and the images uncovered show drawings and artwork of the racing teams of the time.

During the Middle Ages (5th-15th centuries), stables had the primary purpose of defense. These stables were not built for looks but for functionality, and little thought was given to the barn's aesthetics. From the 17th century forward, horse stables were built to compliment the home and create a vision of wealth and prosperity. After all, a person was considered wealthy if they owned a horse. Boy, all these years later, things have not changed when it comes to the perception of horse ownership!

A barn is a sanctuary in an unsettling world, a sheltered place where life's true priorities are clear. When you step back, it's not just about the horses - but about love, life, and learning. ~Lauren David Baker

~August 7~
Expectant Mothers

It was 1947, and a massive snowstorm had hit New York City. What made matters worse was that it was Christmas time. The hustle and bustle of everyday life was at a yearly high with family visiting from out of town, people traveling to holiday parties, and the normal busy holiday shopping. The huge snowstorm that had hit Brooklyn and surrounding cities had left heavy snow several feet deep on all the city streets, which created a dangerous situation for expectant mothers and ill people who needed to get to the hospital.

According to The New York Times, an emergency appeal for horse-drawn sleds and other vehicles was put out on December 26 by radio station WNEW. The sleds were primarily needed to help deliver pregnant women and sick people to the hospitals. The Morro Limousine Company on Prospect Park West was in urgent need of horse-drawn sleds that could make it through the deep snow. All eighteen of its transport vehicles had gotten stuck in the heavy snow throughout the city, and there was no way to get them out at the time. The snowstorm had produced so much snow that vehicles were stuck everywhere, which made it impossible to get through many city streets. The company was receiving 25 calls an hour for hospital transports, but was unable to respond to any of them.

Horse owners everywhere answered the call to help. Soon, horses hitched to sleds were on their way to help the people in need in the areas where a motorized vehicle could not make it through, which turned out to be most of the city. The snow was deep but the horses and sleds went through it with ease. The sled rides to the hospital for any pregnant woman or sick person was done at no charge, and it truly was a Christmas season to remember. It was the year the horses helped deliver babies!

~August 8~
Gulf Of Mares

Horses have always been used in exploration, and the success or failure often depended on the horses that helped make the journey possible. These explorations were very long and treacherous, and in some cases, it drove the men and horses to the point of madness. Some expeditions crossed the vast oceans and many horses were led onto these ships, often ill-equipped to care for the large animals.

On Columbus' first voyage with horses aboard the ship, not one of the horses survived. The ship became dormant at sea, and with the hot tropical sun, they soon ran out of water and the horses died of thirst. Death often came slow and it was so unbearable on the horses that many of the horses were thrown overboard before they were entirely gone. Golfo de Yegues means the Gulf of Mares in Spanish. It is a vast area of the Atlantic Ocean, north of the Canary Islands, named for the massive number of horses that died in the ocean waters over the centuries.

Columbus' second voyage to the New World in 1492 was much different and very successful in keeping the horses alive. Aboard the ships were 15 stallions, 10 mares, and Columbus' personal horses. The weather was better and the crossing was fast. It only took 22 days from the Canary Islands to reach land in the West Indies. They made a stop in Guadeloupe and stayed for six days while the horses were led ashore for exercise and to graze. The horses were then taken by ship to the new colony of Isabella where their journey ended. These were the first horses to make it to the New World. After Columbus, more Spanish explorers came with horses aboard their ships, but many horses did not survive. Many of these early explorers came in search of great treasures in Mexico, while others stayed and devoted themselves to ranching. It was a time in history when the complexities of the horse's health were not known, and man truly did not know how fragile these huge equines were.

~August 9~
Fantasia

In the small country of Morroco, there is an equestrian custom that takes place every year. Morroco is part of North Africa, which is close to the European border. Many men ride their horses every year in a festival called Fantasia (Tbourida), which dates back hundreds of years. In ancient times, the Numidian people participated in Fantasia to show off their waring abilities and the strength and stamina of their horses. The Arab-Amazigh tribes in the 17th century practiced what they called the Cavalry Charge, which was performed by the advanced guard.

The horses commonly ridden in Fantasia come from the Arabian, Andalusian, and Barb breeds. For the men riding the horses, these performances are very important, and they practice often to make sure their horses are ready for the Tbourida festivals. The performances are also provided for weddings and other special ceremonies. The horses are dressed up in stunning traditional Moroccan costumes, which represent their specific tribes along with decorated bridles and embroidered saddles.

For the people of Morroco, Fantasia is considered their "equestrian art" that showcases their ritualistic wargames and, above all else, celebrates the relationship between the horse and rider. The horse is significant to the Moroccan culture in remembering history, and the battles on horseback are displayed through the Fantasia celebrations. Many of the men practice together and they are called Troupes. During their routine, they will fire off their guns simultaneously and show the speed and agility of their horses. The horses used in the festivities are strong and athletic, but they are also known for their graceful movements. The people of Morocco take great pride in their horses, and these performing horses are elevated to a very high status among Moroccans.

~August 10~
Barge Horses

When the Roman Emperor Claudius and his military conquered Britain in 43 AD, they quickly started building large canals for irrigation and land drainage waterways. Soon canals were being built all over Europe and other countries. Horses and mules were used to pull boats loaded with cargo along these canals, and they found out that it was a very effective way to transport goods. These horses were called Barge Horses. A horse used for towing a boat from the towpath had the strength to pull 50 times as much cargo as it could pulling a wagon, because there was minimal friction on the water. By the 1740's, the canal systems had grown, which meant more horses were needed that could pull the boats. The larger horses would pull the large barges that were loaded down, and the smaller horses pulled the smaller boats. Often the horses were used in teams as well, and mules or donkeys were used if horses were not available. The canal transport system was heavily used during the Industrial Revolution and continued well into the 1960's.

The canal boats could carry 30 tons at a time with only one horse towing the barge. Later, mules became the preferred animal to pull some of the barges because they were less prone to accidents or injuries. The average speed of a barge was 2-3 miles per hour, and the horses often walked 20 miles a day with breaks during the day to eat, drink and rest. Goods were transported day and night, which meant there would be a change in the barge horses a few times during a 24-hour period.

One problem that existed was that the barge had a lot of momentum once it got going but no brakes. That meant that sometimes the horses got pulled into the canal. With no way to get out, the horse would drown. Soon "horse slips" were built along the sides of the canals so that a horse could get out of the water quickly and easily and these "horse slips" resulted in fewer horse deaths.

~August 11~
Kasztanka

Field Marshal Józef Piłsudski was introduced to the mare as a service mount in August of 1914. It was said that he fell in love with the chestnut horse instantly and he named her Kasztanka after her chestnut color. Kasztanka was foaled in either 1909 or 1910, and when she came of age and was trained, her owner offered her up to the First Brigade of the Polish Legions. Kasztanka stood at 14.3 hands with four matching socks and a beautiful white blaze. Kasztank quickly became Józef Piłsudski's favorite horse, and he considered the mare a faithful companion in the Polish Legion battles for independence during World War I. The mare was a nervous horse who hated the artillery fire and the chaos around her, but when Piłsudski asked her to go anywhere, she did it with total trust in him and stayed calm and obedient under the harshest of situations. Her loyalty to him was easy to see for anyone that came in contact with the mare.

Kasztanka carried Marshal Józef Piłsudski throughout the entire war. When the war was over and Poland celebrated its independence, Piłsudski rode the mare in parades and made appearances for the next few years. Kasztanka had given birth twice over the years, and on November 11, 1927, Marshal Piłsudski rode Kasztanka for the last time at the Polish Independence Day parade. Just twelve days later, the mare died after a serious injury while on a train headed back to her home where she was stabled. Piłsudski took it extremely hard and wouldn't talk to the officers in charge of her care.

After Kasztanka's death, her body underwent taxidermy and, after several locations was placed at the Belweder Palace museum. The rest of her remains were buried at her stable at the 7th Uhlan Regiment beneath a stone inscribed, "Here lays KASZTANKA, favorite combat mare of Marshal Piłsudski."

~August 12~
The Ferryboat

The horse-powered boat can be traced back to the Romans around 370 AD. Then during the late 1700's and early 1800's, the horse-powered treadmill became the preferred method of propulsion on Ferryboats. Two horses would stand on large flat treadmills down below the top deck. Horses were harnessed together on each side of the deck in opposite directions – one to the bow and the other to the stern. As they began to walk their hooves would catch the channels cut into the wooden flat treadmill, which was connected to a large wheel underneath their feet. As it started to move the wheels in a direction opposite to that of their own forward motion, it in turn would move the tow vertical wheels which were on each side of the boat. These wheels were constructed like paddlewheels and would propel the boat forward. One observer who went down below the main deck to see how the horses powered the boat said, "The horses are covered by a roof, furnished with curtains to protect them in bad weather, and do not appear to labor harder than common draft horses with a heavy load."

There were many horse-powered boats working on the lakes and rivers during this time. Besides moving goods and ferrying people to their destination, these boats were also being used for entertainment. The boats would wine and dine people while the horses worked below deck. The treadmill design was much easier on the horses than the older circular "whim" design, where horses would walk in a circle for hours. There were noted cases where the horses that walked on horse whims instead of horse treadmills would become dizzy and disorientated, and it was said that you would see some of these "boat horses" walking in constant circles out in their pastures. The horse-powered ferryboats came to an end around 1900, which was true blessing for the horse!

~August 13~
A Horsemen's Prayer

Dearest God in heaven, give me the strength to guide my horse.
Make my hands soft and my head clear.
Let my horse understand me, and I him.
My heart you have blessed with a special love for these animals.
Let me never lose sight of it.
My soul you have gifted with a deep need for them,
Let that never lessen.
Always let my breath catch as the sun gleams on an elegant head,
Always may my throat tighten at the sound of a gentle nicker.
Let the scent of fresh hay and a new bag of grain always be sweet to me.
Let the touch of a warm nose on my hand always bring a smile.
I adore the joy of a warm day on the farm,
The grace and spender of a running horse.
The thunder of its hooves make my eyes burn and my heart soar,
Let it always be so.
Dear God, grant me patience,
For horses are harnessed wind and wind can be flighty.
Let me not frighten or harm them,
Instead, show me ways to understand.
Above all, dear God, fill my life with them.
I am not whole without them.
When I pass from this world, send my soul to no heaven without them,
For this love you have given me graces my existence.
I shall cherish it and praise you for it, all the time.
Amen

~Author Unknown

~August 14~
Bits

When man first came upon this strange animal that was big and could run very fast, it is said that they were frightened. They soon realized that the horse was not a fierce man-eating carnivore, and with time, could be trained to be ridden as a weapon of warfare. It is believed that horses were first controlled by means of a rope around the lower jaw or very primitive hackamore. From the first discovery of the gap between the molars and incisors in the horse's mouth to the moment man figured out that they could control the horse when something was put into that open space, the way humans did things would change forever with the help of the horse.

The earliest attempts to design a bit for the horse were made with leather thongs and bone or wood tied to cheek pieces made of antler. The earliest records of metal bits date from around the 14th century BC, and were made of bronze. These bits were found in the region of Luristan, which is present-day Iran. Early bits were very severe as horse training or horsemanship had not developed very far, and riders needed a means of control and quick response when riding into battle.

The first records of the curb bit are from around the 4th century AD. The medieval warhorse was often ridden in a curb bit with an extremely high port and long shanks, which increased the leverage on the curb and the pressure on the horse's poll. This gave the heavily armored soldier complete control of the horse without hardly touching the reins. It wasn't until the Renaissance period that milder bits were introduced, and man discovered he could have a relationship with the horse. In more modern times, nickel was the material of choice for bits until around 1940, when stainless steel largely replaced it. Over the last few decades, bits have come a long way in their design due to our growing understanding of the effect and pressure bits have on the horse.

~August 15~
Road Rage

For those of you that are old enough to drive a vehicle, you are probably very familiar with the term "road rage." Unfortunately, road rage arguments and accidents make the nightly news in today's world. Sadly, things haven't changed much in the last two centuries.

Long before the car, there was the horse and carriage. Between the 1700's and 1800's, the city streets were jammed packed with horses everywhere. There were horses pulling wagons, carriages, and other types of horse-drawn vehicles, plus you had people riding their horses in and out of the congestion. People were always in a hurry rushing to work or running errands and making deliveries. As you can imagine, life got interesting at times with the horses that were expected to do everything to keep a city moving forward.

A few of the most common horse-related issues were speeding, unsafe driving, and new drivers who didn't know where things were located, which ultimately caused confusion. And then you had the drunk driver who was a complete hazard on the roadway. Carriage and wagon accidents became very common often due to a spooked horse that bolted and pulled everything behind him at a full gallop. Crashes were common with young horses that were learning how to maneuver through traffic, and some horses were high-strung and too much horse for the driver to handle. With so many horses it was possible for anything to happen, and it often did. Sometimes a horse would rear and be out of control, and it would feed into the other horses on the street, and soon it became a circus.

There were many people who were very patient with their horses in all the city congestion, but some became angry and developed road rage. Soon it became necessary to arrest and fine any person who drove in a reckless or angrily manner. The city streets were too crowded to deal with angry drivers, and it was very stressful on the horses.

~August 16~
Fire Horse No. 12

Sometimes a horse gives beyond what is humanly possible, and when you come across a special horse like that, you need to make sure it is never forgotten. This is the real life account of Fire Horse No. 12.

It was the early morning of March 30, 1890, in Washington D.C. The fire alarm went off like it had done thousands of times before and the horses were anticipating the next few seconds when their harnesses would be put on, and they would be out the door running full speed pulling the horse-drawn fire wagons. This particular morning as the fire horses were racing down the city streets, they collided with another horse-drawn fire wagon headed to the same place. Quickly assessing that all was okay, the drivers of the hose cart and the heavy steam engine urged their teams forward as fast as they could run towards the fire, as time was crucial. As the horses raced across town, the driver of the hose-cart noticed that one of the horses on his team limped somewhat as he was running. When they arrived at the fire scene, the horse immediately pulled up lame and would not bear any weight on one of his legs. When the driver jumped out of the wagon to look at the sweated-up horse, he made a shocking discovery. The horse had lost its left rear hoof! There was nothing there but bone, flesh and blood. Apparently the horse's hoof had been run over and cut off in the collision with the heavy engine. What is so remarkable is that the horse had galloped almost a full mile on his stump of a leg to the fire. With heavy tears flowing down their faces, the firefighters quickly shot the brave horse to end its suffering.

Not all running by horses is done on the racetrack. It's not always done for prize money or glory in front of a cheering crowd. Sometimes horses run because they know that is what they are supposed to do. And that's exactly what Horse No.12 did. ~Author unknown

~August 17~
Xenophon

Horses are astonishingly beautiful, strong, and yet so fragile both mentally (they never forget) and physically, as many in history have learned the hard way. Many horses have been ruined because man did not take the time to look deep inside the soul of the animal and see what their needs were—which are so simple. Safety, shelter, food, and water is what they need, but equally important is patience with a gentle hand.

Xenophon understood this concept and understood the horse. Xenophon was a soldier, historian, and writer of Ancient Greece and 2,300 years ago wrote these words, *"A horse so prancing is a thing of beauty, a wonder, and a marvel; riveting the gaze of all who see him, young alike and graybeards. They will never turn their backs, I venture to predict, or weary of their gazing so long as he continues to display his splendid action."*

Xenophon's life would be constrained by the warring factions of the Athenian empire and Sparta, but during those battles, he knew the horse was something special and not just a war machine to be tossed aside when done. He was very compassionate for this animal that was willing to be led into battle and serve its master so humbly. He began to study the horse in all areas and later would produce many writings on horsemanship, training, and proper care of the horse. Xenophon goes on to describe in his writings, *"It is a good thing also for a rider to accustom himself to keep a quiet seat, especially when mounted on a spirited horse."*

Xenophon wrote the book *On Horsemanship,* which is known as the oldest written work on the subject of the horse, including the care, training, purchasing, stabling, and grooming of horses.

"And indeed, a horse who bears himself proudly is a thing of such beauty and astonishment that he attracts the eyes of all beholders." ~ Xenophon.

~August 18~
Forty Belgian Draft Horses

When they came down the parade route, no one could believe their eyes. The ten rows of four Belgian Draft horses all hitched up, pulling a wagon down the city streets, left every mouth wide open. The 40-horse team was a sight to behold. Elmer Sparrow had been asked to bring his huge team of Belgians to Milwaukee for the Circus Parade in 1972. Before Sparrow could make the trip, he would need to figure out the logistics since the last time a hitch this big was driven in a circus parade unit was at the turn of the last century. Sparrow lived in Iowa and was well known in draft horse circles, and the thought of bringing his horses to the parade sounded exciting.

There would be a few things to figure out before he was ready for a parade with his horses. Any teamsters (the person who drove the team) who had driven 40-horse hitches were no longer alive. Sparrow studied the details of the harnesses and hitching in photos taken in the 1890's. Then he figured out what needed to be done and started to assemble his team, taking care to put horses with different personalities and temperaments in specific spots. Then he would practice as much as possible with the horses hitched before coming to Milwaukee.

It was a huge undertaking that took a lot of knowledgeable horsemen to groom, hold, and hitch the team for practices before the actual parade. So much depended on the lead horses and the lead lines were 130 feet long to signal the lead horses. The biggest challenge for the 40-horse hitch was turning corners on the parade route. A few outriders on horses traveled next to the 40-horse hitch, plus someone sat next to Sparrow on the wagon to keep the excess reins in working order. What a treat for the people who were there at the parade to witness something so spectacular as a team of 40 beautiful Belgian horses coming down the parade route.

~August 19~
The Jinx

By 1864, Dixie Bill was considered a jinxed horse. He had been through many battles, and death seemed to follow the horse and had become part of his reputation. At the Battle of Wilson's Creek in 1861, the Confederate soldier riding Dixie Bill was killed by an Iowa soldier. Dixie Bill was shot in the neck but survived (the first of four battle wounds). After Wilson's Creek, Dixie Bill was sent with other captured Confederate mounts to Muscatine, Iowa, where Colonel Sylvester G. Hill led the 35th Iowa Infantry. Hill purchased Dixie Bill and, while riding the horse, got word that his 18-year-old son was killed in battle. Then the heartbroken father was shot while riding Dixie bill and was recovering from the bullet wound. Major Abraham John rode Dixie Bill while Hill was recovering, and was killed in a skirmish at Old River Lake, Arkansas. Then, just a few months later at the Battle of Nashville in 1864, Hill was killed astride Dixie Bill during an assault. Afterward, a 33rd Missouri Infantry officer purchased the horse, but when the officer learned of Dixie Bill's bad luck on the battlefield, the horse was offered for sale.

Printed in an Iowa newspaper years later, *"With this record, three riders killed in action, he became hoodoo, and no staff officer could be found who would ride him."* Dixie Bill became known as the horse no one wanted to ride. Then military Chaplain William Bagley purchased Dixie Bill near the end of the war and took the horse back to his farm in Iowa. It was a decision he never regretted. In parades throughout the state, Dixie Bill often was a star attraction, and Bagley enjoyed talking about Dixie Bill's wartime adventures. On October 15, 1881, Dixie Bill died. He was somewhere around 35 years old. He received a grand military funeral where scores of veterans attended. Covered with an American flag, the battle-scarred warhorse was laid to rest by Bagley in his backyard.

~August 20~
World War Two

Though World War Two was the first war equipped with advanced machinery, the horse played a surprisingly huge part in the war effort for both sides. Horses were still used as cavalry mounts, field artillery, and supply delivery animals and as part of first aid and rescue operations. Germany had the largest cavalry divisions, followed closely by the Soviets who had an impressive number of horses in their military. The U.S. Army had requested 20,000 horses for their cavalry in Europe, and that number increased by the tens of thousands in the early years of the war. The U.S. Army Veterinary Corps would care for close to 56,000 horses during their time in service.

For thousands of years, horses have been a major part of battles and wars throughout history because of their size, strength, and speed, but the horse could not withstand the modern weaponry that had been developed and used during World War Two. As the war continued on, the number of horses used in the war effort decreased. In 1943 the U.S Army used 3,000 horses for beach patrol to keep watch for German boats and submarines, and the last remaining cavalry unit to serve ended in 1944. By the end of the war, Germany would be the only country still using a large number of horses, while most of the other countries had become fully mechanized. In all, Germany used nearly three million horses to help in the war effort.

As the modern world was changing and the need for the horse on the battlefield was diminishing, so was the way of life for the cavalry soldiers. Many of the warhorses left a profound impact on the men that would last their lifetime. The horse was a faithful war companion to the soldier.

In their eyes, shine stars of wisdom and courage to guide men to the heavens.
~Jodie Mitchell

~August 21~
Harvesting The Sea

When you think of the ocean and then add a horse into the picture, it almost seems perfect. After all, what could be better than riding a horse on oceanfront property? Believe it or not, on the east coast of Canada, you will find horses pulling baskets through the surf to harvest sea plants (marine macro-algae and seaweed) from the ocean. It turns out that sea plants have excellent nutritional benefits for animal health and fertilizer.

A company in Canada has found a positive way to employ many horses and riders, which is a win-win for both animal and human. The company harvests sea plants from the ocean using 150 draft horses during the harvest season to cover a stretch of beaches 30 miles long. The horses are owned by people who are employed by the company during the harvest season. When the harvest is ripe for taking, as many as 150 people with their horses and baskets may be on the payroll. The company uses draft horses for harvesting the sea plants and after being trained how to pull the basket in the ocean they can be worked each year during harvest time, collecting four different types of sea plants into the baskets. The harvest can run from April to December, depending on the weather. The horses seem to enjoy the work and they love the water. The horses often work five hours a day and are taken well care of.

Horse Shrimping is another job horses have done for hundreds of years in Oostduinkerke, located in the Belgian province of West Flanders. Brabant horses (Belgian draft breed) walk through the ocean waters twice a week, pulling a drag to shift the sand and create a vibration so the shrimp jump into the 23 by 33-foot nets. Workers place the shrimp in the baskets hanging on each side of the horse. There is a huge amount of trust that the rider and horse need to have for each other, as the water can be chest deep. Horse shrimping is a 500-year-old tradition that is still done today.

~August 22~
The Farm Horse

The workhorses of the past are rarely seen pulling a plow or other piece of equipment in our modern world, except in a few communities who still work the land the old traditional way using actual horsepower. But before the early 1900's in the United States and Canada, ninety percent of the agricultural farm work and other maintenance jobs were done by teams of horses—lots of them.

For thousands of years, the planting of grains and vegetables was done manually. Soon new and improved farm equipment, like the double-width harrows, steel plows mounted on wheels, binders, threshers, and combines, meant that man needed real power and the draft horse was the power source of choice. At the same time, the harness was being greatly redesigned and improved for a better fit on the horses, and the hitch was also a work in progress to make the job easier on the animals.

There was a time in history when farmers with smaller farms tended to prefer mares over geldings. Mares could be used both for riding and driving, but mainly many farmers believed they lasted longer and worked harder than the geldings. The mares could also be bred and continue to work during much of their pregnancy. After the babies were born, a farmer could either keep the young horses or sell them for added revenue on the farm. If a gelding came up lame, there wasn't much a farmer could do but wait and see if he got better, sell him, or sadly destroy the animal. It was a time in history when horses were not kept as pets. They served a purpose and if they couldn't work they were not kept around.

"The farm horse worked long days, and a good farmer knew that if he took care of his equines, they would repay him tenfold. For a wise farmer recognized that these huge animals could refuse to plow the field at any time, but still did the work to please the human who had become his partner in life."
~Author Unknown

~August 23~
Circus Maximus

When you think of chariot racing and the fast teams of horses pulling the beautifully decorated chariots, you need to go back to the beginning where this dangerous and often romanticized sport began. We need to go back to the great Circus Maximus in Rome. When Circus Maximus was built in the 6th century BC, it was designed for chariot races along with other types of competition, where the losing competitors often lost their lives at the end of the game. It was common for chariot horses to become severely injured or die in these extreme and desperate competitions, which often determined whether a slave would gain his life and freedom or lose it. These games were put on each year by the Romans for the citizens and their gods, and the bloodier the competition, the more the crowds cheered.

Each summer, the games would take place in the massive complex built of stone with a huge oval track in the center, and it is estimated that this forum could hold up to 150,000 spectators! The Emperor's horses and chariots were maintained with the greatest of care, and there were complete teams including farriers, handlers, veterinarians, trainers, and charioteers. The charioteers (the drivers of the chariot) were often slaves who competed in hopes of gaining their freedom by winning a race. The stakes were high if you were to compete at the Circus Maximus games, and second best was never good enough for the Romans.

During the golden years of the Circus Maximus, many horses were also used for show and what they called "art riding." A charioteer could have up to 10 horses pulling a chariot while performing special maneuvers. During that time, Romans maintained up to 14,000 horses for training and competition in hopes of one day having their horses compete in the Circus Maximus games.

~August 24~
Black Jack

He was foaled on January 19, 1947, and was completely black in color except for the white star on his forehead. His breeding is not clear, but many say he was probably a mix of Morgan and Quarter Horse. The U.S. Army Quartermaster purchased Black Jack on November 2, 1953. He would be the last of the horses to have a military brand on his left shoulder and his U.S. Army serial number 2V56 on the left side of his neck. The Army sent Black Jack to Fort Myer as a mount, and he quickly earned the reputation as being a difficult horse that often refused to do his job. He turned out not to be suitable for riding and wouldn't pull anything, so parades were out of the question! The one thing Black Jack had going for him was that he was black and beautiful. So the Army, as a last attempt, sent him off to do a funeral procession as the caparisoned horse—the riderless horse that walks behind the casket with the boots facing backward, symbolizing the rider's last ride.

From that first funeral, Black Jack's career was secured as he made the perfect caparisoned horse. Black Jack would become famous as the horse that symbolized the sacrifice of so many. He walked in over 1,000 funeral processions, including John F. Kennedy, Herbert Hoover, Lyndon B. Johnson, and General Douglas MacArthur.

Black Jack died after 29 years of military service on February 6, 1976. He was buried at Fort Myer with full military honors, and Black Jack is only the second horse in U.S. history to receive such an honor. Black Jack would be the image that many would take home with them after saying goodbye to their loved ones. What an incredible honor that was bestowed upon this horse.

"A nation that does not honor its heroes, will not long endure."
~President Abraham Lincoln

~August 25~
Lewis And Clark

America was very young, and it was a great time of exploration for the nation. Meriwether Lewis (1774–1809) and William Clark (1770–1838) were chosen by President Thomas Jefferson to go forward with an expedition in 1804 that would carve out a route and passage between the Atlantic and Pacific Oceans. They were also to trace the boundaries obtained in the Louisiana Purchase and to claim the Oregon Territory. This expedition would take two and a half years to complete. It is said that Lewis and Clark would not have been successful without the horses that took them through the vast and often harsh terrain for thousands of miles to open up the west.

What started off as a very slow expedition on foot changed with the purchase of horses from the Shoshone Indians near the edge of the Rocky Mountains. The men were not prepared for the incredible height and steep terrain of the mountains, and with the newly purchased horses, they were able to cross the Rocky Mountains and reach the other side before winter set in. Riding on the back of their tired horses, they would go on to fulfill the mission that was given to them for the nation's future. The horse's role in the Lewis and Clark expedition is so important, and the horse is finally being recognized as one of history's major players in the growth of what was our very young nation.

The one thing that is humorous is the fact that Lewis and Clark were not very good horseman. They were often viewed as "pathetic and clumsy riders" rather than accomplished horsemen. It was as if the horses took care of them even though the horses were equally exhausted and hungry. It was said that on the expedition, Lewis and Clark learned to be horse traders, horse doctors, and often horse breakers and trainers, as many of the horses they acquired from the Native Indians were somewhat wild at first!

~August 26~
The Shunting Horse

In 1920 there were over 19,000 horses working at railway station yards across Britain. Charlie was a "Shunting horse" that lived at Newmarket railway station and pulled train boxcars and coaches into position. He retired on February 21, 1967, as the last shunting horse. Horses had been used to haul boxcars from the earliest days of the railways, and Newmarket was the last British railway depot to withdraw the shunting horses. They were retained there to move special vehicles used for transporting racehorses along with other good and supplies coming by train. Although locomotives could move heavier loads, horses were cheaper and more flexible, so they were kept on for many years to shunt at the smaller depots.

Charlie and his stable mate Butch also had the job of shunting railway wagons. Railway shunters break apart and join the coaches and wagons together at the yards. The pair worked seven days a week maneuvering wagons in a way that no engine could compare. With all of the modernization happening in 1964, Charlie and Butch still proved to be more useful at their job than any engine.

The public had a special affection for the railway horse. For many people living and working in the city, the farm horse was a distant creature not often seen, but the railway horse was different. The railway horse was a part of daily life and a comfort to see in a fast-changing world. Charlie retired to a loving home with his stable mate Butch. Many retired shunting horses did not have such a good ending. Some were euthanized for food, while others worked different jobs. Local newspapers printed stories to create campaigns to save the railway horses in their towns and cities. With the public's help, many would buy retired railway horses and then rehome them with regular inspections to ensure the horse's welfare. When Charlie retired, a way of life at the railroad ended forever.

~August 27~
The Gelding

Castrating or gelding horses has been done for centuries and the term gelding, which means a castrated male horse, originated from the Old Norse word "geldingr." The procedure of gelding horses has always been known to quiet down the stallion and make him less aggressive with other male horses. And, of course, it takes away his drive to breed mares. But some of the history behind the procedure of gelding a horse was interesting and disturbing at the same time.

Aristotle mentions the gelding of horses as early as 350 BC in some of his writings. The Scythian people were believed to be the first to castrate their stallions, but little information on how they performed the castration is available. The Mongolian people have a unique and ritualist way of gelding their stallions. The young stallions are not gelded until two to three years of age. The young colts are rounded up, and one by one, they catch them and tie their legs together. Then the horse is pushed onto his side. They use a knife that has been boiled in water and then cut off the testicles. After the testicles have been removed, they rinse the area that has been cut with mare's milk which is believed to promote healing. When the castration of all their horses is done for the day, they take a testicle, puncture it with a knife and insert a rope through it. The rope is then tied to the tail of a newly castrated horse. It is believed that when the testicle has dried up, the area will be completely healed. The remaining testicles are cooked and eaten by the head male of each family. They believe it will bring each man the strength of the stallion.

Today, castrating stallions is very commonplace, and with modern medicine, it is done basically pain-free. The reasons for gelding a horse have stayed the same, but the instruments and medical care have changed. No testicles hanging on my horse's tail!

~August 28~
Vonolel

Vonolel was a beautiful grey Arabian horse who was very fast and agile. He was purchased in Bombay, India by Field Marshal Lord Roberts, who bought the horse shortly after the Lushai Expedition of 1871-1872, while he was still a major in the military. The Arabian was named after a revered chief of one of the local tribes. Vonolel carried Roberts on the 300-mile march from Kabul to Kandahar during the Second Afghan War (1878-80). The pair were inseparable and seemed the perfect match between horse and man. Lord Roberts was only 5 feet 4 inches tall, while Vonolel was a little bigger than a pony.

Vonolel turned out to be Lord Robert's only reliable horse during the entire war and carried Roberts on the march from Kabul to Kandahar. After the war, Vonolel went home with Robert's and became a familiar sight at ceremonial parades and other events. He accompanied Roberts to Ireland, where he served as Commander-in-Chief from 1895 to 1899. Roberts said of his beloved horse, "During the 22 years he was in my possession, he traveled with me over 50,000 miles and was never sick nor sorry."

The Queen awarded medals to her officers and soldiers who had taken part in the Afghan campaign and in the expedition to Kandahar. She did not forget Vonolel. Lord Roberts hung the medal with four clasps and a bronze star around the Arabian's neck.

Vonolel died in 1899 at the age of 29 years old, and it was said that Lord Roberts was heartbroken. The horse was buried at the Royal Hospital in Kilmainham, Dublin. Today, many people walk the grounds of the Royal Hospital in Kilmainham and will pass a small grave without noticing what is written on it. And yet, this grave is probably one of the most unique and special grave sites in all of Dublin. It's the grave of a very brave and courageous horse, Vonolel.

~August 29~
Faithful Until Death

The horses and mules did what was asked of them often without complaint. After weeks of bombs, shelling, and the smell of death all around them, many horses seemed as if they had retreated deep inside their heads just to survive. For the men who took care of these brave warhorses, many had become tightly bonded with these animals that had been drafted into World War I. The men did whatever they could to help keep the horses and mules as comfortable as possible under horrific circumstances.

Life was hard, dangerous, and often short for the horses serving on the Western Front. Most horses and mules were tied in open fields (there were no shelters), which exposed them during the winter months to horrendous conditions. Lieutenant-Colonel David Sobey Tamblyn, a veterinary surgeon, wrote these words, *"Nothing more distressing could be witnessed than a concentration of transport animals, during wet seasons, in fields where the mud was over their knees and hocks. The Horses were wet and cold for months at a time, and the hay was trampled into the mud. Under these conditions, debilitated horses, which were propped up by the mud, died on their feet."*

The situation was made far worse by the mandatory body clipping of the horses as a preventative measure against mange and lice. Because horse blankets were not always available, the practice of clipping the horses resulted in a greater number of horses dying due to the constant cold, wet weather. In 1918, clipping was limited to only the horses' legs and stomachs to help keep the horses warm.

When Spielberg's film War Horse came out in 2011, it did what should have been done decades before. It brought to the forefront the brave and courageous equine heroes of the war. The horses came from all over the globe in the millions. They had no choice and most never went back home after the war. They are the unsung heroes of the war and they were faithful until death.

~August 30~
Dream Alliance

Sometimes, all a town needs is hope and a dream to change its course. Such was the town of Cefn Fforest, Cawerphilly, a village in one of the poorest mining areas of Wales. Jan Vokes and her husband lived in the town that once was thriving, but now not much was left since the four coal mines surrounding the area closed down. The closing of the mines affected every business in the small town and as more businesses closed their doors, more people left. The ones who stayed watched their town die and with that, their dreams.

Jan, who was 61 years old, still worked every day cleaning at different places and had a second job working at a store. Her days were long, but at least she had some income coming in. Jan and her husband rented a small slag-heap (waste matter from the coal mines) that normally was used to grow vegetable. But Jan had an idea. Against all reasonable odds, she wanted to breed a racehorse for the Grand National. Jan and her husband Brian pooled their money and bought a mare called Rewbell, who was considered possibly, "the worst racehorse in Wales." Jan knew they didn't have the money to breed and train a young racehorse so they offered a syndicate to a few of their friends in town. After their first meeting, they had a 23-strong syndicate of investors who were common everyday folk which makes the story that much better!

Jan didn't give up on the dream. Rewbell gave birth to a foal they named Dream Alliance and the young colt was raised on their slag-heap allotment. Dream Alliance would grow up in the poorest of towns, in the humblest of surroundings, to become a Grand National Champion in 2009, racing against million-dollar racehorses with the best bloodlines money could buy. It's the remarkable true story of a horse that brought a little town back to life, and gave the people something to hope for. Dreams do come true.

~August 31~
Horses In Art

If you have ever walked into a person's home that loves horses, then it is guaranteed you will probably find some form of artwork depicting a horse. I have horse pictures hanging all over my walls, along with horse plates, horse statues, and pictures of my daughters with their horses! History has proven quite well through art that no matter your station in life, no matter the continent, culture, or century, the obsession with the horse has affected humans in a deep and spiritual way.

The earliest known images of horses are found in caves in France and are estimated to be thousands of years old. The "Panel of Horses" is considered a masterpiece for its time. Drawn in charcoal and clay, it depicts horses in a way that feels modern because it conveys both dimension and motion. Ancient artifacts of the Hittites and Ancient Egyptians both showed horses pulling chariots and participating in competition. Ancient Greece depicted horses on black plates and vases to show off their military and nobility. During the 3rd century, 600 full-size Terracotta horse sculptures were placed in the Tomb of Qin Shi Huangdi, who was the Emperor of a unified China. They were buried with him and today it is considered a masterpiece. The Ancient Romans loved to create statues of their leaders on horseback, and horse artwork wasn't limited to drawings, paintings, and statuary. The enormous 11th century Bayeux Tapestry contains dozens of embroidered wartime scenes leading up to the Norman conquest of England, and features 190 horses. In the last few centuries, horses have been the inspiration of Native American artwork throughout the west. Today's artwork often portrays horses in sport and competition, but nothing will ever compare to the beauty of the horse in its natural surroundings. Horses have captivated our hearts, and artwork in all its various forms, is a beautiful way to honor them.

~September 1~
Barrel Racing

Women have been barrel racing in rodeos for decades but the early rodeo competitions looked much different for the ladies who rode horses. In the 1880's, Buffalo Bill Cody hired Annie Oakley, considered the best-known female gun handler of the day. Cody discovered quickly that people would flock to his Wild West Shows to see a lady ride a horse and shoot a pistol!

In 1931 in Stamford, Texas, the rodeo organizers decided to allow girls 16 years and older to compete in a special event in which they would ride a figure eight pattern. The pattern wasn't timed and it was more like a western pleasure class. The girls would also lead the parade, ride their horses in various rodeo events, and be available to talk and dance with the cowboys at the dance held each evening. It was less about riding skills and horsemanship and more about adding a feminine touch to a man's sport, and the ladies would help by bringing in the cowboys and the audience.

The next year the young ladies were given prizes for the nicest looking horse, most attractive riding outfit, and best horsemanship. The horsemanship again was demonstrated by riding a figure eight pattern around barrels with style and grace. In 1935 the Stamford event changed the figure eight pattern to a cloverleaf pattern, but it wasn't until 1949 that it became a timed event, and from there the sport grew like crazy.

Barrel racing has come a long way since the days of pretty riding clothes and dances with cowboys. In the last 70 years, the sport can boast prizes equal to all other rodeo events. Beginning as a way to emphasize a lady's beauty, rodeo attire and horsemanship is now viewed as a serious sport that requires actual work and athleticism for both the rider and their horse. It would be safe to say barrel racers have brought the sport to a very professional level, and the horses used in this sport are true athletes in every way.

~September 2~
Horse Manure Crazies

The truth is you can't have a horse book without a page about horse manure! If you love horses and want to know everything about them, then you need to know how the poop that comes from the back-end of the horse has contributed to civilizations, even if it sounds crazy.

Jockeys needed to be below a certain weight to race horses on race day. One pound over the limit could mean a day off from the races. In the 1920's in Tijuana, Mexico, the jockeys took losing weight to the next level. They discovered that if they sat in a pile of hot horse manure covered up to their neck for an hour or two, they could sweat off a few pounds. This might be considered the first modern sauna.

In 1981, the royal wedding of Prince Charles and Lady Diana took place. The carriage horses used in the wedding were fed colored dyes in their feed so that their manure would match the wedding's color scheme and therefore look more aesthetically pleasing on television.

In 1783, two French inventors used horse manure along with chopped wool and straw to successfully launch the world's first hot air balloon. The balloon stayed airborne for eight minutes with a sheep, a duck, and a rooster aboard. They all survived!

In 1735, cooking chefs used a "horse manure oven" as a way to cook their food. In the book The Modern Cook, they were advised to, "Take a good ham, cleanse it from all nastiness about it, take off the rind, spread a cloth, in one end of which you put the thyme, sweet basil, and bay leaves; then put upon it the ham, facing downwards, season it top and bottom alike. Lay one fold of the cloth over it, sprinkle it with some brandy, and fold it up. Then bury it in horse dung for 48 hours." Afterwards, take it out and enjoy!

~September 3~
Where To Put Them All

Where do you put hundreds of thousands of workhorses to eat and sleep in the city? This was a major problem for many large cities in the United States and England during the 1800's and early 1900's. Horses were used for everything, from pulling wagons to street clean-up. They pulled the paddy wagons and fire trucks, they delivered vegetables, common goods and beer daily, and that was only the start. You had the ice wagons, milk wagons and everything in-between.Basically anything that needed to be moved or delivered, including people, was done by the horse. Horse-power is what made the cities flourish and grow, and many of these horses worked six or seven days a week. So where do you put them all at the end of their work day or on their days off?

When we think about the horse stable, we often think about what we are familiar with today. Beautiful stables with large fields of green grass in the quiet setting of the country. But that was not the case for the workhorses of the past. The horses that lived and worked in the cities daily also ate and rested in the same city each night. Many of the larger cities had "horse districts" where the horses were stabled in buildings that would otherwise be used for people or businesses. Stalls along with everything needed to care for the horses were built inside the buildings. The streets that housed the horses were usually side streets away from the main thoroughfares. Horses learned to walk up ramps to second stories where they were housed, or they walked down a ramp to live in underground stables.

The horse's care or comfort was not a top priority for most people in the city. After everything closed down for the day, the horses were walked back to their "homes" and kept out of sight until the next day to do it all over again. It was a time in history when many horses lived in the most unnatural environment.

~September 4~
Big Game And Fast Cats

Thousands of years ago, hunting on horseback looked much different with man and his horse. The horse was a true game changer for how man hunted big and small game, but in some tribes or civilizations, the horse was only half the story.

In the ruling classes, hunting on horseback was encouraged while, at the same time, it taught the younger men good war tactics using spears and other weaponry. It was also common to use other animals to help in the hunt, including hounds, birds of prey, and even big cats. Horses were forced to undergo a new kind of training where they had to learn to work alongside their animal hunting partners, who were natural predators. The horses that were trained for these hunts needed to have a good mind and speed, but equally important, they needed to have courage. It took a brave horse that was willing to listen to his master and run as close as possible to a large animal that was being hunted. Stone carvings in the Middle East show many images and writings of horses that were used in the royal lion hunts around 2,600 years ago. In the 4th century, Iranian kings built large game parks where hunters on horseback could hunt animals like bears, leopards, and wild boars.

In Central Asia, India, and the Middle East, big cats like the Lynx and Cheetah were trained to help in the hunt. These meat-eating cats were trained to ride behind the hunter on the rump of his horse. When an animal was spotted, the cat jumped off the horse and ran at full speed after its prey. Horses that were normally preyed upon by big cats were now forced to work side by side with these felines in the most unnatural way possible. History doesn't tell us what some of the outcomes were for the horses, but with more excavation, maybe the ancient sites will tell the complete story. But for now, all we can do is try to envision what that must have been like for the horses of that time.

~September 5~
Long Live The Friesian

The magnificent Friesian horse will leave you in awe with their long black wavy mane and tail, and their walk, trot, and canter, which looks like a dance when they move. The Friesian is truly a one-of-a-kind breed and the history behind this black beauty is amazing. The Friesian horse originated from Friesland, a province of the Netherlands. It is one of Europe's oldest breeds, and its lineage can be traced back to the ancient horse Equus Robustus. Equus Robustus was a massive horse that once roamed Northern Europe around 3,000 years ago.

The monks were well known for their superior horse breeding in the Middle Ages and crossed the draft-type Equus Robustus descendants with lighter horse breeds. The result was the Friesian horse, one of Europe's first pure horse breeds and one of the world's first warm-blooded horses. The Friesian became known for its incredible strength, flowing movement, along with a very willing and kind disposition. Armored knights preferred Friesians for their strength and endurance when going into battle. William the Conqueror used horses showing a remarkable resemblance to Friesian stallions at the Battle of Hastings in 1066. Friesians carried European knights to the Middle East during the Crusades, and the royal monarchy heavily imported the horses during the 16th and 17th centuries.

Sadly, by the 1800's, very few purebred Friesians could be found. In 1879, with great effort, the first Friesian studbook became available for registered stallions, but by 1913 there were only three registered purebred stallions left available for breeding! Over the next fifty years, the people of the Netherlands worked diligently to bring back their amazing Friesian horse. With a lot of hard work and careful breeding, the Friesian horse has made a spectacular comeback.

~September 6~
Horseball

Horseball, originally called Pato, has to be one of the craziest equestrian sports ever invented, and I would bet the horses would wholeheartedly agree. What is even more absurd is the origin of this sport that involves the horse, the rider, and a duck! Yes you read that right, a duck! Let me say it one more time—A DUCK!

Today's equestrian Horseball is basically a bunch of people riding around on horses and tossing an odd-shaped ball with handles on it to each other's teammates. But a few hundred years ago, instead of a ball, the players tossed around a duck. The original version of Horseball, known as Pato, was very popular in Argentina, and the participants used a real live duck in an enclosed basket as the ball.

The live duck version of Pato became illegal to play very quickly due to a high death rate among the players. One can only imagine why there was such a huge death rate, but possibly due to the horses freaking out from the loud squawks and wildly flapping wings, or the duck getting loose and attacking the players and horses! I am sure many riders hit the ground hard with all the chaos happening. Still, it didn't stop the Argentinians from having the time of their life. And even though it became illegal to use a live duck, the new version of the game took off, and they made Pato their national game using a ball with handles attached. Quickly there was a significant drop in fatalities and the sport was reborn as Horseball. Now that the game didn't involve the death of a duck or human, more and more people began finding Horseball rather fun causing it to spread across Europe and eventually overseas.

For a sport that may have started with a live duck, Horseball has become an equestrian favorite among Argentinians. I am sure the horses are glad they don't have to run around with their rider holding an angry duck!

~September 7~
How Many Hands?

The buying and selling or horse-trading of horses became an important part of most civilizations once the horse was domesticated. In order to measure horses accurately for selling, a system was created by using a man's hand to measure the height of a horse. Egyptians used their own body as a unit of measurement and their hands were part of the equation. They measured the height of a horse starting with the distance from the ground to the top of the horse's front leg, using fists or open hands as units of measurement. This practice was widely used but not very accurate. After all, the size of a man's hand or foot varied with each person. There were also other problems with accuracy as some civilizations measured with just the four fingers held open wide, while others included the thumb as part of the measurement. There were no standard measuring tools in ancient societies, and using a man's hand to measure the horse seemed the easiest, but improving the way a horse was accurately measured needed to be found. Even though we have a better and more accurate way of measuring a horse today, the original language of calling it a "hand" is still used almost 3000 years later!

In the 1500's, King Henry VIII standardized the hand measurement at 4 inches. Having a consistent width allowed buyers and sellers of horses to have a standard reference. They seemed to understand that the withers stayed at the most stable position on a horse's body which made it ideal for measurement back then, and is still true today. One hand is considered 4 inches, so a 15-hand horse is 60 inches tall.

In the United States, the hand remains the primary unit of measurement, as in most English-speaking countries such as Britain, Canada, and Australia, while other European countries and the Federal Equestrian International (FEI) use meters.

~September 8~
Star

Paul Revere may have ridden all night to warn people that the British were coming, but Sybil Ludington also rode all night and twice as far with her horse when she was only 16 years old. I am talking about the all-night ride where Sybil Ludington rode her horse Star across miles of countryside to get the word out that the British were coming in 1776. I wanted to celebrate the female version of Paul Revere and her amazing horse Star, who ran all through the night in rainy weather and complete darkness with the only light coming from the lanterns at the houses they would pass. There were many couriers trying to get the word out that the British were heading towards the village of Concord, but Sybil and her horse went farther than most on those famous rides.

Star belonged to Sybil and she trained the horse herself. She named the horse after the marking he had under his forelock. Sybil was an expert rider and Star would do anything Sybil asked. Sybil had watched her father train the militia at their farm, and she had helped often by running errands for her father. She knew where each soldier lived and she knew the landscape very well. Then, as word had come in that the British were near, Sybil, with her father's permission, rode one night starting around 9 p.m. until dawn to warn the people. Only a small part of Sybil's 40-mile ride was on the main roads. Most of the roads had become too muddy, and at times, she had to dismount Star and lead him. Like Paul Revere's ride, Sybil Ludington's journey was an inspiration to the troops and the colonists. Later, General George Washington came to Ludington's Mill to thank Sybil personally for her all-night ride.

Today a statue honoring Sybil and Star stands in Carmel, New York, along with historical markers mapping the route of their ride. Star was one of the horses who did his part on a cold, rainy night to carry his young rider for American independence.

~September 9~
Face Protection

Face protection for horses in the military or police force is not a new idea. The Saffron face covering (ancient face protection) dates back to early Greece, but we are probably more familiar with the images of the medieval knight riding his warhorse and his steed is covered from head to toe in metal or leather barding. The most interesting part of the body protection was the very intricate and detailed Saffron that was carefully put on the horse's head. These metal face coverings were not only supposed to protect the warrior's horse, but they also wanted the horse to look fierce, intimidating, and show a spiritual presence.

During the medieval period, jousting was a way for men to show their strength and possibly be noticed by the king. Jousting was also entertainment for the nobility and the commoners. Well-trained horses for jousting were expensive, and if a lance was to hit the horse's face, it could easily put their eyes out or worse. The "blind" Saffron covered the horse's entire face, including his eyes, so that he was completely protected and it also kept him from shying away from the opposing side's lance and other forms of weaponry. Yes, you read it right, the horse was completely blind when the Saffron face covering was put on his head, and that is how the knight would ride his horse in competition.

Today's equine face protection is made to be much more comfortable for horses. Police horses will often have to put on heavy-duty clear face protection during crowd control, riots, or other emergencies, but it is of the utmost importance that the horse becomes very comfortable in wearing the face protection before he is ever asked to work with it on for long periods. Thank goodness the well-being and comfort of the horse is considered first when deciding what kind of protection they will wear on their face.

~September 10~
The Fox Hunt

Fox hunting began for very practical reasons. Horses were ridden to hunt along with dogs that could smell out animals that would be killed for food and for the hides to keep warm. The other added element was that fox hunting was believed to help the men in the military become far better riders and horsemen. Fox hunting was also used for pest control as foxes were numerous, and they were often killing farmer's animals.

In 1668 George Villiers, the Duke of Buckingham, established the first official fox hunt and the traditional sport still takes place to this day. Throughout the centuries, fox hunting on horseback began to evolve and change from a way of finding food, military training, and pest control to becoming a leisurely activity for the wealthy.

Eventually, the fox hunt was modified for military training, in which it was called "drag hunting." For drag hunting, they would set out chemical scents instead of using a live fox or other animals. The dogs would go after the scents and the riders would follow. Jumps and obstacles were set up for the sole purpose of the military to jump and maneuver as they galloped through the fields. This was used by the British Army to train the troops before they were sent off to war.

Today hunting live foxes is banned in the UK, as well as most of the world due to the violent death of the fox. But the "fox hunt" by drag hunting is still done all over the world and is very popular since no animals are harmed. It takes special horses that are calm, yet very athletic and have the stamina needed to run the course through obstacles and jumps, alongside the numerous dogs barking and running all around. The horse breeds used for fox hunting vary, and much might depend on the country. The UK is known for its formality and you will see more Thoroughbreds or Warmbloods, while in America, you could see just about any breed of horse.

~September 11~
Vehicle Names Inspired By...

A car named after a beautiful horse can create magic, and the car manufacturers knew this better than anyone. The influence and inspiration equines have had on us and our vehicles is amazing.

- The Ford Bronco was originally built in 1966 and continued to be built until 1996. It was recently redesigned in 2021, and the Bronco horse logo is still the same!
- In 1971, Ford created the Pinto car named after the Pinto horse. It was a smaller car and was tame by vehicle standards.
- In the early 1960's, Ford designed the Mustang car and the name fit perfectly. The Mustang was considered the first of the "pony" cars. It was small, sporty and designed for high performance.
- In the 1970's, Subaru made a car known as the Subaru Brumby that was sold in Australia. It was named after the wild Brumbies (horses) from down under.
- In 1975, Hyundai designed a small car they appropriately named the Hyundai Pony as it was small like a pony.
- In 1999, Hyundai designed a car named the Equus. Equus is the Latin word for horse.
- In 1959, the Austrian company Steyr-Daimler-Puch built a small work truck named the Halflinge, after the Haflinger horse.
- The Pinzgauer is an Austrian military vehicle that has been in production since 1971. This vehicle was named after the Austrian breed of draft horse with the same name.
- In 1971, Dodge started selling the Dodge Colt.
- In 1964, Dodge designed the Charger, which was named after the medieval horse (called a charger) that was used for battle.

One can get in a car and see what man has made. One can get on a horse and see what God has made. ~Author Unknown

~September 12~
Surprising Statistics

For the people who think that the horse hasn't contributed to the world economy, take a look at some of the newest numbers and statistics that prove how important the horse has been, even after the Industrial Revolution changed how horses were used. The horse is here stay! Here are some of the latest statistics.

- There are about 9.2 million horses in the U.S.
- The horse industry is worth 40 billion a year. Horse racing contributes about 15.6 billion to the economy each year.
- The horse industry employs 1.74 million people.
- Texas has the highest population of horses—767,100. California is next—534,500. Third is Florida—387,100 horses. Rhode Island is the lowest with fewer than 4,000 horses.
- Each year, roughly 7 million Americans go horseback riding.
- In the United States, most horse owners are married females between the ages of 38–45.
- In the UK, horse racing is the most attended sport, except for football. 7 million people come to watch yearly.
- The Quarter Horse holds the largest registry in the world, with over 2.5 million registered horses.
- A Thoroughbred racehorse named Fusaichi Pegasus sold for $70 million in 2000 to a breeder after winning the Kentucky Derby.
- In 1890, the horse-drawn cab traveled at around 6 miles per hour in New York City. In 1990 an automobile cab in New York traveled around 6 miles per hour! All I can say is…very interesting.

~September 13~
Unusual Inventions

The horse has been the inspiration of countless inventions either for humans or to make life easier for the horse, even though most human inventions are probably not what the horse had in mind. But with each invention, good or downright silly, it's still fun to look at what people have come up with.

In 1949, a saddle with a built-in radio was invented that was way before its time. You could buy the saddle for $295.00 and up, depending on the extras you put on the saddle. That was a lot of money back then, but you would have the luxury of listening to tunes while you ride. There probably weren't that many radio stations to choose from at the time, but it was still a clever idea!

In the late 1800's, Hubert Cecil Booth created "Puffing Billy," a carpet cleaning machine that was about the size of a full-size carriage cabin. A horse was hitched to the Puffing Billy and pulled the machine from home to home to clean and vacuum carpets. It is where we get our in-home carpet cleaner companies of today!

The Horse Speeding Vehicle, created in 2003, is one of the most abstract ideas or inventions that involve horsepower. Instead of the horse pulling a cart or carriage, he would be led up on the four-wheel machine that he would power from on top to make it move. Not sure what the purpose was for, but after the patent was submitted, it was put in abandoned status. Probably a good thing for the horse!

In the 19th century, someone had the idea of making a machine that would do all the work of brushing your horse. All you needed to do was secure the horse in front of the machine, which was a huge contraption with metal arms and brushes attached at the ends. It looked like a metal octopus! I'm not sure how the horse liked it, but I would guess probably not very much.

~September 14~
Horses Of The Civil War

The Civil War (1861-1865) would have looked much different without the help of all the horses. They were used to carry the soldiers, pull artillery, and carry food, supplies, ammunition and so much more. No one could imagine what these equines would endure during this long battle between the North and the South.

The lifestyle and culture was deeply embedded into the daily life of horse ownership. In the South, horses were a vision of having elite power, and in the North, horses were a part of the fabric of work and industrialization. To the owners of both sides, the horses in their care were of the utmost importance, and when the war broke out, it greatly intensified. These warhorses worked hard and long hours, and a race to acquire a position against the enemy had no room for gentle treatment.

When the war broke out, both sides needed as many horses as possible, taking them from farms and cities and even using children's ponies to pack in the enormous amount of supplies. At the beginning of the war, the military knew how important it was to make sure all the horses had good hay, grain, and water but as the war continued, supplies ran out, fields were cut dry of forage, and water became difficult to manage. Most of the horses died of exhaustion, sickness, and multiple gunshot wounds. Both sides knew that if you took down the horses, then you had a chance of winning each separate battle. The most accurate numbers are not known of how many horses, mules, donkeys, and ponies died during the Civil War, but it is estimated to be in the millions. In the end, the horses were among the victims of all of it.

They shall not grow old, as we that are left grow old. Age shall not weary them or the years condemn. At the going down of the sun and in the morning, we will remember them – the warhorse. ~Author unknown

~September 15~
Queen Of Diamonds

Working in the horse industry and having my own business in the 21st century has its share of challenging days, but for the most part, it's a nice life. Horses and the farm keep me pretty busy because, as you know, if you are taking care of horses, there is always something that needs to be done. I am thankful for my husband, who does the brunt of the work without ceasing. Now if I was working in the horse industry in the 1800's, my life would look a lot different. Being a businesswoman back then was not the norm.

Meet Kitty Wilkins, horse-trader and businesswoman. Kitty grew up out west in the late 1800's around her father, who was a smart businessman and she watched and learned. During her teen years, she excelled at riding (side-saddle) and learned as much about horses as she could during those years. She had the best of both worlds when it came to her family and learning about the world of business. Her father had started a cattle and horse business, and at 20 years old, Kitty watched her dad and quickly came up with her own marketing strategies for selling horses. She could recognize excellent horse stock, and she would tell her customers that she would never sell an unfit horse. As her father aged, Kitty took over the Diamond Range Ranch, and selling horses became her profession which she excelled at. Kitty started purchasing stallions from around the world to develop her strong breeding stock and became well-known for the great horses she bred and sold. Her horses were of such good quality, that soon her clients were coming from all around the United States and Canada to buy her horses. Her ranch provided the U.S. with thousands of the horses used in World War I. Through her stallions, she bred for a couple different horse markets including draft horses for heavy work and Morgans for riding and carriage. She truly was a horsewoman of excellence and is remembered as the Queen of Diamonds.

~September 16~
Colonial Life

Colonial life and the people of that time loved their horses and used them for everything. But as things started to get out of control with the horses, new laws were being written up. In 1674, Plymouth, Massachusetts, enacted a law prohibiting the running of horses in any streets. The people of Plymouth grew tired of horse racing in their villages and created an ordinance forbidding it. However, the large fines or being put in the "stocks" did not discourage the colonists from horse racing. Connecticut later passed a law that demanded the forfeit of a man's horse along with a fine of 40 shillings (approx. $1.92) if he was caught racing in the streets.

As the need for higher quality horses grew and to help ensure that only the best horses would be bred, in 1668, Massachusetts decreed that only horses "of comely proportions and 14 hands in stature" could graze on town commons. In 1687, a law in Pennsylvania was enacted by William Penn, which set a minimum height of 13 hands for free-ranging horses, which is unusual since that would be the size of a modern-day pony. Any horse older than 18 months and less than 13 hands had to be castrated. By the 1700's, the number of horses had grown substantially, and the colonies were being overrun by stray horses. In 1715, Maryland approved a law that any old stray horses could be shot on sight.

Early American roads were only passable on foot or horseback, and many colonists couldn't afford a horse, so a system of "Share a Horse" and "Ride and Tie" was born. How it worked was one man rode on a horse while the other man began walking. After a set distance, the rider who was ahead would dismount, tie the horse to an object and start walking. When the other man had walked the distance to the tied horse, he mounted and rode past the original rider to the next tying point. In this system, each man got to ride part way, and the horse even got some rest!

~September 17~
Chernobyl's Wild Horses

The existence of wild horses in Asia has been known since the 15th century. But it wasn't until 1881, when a smaller type of horse was formally identified using scientific studies of a skull and skin collected by Russian Colonel Nikolai Przewalski. The horses were known to the local people as Takhi, which meant "holy" in Mongolian, but were renamed to what we are familiar with today – The Przewalski's horses.

In 1986, the Chernobyl Nuclear Power Plant disaster happened in Ukraine. This accident, which was the largest ever at a nuclear site, led to the creation of a 4,700 km exclusion zone in Ukraine. A total of 350,000 people had to be evacuated from the area, and experts predicted that the radioactive contamination would leave the area uninhabitable for thousands of years. Chernobyl had been labeled a nuclear wasteland where no life would survive. Then came the Przewalski's horses.

In Colonel Przewalski's time, these wild horses were already rare in the steppes (grassland areas) of Mongolia and China. Overgrazing and hunting by humans caused the horses' final decline. The last wild Przewalski horse was spotted in the Gobi Desert in 1969. The situation was bad for the captive Przewalski's horses as well. In the 1950's only 12 survived in European zoos. However, they became the foundation for a breeding program that has managed to rescue the horses from extinction and release them back out into the wild. Three decades later, Chernobyl holds a diverse and growing animal community, and the wild Przewalski's horses are proof of it. Today, the number of Przewalski's horses has grown to around 2,000 worldwide. To the surprise of many, small herds of these wild horses wandered into the nuclear exclusion zone and began to breed and thrive, and these horses are increasing in number and doing quite well!

~September 18~
The Horse Trail

Many horse owners love to trail ride on horseback as a day trip or even a long vacation. It's relaxing for the horse and rider and a great way to see the beautiful scenery God created. But as with everything else, the horse trails of today had to be fought for, as they were disappearing when the motorized off-road vehicles took over the landscape. It took a lot of work by many people decades ago to regain access to the trails for the horse and rider.

Trails and horses have always been a part of America. The Europeans came with their horses, and then shortly after, the Native Americans became excellent horsemen. Most states in the union didn't have a park system in place, and horses were still being used as work animals up until the 1940's. Very few people rode for pleasure. As the development of cities and paved roads increased, the horse and trails decreased. Then in 1944, Equestrian Trails Inc. was established as a nonprofit organization with its mission and charter stating, "Dedicated to the Acquisition and Preservation of Trails, Good Horsemanship, and Equine Legislation."

After World War II, Americans found themselves with more time for relaxation. In the 1960's, it was realized that horse trails in parks were severely limited and things needed to change. The workhorse was no longer needed in most areas, and people were instead riding horses for leisure. By 1970, the horse population had doubled, and horse owners started lobbying for horse trails in state parks. It came with a fight between the people who wanted the horses and those who did not, but it was worth fighting for. The movement grew with huge publications like The Western Horseman, Equus, and Appaloosa News joining in. Since those days, many public parks now have horse access, and even though there are still battles in some states for trail access, the horse and rider are here to stay.

~September 19~
The Ultra-Race

So the question that has plagued man for centuries is…who is faster—the horse or man? Many men believed that humans were faster over long distances because the horse would become winded and burnout, but man knew how to pace himself over a long distance.

The talk about men running against the horse was common centuries ago when horses were the only mode of transportation. In 1818 in England, Mr. J. Barnett took on a bet that he could beat a horse in a 48-hour race. After the first 24 hours, the horse had covered 118 miles, and Barnett had gone 82 miles. After 48 hours, the horse won, covering a distance of 179 to Barnett's 158. Barnett believed he could have won if the race was another day longer, since the horse was completely exhausted.

Then in 1880, a 6.5-day event putting horse against man was held in Chicago. Fifteen men and five horse/rider teams competed with a crowd of 4,000 spectators. The runners and horses started off, and after the first day, the leading horse had covered 130 miles and the leading man 117. By hour 48, the top horse, Speculator, had reached 220 miles and the top runner, 195 miles. Five days into the race, a runner took the lead, but on the last day, Speculator had taken back the lead but collapsed and died soon after. The new horse in the lead was Betsy Baker, but she was exhausted and would no longer respond to her rider whipping her. She was fed a "dose of champagne," hoping to revive her a bit, but in the end she couldn't even walk. The runner won. He covered 578 miles in 6.5 days, and the mare, Betsy Baker, finished in second with 563 miles.

Ultra-races between man and horse have continued even through the 20th century. The one thing that has significantly improved is the care of the horses that are entered into these competitions. No "champagne" concoction for today's equines!

~September 20~
Pick-Up Horse

The rodeo pick-up horse has a critical job when it comes to helping the cowboys who are riding broncs. These horses are stoic and genuine athletes, but at the same time, they are very sensitive and listen to their riders every signal. It is truly amazing to watch the teamwork between the pick-up horse and his rider.

The responsibility of picking up the competition cowboys after their saddle bronc or bareback ride has gone the full eight seconds is huge. Speed and accuracy are vital while trying to get up close to a bucking horse to help the cowboy off. Reaching up close to grab the bucking strap takes a horse that has nerves of steel and doesn't get rattled. It's an extremely fast pace for those few seconds when two things are happening at once. It's like trying to hit a moving target because the bronc is still bucking and the pick-up horse needs to stay right by his side until the job is done.

Usually, pick-up horses and their riders work in teams, and some of the teams have been working rodeos together for a long time. They know each other's horses and they each know their own horse's strong points and weaknesses. Most pick-up riders prefer taller horses because it makes it easier to get up close to the cowboy on the bronc at an equal level, and help him off as fast as possible. Gary Rempel, Canadian Cowboy of the year in 2009, was quoted in an article saying, "I need a horse that's got a little bit of size, around 15.3 to 16 hands, and they need to have speed. They have to have attitude and personality and take a little bump now and then, and they need to be able to take the pressure and the noise of the crowd. It can be easier for some than others. Some horses really like their job, and there are times when my horse has done his job so well that by the end of the day, I can't even remember being on him." The pick-up horse is by far one of the most admired athletes on the rodeo circuit.

~September 21~
Twenty-Mule-Team

Mules were a vital part of the expansion of many businesses across the United States and were often the preferred choice of beast of burden because they seemed hardier than the horse. The Twenty-Mule-Team hitches worked for the Harmony Borax Works Company in Death Valley, California, and were the reason the Borax Company became successful and prosperous. These massive hitched mule teams pulled heavy wagons loaded with Borax (a natural mineral known as sodium borate) from Furnace Creek to the railhead near the Mojave Desert. It was a grueling 165-mile, 10-day trip across barren desert roads. Borax was widely used as a household cleaner and detergent booster for cleaning laundry back in the day.

The Muleskinner was the driver of the hitched wagon, and many muleskinners preferred driving the mules instead of draft horses. In fact, some would even say the mules were much smarter. The wagons that the twenty-mule teams pulled were 16 feet by 4 feet and 6 feet deep. They weighed 7800 pounds empty and 36 1/2 tons loaded. The back wheels of the wagon were 7 feet tall, and the front wheels were 5 feet, and each wheel weighed 1000 pounds! What made the job even harder for the men and mules was the excessive heat in the Mojave Desert. The teams could only travel at most 17 miles a day and water had to be brought along to make sure the mules had enough to drink. It was a major undertaking. The temperatures were well into the 100's much of the year and it was a slow trek across the desert, but the mules seemed to handle it well.

Although the mule teams only ran for a total of six years (1883 to 1889) they became a symbol of the Old West. This is primarily due to a very successful advertising campaign that heavily promoted the Twenty-Mule-Team Borax Soap. The Twenty-Mule-Team is an important part of America's history.

~September 22~
Buzkashi

Horses have endured a lot through the ages, but some of the equestrian sports that have evolved can downright leave a person speechless. If you grow up in Afghanistan and like to ride horses, then there might be a good chance you will learn to play an intense equestrian sport called Buzkashi.

This national game is believed to have originated in Afghanistan since the days of Genghis Khan, the Mongol warrior whose army swept across Asia in the 13th century. Played against other riders on horses, Afghanistan's national sport Buzkashi, is fast and extremely physical for both horse and rider. However, what grabs people's attention is the dead goat. This traditional game is played on horseback with a headless goat carcass that players maneuver around the playing field. Buzkashi (pronounced 'booz-ka-shee') literally translates as "goat pulling or dragging" in Persian. One theory for the game's origins is based on Afghan tribes galloping on horseback to steal a rival tribe's goat from their flock. That would explain the physical and sometimes violent riding that makes up a large part of the game.

There are two types of horses in Afghanistan. One is the Qatgani type which is smaller but very strong, from the province of Qataghan, and the other breed is raised in the steppes of Faryab and Balkh provinces which are larger in size. The Buzkashi horses are well-trained, fast runners and are highly valued, and only stallions are used in the game. Riders usually wear heavy clothing and a helmet to protect themselves from whips and boots coming at them from the other players. The game embodies the Afghan's love of horses and the thrill of the ancient sport. It takes years of training to reach the necessary skills to play the game safely. For many young Afghan boys, it is their dream to grow up and be a champion Buzkashi rider known as a Chapandaz.

~September 23~
The Shahzada

The Australian endurance race is called the Shahzada after a stallion that was known to have a huge heart and incredible stamina to go any distance that was asked of him. The purebred Arabian stallion was imported to Australia, and his name was Shahzada. Few competitors could keep up with the stallion during the tests that were held in 1920, 1921, and 1922. The distance covered during these marathon tests were 250, 300, and 500 miles and each ride was held over five days. Shahzada had won the first and third tests beating the other horses easily, and came in second over the 300 mile distance. Shahzada had gone the 300 mile distance in 37 hours and 29 minutes.

Today the 250-mile Shahzada marathon is held over five days at 50 miles a day. Each horse and rider has to be approved to enter the race since it is not for the beginner rider or horse. It is grueling on the horses and just as hard on the riders. It's not the five hundred-mile distance the riders completed in 1922, but today it represents one of the longest endurance rides in the world. During these rides, there are twice-daily vet checks which are extremely stringent as every horse's welfare is of the utmost importance. The horse comes first above all else in this race.

The mountains of Yengo National Park and the rocky and often steep hill climbs like "Prestons Hill" and "The Steps" are true tests of the rider and his horse. Then add in the river crossings, and rough terrain and a person will quickly realize that this endurance ride is not for the amateur rider or novice horse. Rain and sleet are common, and the weather changes quickly from the hot temperatures in the lowland to the low 20's in the mountainous areas. This is serious endurance for the test of will, spirit, and endurance of both man and horse and the Australian endurance community regards every competitor and horse as a true winner.

~September 24~
The Fire Horse

For most of history, there was a genuine need for horses in the workforce. Horses became a major form of transportation and one of the most important jobs a horse could have was pulling the wagons for the fire departments.

The period from the Civil War to the early 1920's is known in firefighting as the era of the fire horse. Before that, men pulled the wagons that transported the water tanks, ladders, and equipment. The first documentation of horses pulling a water wagon to a fire was before the Civil War.

In the beginning, horses in the fire station were not accepted with open arms, but as equipment became heavier, the need for real horsepower was realized. As their presence in firefighting grew, the firefighters came to respect and love the hard-working and brave fire horses. The fire horses were often treated very well, and most firemen wanted their fire horses to be bathed and well-groomed. Buying and training one fire horse was expensive and cost as much as ten firemen, but a team of horses could reach the fire much faster and pull ten times the weight. A horse had to meet certain criteria to be considered as a fire horse. The horses were usually Percherons or heavy draft types and the training was rigorous, taking up to two years. A fire horse's career usually only lasted about four to eight years, but some fire horses worked many years beyond that. A fire horse would fall into one of three categories: lightweight at 1,100 pounds used for the hose wagons, middleweight at 1,400 pounds used for the steam engine wagons, and heavyweights above 1,400 pounds pulled the hook and ladder wagons. Not only did these horses become the firefighters trusted partners, but they also were revered as heroes by everyone.

It takes courage to grow up and be a fire horse, said the old steed to the rookie.

~September 25~
Silver

The stallion's real name was White Cloud, but his Hollywood screen name was much better known. He was called Silver in The Lone Ranger television series that ran from 1949 to 1954. Silver was thought to be one of the most popular horses of all the western shows on television. White Cloud was 12 years old, pure white and stood 17+ hands tall. He was owned by wrangler and stuntman Bill Ward, who was a stand-in as the stuntman for Clayton Moore, who played the Lone Ranger. During the series, Silver also had a stunt double by the name of Traveler, who stepped in for the more complicated parts. Bill Ward also owned Traveler, who played Silver for stunts requiring action scenes. Bill Ward would dress as the Lone Ranger, ride Traveler during all the chase scenes and do other stunts like leap off the horse at a full gallop. Over the next decade, a third horse would play "Silver" on the show. His real name was Hi-Yo Silver, and he also did many of his own stunts and made special appearances.

In 1957 White Cloud won the Patsy Award (Performing Animals Television Star of the Year) for excellence in television. White Cloud retired and lived out his life at the Ace Hudkins Stables in California. He passed away in 1959 at the age of 21 or 22. Hi-Yo Silver retired and lived at the Wayne Burson Ranch. He passed away in 1976 at the age of 29.

Traveler (the original stunt horse for Silver) became the USC College football mascot in 1961 and was at every home game for many years. The beautiful white horse would appear at all the USC home football games with a Trojan warrior riding him in the arena. He became the most famous and iconic symbol for USC and college football.

Of all animals kept for the recreation of mankind, the horse is alone capable of exciting a passion that shall be absolutely hopeless." ~Bret Harte

~September 26~
Search And Rescue

The amazing thing about horses is that they can travel in places that a motorcycle, vehicle, or off-terrain vehicle can't get into. The horse still dominates when it comes to going into deep forests or mountainous areas thick with brush, rocks, ravines, and downed trees. Even with all the modern technology in the world, the horse is the one to get the job done in emergency situations where no other option is available. I am so glad to see that even in the 21st century there are people that still understand the importance of the horse in search and rescue efforts.

For the first time since 1990, in the state of Connecticut, a fully trained team of 25 riders and their horses became part of the Horse Guard for search and rescue situations. Before 1990 each state had people who would volunteer, but now they have a deployable team that has trained extensively for this. Often a search party on foot doesn't get to the lost or injured person in time but on the back of a horse, they can cover more ground much faster, which will increase the chances of finding the person sooner. The horse has a heightened sense of smell, and incredible eyesight and hearing, which means they will often see or hear something before the human does. Sometimes all you need to do is follow where they are looking and the direction of their ears. Peter J. Vernesoni, who started the search and rescue team, said, "Horses are animals that are preyed upon, so they're wary of potential animals trying to prey on them."

The horses are tested through different types of terrain, including water, downed trees, over tarps, railroad tracks, and up steep inclines. The horses need to be calm and steady no matter the situation. Many states have search and rescue teams available at a moment's notice, and it's awesome that so many people see the value of the horse and that they can help save lives.

~September 27~
Off To School

For thousands of years, children all around the world have gone to school to learn reading, writing, and math, among other things. For many children throughout history, going to school meant you would have to travel miles to get to the schoolhouse. Before the motorized school bus, there was the horse to help them make it to school on time.

The earliest form of a school bus was called a "kid hack or school hack." The horse-drawn hack could carry a lot of children and get them to school and back home quite easily, which would free up their mother to cook dinner and take care of the other household chores. In the 1800's, schoolhouses were far apart and often in rural areas. Children that lived far from school would either walk to a location to hop on a horse-drawn school bus or, if possible, it would stop by their home and pick them up. Some school hacks were repurposed farm wagons, and some were specially built to transport children with bench-style seating around the perimeter. To avoid scaring the horses, the children would enter the hack through the back end.

Another way to get to school was the family horse. Since families were large, you would often see a bunch of siblings riding one of the farm draft horses to school. Often the horses would spend the day in a fenced-off part of the school ground, usually called the "horse paddock." Back in the days before motorized school buses, one of the most common excuses given by a child who was late for school would be, "I couldn't catch my horse!" For some children in very rural areas in the Midwest, especially in ranching communities, riding their horse to the bus stop and waiting for the school bus was part of the commute. At the end of the day, their horse would be waiting along with their mom or dad, ready to ride back home.

~September 28~
The Circus Horse

The Circus is in town! People young and old loved to hear those words shouted in their hometown when the circus pulled in to put on a show. The circus as we know it today has its roots in Great Britain during the 18th century. Philip Astley (1742-1814), the son of a cabinetmaker, decided he wanted to be a horseman since men on horseback were regarded as strong and brave at the time. At six feet tall, Astley looked impressive atop a horse and easily started earning a living as a horseman with his white horse. He would perform trick riding and swordsmanship that he had learned in the military and he would perform on his horse anywhere people would gather. Soon he became well-known for his acrobatics on his horse. He started adding even more balancing tricks, a second horse and a female equestrian named Patty, who became his wife. He added clowns, magicians, tumblers, and rope dancers, but performing on horseback was the highlight of the show. Astley is remembered for starting the first modern circus.

Circuses grew in Europe and America between the 18th and 19th centuries with more and more death-defying acts, skimpier outfits on female equestrians and acrobats, and larger-scale performances of plays or poems recreated as stories acted out by the performers and horses. People especially loved women who performed feats on horseback, viewing these women as strong yet feminine at the same time, and able to control the mighty horse and look very feminine while doing so.

Many circus companies opened and traveled the globe with many different attractions, but the beautiful white performing horses have always been a crowd favorite for both young and old. It would be safe to say that the horse was a great instrument in bringing the circus to life, and it had a huge impact on how people viewed these amazing equines.

~September 29~
Packhorse Librarians

The Nation had plunged into a depression, and Kentucky was one of the hardest hit states in the country. Thousands of families living in rural and mountainous areas like the Appalachia Mountains had very little food or contact with the outside world. On top of it, a huge percentage of these families had children or parents who couldn't read. The librarians of the day understood the importance of reading, and in 1935, the Packhorse Library Project was established to bring reading materials to families in these rural areas.

Librarians at the time were almost always women, and many were young mothers. These ladies would gather books and newspapers from the library and head out on long routes on the back of their horse to deliver reading materials to the families in the Appalachia Mountains. Librarians were often alone and traveled 50 to 80 miles a week along muddy trails, river beds, and rough terrain to reach the most remote residences and schools in the mountains. Sometimes the trails were so steep that the librarian had to get off and walk alongside her horse over the treacherous footing. And sometimes, there was no trail at all, and the librarian and her horse had to make their own path. These librarians took their job and mission seriously and traveled year-round no matter the weather. Besides carrying the librarian, the horse carried the saddle bags loaded with reading materials and anything else the librarian might need, including a gun and food.

During the height of its program, the Packhorse Library Project served over 100,000 Kentucky residents who would not otherwise have books or newspapers to read. In 1943 the Packhorse Library ended, but a few short years later, it was replaced by motorized bookmobiles. You can say that the horse was the original bookmobile!

"Courage is being scared to death but saddling up anyway."

~September 30~
The Vaquero Tradition

In the mid-1700's, the Vaqueros came to America and brought along with them their incredible horsemanship skills and traditions. They landed in California among the large cattle ranches and soon were teaching the ranchers of the area a new way to train the ranch horses. Vaquero in Spanish means, "herdsmen or one who tends cattle on horseback," and that is where we get the word "cowboy."

The vaquero horsemen believed in harmony between the horse and rider, and they wanted to do it right. These men did not rush to finish a horse while it was in training to be a ranch horse. Instead they prided themselves on going slow and teaching each horse according to their personality and ability, and the results were horses that loved their masters and their jobs. The goal was to have a horse that was soft and light in the bridle and would respond with the lightest tap from the reins.

The vaquero's believed in training the horse out in the open fields among the brush and various landscapes. It was a way of helping the horses gain their confidence and become used to any unusual movements from animals jumping out of the bushes or running across an open field. The things that seem to spook "city horses" would not even make a vaquero horse flinch.

The vaquero tradition is still being taught today to horses but has been modified slightly from the 1800's. Today's trainers use equipment on the horse that is much less severe, but the core foundation and principles are still the same.

Sheila Varian, who had kept the vaquero training method alive for many years, was quoted in a magazine saying, "To make one of these horses, you can't ride in an arena, and you also can't ride down a trail. God put lots of bushes, trees, ledges, and creeks on this earth for me to train my horse around."

~October 1~
Holiday Horse Shortage

The year was 1928, and it was a very busy November in Brooklyn, New York. The holiday rush kept the customers and business owners in a wild frenzy, with Christmas just around the corner. Postmaster Albert Firmin was expecting record-breaking mail volume with the upcoming holiday season less than a month away, and he needed to start putting plans in place to ensure everyone got their holiday mail and packages before Christmas day. He put notices in the newspaper as a reminder to the public to mail their Christmas gifts and cards early. He hired 3,000 additional clerks and 1500 extra mail carriers to handle the heavy volume that would come into the post office. Motorized vehicles were becoming more available, and he asked for 60 more mail trucks to add to the existing fleet, but he knew that wouldn't be enough. What he needed was horsepower!

Postmaster Firmin planned to hire 200 horse-drawn carriages and wagons. What he wanted was dependable people and horses, and if he could find them, he felt confident everything would run smoothly. The horse-drawn carriages and wagons would be used to deliver the regular mail in the downtown district where traffic was slower, and also to the residential areas. Although it was normal each holiday season for the Brooklyn Post Office to supplement its motorized fleet with horse-drawn vehicles, for some reason there was a shortage of horses in 1928. He could only find workhorses hitched up to wagons at laundry facilities. They were used for delivering clean laundry to hotels and other places. It appeared that laundries were the only businesses in Brooklyn that were still using horses. He hired as many horse-drawn vehicles as possible from the laundries and figured most people would be okay with their laundry being late, but they would be frantic if a Christmas card or package didn't arrive before December 25th. Horses to the rescue again!

~October 2~
The Omnibus Horse

The Omnibus originated in the 1820's as a horse-drawn vehicle that transported people along the main streets of Paris, France. By the end of the 19th century, there were well over 10,000 Omnibus horses used by the London General Omnibus Company to carry passengers. Eventually Omnibuses found their way to the larger cities in America.

The buses came in different sizes, but many of them were quite large and very long and could hold up to 28 passengers, which meant large draft-type horses were sought after and in high demand. These buses would move along the city streets at the speed of about 7-8 miles per hour, and was one of the most demanding jobs a horse could ever have. The horses traveled on average about 12 miles per day and due to all the stopping and starting, which was very hard on a horse's body, an Omnibus horse usually only lasted about five years. They also needed to be stabled, fed, watered, and cared for every day, and a horse's fate depended on the Omnibus Company's owner. Some of the operators took excellent care of their workhorses and had large teams of horses at the stable so that the horses could be rotated out during the day to rest and eat. Other operators worked the horses to the ground, and often horses would collapse in the streets from exhaustion. The horses worked in all types of weather and temperatures, and their days started very early and ended late in the evening.

Tramways eventually took over, and then the motor coach came, but the horse-drawn Omnibuses remained a common sight on Paris streets for many years. The very last horse-drawn Omnibus, the Impériale, made its final trip on January 11, 1913, accompanied by a crowd of people who came to say goodbye. The last two Omnibus Percherons were put out to pasture in the countryside, and the streets of Paris never looked quite the same again.

~October 3~
The Horse Phase

If you love horses and I mean genuinely love horses like an obsession, then you will probably never grow out of the phase of wanting to be around them. I know that is hard for some boyfriends and spouses to understand, but it's the cold hard truth. I am laughing as I write this because I remember a situation in my mid-twenties involving a guy I was dating for a very short time. I had met him while I was in my country-western dance phase, and we went on a couple of dates. Then one Saturday, I was going Team Penning and I told him I wouldn't be around. I remember exactly what he said to me just like it was yesterday. He looked at me and said, "When are you going to grow up and grow out of this horse phase, after all, it's just a phase."

Well almost forty years later, I'm still in the "horse phase" and God sent me the most wonderful man to share my horse passion with. I am glad I listened to the Lord and followed my dreams and waited for the perfect man for me. Horses are not a phase for people who are crazy about them, and it's not something you grow out of as you mature!

For the people still waiting for their perfect mate to go through life with, relationships are more than dinner and movies, nice clothes, and cars. It is about something so much deeper. It's about your passions and desires and working together to achieve them.

For me, it's about taking care of the horses daily on our farm alongside my husband. My phase turned into a passionate career, and I want to make sure I do my best with what the good Lord has entrusted to me.

In my mind, I will always be that little girl who pretended to be riding a big white horse with the kitchen broom. I also believe horses have brought many couples together throughout history!

~October 4~
The Unique Relationship

The relationship between the horse and human is unique on so many levels. We have asked the horse to give so much of themselves for thousands of years, and the bond is at times unbreakable. We love horses and we hope they will love us back, but sometimes we forget that they are a horse first, and they look at things much differently than we do. Even from the days of mounted warfare and workhorses to our modern-day existence where we have the privilege of enjoying the horse in a much more positive and casual manner, the relationship never changes. It is built entirely on trust between horse and human, and if we can understand that first and honor their God-given ways of existing and communicating, then we are one step closer to creating a bond that is rare but very real.

The one thing many people either don't understand or they forget in the heat of the moment is that horses watch us and sense what our mood is. For the horse, it's about the relationship and trying to please his human. But that means that we need to communicate in a way that they can understand, and be patient when they are clearly showing us they are confused.

When God created the horse, He knew exactly what he was doing. He gave us a helper to make our lives easier, and after thousands of years of hard labor, the horse has brought us into the 21st century. Just think about that for a moment. The horse has carried man and his belongings for over 5,000 years and we have only had a little over 100 years without the need for the horse as a beast of burden. It gives me chills when I really think about it. We are the luckiest and most blessed among generations because we get to have a relationship with the horse built on pure enjoyment and not survival. That is something truly to be thankful for.

~October 5~
The Farrier

The old saying, "No Hoof, No Horse!" couldn't be a more important statement, and the farrier who takes care of your horse's feet is equally paramount! After all, a good farrier is worth their weight in gold. The history of the farrier is, in many ways, like the history of the horseshoe. We know that there were farriers during the ancient Roman period, but exact origins are hard to pinpoint.

The need to keep a horse's feet trimmed or shod came with a learning curve for every culture that has come before us. The Roman Empire had farriers on staff to keep their cavalry horses shod and sound both at home and on military campaigns. The Roman writer, Vegetius, mentions in his writings, "the smiths of all sorts," when talking about the farrier. These men were considered to have a specialized trade necessary to the army in regards to keeping the horses fit for warfare. They were exempt from battle and routine military tasks like patrol or ditch digging. That shows us how vital the farrier was during that time.

One of the jobs of a military farrier was "the humane dispatch of wounded and sick horses," which meant the farrier had the responsibility of deciding which horses were ready for battle and which ones were not. Taking care of the horse's feet was connected closely to the task of making sure that the "whole horse" was in good fighting shape. Early on, the farrier also took on the role of the veterinarian and was considered by most men to be both.

It is suggested that William the Conqueror's farrier was given a coat-of-arms and the surname de Ferrers, from which our modern "farrier" comes. There have been other opinions that the word just comes from the Latin "ferrarius" meaning iron. Either way, the coat-of-arms the De Ferrers family received has six horseshoes on it and suggests that the craft of farriery was very highly respected among all trades.

~October 6~
Branded For Life

Branding cattle has been done for thousands of years. Painted pictures and carvings depicting cattle roundups and brandings have been discovered on the walls of Egyptian tombs, and they can be traced back to around 1900 BC. The first introduction to branding in the Western Hemisphere was done by the Spanish conquerors of the Aztecs in South America. The brands were placed on the hips and shoulders of their horses and cattle. In 1519, explorer Hernán Cortés settled in Mexico and began branding his livestock. The first brand was of the three Latin crosses representing the Father, Son, and Holy Ghost. Branding was done as a symbol of ownership and to deter horse and cattle thieves.

It became standard practice to brand horses on their left or right hip or shoulder using capital letters and numerals, often in combination with symbols. Although fire branding is still done on commercial ranches, gas and freeze branding (which uses dry ice or liquid nitrogen) are often used on horses and registered cattle herds. Captured Mustang horses available for adoption through the Bureau of Land Management must be freeze-branded. Tattooing, microchipping, ear notching, tagging, iris-recognition technology, and semi-permanent paint branding are also slowly being implemented.

Most breeds of horses racing in the United States are required to have a lip tattoo (a type of branding) for identification purposes. This needs to be done before their first race. This tattoo in placed inside the upper lip and is linked to the registration papers to identify the horse and owner. The lip tattoo originated in 1947, and was so effective that now most states require a tattoo on all racehorses. You can also find lip tattooing in Standardbreds, Appaloosas, Arabians, and Quarter Horses because these breeds are also used for racing.

~October 7~
The Horse's Prayer

Written in the 19th century, The Horseman's Prayer is a plea from a carriage horse to his master. The Author is unknown.

Feed me, water and care for me and when the day's work is done, provide me with a clean shelter, a clean dry bed and a stall wide enough for me to lie down in comfort. Be always gentle to me and talk to me; your voice often means more than the reins. Pat me sometimes that I may serve you more gladly and learn to love thee.
Do not jerk the reins, and do not whip me going up a hill. Never strike, beat or kick me when I do not understand what you mean, but give me a chance to understand you. Watch me and if I fail to do your bidding, see if something is wrong with my harness or my feet. Don't draw the straps too tight. Give me freedom to move my head. If you insist on me wearing blinkers to keep me from looking around, at least see to it that they do not press against my eyes.
Don't make my load too heavy and don't leave me tied up in the rain.
Have me well shod, examine my teeth when I do not eat; I may have an ulcerated tooth and that you know is painful enough.
Do not tie my head in an unnatural position, or take away my best defense against flies by cutting off my tail.
I cannot tell you I am thirsty, so please give me pure cold water frequently. Do all you can to protect me from the sun and throw a cover over me when I am standing out in the cold.
Don't force an ice cold bit into my mouth, but warm it first in some water or in your hands. I always try to do cheerfully the work you require of me and day and night and I stand hours waiting for you. And finally, my master, when my useful strength is gone, do not turn me out to starve or freeze, or sell me to a cruel owner to be slowly tortured and starved to death. But do thee, my master, take my life in the kindest way. And your God will reward you here and thereafter. May you not think me irreverent if I ask this in the name of Him who was born in a stable. Amen

~October 8~
Big Ben

Big Ben's contribution to the world of show jumping is unparalleled, but what makes this horse's story even more remarkable is that he conquered the show jumping world against all odds. Big Ben had a modest beginning like many heroes we read about. He was passed over as a show jumper because many trainers thought he was too tall and large at 17.3 hands. Big Ben was a seven-year-old Belgian Warmblood when Ian Miller saw the giant horse for the first time, and he knew instantly that this was the horse he had been waiting for.

Big Ben came home with Ian, and soon the two were training and competing, and quickly they had qualified for the 1984 Olympics in Los Angeles. That was the beginning of a legendary partnership between the two. Big Ben's career spanned nearly a decade, including being a Pan American double gold medalist, Du Maurier International Champion, plus competing in over 50 major Grand Prix shows. He won everything, and he had the unique ability to jump large fields outdoors with any kind of footing, and it didn't matter to him if it was raining, windy or hot. He would make the jumps without a care in the world.

During his years of competition, Big Ben also dealt with a lot of adversity. He had gone through two colic surgeries to come out even stronger. He had also survived a horrific trailering accident where the trailer tipped over, but Big Ben went on to dominate the Grand Prix only two months later. His ability to overcome obstacles on and off the jump course made everyone fall in love with him. Big Ben was officially retired in 1994 and was made an honorary member of the RCMP Musical Ride of Canada and was inducted into the Ontario Sports Legends Hall of Fame. In 1999, the Canada Post issued a postage stamp to commemorate Big Ben's impact on Canadian history and to honor his accomplishments.

~October 9~
The Shire

The role the Shire horse in man's pursuit of conquering countries, working the land for agriculture, or entering the new world of the Industrial Revolution is hard to describe in a few short sentences. This cold-blooded, heavy horse has been a part of world history since around 1066, when brought to England after the Norman Conquest. This horse was called the "The Great Horse," and in medieval times, it was highly important to increase the number of these gentle giants to carry knights in full armor. The more of these large horses a kingdom had ready for battle, the stronger the kingdom.

Britain and other countries depended so much on the Shire horse and their strength, that at one time, there were millions of these horses working every job imaginable. They worked in the fields, in towns and cities, on docks and landings, on canal towpaths, and for mills and railways. Shires were used during the first half of the 17th century when work began on draining the Fens, a naturally marshy area of landmass in England. A massive wide-footed horse was needed due to the extremely muddy and wet conditions in which the horses would be working in for long hours. The Shire horse provided the strength required for the heavy work. Their even temperament, gentle spirit, and the ease of training them kept them in high demand .

During World War I & II, the Shire became a warhorse pulling heavy artillery for miles daily in appalling conditions. The Shire horse nearly became extinct after World War II, and it was only due to the strong dedication of a few breeders that the number of Shires finally started to grow again. The Shire has humbly showed us what a great horse looks like under all circumstances.

~October 10~
Ghost Horses Of The Desert

The Namib Desert in southwest Africa is known as the land of ghosts. It is vast and inhospitable, and some have called it a wasteland where no one can survive. Along a strip of beach called the Skeleton Coast bears the remains of shipwrecks washed up on the shore from another time in history. Drive inland and you'll encounter one of Africa's most famous ghost towns and the "ghost horses" of Namib. The massive Namib Desert is one of the oldest deserts in history, dating back thousands of years. The hostile terrain has made Namib one of the least populated countries in the world. But amid this unforgiving land, there is evidence of a once thriving human settlement. Kolmanskop was once a booming diamond mining town, but miners soon found diamonds under less harsh conditions further south, causing the town to close down overnight.

The town of Kolmanskop is not the only ghost of Namib. An equally iconic symbol of the region is the population of around 150 wild horses which have adapted to the barren wasteland. These horses are able to go without water longer than domestic horses while surviving for generations on the edge of the desert. The horses are not originally from Southern Africa, and it is still a mystery how the horses came to be in Namib. The most likely theory is that the horses were military horses used by both the Germans and South Africans and were abandoned in the chaos of World War I. But the miracle is that they survived and even thrived, living in the harshest conditions on earth. It is believed that once the horses found water, they stuck close by and ate the local grasses and shrubs. They learned to adapt to sandstorms and protect themselves from the elements. For generations the horses have existed and remained largely out of sight from humans, and they have become known as the Ghost Horses of Namib.

~October 11~
To Pace Or Trot

Harness Racing, or Road Racing (as it was called up until a century ago), has fueled man's spirit to compete and be victorious. Men throughout history have always loved a good race or competition, and the horse has always been the centerpiece of those dreams. It started with chariot racing and has grown, been modified, and refined depending on the culture and civilization.

The origin of harness racing and the two different types of horses, Pacers, and Trotters, is unique. When people think of harness racing, they usually think of the tall and lean Standardbred. What they may not know is that these amazing horses can be bred to either pace or trot, and at times, a horse will come up through racing lines that can produce fast times in both gaits. The most unique part of this type of racing is that only certain horses have the "gait keeper" mutation gene, which produces the ability to pace. This gene was only discovered recently, but now they can trace this gene to certain horse breeds throughout history.

These harness racing horses are fast and often reach speeds of 25 to 35 miles per hour and, occasionally, even a little faster! It is said that the Pacer can move faster than the Trotter when both are in peak condition. Both Pacers and Trotters have earned their rightful place in helping shape the world of horses and long-standing traditions that we still enjoy to this day. Just watching one of these beautiful horses do what they were created to do is quite impressive.

"My life is parallel to a racehorse. They have blinders on to keep them from being distracted in the race and keep them focused on winning the race. That's kind of like my life. Focus on the goal, not the things coming at me from the side." ~Reggie Bush

~October 12~
A Second Chance

There are many opinions about prosthetics for horses, but what I wanted to share in this book is more about what horses have experienced at the hand of humans, and not so much my personal opinion. Until recently, when a horse had broken a leg or had a severe hoof injury, the only option was to humanely euthanize the animal. With the size and weight of a horse, they cannot walk on three legs like a dog can, and there were no other options until prosthetics were invented for the horse. Today, so much progress has been made in the field of medical technology for equines. Equine veterinarians, researchers, and inventors keep looking for ways to help horses when the only option is amputation. Prosthetics for horses is much different than prosthetics for humans—for the simple reason that the horse's anatomy is much different. For a horse to be eligible for a prosthetic, an extension must be attached by nails to the bone first to ensure the horse can support all its weight on the leg without affecting his stump. The healing process will last approximately one month, and during that time, the equine specialist will make sure the horse is doing well and there are no signs of infection. Then, if everything looks good, it is removed and placed directly on the stump, and then the prosthetic will be fixed there.

Horses speak volumes through their body language and will express how they are feeling. In some individual cases, the horse did not do well with a prosthetic and needed to be euthanized, but in other situations, the horse did remarkably well. The welfare of the horse must be the priority for all involved. If at any time the horse is showing signs that the prosthetic is not working, then alternative decisions need to be made for what is truly best for the horse, even if it means saying goodbye. For some horses, prosthetics have given them a second chance at life.

~October 13~
Funeral Horses

In London, it was common to see a team of solid black horses pulling a distinctive wagon or carriage called a hearse during a funeral. Its windows were large and the fittings on the hearse were often made of silver. When you would see these teams of black horses with their gleaming coats, you instantly knew that someone had died. These funeral horses were called the Black Brigade, and they were always Flemish stallions that came from Belgium. Each horse's training lasted about a year, and once trained they would work for about six years.

Job Masters was well-known at the time for owning many Black Brigade horses, and he rented the horses out to undertakers when needed, which was quite often. During times of severe sickness like cholera, where there were many deaths, these horses rolled out with their undertakers several times a day. To ensure these stallions' coats stayed glossy, their diets were restricted. These horses generally ate hay, oats, and even rye bread. Once a week on Saturday nights, a mash of linseed and bran was also fed to them. To guarantee that no babies of a different color would accidently be born, these stallions were kept away from all the mares.

In America, funeral horses often became a valued asset to a town or city. This meant that if a funeral horse died or a new funeral horse was purchased, the town's people read about it in the paper. It was a big deal. On top of it, the town looked up to any undertaker with an intelligent team of horses and they usually received more business. Although great emphasis was put on the training of funeral horses, there were still plenty of accidents. Teams would spook and take off carrying the casket, and on more than one occasion, the runaway funeral team would collide with another coach or wagon with horses. This never ended up well for the deceased in the casket, the family, or the undertaker.

~October 14~
The Requisition

Big, strong horses were needed more than ever during World War I. During that time, around three million horses were at work in Britain, pulling wagons for businesses, agriculture, and transportation. When the war broke out, it was quickly realized how important the horse was needed for the war effort, and with so many warhorses becoming injured or dying daily, England soon found itself short on horsepower. They quickly drafted a letter requisitioning horses from the public in a state of emergency. The army now had permission to take any horse that appeared to be healthy and strong enough for the war effort. The only exceptions would be the horses that were needed for specific jobs like farm work or other essential jobs. Within the first months of the war, 120,000 horses were taken from the civilian populations alone under the Impressment Act, but it would not stop there.

The requisition of horses did not sit well with much of the public because their horses were valuable to them and necessary for their small businesses and transport. In one such situation, a Remount Army Officer arrived at a paper mill to look at the horses. A young boy who worked at the mill was quickly instructed to take one of the prized stallions and hide the horse in one of the outbuildings. There were other similar stories of civilians hiding their horses throughout Britain. The public became angry at the protocol for taking horses because it became clear that the rules were not fair to all people. Some people had all their horses taken even though they used them for agriculture, while others had none requisitioned if they had connections or government contracts.

Soon the angry public went to the newspapers to speak their mind. The government quickly modified some of the protocols for taking horses from civilians during a time when horses were what kept Britain and its businesses alive and going every day.

~October 15~
Therapy Horses For Veterans

Horses have now taken on a new role for war veterans who suffer from PTSD, otherwise known as Post Traumatic Stress Disorder. Men and women, who have served their country in the harshest environments, often come back with some mental stress related to what they experienced. For many veterans, the therapy horse has become a way to help them heal mentally and physically. It was realized that horses had a way of calming humans just by their presence. The pressure of adjusting to civilian life is often too difficult for some veterans, and the quiet and simpler way of life with horses seems to be a huge key in helping many. The horses are very aware of a person's stress and personality, and a good therapy horse can stay calm while the human learns to relax. For many horse owners around the globe, they are now using their horses to help heal veterans in their country.

Recent studies have provided evidence that veterans have come out of depression or PTSD faster with horse therapy than other common therapies. One study enrolled 63 veterans with PTSD in weekly 90-minute sessions led by a mental health professional and an equine specialist, who helped them learn about horses and their behaviors. More than fifty percent of the participants showed a reduction in PTSD at the three-month follow-up. Dr. Fisher (who led up one of the studies) was quoted saying, "Through horse-human interaction, veterans can relearn how to recognize their feelings, regulate emotions, and better communicate as well as build trust, and come to trust themselves again—all valuable tools to help them succeed with family, work, and social relationships."

It's beautiful to witness the trust and bond that develops between the veterans and the horses used in therapy. The warhorse of the past now has a beautiful new role in helping veterans heal.

~October 16~
The First Equine Veterinarians

Before the horse was domesticated they were used for food. Once man realized that he could tame and ride these huge animals, the horse became a war machine above all else. Soon horses were being used for conquering enemy tribes and nations, plowing fields for agriculture, and pulling wagons and carriages. Even in the earliest civilizations, people realized that it was much more costly to replace the horse than to take good care of it. Men started learning how to heal injuries and nurse a sick horse back to health. There are Chinese writings of medical procedures for horses, dating back to 2500 BC. The Egyptians painted pictures in 3000 BC of men taking care of injured chariot horses. Indian art from around the same period shows images of men and women caring for sick horses.

Fast forward a few thousand years, and on December 16, 1776, General George Washington issued an order stating that a farrier be included on every roster for each new regiment. Washington recommended that the farrier be responsible for the medical care required by cavalry horses since they had medical knowledge of the horse's whole being. These appointed farriers were the first veterinarians in the U.S. Army.

During the Civil War, the army discovered the importance of veterinary care for the horses used in battle. Unfortunately, some of the officers didn't recognize the position of the "Veterinary Sergeant," and instead, due to complete stupidity and pride, gave each soldier a copy of the book titled, *Each Man Is His Own Horse Doctor*. The results were disastrous for the sick and injured horses, which led to the death of many horses. It was definitely a time of trial and error. Things began to change soon afterward for the betterment of the horse. Equine veterinarians have come a long way with their knowledge about horses, and today's horses have never been more cared for by the doctors who treat them.

~October 17~
The Bathing Machine

In 1753, the Bathing Machine was invented. It was a large wooden hut on wheels that was pulled into the ocean by a team of draft horses. It was probably one of the craziest inventions ever made, but necessity is the mother of invention, and it was during a time in history when men were not allowed to see women in their undergarments when swimming. Swimsuits had not been created yet.

During the Renaissance period, it was common to find many large horse-drawn wooden bathing machines on the beaches. Women would use these bathing machines on one end of a beach, while farther down the beach were more horse-drawn bathing machines for the men. In Britain, it was illegal for men and women to swim together during the 18th century. Modesty was of the utmost importance, even required, and this allowed the women to walk into the hut fully clothed and change into bathing clothes (undergarments) in private. The men would do the same thing in their bathing machines. Then the teams of horses would pull the huts out into deeper water and the gentlemen and ladies would each exit the back of their huts into the water. The teams of horses standing in chest-deep water would then be unhitched and the driver would ride them back to shore. When the men or women were ready to return to shore, the driver would take the team of draft horses back out, hitch them back up, and pull the large bathing machine back in.

Although it was hard work for the horses, the salt water often healed any cuts or lameness issues. At the height of the bathing machine's popularity, you would find hundreds of wooden huts on wheels with horses hitched, ready to cart men or women out into the water. Horse-drawn bathing machines remained in use for the next 150 years throughout Europe, the United States, and Mexico.

~October 18~
Uniting Over Horses

European horse shows are typically quiet and reserved events and have been for many decades. But in Israel, you will experience a different kind of horse show where people are cheering, clapping, and highly excited for the horses they are watching. What makes these horse shows even more unique is that Jewish, Israeli-Arab, and West Bank Palestinian breeders compete against each other and get along. They will spend all day together looking at each other's horses and sharing breeding information about the stallions and mares. It's as if the horses have brought people who are normally at odds with each other together with a shared passion.

One of the most established and well-known horse stables in Israel is owned by Chen Kedar. It is called Ariela Arabians, and when Kedar goes to horse shows with his beautiful horses, he says you will see people from every background and ethnicity sitting down and talking for hours about their horses and the pedigrees and sharing horse stories. Chen Kedar has also sold some of his best Arabians to countries like Bahrain and Qatar with whom Israel does not have diplomatic relations. Between the Palestinian territories and Israel there are around 8,000 registered Arabian horses that are part of the World Arabian Horse Organization.

Israel's Arabian Horse Society of breeders is truly a community that has come together because of the Arabian horses. Both the Palestinians and Jewish breeders fully understand and realize that what they have created with open dialogue concerning the horses is highly unusual, and it is to be respected and appreciated since the rest of their worlds are separate and often in opposition with each other.

It was said by one of the Taha breeders, "Horses set an example of living together that politicians failed to accomplish. You need a clean heart to breed these horses."

~October 19~
The Musical Ride

Canada is known for the Royal Canadian Mounted Police (RCMP), more famously known as the Mounties. They are recognized for riding their horses in bright red uniforms and brown Stetson hats. The RCMP came into being to keep order in Canada in the 1800's. The Mounties performance, known as the "Musical Ride," consists of 32 riders and horses and has its roots all the way back to the 1800's. Today a select group of officers and their horses perform intricate routines to music each year for crowds all across Canada. People love their Mounties, but the horses are the true heart of the Musical Ride.

The Musical Ride horses are bred for color (only solid black horses are allowed), temperament, and conformation. Height is also important, and only horses between 16 and 17+ hands will be accepted into the program. Thoroughbreds have always been the breed of choice, but in 1989 black Hanoverian mares and stallions were bought in to improve the breeding program. Warmbloods were chosen because of their great temperament and they tend to stay very calm. Warmbloods are also incredibly athletic and have great stamina to perform the intricate movements required in the Musical Ride performance.

At six years old, the horses begin training and take their first trips with the troop when they are ready. They will remain a part of the Musical Ride for as long as they are healthy and strong. Great care is taken to ensure the horses stay healthy and are mentally well-balanced. There are no grooms that travel with the Mounties. Instead, each officer cares for their own horse, including grooming, tacking up, feeding, watering, cleaning stalls, and warming and cooling out before and after each ride. A strong bond happens between the officers and their horses, and you can see it in their performances as they dance as a team to the music.

~October 20~
The Bond

The bond between a cavalry soldier and his horse during wartime was often so strong that a soldier might never get over it if his horse got seriously hurt during the fighting. Not only did the soldiers ride their horses into battle, but they cared for the horse's every need, including nursing them back to health when they became sick or injured. The soldiers would sleep with their horses out in the field and cry on their necks when they couldn't take it anymore. The horse wasn't just a war machine, he was a faithful companion for the young men who were far from home and who often felt very alone and scared.

During World War I, the horses endured horrific conditions while being forced to work every day for the war effort. Horses were dying of exhaustion and sickness. Even the smallest of injuries often turned into serious infections that would end up killing the horse because the soldiers did not have the proper medical supplies to help the poor animals. The Royal Army Veterinary Corps did the best they could to help as many horses as possible, but they could not keep up against the artillery and machine gun fire that was literally tearing horses apart daily. The harsh winters and lack of food also took a heavy toll on many horses who just gave up and died.

The relationship between the men and their horses grew even stronger as the war continued. The men did their very best to take care of the brave animals through the hellish nightmare they were all living. When the war was over, some soldiers went home broken from what they witnessed daily with the horses. Very few horses ever went home, but for the ones that did, it was a celebration. The close bond between the soldier and his horse will never be forgotten.

~October 21~
Winter In The City

In our modern world, we hardly notice the inconveniences of a winter storm, ice, or freezing temperatures when we drive our vehicles into the city. We have huge snowplows that clear the snow immediately, and the roads are salted when the streets become icy. If we are lucky, we can park our vehicle in a covered parking lot so that we never have to walk through the white stuff when going to the mall or our job. We have it pretty easy. But that's not how it was years ago when horses pulling carts, wagons, and carriages ruled the road. Wintertime was a hard and dangerous existence for the horses that worked every day in the big cities.

The snow made it much harder for the horse to pull anything through the city streets. It was not easy to remove the snow from the streets and it often turned to ice, making it even more difficult for the horses to gain their footing. Workhorses quickly became tired due to the extra weight of pulling their wagons through the thick snow, and if a horse slipped (which happened a lot), the horse would go down, and then it was even harder to get the tired animal up again. The horses worked no matter the weather, and often they would become wet from the rain/snow mix, and between the exhaustion and frigid temperatures, many horses got sick and often died. The carriages and wagons were made of wood, and shafts would often break from the weight and strain of going through the heavy snow. It was common in the wintertime to see a wagon or carriage with a broken shaft, stuck for hours while the horses stood there in the bad weather. The weakest animals would shiver, unable to contain their heat, and some horses died right where the wagon broke down. It was a very hard existence that took its toll on many horses who worked in the cities in the 19th and early 20th centuries. It was a blessing when advocates for the horses started lobbying for better laws to protect all equines, no matter their station in life.

~October 22~
Cloning

If you have been around a barn or show pen long enough, you will eventually hear someone say, "I sure would like to clone that horse." There are different opinions about cloning, but whether you agree or disagree with it, cloning is a part of our modern world and when it comes to horses, it is worth talking about.

What is cloning? If you look at a dictionary definition, the simple description would be, "A clone is an individual grown from a signal cell of another individual. The new animal is genetically identical to the parent cell donor." The University of Idaho did the first cloning of an equine in 2003. The cell taken from a 45-day-old mule fetus was used to produce a mule by the name of Idaho Gem. During that same year, two more mule clones were born a few months later. Then a group of Italian scientists announced they had cloned the first horse named Prometea, a Haflinger filly.

So why would anyone want to clone a horse? Some think cloning a horse of exceptional confirmation and traits, but is unable to breed, could help the industry. Others look at it as a way to ensure that particular breeds do not become extinct. Some groups have objected to cloning as a way to breed horses. The Jockey Club will not allow horses that have been cloned to race or be registered, and the American Quarter Horse Association has put in a similar rule against cloning.

For the equestrian sports that do not have breed restrictions, there might be a market for a cloned horse, but it is going to cost you a pretty penny. Cloning is not cheap. Maybe some things are better off left to God and nature and let the great horses that have passed away be immortalized in books, movies, museums, and artwork. Because, as we all know, most of the time the sequel is never as good as the original. Just something to ponder.

~October 23~
The Treadmill

The horse-powered treadmill is not a new invention. The treadmill was first used centuries ago. The Romans used treadmills, first powered by slaves or oxen, to grind their grain and other foods. Then in the early 1800's, the treadmill exploded with the use of real horsepower. Soon larger treadmills powered by horses became standard equipment, and they helped make life on the rural farms and city businesses much easier. In 1851, the Beavertail Lighthouse in Jamestown, Rhode Island, got a new fog whistle. It was the first to use a horse-powered treadmill to power the loud whistle.

The horses were trained to walk on the treadmill, and depending on the connection of the shaft and gear box, they could churn butter, grind grains, and pump water. The treadmills were usually inclined, and that helped the horse walk at a steady pace. As it moved, the horse would naturally walk forward. The larger horse-powered treadmills could even power an entire sawmill. The most challenging part of the treadmill was finding horses that were not scared of it and would walk up the incline to the end of it. I am sure there were plenty of accidents as man continued to find new ways to help keep the horse safe while walking on it.

Since the days of using horse-powered treadmills for farm work and businesses, the treadmill has changed a lot. Now with electricity, the treadmill is no longer a working piece of machinery that is powered by the horse. Instead the treadmill is now designed to help the horse. Today horse treadmills are built to give the animal exercise, evaluate medical conditions, and used for rehabilitation. There are still some groups of people that use horse-powered treadmills on their farms. But for the rest of us, the treadmill is now a piece of exercise equipment that sits in our homes with clothes hanging over it!

~October 24~
Combined Driving

The equestrian sport of Combined Driving is unique and will keep you on the edge of your seat! In this sport, the drivers and horses compete in three phases: 1st phase is dressage, 2nd phase is marathon or cross country, and the 3rd phase is obstacle or cone driving, all while pulling a carriage. Depending on the class, a driver can choose to have his vehicle pulled by 1, 2, or 4 horses or ponies.

The three-day event competition begins with a dressage test that gauges the horses' ability and athleticism, followed by a cross-country marathon requiring them to navigate various hazards until reaching the end. Then each team completes an obstacle test following a course marked with cones, and this is all done while pulling a special carriage built for quick turns and speed. It takes nerves of steel and horses that are strong, agile, and can put on the speed when asked to go through a difficult course.

Combined Driving is a newer sport in the United States, but in terms of history, it is not. The sport has roots centuries before in the maneuvers military teams would practice while traveling cross country or in crowded cities. The fast chariots of the Assyrians, Romans, and Greeks are the earliest accounts of Combined Driving. Controlling a team of horses at a fast speed with sharp accuracy proved to give an edge in battle. Centuries later, competition between friends and neighbors became common on Sunday afternoons when there wasn't much else to do. Historically all the racing and competition throughout the centuries has contributed to Combined Driving and helped make the sport what it is today.

In 1970, Prince Philip fell in love with driving horses after retiring from playing polo and developed the first international rules for Combined Driving. This fast and very elegant sport took off from there and has become popular in many countries.

~October 25~
The Golden Horse

The Akhal-Teke breed became known as the horse of many names due to the legends that have followed the glistening horse. They were most often called the Turkoman or Turk horse of the Middles Ages. Thousands of years ago, they were known as the Nisean horse and sought after by Persian royalty. The Russians called them the "argamak" meaning sacred horse. Today, the people of Turkmenistan regard them as a national treasure, and the horse is called the Akhal-Teke after the oasis (called the Akhal) in Turkmenistan. The Akhal-Teke breed is over 3,000 years old, and they were so desirable that they quickly became the catalyst for several battles in 104 BC and 102 BC that became known as the "Wars of the Heavenly Horses" between the Chinese Han Dynasty and the Persian Empire.

What makes this breed so unique is the horse's physical appearance. It is often called the "golden horse" due to the horse's glimmering sheen and it's as if the horse has gold dust sprinkled all over it. The Akhal-Teke horses lived closely with the Central Asian nomadic tribes, and it was common for the horses to live in the tents with their masters. The horses often lived on little food, but the food they ate was very high in protein. Due to the region's lack of forage and the migratory lifestyle of the people, the herds were kept small. These horses were known for their incredible speed, stamina, and courage, making them essential for warfare and travel. A great number of these horses died during WWI and WWII, and Bolshevism brought an end to private ownership, so the horses were placed in state-owned breeding farms. Rather than surrender their beloved horses, many tribesmen fled with them to Persia and Afghanistan. The Turkmenistan breeders worked hard to bring back the Akhal-Teke when it was close to extinction. The Akhal-Teke is truly one of God's most beautiful equine creations.

~October 26~
Train Race

It was a new idea to have a locomotive steam engine carry passengers or freight to a destination. The B&O railroad intended to change the course of history by hauling people and goods of all kinds with its iron-horses. The horse-drawn wagon rails had been in very high use in most cities, and many people didn't see the need to improve on something that didn't need improving when it came to transportation. Engineer Peter Cooper knew he could better people's lives if they would give him a chance with his little locomotive, which he called the Tom Thumb. He thought the best way to show people what this locomotive could do, was to have a race between his iron horse and a real horse.

The B&O railroad company arranged a demonstration of the Tom Thumb on the 13 miles of track it had completed in 1830. The locomotive had covered the distance from Baltimore to Ellicott Mills in an hour, and had reached a top speed of 18 miles per hour! On the return trip, the little locomotive was met by a very familiar open-air passenger car that was hitched to the strongest and fastest draft horse. The horse and car were on the adjacent track, and the race began. The horse-drawn car pulled ahead as the tiny engine struggled to build up steam. Then it got going and soon it was chasing the horse, and sure enough, the Tom Thumb pulled ahead. Then the most unfortunate thing happened. A drive band slipped in the locomotive, and the engine slowed to a crawl. The horse-drawn car quickly pulled ahead and by the time the engineer repaired the damage and gained speed, it was too late. The horse was too far ahead and won the race.

It is true that the first race between a horse-drawn car and a locomotive came out with the horse as the winner, but it didn't stop progress from taking place, and soon the horse-drawn rails were replaced with locomotive rails.

~October 27~
Hollywood Horses

The horses of Hollywood have carried actors on cattle drives and through the Arabian Desert, gunfights at the OK Corral, and on racetracks. They have pulled chariots and carriages for movies and television shows, and that is only a fraction of their acting skills! Horses have been in more movies than can be counted, and are considered a major part of the film industry. Let's face it, without the horse, many movies would just not be the same and, in fact, downright boring. Some of the most well-known actors fell in love with their equine co-stars and made sure after their roles were over, that their acting partner was well-taken care of for life.

Lorne Greene played Ben Cartwright on the western television show Bonanza, from 1959-1973. It was said that he didn't much care for horseback riding or even horses, but when Bonanza was canceled in 1973, Lorne Greene purchased Buck (his longtime equine co-star on the show) because he was worried that the horse would end up in a bad situation or abused. Greene then donated Buck to a therapeutic riding center where Buck taught children with disabilities how to ride until his death in 1992 at age of 45!

It was said that James Stewart loved animals, and he especially loved a horse named Pie. Pie had been his equine co-star in 17 films until Pie's retirement at the age of 29. After Stewart finished shooting the movie Bandolero, which was the horse's last movie, Stewart tried desperately to buy his equine co-star from the owner, but she flat out refused him every time he asked. Stewart had an incredible bond with Pie, and when the horse died, he paid all the expenses to give the horse a private burial and to ensure the horse's dignity.

"It was almost a human thing between us. I think we liked each other...I really talked to this horse and I know he understood that I loved him. I loved the horse." ~James Stewart

~October 28~
Sefton

It was a special assignment for the horses of the Household Cavalry Regiment that served the Queen of England. Sefton was a British Army horse (Thoroughbred/Irish Draught-Cross) who had served for many years. On July 20, 1982, during the Changing of the Guard, the IRA exploded a car bomb in Hyde Park that took the lives of four men and seven horses. Sefton was one of eight horses still alive but severely injured by the blast. His injuries included a severed jugular vein, a wounded left eye, and 34 wounds covering his entire body. Sefton was the first horse to be brought back to barracks, where he underwent an emergency operation lasting over 90 minutes to save his life, and then an additional 8 hours of surgery (a record in veterinary terms in 1982). Each of the injuries he'd sustained had the potential to be life-threatening, and he was given a 50/50 chance of survival. Over the following months Sefton made remarkable progress, and his attending equine assistant was quoted as saying, "He took everything in his stride." Sefton received enormous amounts of cards, mints, and large monetary donations while he was in the hospital, and the gifts were enough to pay for a brand new surgical wing at the Royal Veterinary College, which was named the Sefton Surgical Wing.

After Sefton recovered from his injuries, he returned to active service. Sefton became one of the first horses inducted into the British Horse Society's Equestrian Hall of Fame, and an annual award was named after him. He was also awarded "Horse of the Year." On August 29, 1984, Sefton retired from the Household Cavalry and moved to the Home of Rest For Horses, where retired cavalry horses who serve the Royals live out their days. Sefton lived there until he was 30 years old, and had to be put down during the summer of 1993. Sefton will always be remembered as a courageous horse who served his country well.

~October 29~
Sea Biscuit

All though he descended from the proud line of Man o' War from his famous sire Hard Tack, he seemed to be missing the genes that great racehorses were made of. He was small for a Thoroughbred at only 15.2 hands with a thick neck and short stubby legs, and many thought he wasn't much to look at. In fact, his first trainer felt the horse was incredibly lazy and told his rider to whip him continuously, hoping the horse would learn to run fast. The horse never did. Instead he became angry and soon earned the reputation of being a very difficult horse to handle. By the time Charles Howard saw the horse, he was beat up, and his eyes had a hollow look about them. Howard's trainer saw something different in the little horse. His name was Sea Biscuit.

They brought Sea Biscuit home and started feeding him good hay and grain and let him be a horse again for as much time as he needed. His trainer knew that a companion would be good for Sea Biscuit, so they brought in an older horse called, Pumpkin, who would end up being Sea Biscuit's lifelong companion. The two became inseparable, and wherever Sea Biscuit was, so was Pumpkin.

Sea Biscuit's rehabilitation began working, and in 1936 he started racing again. This little horse was beating huge Thoroughbreds on racetracks all over the country, and he soon became America's sweetheart. His biggest race was a match race against the Triple Crown Winner, War Admiral, who was nearly 18 hands tall. People came from all walks of life to watch the race, during a time when our country was still in a depression. Sea Biscuit was considered the underdog against the huge War Admiral, and even though many people were rooting for Sea Biscuit, they placed their money on War Admiral. Sea Biscuit won by four lengths in the race of the century! He will always be remembered as the little horse that didn't know he was little.

~October 30~
The Horse Logo

Centuries ago, knights would put drawings or paintings of rearing horses on their coat-of-arms because it was believed to bring them success and glory on the battlefield and in tournaments. Fast forward to the early 20th century, and the fighter pilots wanted a horse painted on their airplanes. The familiar bucking horse and cowboy image was first put on fighter planes during World War I. There were at least three real-life horses that became the inspiration behind the airplane logos and artwork of those early warplanes.

George Ostrom created an emblem for the regiments when he was stationed in France in 1918. Ostrom loved his horse Redwing and entered a contest that his commanding officers were putting on for the best emblem to represent individual regiments. Ostrom painted a picture on a drumhead of Redwing bucking with a cowboy on his back. His design won the contest and became a famous logo that was painted on many of the fighter planes. It also became the original logo for the state of Wyoming.

Francesco Baracca was a courageous fighter pilot and a true aviation war hero of the First World War. He had a black rearing horse on the fuselage of his fighter plane. Later in 1923, Paulina Baracca, the Fighter Ace's mother, met Enzo Ferrari—the Ferrari car maker. She asked him to put the black rearing horse that was on her son's fighter plane on his cars, and history was made! The original horse logo on the Ferrari cars has never changed and is one of the most recognizable horse logos in history on one of the most expensive cars in history!

There have been warplanes called Crazy Horse, Wild Ass, and Pegasus, to name a few. Then the P-51 Mustang was designed and built and became known as the fastest fighter plane in World War II and was named after the Mustang horse. It doesn't get any better than that!

~October 31~
Retirement

Trooper and Detective John Reilly were a mounted police team for an entire decade in New York's Central Park. Detective Reilly turned 63 years old and it was the mandatory retirement age for the police in New York. Trooper had worked for the force for 11 years and it was now time for his retirement also. Together they would take their last ride on the force.

Sunday through Thursday for ten years, detective Reilly would get to the stable early in the morning and check in on Trooper, and then the day would begin. He would groom Trooper, while checking him all over to make sure he didn't have any new cuts or injuries, and to ensure he was feeling good and ready to take on the day. He would tack him up and away they would go to Central Park. The pair patrolled Central Park year-round no matter the weather, and they became a constant in a changing world. The presence of Reilly and Trooper was a crime deterrent, and it made the park visitors feel safer. The daily sound of the clip-clop of Trooper's shoes became a familiar and somewhat soothing sound for many people who came to the park often. Over the years, Trooper had become kind of a Central Park celebrity as many people loved to take pictures with him and pet him. Reilly said that Trooper was an exceptionally smart horse and was always very alert to what was going on around him. He was also a very calm horse who didn't overreact to situations. Trooper listened to Reilly and trusted him. Congratulations to both Detective Reilly and Trooper! Enjoy your retirement .

Through all four seasons and the best and worst the weather could bring, they have done their job faithfully so you could feel safe. The sound of their clip-clop each day brings a comfort to all, and when it's finally time for retirement, it is well-deserved. Thank you to the police horse, good and faithful servant.
~Author Unknown

~November 1~
Horses In Mythology

Horses were so revered in past civilizations that many of the stories passed down grew into larger-than-life legends and are still very well known today. The horse's impact on humans since the beginning of time cannot be underestimated, and in some ways, it makes them even more magical. We love everything about the horse, even the mythology that has been passed down for many centuries. Here are some Mythical horses you might be familiar with.

Pegasus is the mythical winged horse of Greek mythology. Pegasus carried heroes on to great adventures and earned a place in the stars as a constellation. It was believed that Pegasus could create water streams wherever he struck his hoof. At least two famous springs in Greece, both named Hippocrene "Horse Spring" were widely believed to have been created by Pegasus' hoof.

Llamrei was a mare owned by King Arthur. According to the Welsh tale, Culhwch and Olwen, in Wales, there is a hoof-print etched deep into the rock "Carn March Arthur" or the Stone of Arthur's Horse. The hoof print is said to have been made by King Arthur's mare when she was pulling a monster from the lake.

Skinfaxi, meaning shining mane, is the horse that pulls Dagr's chariot every day to light up the sky and the earth below, while Hrímfaxi, meaning frosty mane, pulls Nótt's chariot every night. In Norse mythology, these magnificent horses were what brought daylight and nighttime to earth. The Norse god, Odin, was also said to ride an eight-legged Icelandic horse called Sleipnir, who was the king of all horses.

Balios and Xanthos were a team of immortal chariot horses which Peleus received as a wedding gift from Poseidon at his marriage to the goddess Thetis. The horses pulled the chariot of the couple's son Akhilleus (Achilles) during the Trojan War.

~November 2~
Wells Fargo Stagecoach

Gold was discovered in California in 1848, leading to a massive migration of people to the West. Businessmen like Henry Wells and William Fargo saw a once-in-a-lifetime opportunity, but it wasn't with a pick or a pan. Their riches would come from a stagecoach and a shotgun. The Wells Fargo Company was born in 1852, which would heavily impact the history and development of the Old West. The company's primary business was to provide delivery and banking services specifically for new settlements in the West, and they would use their stagecoaches to deliver or move gold and cash. This is where the shotguns came in.

During the California Gold Rush, Wells Fargo stagecoaches and horses were gold-haulers. The stagecoaches spread out to the various mining camps and collected large quantities of gold dust which was hauled quickly back into the cities. The horses were called "The pride of Wells Fargo service," and it was the horses that made their stagecoach business very successful.

Wells Fargo believed in the importance of taking good care of its horses even in the 1860's. This was during a time when stagecoach horses were often underweight and overworked. Wells Fargo made sure the horses were healthy and well-fed, and formalized new policies to ensure that, as the company grew, the Wells Fargo horses in thousands of towns across America would be guaranteed the same excellent care. Drivers needed to check the horses for signs of injury and replace worn-out equipment. Horses were given plenty of water to drink in hot weather and also sponge baths. During the wintertime each horse was blanketed to keep them warm. The stable foreman ordered plenty of hay and oats, but they also bought molasses, carrots, and alfalfa to add nutritional value and treats. Wells Fargo gained an excellent reputation as a humane company that cared for its horses like they were precious metal.

~November 3~
Baśka

Since the 16th century, horses have worked in the Wieliczka salt mines in Poland. The horses worked hard pulling heavy trolleys filled with salt and powering treadmills to send the salt up to the opening of the mine. There were over 100 horses still working the Wieliczka mine just in the last century. To get the horses down deep below the earth's surface, the horses were put into special harnesses that held their legs tight against their body so they couldn't hurt themselves while going down. Once the horses were lowered down into the mine, they spent the rest of their lives there, except for special situations where they were brought to the surface or were retired. Some of the horses could not adapt to the mine environment and went crazy. On average the horses worked about 10 years in the mine, and a few worked over 20 years without ever seeing the light of day until they were retired. The horse's work was very hard, but the miners appreciated them, and it is said that they were well taken care of. The mining authorities required good working conditions and rest for the horses. There was a great emphasis on keeping the horses safe in the mines, and horse-friendly routes called "horse roads" were built to help them move through the tunnels easier.

In the 20th century, the development of mine mechanization gradually limited the use of horses underground. In the 1970's only two horses remained. The last mare, Baśka, left the Wieliczka salt mine on March 14, 2002. Baśka worked in the Wieliczka mine for 13 years. When she went to the surface, she was 16 years old. They brought her up at nighttime so that her eyes could slowly adjust. The miners said goodbye to her "like a real miner" with the traditional miner's greeting, "God Bless." Baśka enjoyed retirement and passed away on December 20, 2015, thus ending the history of horses in the Wieliczka salt mines.

~November 4~
Shipping Warhorses

During World War I (1914-18), horses were needed for the war effort. The transportation and care of the horses was of great importance, and it led to new problems when it came to shipping a massive number of horses and mules by ships. Prior to the war, a census of British horses had been taken, identifying how many were available and what type of work they were suitable for. In the first few months of the war, the Army requisitioned around 120,000 horses from the civilian population. By the middle of the war, more horses and mules were being sought overseas. Soon they were buying horses from around the world, especially from America and Canada. More than 600,000 horses and mules were shipped across the Atlantic Ocean.

Traveling by sea was extremely dangerous for the horses and mules. Not only was it hard on the animals, but it was a completely unnatural way for them to live. Once on board the ships, the horses and mules were walked down below deck and led into tiny stalls in very cramped spaces. These areas were dark with poor ventilation which created respiratory problems for many of the animals. The horses and mules were given regular health checks, but despite the best efforts, many suffered from "shipping fever," a type of pneumonia. Thousands of horses and mules died aboard the ships mainly from disease, sickness, or injury caused by rolling vessels. In 1917, more than 94,000 horses were sent from North America to Europe, and 3,300 were lost at sea. Around 2,700 of these horses died when submarines and other warships sank their vessels. In 1915, the horse transport SS Armenian was torpedoed by a U-boat off the Cornish coast. Although the surviving crew was allowed to abandon the ship, the vessel housed 1400 horses and mules that perished with the ship. Today these brave horses and mules are finally being recognized for their sacrifices made during the war.

~November 5~
The Hairless Horse

One of the most beautiful things about the horse is its coat, mane, and long flowing tail. But what if your newborn foal is completely hairless? Sounds crazy, but it happens. Hairless horses do exist, but it's rare, and it is due to a genetic mutation. The Akhal-Teke horses have birthed more hairless horses than any other breed, but there is no actual hairless horse breed. The heartbreaking part of having a foal that is hairless is that they rarely live long, and they often have a long list of health problems. Scientists have coined the term "Naked Foal Syndrome," or NFS.

The first known hairless horse was discovered by a merchant named Lashmar in the 1860's, who was traveling in South Africa when he spotted a horse with absolutely no hair on his body. He described the skin of the horse as feeling like "India-rubber with no hair follicles."

Blue Bell was another famous hairless draft-type horse in history who was nicknamed the "India Rubber-Skinned Horse." Her owner saw a money-making opportunity and advertised Blue Bell as "The $25,000 Hairless Wonder," and people would travel from all over to see the hairless mare.

Even in the 21st century, there have been documented accounts of foals that were born hairless. While a foal that is born hairless is often considered bad news, there have been some hairless horses that have beaten the odds. A Percheron by the name of Harry was born completely hairless, and lived well into adulthood without any major health problems. It was discovered that Harry started losing his hair while in the womb. Handfuls of hair were found in the amniotic sac when he was born. Harry had to deal with sunburn, windburn, and insect bites, but for the most part, he lived a very quiet and normal life as a companion horse. Harry was the exception to the rule for the hairless horse.

~November 6~
The Rescue Of 5000

During World War I, the number of horses requisitioned for the war effort was staggering. Overnight the lush green landscape of England was void of horses. The city streets were eerily quiet with only a few horses left behind that were needed for hauling goods for business and agriculture. Not only was it a horrific time for the horses, but also for the British people. They deeply loved their horses and were dealing with the great loss, wondering if their horses would ever come home. Near the war's end, it became evident that the horses were never returning, and most died from horrible conditions on the frontlines. The British people had sadly begun to realize that they would never see their beloved horses again. What made the situation so much worse was that tens of thousands of these horses were instead sold to Egypt after the war. These once proud warhorses were now forced to endure many more years of extremely hard labor in a foreign land, with extreme heat and a language they did not understand.

One woman alone set out to rescue 5000 of these horses that had been sent to Egypt. Her name was Dorothy Brooke. Dorothy and her husband had traveled to Egypt in 1930, and that is where she discovered thousands of the former warhorses still alive, but enduring horrific conditions. Many were emaciated and weak from the lack of food, and their scars showed the hard work they performed daily in Egypt. These tired old horses were now just hollow shells of what were once brave and courageous steeds, willing to do anything for their riders in battle. Brooke set out over the next three years to campaign and raise enough money to buy 5000 of these horses and get the proper care they desperately needed. She not only bought 5000 horses, but in 1934 she opened the Old War Horse Memorial Hospital in Cairo, which is still a working equine hospital today.

~November 7~
What Bravery Looks Like

The day finally came when a beautiful, perfect foal was born. His owner, Jeanette, was so delighted for this was her future dressage horse. She would call him Valiant, and little did she know that a few years later his name would prove even more fitting for him—for he would demonstrate what bravery looks like.

Valiant proved to be a strong, energetic young horse and often gave his owner the ride of her life, sometimes leaving her on the ground. She waited patiently for the day when he would settle down. Then one day years later, Valiant stepped on a horseshoe nail. The puncture was deep, and her vet came out quickly. Jeanette was given penicillin to administer for a few days, thinking it would clear up any possible infection. The next day Jeanette came to check on Valiant, and as he lowered his head, she noticed that his eyes were cloudy. She called her vet again, but this time the diagnosis was heartbreaking. Valiant had contracted uveitis or "moon blindness," an inflammation of the eyes that can lead to partial or complete blindness. Valiant was sick for many weeks and his eyes were in pain. The healing process was slow and Valiant pulled through, but not without the total loss of his eyesight. Jeanette needed to make a decision. What was she going to do with the horse she loved so much, but was completely blind? She had two choices. Either put him down or give him the best life possible. She chose the latter, and after giving Valiant as much time as he needed to adjust to his blindness, she decided to try riding him again. It was a very slow process built on trust, but soon the two became inseparable and started competing. Valiant rode as if he wasn't blind, and he listened intuitively to Jeanette's voice. Valiant lived for more than 20 years with blindness, but it never stopped the spunky horse or his owner, and they became an inspiration to so many and proved anything is possible with time, patience and love.

~November 8~
The Scythian's Horse

The Scythian people were accomplished horsemen by the 7th century BC. Their kingdom included southern Siberia from the Black Sea to the edge of northern China. The horse was an essential part of their life, and they had become excellent at breeding large herds of horses for work and riding. Before the horse's domestication, they were mainly kept for the mare's milk and hides. Once these fierce people could ride this animal, they were able to travel much farther and quickly they became a powerful force against any opposing tribes.

The Scythians bred fast, athletic horses, and the horse became a partner and companion to man, not just a beast of burden or food. These nomadic people believed that the horse was an extension of themselves, and because they believed in an afterlife, they would be buried with the horses they owned, and the horse would take them into the next world.

During recent excavations, there have been found, as many as 200 horses buried with human remains, and the horses were tied together with rope. It is said through writings that Scythian tribes sacrificed horses as a way of paying respect to each other. For them, it was one of the highest honors a person could have bestowed upon them. The more important a person was in the tribe, the greater number of horses that were sacrificed. Today, they have found horses preserved within the frozen ground and dressed in their ceremonial regalia. The magnificent costumes that were put on the horses, along with elaborate horse tack, were believed by these ancient people to transform the horse into a powerful steed that was ready to carry the dead into the next world. For the Scythian people, the horse was undeniably valued and revered in many ways. The Scythian civilization stayed powerful for over 500 years, and it is contributed to the horses that were a major part of their culture.

~November 9~
"The Galloping Horse"

Eadweard Muybridge was a photographer who took a series of photographs of an exercise rider on a galloping Thoroughbred horse, as a photographic experiment on June 15, 1878. The horse's name was Sallie Gardner. Leland Stanford owned and raced Standardbreds and Thoroughbreds and became interested in photography, so he hired Muybridge to take pictures of his horses.

Much of the talk or debate from racehorse owners at the time was about one question. When a horse is galloping, are all four of the horse's feet off the ground at the same time? It was hard to tell when a horse was at full speed, and there wasn't enough substantial proof just from the human eye. Stanford wanted to study the horse's gait to see if all four of the horse's feet were off the ground at any time. His goal was to improve his racing horses' speed and endurance, and photography seemed to be a way to visualize what needed to be done.

Muybridge arranged 24 cameras along the track in a line parallel to the horse's path. Each camera was set 27 inches apart. To activate the shutters, the horse would trip the wires as she ran past, causing the camera to activate, and the photographs would be taken in increments of approximately one twenty-fifth of a second. The jockey kept the horse at a steady pace for one mile. When the individual photos were developed and run in sequence, they clearly showed the movements of a galloping horse, and at one point in the horse's gait, all four hooves were off the ground simultaneously.

The photographs were first projected onto a screen in 1880 when Eadweard Muybridge gave a presentation at an art institute in California. This was considered the first exhibition of a motion picture ever made.

So, if you enjoy watching a good movie, then you can thank a horse, a Thoroughbred mare, of course!

~November 10~
The Outrider

Racetrack outriders and their horses have an enormous job. They are there to help keep the jockey or exercise riders safe during workouts and at the actual races. On race day, the racehorses must prove to the veterinarian they are sound, fit, and ready in all ways to be entered into the races. At this time, the outrider horses are ready to go with their riders in case a horse gets loose, or something else happens. There are normally around a dozen races scheduled daily, depending on the track. Each race runs in just under two minutes, but the outrider's day starts long before the actual races begin.

The outrider and their horse parade-marshal each racehorse, meaning they lead the horses running in each race past the grandstand for the people to view. Once the racehorses are on the track, many of them become very uptight and often need a calm horse to stand close to them before they load into the gate. The outrider horse will be used to pony the racehorse if the jockey needs assistance getting his horse to the gate or after the race is over. Just having the outrider horse there can calm the nerves of the racehorse for those few moments.

The outrider horse needs to be calm and have nerves of steel with so much going on with the racehorses. A good outrider horse needs a lot of speed for when you have to go after a runaway horse that has lost his rider. Running at full speed after a runaway racehorse or harness horse can be dangerous, especially when you need to get close enough to the horse to grab the reins. It takes a steady horse that can handle that kind of pressure and excitement all at the same time. The outrider horse should be well-suited for the job and once he starts to really learn what his job is, it will become second nature to him. The outrider horse is an essential part of the racing industry and has helped make the sport much safer.

~November 11~
Hot/Cold/Warm

The origin of hot, cold, and warm-blooded horses is interesting, and when you to look at the bigger picture of how history has played into the different breeds and types of horses, it all begins to make sense.

Most hot-blooded horses evolved in hot-desert climates such as the Middle East and North Africa. These horses had thinner skin, and light coats and did very well in the hot temperatures. The Arabian would be the best example of a hot-blooded horse. It wasn't until the 16th century that the Arabian reached the European continent. Soon they were crossed with the horses in Europe, and the Thoroughbred breed was born. Hot-blooded horses often have a more intense personality but are very willing to please their owners. It was discovered that hot-blooded horses have a faster metabolism, making them harder keepers than cold-blooded equines. Hot-blooded horses also have higher red and white blood cells, hemoglobin, and packed cell volume compared to cold-blooded horses. So if you are having difficulty keeping weight on your Thoroughbred, it could be because of his hot-blooded lineage.

Cold-blooded horses that were bred in the coldest areas developed heavy coats to withstand the harsh climates. They are usually larger horses with some bulk to their body and have gentle and willing personalities. Cold-blooded horses were used early on for farming and warfare, and through constant breeding over the centuries, the horses grew even larger than their equine ancestors.

Warm-blooded horses are often said to be the best of both worlds. They are strong and athletic but calm and easy to train. When the cavalry returned to Europe from the Middle East and Africa, they brought along the Arabian horses that were captured in the battles. This time the Arabian was being crossed with horses to create the warmblood breeds we are familiar with today.

~November 12~
The Beer Wagon

The huge gentle horses had already been fed their morning hay, and now they were being brushed and harnessed to start the day's work. It was only 5 am, but the brewer's horses worked six days a week and rested on Sundays. Depending on their beer routes, these horses would work 12-16 hours a day. It was a very hard life for these heavy equines back when they were the only mode of transportation for delivering beer.

The Shire horse was the most preferred choice because of their size and strength. They needed a large horse, and the Shire weighed close to two-thousand pounds and stood 17+ hands high. The horses needed to be able to pull the heavy beer wagon that weighed about two tons empty, but when loaded with 25 barrels, could weigh between five to eight tons. They also needed a quiet horse with a calm disposition that was willing to stand for long periods hitched to the wagon. The Shire was ideally suited for the job.

Because the beer wagons were so heavy when loaded, the drivers and owners of the horses had to pay close attention to the horse's feet. The horses were pulling heavy loads along all types of roads, including cobblestone which was uneven and hard on their hooves and legs. Custom horseshoes were designed for these large horses to keep their feet strong and prevent lameness, but unfortunately, not all owners cared enough about their horses to ensure their feet were in good condition. The brewer's horses usually worked in teams, either side by side or in tandem, and much depended on where they were going to be making deliveries. The streets were crowded in the larger cities, and being able to turn the wagon around in very tight areas was important.

Today all over the world, draft horses still drive brewer wagons but this time it's just for show. It's a wonderful way to pay tribute to the great brewer horses that came before them.

~November 13~
Horse Fighting

Mindanao is the second largest island in the Philippines, where horses are used for a sport not found in any other part of the world. It is the sport of horse fighting between stallions. The Mindanao Lumads "indigenous people" have been pinning stallions up against each other in this ethnic sport for the last five hundred years and still practice it today.

Horse fighting is one of the events at the Kadayawan Festival held in the Philippines each year. The people gather and sit out on the edges of the field where the fight will take place. A mare that is in heat is brought out to the field and tied up between two bamboo poles so she cannot escape. Next, the two stallions are brought near the mare. Once the stallions take notice of the mare, their natural instincts take over and quickly become aggressive towards each other. The fighting usually begins with loud squeals, nostrils flared, and the stomping of hooves or striking out at each other. But soon, the stallions become more aggressive as they bite each other's necks and use their hind legs to kick. The winning stallion is the one that lasts the longest and doesn't flee.

Without the mare present to stimulate the stallions, they probably would not fight with each other. As the stallions fight they tend to stay close to the mare, which has proven at times to be very dangerous for the mare that is tied up and cannot get away. The fights between stallions can be quick or last well over thirty minutes. The sport basically emulates what horses would do in the wild, but under a controlled environment for the purpose of entertainment. During these fights, bets are made, and money is exchanged. An effort has been made to stop this sport from continuing in the Philippines. In 1998 The Animal Welfare Act outlawed all horse fighting throughout the Philippines, but on tribal lands, the sport continues.

~November 14~
Today's Logging Horse

We've come full circle regarding logging and using good old-fashioned horsepower. The days of massive logging done by teams of draft horses in the wintertime is now a part of history, but hopefully will never be forgotten.

Today, we see a new generation of loggers who are getting back to a simpler way of life and using horses for logging, not only for the pure love of it but to do their part in preserving the earth and environment. For some of these modern-day loggers, it feels refreshing to work with your hands and do things the way they were done a century ago. For others, it's become a viable business where draft horses are used for clean-up after storms where downed trees need to be cleared. The horses can get into areas that trucks cannot, and pulling out the logs with real horsepower is gaining popularity. It is a win-win for everyone, especially those who love this way of life and the horses they work with daily.

The number of people who are walking away from their high-paying city jobs to put on a pair of jeans and a hard hat and start something new is growing. The thrill of searching for the perfect horse or team is all part of the journey, and the bond between the people and these huge horses is something that is undeniably evident by how they care for the horses and how they talk about them.

To watch these huge draft horses pulling logs out of the woods takes us back in time to a life that was simple and much quieter. It was a time when you didn't hear the noise all around you. The only thing you heard was the soft nicker as your horse saw you walking toward him or the sound of his huge feet hitting the ground with each step as he pulled the logs. It's the sound of power and gentleness all wrapped up in this amazing animal. Some things just never get old.

~November 15~
Horse Bells

Horse bells have been used to adorn horses since around 800 BC. They were often used for decorative purposes for people of higher social standing, but they were also used for very practical reasons as well. In the 1700's and 1800's, horse bells were used on pack horses traveling narrow trails through the mountains. Bells were used up through the 1900's on the horses that pulled wagons along winding country roads in southern England and Wales.

During the medieval era, highly decorated knights would be given a bell, plated with gold or silver and engraved with the coat-of-arms and inscription, which was presented as a gift or award for outstanding service to the king. The large bell (Crotal) would often be 5½ inches in diameter and tied to the knight's saddle. The bell would sit high on the horse's rump as the knight rode his horse. The horse's movement would motion the bell, and it would jingle for all to hear. It was also believed that bells thwarted off evil spirits, protected against disease, and they were often worn on horses for good luck. Many people who had acquired wealth put bells on their horses purely to show off their accumulation of land, homes or objects of value. The bells on a horse became a symbol of a rich life and excellent social standing.

Often people would adorn their horses with bells to enhance their beauty. In the 1800's, people started putting bells on horse sleighs for decoration while traveling to their destination. The strong association of horse bells with Christmas and winter fun led people to gradually call them "sleigh bells." The famous song by James Lord Pierpont in the 1800's was called Jingle Bells and, of course, it's about a horse and the bells he wears while pulling a sleigh. Today, the horse and sleigh bells have become a symbol of a good life shared with family and friends, especially during the Christmas season.

~November 16~
Bess

Over 10,000 horses were drafted into World War I from New Zealand, and a four-year-old black Thoroughbred mare was one of them. Her birth name was Zelma. The New Zealand government was purchasing horses for the war effort, and they were requesting geldings as their first choice and mares second. The horses needed to be between 4-7 years old, 14 to 15.2 hands tall, and strong. Captain Charles Guy Powles saw Zelma and purchased her for his mount. Powles quickly renamed her Bess, and she would prove to be just as strong as any gelding, and have the fight in her to keep going under the most horrific conditions. In October 1914, Bess and Powles left New Zealand bound for Egypt, along with 3,815 horses that were being transported in rows of cramped stalls aboard a ship. During the trip, the men had to rub the horses' legs due to swelling. They would also exercise them daily on coconut matting on the deck. Over a hundred horses got sick and died on board the ship and their bodies were thrown overboard. Once they reached Egypt, the conditions on the ground were even worse.

The terrain was extremely harsh, and there were often shortages of food and water for the horses. The weather was unbearably hot, and the burning sand and dust wore out the men and horses. Many horses died while others were too weak to continue. The men became emotionally and physically dependent on their horses and often used the horses' shadows to get protection from the scorching midday sun. Somehow Bess had survived the war and was one of just four horses that made it back home to New Zealand. Powles kept Bess and took good care of her. She had several foals and lived a good life. Bess died in 1934, and Powles buried her with two memorial plaques on stone that listed the places where Bess served during and after the war, along with an inscription that read, "In the Name of the Most High God."

~November 17~
Old Charley

One of the favorite horses of William F."Buffalo Bill" Cody was Charlie. He was his scouting horse in the late 1800's, and then became Cody's star horse when the Buffalo Bill's Wild West Show opened up. Cody would tell people that Charlie was an animal of almost human intelligence. The Wild West Show became so famous that Cody and Charlie traveled across America and then to Europe to perform. While in London, Charlie attracted so much attention that many members of royalty asked to ride him. Among these was the Grand Duke, who several times rode him in a "chase" after Buffalo Bill's herd of buffalo that were part of the show. Afterward, the Prince of Wales visited the show's stables and wanted to meet Charlie, and by this point, the horse had become a celebrity. Charlie would race at full speed around the arena while Cody shot dozens of glass balls that were tossed up as turrets. Charlie appeared to be at his best when Buffalo Bill rode him at the "command performance" at Windsor Castle. But on the journey home to America, when the ship was in mid-ocean, Charlie became very sick and died. Charlie's body was taken to the main deck and covered with an American flag. Cody stood alone next to the lifeless body and was heard saying in part:

"Old fellow, your journeys are over...Obedient to my call, gladly you bore your burden on, little knowing, little reckoning what the day might bring, shared sorrows and pleasures alike. Willing speed, tireless courage...you have never failed me. Ah, Charlie, old fellow, I have had many friends, but few of whom I could say that...I love you as you loved me. Men tell me you have no soul, but if there is a heaven and scouts can enter there, I'll wait at the gate for you, old friend."

When the band played, Old Charlie was slowly lowered into the waves of the Atlantic Ocean.

~November 18~
Making House Calls

Up through the early part of the 20th century, doctors often made house calls to sick patients by way of horseback, or horse and buggy. Unless you lived in town or a larger city, access to a doctor was not easy, and traveling doctors on horseback was often the difference between life and death, if the injury or illness was serious. If a town or settlement had a doctor living within a day's journey, settlers often expected the doctor to come to them. Doctors traveled very long distances on foot, on horseback, or with a wagon and carried everything with them no matter the situation.

Soon, nurses started making house calls to help assist the doctors' heavy client load. By the mid-1930's, nurses on horseback became a familiar sight. They would be dressed in blue-gray uniform coats, breeches, white shirts, ties, caps, and knee-high riding boots, and their saddlebags would be packed full of supplies for almost any medical emergency. When poor children in the Appalachian Mountains and other rural areas asked where babies came from, they were told, "The nurses bring them in their saddlebags." These nurses traveled in all kinds of weather on their horses, and sometimes the terrain was so harsh they would have to get off and lead their horse across the unmarked trails.

During those years, a nursing service was created to help the medical staff, but to also make sure the horses were ready at a moment's notice. These staffers were called "couriers," and it was their job to care for the horses, making sure they were well fed, healthy and ready to go day or night. They also kept riding tack in good condition, delivered supplies to the outlying clinics, and sometimes accompanied the nurses on their rounds. The horse's care was of utmost importance, otherwise the nurses and doctors might not make it on time to deliver a baby or save a life. Horses were a vital part of the health care system back in the day.

~November 19~
The Steeplechase

The first Steeplechase race was held in County Cork, Ireland, in 1752. Two horsemen, Cornelius O'Callaghan and Edmund Blake, challenged each other to a friendly match race to see who had the fastest horse. The race would cover approximately 4½ miles from Buttevant Church to St. Mary's Doneraile, whose tower was known as St. Leger Steeple. Church steeples were the most noticeable and tallest landmarks on the landscape, and the sport took its name from the race between these two men that ended at the church steeple. After that race, the Steeplechase was born.

Steeplechase horses are usually Thoroughbreds and are typically a little older than horses that race on the flat. While most racehorses have experience flat racing, a Steeplechase horse must possess endurance and a natural jumping ability. A need for stamina is a must as Steeplechase races are much longer than flat racing. The Belmont Stakes is the longest race of the Triple Crown at 1.5 miles, where Steeplechase races are two miles in length or longer. These races also include many jumps over hedges and water, which is quite a difference from flat racing.

The training of a Steeplechase horse also called "chasers," requires time and patience, as the horse needs to become mentally mature with age and must learn to run fast but also be willing to jump anything in front of them without hesitation. It is especially important that they are NOT scared of water! The horses are often trained in open fields where they are asked to jump numerous objects with changes in scenery and they usually don't start their career until they are around 4 or 5 years old.

The Steeplechase race may have originated in Ireland over a bet between two men, but it gained popularity in England, and then it jumped the pond to America, where you can find Steeplechase races in many states, especially on the east coast.

~November 20~
The Colonial Pacer

These horses were often called the "Colonial horses," but their recognized breed name is the Narragansett Pacer, which comes from the area in which they were bred—the Narragansett Bay area of Rhode Island. George Washington owned a couple of Narragansett Pacers and was known to race his horses a time or two. The Narragansett Pacer is said to be the breed of horse that Paul Revere rode on his famous midnight ride to warn the people that the British were coming.

The origin of the Narragansett Pacer has been disputed for centuries, and it is believed that the breed originated from the English and Dutch horses which arrived in Massachusetts between 1629 and 1635. These smooth saddle horses became famous quickly for their comfortable gait, great stamina on long rides, and being extremely sure-footed. They were bred in large numbers in the 1700's.

These horses were basically the only means to get to town, see a doctor, or visit a neighbor in an area known for cold, wet weather much of the year. Due to the poor weather conditions, the roads were often rutted and uneven, and the Narragansett Pacer seemed to travel with ease on the roads that were usually in horrible condition. These horses were small in stature at around 14 to 14.3 hands tall, but had tremendous endurance and a very spirited personality.

As colonial roads were improved, people began driving carriages more and rode less. As the lifestyles of the colonials changed and carriage driving became a more preferred way to travel, eventually, the Narragansett Pacer became less and less until the breed became extinct. The Narragansett Pacer is known as the first horse breed to be developed in America, and is one of the founding breeds of today's Standardbred.

~November 21~
The Brumbies

When you think of the wild horses in Australia, two things might come to mind. First, one of the best horse movies ever made, The Man from Snowy River, and second, the wild horses that live in the outback known as Brumbies. These feral horses that roam the countryside are thought to have originated from some of the horses left behind and named after Sargent James Brumby. When Brumby, who was a soldier and farrier in the outback in 1791, was later transferred, some of the horses proved impossible to catch, so they left without them. Prior to this time, there were no native horses known to Australia due to the harsh landscape. It is said that the very first horses came over on the first ship from England in 1788. The vessel carried seven horses total, both mares and stallions.

The Brumby horse can be traced to the Capers breed from South Africa, Timor Ponies from Indonesia, British Draught horse, as well as Thoroughbreds and Arabians. Brumbies are rarely consistent in size and they come in a variety of colors, which makes them even more fascinating. Brumbies are considered feral horses because they came from domesticated horses. They have adapted and survived in their surroundings quite well and have produced hardy offspring. They are very social horses and live in groups called "mobs" or "bands" (we call them herds here in the west), and now live in most parts of Australia. The Brumby became a sought-after horse for both WWI and WWII because they were strong, very adaptable, and easy to train. What made them even more popular was that they had a wonderful temperament and a courageous spirit. But, as warhorses were replaced with motorized vehicles, the Brumbies were used less and less and left alone to free range and multiply. Today the Brumby is considered an icon and national symbol of Australia, and these horses have been immortalized in art, books, and movies.

~November 22~
Today

Today I was put into a box that moved and taken away from everything I ever knew. It was noisy, and my body trembled as I munched on the hay that was placed before me. I did not make a fuss because I wanted to please the people I knew.

Today was a long day, but my new surroundings seemed pleasant, and the voices I heard and the new humans in front of me had a kind face. I will listen and try to understand what they are asking me to do.

Today I am meeting my new horse mates outside. I hope they are as fun as my old friends from my previous home. With all the new horses running around me, it is a little overwhelming, but I will look for a mate to hang out with.

Today I recognized the same people who brought me here yesterday. They have a small human with them that has a high-pitched voice and a loud giggle. She keeps putting her arms around me and touching me all over. There is something about her that I like. She also keeps feeding me carrots.

Today this little human whom I have grown to love and wait for every day took me on a trail ride. It was so fun to be out with other horses walking down a path with the cool breeze and sun shining. She is gentle with me, and I will take care of her.

Today my body is sore, and my coat has faded. My days are peaceful and quiet. I hardly see my human anymore. She is busy with little ones of her own. I look for her daily and wait for her vehicle to pull up to the farm. My days are becoming short, but I am blessed to have been sold so many years ago to a wonderful family who has taken care of me all these decades.

Today I will take my last breath. I hope I have been a good servant and trusted partner for my human and her children. I tried my very best all these years.
~Author Unknown~

~November 23~
Cortés

Just 25 years after Columbus came to America, the Spanish explorer Hernán Cortés brought sixteen Iberian horses to the New World. Iberian horses originated from the Iberian Peninsula, which included the Andalusian and Lusitano horse breeds. These horses were kept for exploration and warfare. As some of the horses got loose or were abandoned, they continued to breed, eventually becoming feral. It is believed that the direct origin of today's feral Mustangs found in the United States came from Cortés' original sixteen Iberian horses.

In 1618, two Franciscan missionaries, Bartolome de Fuensalida and Juan de Orbita, headed out from Merida to convert the Itza people. Six months later, they arrived at Tayasal, where the Itza ruler received them in peace. The ruler showed the missionaries an idol in the form of a horse they had named "Thunder Horse." It turned out that when Cortés had visited Tayasal on his journey, he left one of his horses, who had become very lame, with the Canek leader (priest-king) of that day. Cortés promised to return for the horse himself or send for the horse. After Cortés' departure, the Itza people treated the horse as a god, offering it fowl and other meats along with native flowers and plants to eat. Soon the horse became very sick and died. The Itza people became terrified at the death of a god on their hands, so they made a stone idol of the horse to prove they were not responsible for the horse's death. When Father Orbita saw the idol, he became so angry at the idolatry that he smashed the statue into bits. The people became very fearful and didn't want the death of the horse to start a massacre of their people.

It is believed that the horse helped Cortés conquer the Aztecs for his home country of Spain. That defeated empire is now known as Mexico. *"We owe it all to God and the horse,"* said Hernán Cortés.

~November 24~
The Last Fire Horse

Fighting fires with horse-drawn equipment will no doubt go down as one of the most courageous times in history. Not only for the men but also for the horses that heard the fire bell, stood calmly as they were harnessed, and then took off at a blazing speed. These fearless horses did this day in and day out, no matter the hour or the number of calls they had already been on that day. When you think about it, it is only a truly remarkable animal that is willing to run into danger and keep his head about him at all times.

Sadly the days of horse-drawn fire equipment were coming to an end as fire departments were becoming completely motorized. On December 20, 1922, the fire commissioner, firefighters, Jiggs the firedog, and the public waited at Borough Hall to pay their final homage to the fire horse. The last five horses, Balgriffen, Danny Beg, Penrose, Waterboy, and Bucknell, were going to make their last run through the city streets and would be honored at the end.

At 10:15 in the morning, the Assistant Fire Chief rang the fire alarm. Balgriffen took his familiar spot in the middle of the hitch for the engine, with Danny Beg and Penrose on each side for the last time. Waterboy and Bucknell stood in place and were hitched to the hose wagon. Soon the horses were running at full speed down Fulton Street and along Court Street, and then to the rear of the Borough Hall. The five horses came to a halt and stood quietly as they had done so many times before. The ceremony ended as wreaths were placed on each horse, and press photos were taken. Tears were streaming down the firefighters' faces as each man had grown to love and respect each of these horses. Balgriffen, Danny Beg, Penrose, Waterboy, and Bucknell were retired to either light duty on Blackwell's Island or to a lovely farm operated by the ASPCA (The American Society for the Prevention of Cruelty to Animals).

~November 25~
Extinct Equines

Throughout history the horse has evolved into many equine breeds. Some of those breeds have endured cultures, war, and environment and have grown even hardier, while others have died out. I think it is important to mention some of these breeds that no longer exist.

- The Galloway pony is now extinct but was once native to Scotland and England. It was said to have "good looks, a wide, deep chest, and a tendency to pace rather than trot." Galloway ponies were bred in Swaledale during the 18th century, to haul lead ore. The Galloway pony heavily influenced other breeds like the Newfoundland pony, the Highland Pony, and the Fell pony of England. The Galloway pony died out through extensive crossbreeding.
- The Quagga lived in South Africa and was a subspecies of Plains Zebra. After the Dutch settlement began, the Quagga became heavily hunted as it competed with domesticated animals for forage. While some individual horses were taken to zoos in Europe, breeding programs were unsuccessful. The last captive Quagga died in August 1883.
- The Hagerman Horse also called the Hagerman Zebra or the American Zebra was a North American species, and it was one of the oldest horses of the Genus Equus. It was discovered in 1928 in Hagerman, Idaho, and is now the state fossil of Idaho.
- The Syrian Wild Ass is an extinct subspecies native to the Arabian Peninsula. It was known to be untamable and was compared to a Thoroughbred horse for its beauty and strength. The last known Syrian Wild Ass was shot in 1927 near an oasis in Jordan.
- The last wild Tarpan horse, a mare, was accidentally killed when trying to capture the horse in 1890. The last Tarpan horse in captivity died in Russia in 1909.

~November 26~
That Beautiful Mane

There is nothing more gorgeous than a long flowing mane on a horse. It almost makes the horse look magical. But there is so much more to the mane of a horse. First of all, the word mane comes from the Proto-Indo-European root "mon." This means either "neck" or more specifically, the nape of the neck. This evolved into "manu" in Old English and then into the word "mane," which we use today.

The mane provides a protective layer to help horses stay warm and dry. It helps keep the head and neck dry, which is important in keeping the horse warm. The mane also helps maintain the horse's body temperature, insulating the major blood vessels around the head that carry blood to the brain.

When it comes to a horse's mane, the male has thicker hair than the female. Many would assume it has to do with attracting a mate, but on the contrary, it is all about survival. Stallions out in the wild will often fight each other for dominance. When two stallions fight, they will bite each other on the neck and throat area to bring the other horse down. A thicker mane provides protection for the rivaling stallions. "Survival of the fittest" physical traits like the mane and tail will be passed down to the foals being born. The breed of the horse also will determine the thickness of the mane, but most wild horses naturally have thicker manes.

Horses have many different coat colors, and often the mane and tail will determine the correct color type of the horse. For example; both bay and chestnut horses have coats that are brown to reddish-brown, but a bay horse will have a black mane, tail, and lower legs, known as "points." With a chestnut horse, the mane and tail will be a lighter shade or the same color as the body. The horse's mane tells us a lot about the breed of horse and their descriptive color. It's all in the hair!

~November 27~
Horse Of A Different Color

The numerous colors that grace the horse have been symbolic in many cultures since the beginning of creation. But for someone like me who is in love with horses, certain colors of the horse make me feel good. I think that would be a true statement for most people. It is said you should never buy a horse just because of its color, but the truth is, the color of a horse has always impacted our decision whether it is a good or bad one. I thought it would be fun to look into what others have said about the colors of the horse.

- Black horses are often thought of as having mystery surrounding them. For many cultures of the past, they symbolized war, strength, and death. The truly black horse is a sight to behold.
- White horses are symbolic of honesty, truth, and innocence. They take our minds to a place of royalty and love, and show us what untouched beauty looks like.
- Grey horses are the perfect blend of black and white and have been thought of as a symbol of neutrality. They have a calming effect on us and help us to see the entire picture. Their grey color has been said to give us the feeling of strength, and that anything is possible.
- Red/Brown horses keep us rooted and bring us back to the earth and what is important. They symbolize passion and inspiration. It is said that a horse with more red in its coat than brown will often have a fiery sprit.
- Dappled/Multi-Colored horses symbolize a free spirit, variety, and flexibility in personality and how we should live. When we encounter a multi-colored horse, it somehow sends us back to a time before modern cities, rigorous schedules, and stringent rules of society.

~November 28~
Horse Soldiers

The Horse Soldiers were members of the first U.S. Army Special Forces unit to enter Afghanistan following the September 11, 2001 attacks. In the weeks following 9/11, this hand-selected detachment of twelve Green Berets from the 5th Special Forces Group later named the "Horse Soldiers," entered Afghanistan on horseback. Their mission marked the first time U.S. troops rode to battle on horseback since World War II. Their job was to help liberate Afghanistan people from the Taliban without using tanks or trucks; instead, they would use horses.

When the Berets got the word that they would be riding local horses on their mission, they were stunned. The twelve soldiers would be riding horses into dangerous territory, but before that, they would need some quick lessons about horses and how to ride them. Only one of the soldiers had a lot of riding experience, but most of them had none at all! There was so much to think about for the soldiers besides learning how to ride a horse. It was a painful process (especially their back-end) sitting in a saddle for many long hours. Furthermore, the saddles and riding gear were not designed for the size of the American soldiers. The Americans were larger and heavier than their Afghanistan counterparts. The horse tack was in very poor condition, with the leather straps and stirrups breaking often. When something broke, you used whatever you had available to fix it. The stirrups on the saddles often broke but became an easy fix with the men's parachute cargo straps.

The good news was that the horses were very familiar with the terrain, extremely surefooted, and were very patient with their new American riders. The horses could handle being ridden both day and night, and the sounds of artillery fire didn't bother them at all. They were tough Afghan horses who did their job well, and the mission was accomplished with great success.

~November 29~
The Mounties

If you have been on this earth a few decades, then you are probably familiar with the phrase, "The Mountie always gets his man!" But who are the Mounties, and how did they come about? The North-West Mounted Police was created by the Canadian Parliament in 1873, but was quickly changed to the Royal Canadian Mounted Police, otherwise known as the Mounties.

Driven by heavy taxes on whiskey, many "hooch bandits" moved up to Canada from the U.S. in the 1800's, since so much of the region was growing with the Klondike Gold Rush of 1896. The gold rush and bootleggers quickly created a need for law and order, and soon the Mounties were called in. Since their inception, the Mounties have been associated with horses up through the middle of the 20th century. With such a vast area to patrol, horses were the only way to get around fast. Soon the Mountie's horsemanship skills became legendary, and you never saw a Mountie without his horse. The use of horses for regular duties decreased in 1936 as motorized vehicles took over, but every Mountie was still required to know how to ride a horse until 1966.

Since 1938, all Royal Canadian Mounted Police horses have had to be black. Assistant RCMP Commissioner S.T. Wood admired the household guard of King George VI on a trip to England, and he liked how nice the bright red jackets looked atop the black horses. When he became commissioner, he decided that every Royal Canadian Mounted Police horse had to be black. Since then, Mountie horses have to meet very strict size and appearance criteria. Besides being required to be all black with an occasional white marking on the face, the horses need to stand between 16 and 17.2 hands tall. The horses are a cross between Thoroughbreds and Hanoverians, and currently, they are all bred at one breeding farm in Pakenham, Ontario.

~November 30~
The Lesson Horse

Any person who loves horses remembers their first lesson horse. Whether it is the young school girl who impatiently sits in the car as her mother drives her to the barn, or the older adult who has raised her family and is now doing the one thing she has always wanted to do—ride a horse.

It takes a special horse to be the "first horse" for young and old alike, and the lesson horse is a gift from God. Not all horses make good lesson horses because many don't have the tolerance of letting different people ride on their back with mixed signals coming from each rider. Some horses need a confident rider because a nervous rider often creates anxiety in a less confident horse. Finding the perfect combination of confidence and patience in a horse is essential, and those horses are extremely important for future generations of equestrians. After all, we all start off as beginners when it comes to riding and horsemanship.

Lesson horses are the unsung heroes that often go unnoticed. They are usually not the flashiest horses or the horses that are blue ribbon winners in the show ring. But they have something that many horses do not—they have a smart intellect that understands their inexperienced riders. They instinctively know when to walk slowly and when it's time to take it to the next level. A great lesson horse gives confidence to the timid rider and is not going to let anything happen to the child on their back. A great lesson horse will sift through the often confusing cues to figure out what a beginner rider is asking.

For every horse that has ever been a "lesson horse," he will forever be a beautiful memory to the people who came weekly to the stable with excitement in their eyes to see and ride their favorite horse. God knew exactly what He was doing when he created the lesson horse, and we are forever thankful for that.

~December 1~
Pinto

The horse's name was Pinto and he is the only horse to have ever walked the entire distance of the United States while hitting each capital along the way. The total distance covered was 20,352 miles. Pinto was a little horse with a big heart that would go the distance for his owner.

In 1912, George Beck decided to make history by riding his six-year-old horse, Pinto, a 15-hand Morab gelding, from his home on Bainbridge Island to every state capital in the union. Beck had talked three other guys into joining him, and in the process, they were hoping to find fame and fortune. Led by Beck, they called themselves the Overland Westerners, and the group planned to finish their adventure at the 1915 World's Fair.

Unfortunately, the trip did not go as easily as Beck had envisioned. The group spent the next three years sore, cold, hungry, and broke. Beck would make a little money along the way by riding Pinto in exhibitions, but for the most part, the men were penniless just about all the time. Many problems plagued the other three men and their horses throughout the entire journey. The other men had gone through 17 horses, either because of lameness, exhaustion, or death, but George Beck was still riding Pinto.

Once in a while Pinto was used as a pack horse on their journey, but while crossing a deep river, he fell and couldn't get back up. Beck worked fast to help his horse and finally got him up with no severe injuries. Pinto was the only horse to complete the trip in its entirety. Finally three years later on June 1, 1915, the group arrived in San Francisco, but there was no celebration of their arrival. Times were changing fast and people were more interested in motorized cars and the thought of seeing an airplane. Pinto's travel across the United States is considered the longest documented journey of the 20th century.

~December 2~
Horsehair

Horsehair has been used for many different things throughout history, and even after its death, the horse continues to give us so much.

- Horsehair plaster! I bet you have never heard of this before. The purpose of the horsehair itself was to act as a bridging agent. It helped control the shrinkage of the plaster and hold the plaster "nibs" together.
- During the Civil War, horsehair sutures became the standard choice, as other suture materials ran out as the war progressed. They realized once they boiled the horsehair, they had less infection, and they learned about sterilization during that time.
- Until the early 20th century, horsehair was used to stuff upholstered furniture and for furniture designs. Prussians opened their first horsehair fabric manufacturer in 1762 in Breslow, and today horsehair is still being used for furniture and fabrics all over the world.
- Strands of horsehair can be used separately or woven together to form lengths of strong lines suitable for many uses: fishing lines, bows for violins, cellos, and other stringed instruments, and wigs to name a few. Paint brushes are commonly made with horsehair.
- American Indians used the hair of their greatest horses in weaving and pottery to honor and immortalize them, just like we do today with horsehair jewelry from our beloved equine.
- Horsehair clothing was originally called crinoline in the 1850's. Horsehair got its name from the prefix "crin," which means horsehair in French. Crinoline was used to add volume and stiffen hemlines, sleeves, hat brims, costumes, and collars.
- Nearly all catapults used in ancient medieval artillery operated by a quick release of the twisted cords of horsehair that were attached to the wooden beams. This created a powerful force to be reckoned with. Now that's impressive horsepower!

~December 3~
Coconut Roll

Bronc riding has come a long way since the days when cowboys hopped on wild horses to "break them out." Today's rodeo horses are specially bred for saddle and bareback bronc riding, and they are a huge part of the thrilling sport we call Rodeo. There is nothing more exciting than watching a powerful horse use their muscles to try to get the cowboy off his back. The best part is most of these equine athletes are very well cared for behind the scenes.

One special mare has gone down in Rodeo history as one of the toughest and successful bareback broncs ever. Her name is Coconut Roll and she has earned respect and admiration from all cowboys that have competed on the Rodeo circuit. One cowboy said, "She was a very special mare and her competitive spirit was obvious to everyone." Coconut Roll knew her job well, and when a cowboy drew her name, he knew he was in for a tough ride, but staying on might put him in the lead. Coconut Roll bucked her way into the Canadian Finals Rodeo 11 times and the National Finals 10 times. Coconut Roll knew it was show time when she got in the shoot and the flank strap was put on. She looked fierce during those eight seconds, but when the buzzer went off, she knew her job was done.

In 2010 Coconut Roll was retired after the Canadian Finals Rodeo and returned home to the ranch where she had been raised. She had a colt named Grated Coconut that grew up to be equally as talented as his mother. Coconut Roll threw babies that had the sweetest temperaments when at home, but when it was time to work—game on! Coconut Roll lived out her days on thousands of acres. This legendary bareback star earned her place of honor, buried at the gates to the Stampede Ranch with her own tombstone, alongside the other much loved and celebrated bucking legends.

~December 4~
Eventing

The equestrian sport of Eventing is often viewed as the pinnacle of equine athleticism. Some may agree while others disagree, but one thing that can't be disputed is the fact that the horses used in Eventing are both physically and mentally amazing. After all, it takes a lot of stamina and a good sound mind to compete in the sport, which is a combination of Dressage, Jumping, and Cross Country. The horse has to mentally change gears for all three events, and that is not an easy task. You could call it the equine version of the Triathlon.

The origins of Eventing can be traced back to the military, as so many other equine sports have. Fox hunting in the 19th century also played a large part in forming the sport, but it has evolved greatly in the 21st century. In 1912, Eventing became an Olympic sport at the Stockholm Games. At the time only amateur riders who were in the military could compete. The main goal was to test the cavalry on their fitness and horsemanship. Dressage showcased the connection and communication between the horse and rider in the arena. Both the stadium jumping and the cross-country gave the judges a view of the stamina, steadiness, and speed of the horses that would be needed for battle.

A lot has changed and improved in the world of Eventing competition. A few decades later, both non-military and women were now allowed to compete in Eventing and the sport grew even more. The military horses that competed in Eventing a century ago are now the show horses of today. They have never been on the battlefield but are just as athletic with the greatest of stamina, and it gives us a glimpse into what the powerful warhorses of the past were like. When you put the history of the past with the horses of today, it stops nothing short of an overabundance of goosebumps and admiration for the horse.

~December 5~
Side-Saddle

For thousands of years, women were not allowed to ride horses in many cultures. Around three hundred years ago, Britain introduced "The Hunt," to train military officers for mounted warfare. Chasing foxes over fences and downed logs was a great way to gain balance in the saddle for the less coordinated soldier. Soon, the ladies who were bored at home pressured their husbands to let them come along and watch. It wasn't much longer before the ladies also wanted to ride. That is when the creation of the Sedan Chair came to be. This huge wooden chair sat on top of the horse's back (with great discomfort to the horse), and the women would sit in this chair with their legs together, which was required at all times. After a few serious disasters with the sedan chair and horse, the side-saddle was born out of necessity and safety.

The side-saddle enabled a woman to be in much better control of her horse while still keeping her legs together as the culture required. They even developed a machine that wealthy women could hop on in the privacy of their own home, and practice how to ride in the side-saddle without anyone watching. From there, the side-saddle spread to Europe, Australia, and other parts of the world.

Soon women were riding their horses while sitting atop a side-saddle and doing many of the same equestrian activities that men were doing. They would jump their horses while riding side-saddle and work cattle in the outback riding side-saddle. Even a few women like Sharp Shooter Annie Oakley rode side-saddle in Buffalo Bills Wild West Show, and Therese Renz of the Renz Circus family of Berlin rode side-saddle while jump-roping with her horse. Once women were able to ride, it soon opened doors for new adventures and conquests for women, all while riding a horse side-saddle!

~December 6~
The Western Saddle

It's hard to imagine the Old West without the cowboy and his saddle. To the cowboy, his saddle was just as important as his horse, and that meant he needed to make sure it was well-made and fit his horse like a glove. A cheap saddle would make a horse sore in an hour, but a well-made saddle would keep a horse moving cattle for miles and not be worse for wear at the end of the day. A cowboy's saddle was so crucial to his livelihood that the phrase, "he sold his saddle," signified that a man was finished as a cowboy.

The western saddle, as we know it, is thought to have its origins all the way back to the Sarmatians in the 4th century. These nomadic people lived in central Asia. When the Moors attacked Spain in 711 AD, they arrived riding in saddles built for battle. These saddles had high cantles for protection and longer stirrups to accommodate riding with armor. Later on, the Spaniards took this basic saddle design and adapted it to what became known as the Spanish War Saddle. This saddle had a wooden frame or tree, was well padded, and covered in velvet. As the Spaniards transitioned from the battlefield to colonial expansion and exploration, their saddle evolved into a stock saddle that started to resemble our western saddles of today.

When the saddle began to be used in cattle country during the early part of the 1800's, there were still a few more changes made to the cowboy's saddle. The tough wooden tree, the high pommel, and cantle were kept but with slight changes. The cantle was changed for the riders comfort and lowered for easier mounting and dismounting and the velvet was replaced with leather which was more durable. The pommel was changed in size, tilt, and material until it became the horn used to secure a rope. Today's western saddle is as important as ever and still evolving for the many different types of riding disciplines.

~December 7~
Horse Diving!

There have been many sports that horses have been forced to endure throughout history, but it is hard to think of one that tops the charts more than horse diving. Horse Diving was invented in the 1800's by William "Doc" Carver, who had worked with Buffalo Bill and his traveling show. It is said that he got the idea from crossing Nebraska's Platt River in 1881. As the bridge broke, his horse fell into the water and swam away. It inspired him to go out on his own with a new show—Horse Diving! His diving show involved a horse and rider walking up a 60-foot-high ramp and jumping off into around 11 feet of water. In the 1920's and 1930's the show became wildly popular as they traveled the states. It was eventually brought to Steel Pier in Atlantic City, New Jersey, replacing the Elk Diving act put on by nearby Million Dollar Pier. It became an instant success, with horses and riders putting on four shows daily, seven days a week. Horse diving proved to be very dangerous for the divers and horses. One young girl, Senora Webster, and her horse Red Lips had a tragic landing in the water after both horse and rider fell off the dock. The landing was so hard that Senora lost both of her eyes. She became completely blind but continued to dive off the docks on the back of a horse for years to come. She was the inspiration behind the 1991 Disney movie, Wild Hearts Can't Be Broken.

Soon pressure from many people for the concern of the horses resulted in the Steel Pier Act being shut down. While there have been attempts to revive it in 1993 and 2012, none have succeeded, given the outrage by so many people and animal rights groups. The fact is people today don't want to see a horse forced to dive into a pool of water!

If you gain the horse's trust, then the responsibility for his safety has increased tenfold. For a horse that trusts his owner will follow him anywhere.

~December 8~
The Show Stealer

Horses played a prominent role in the circus in the early days. To announce that the circus was in town, horses and performers in costumes paraded through the town to let people know there was going to be a huge show under the Big Top. The circus was heavily dependent on the horses for much more than just performing in their acts. For many horses the work was long and physically demanding. In the early 1900's, the Barnum and Bailey Circus used 750 horses for working and performance. Ringling Brothers had 650 horses during the same time. The circus was moved almost entirely by horses from town to town at first, then later, to and from the railroad yards. They used Percheron horses to pull the wagons and carriages to the fields where they would set up the Big Top. And soon, the dappled gray Percheron became one of the trademarks of the Ringling Brothers Circus since these draft horses were the muscle behind the circus.

The show stealers have always been the horses. The variety of circus horse acts ranged from electrifying feats of acrobatics to elegant classical riding. Most of the horses used were either stallions or geldings since they tended to be more athletic than the mares. Great amounts of time and patience were spent in training horses to perform complex moves. One owner of an English circus very simply summed up the requirements necessary to train a performing horse: "Patience, understanding, and carrots."

One of the most famous performing horses was Black Eagle. He performed with the American circus Howes and Cushing. Black Eagle was billed as "The Horse of Beauty." He could waltz, polka, and stand on his hind legs. The horses that traveled with the larger circuses usually worked hard, but had a good life and were treated well. The smart circus owners knew the value of their most important asset, which was the horse.

~December 9~
Phar Lap

In 1926, he was purchased for $336.00 and shipped to Australia from New Zealand. When the horse arrived in Australia, his new owner David J. Davis was not impressed at all. The horse was skinny, clumsy, and had warts all over his head. Davis was angry at the trainer for purchasing the ugly horse, but the trainer saw something special in the animal. Davis didn't want to stick more money into the racehorse, so he leased him to the trainer for the next three years, and the trainer would pay all the expenses and keep any prize money. The trainer knew the horse's bloodlines and saw a champion in the horse, he just needed a chance. The horse's name was Phar Lap which in Thai means "lightning," but around the stable, he was simply known as Bobby.

Phar Lap proved Davis wrong when he started winning all his races with ease. He became untouchable on the racetrack. Phar Lap's wins seemed to anger the bookmakers, since they had to pay out a lot of money with each win Phar Lap had on the track. It outraged them so much that the horse was even shot at one time, but survived. Davis eventually took Phar Lap back and had his champion horse shipped to California with no expenses spared. Phar Lap had a luxury box stall and plenty of room to roam on board so that the trip was easy on him. Phar Lap continued to win in California up until his untimely death. Mystery still surrounds the death of this great horse, and to this day, it is not known if it was accidental or deliberate.

After Phar Lap's death, an autopsy was done, and it was discovered that his heart was one of the largest hearts ever found in a racehorse. (October 4, 1926 – April 5, 1932).

If they say it's impossible, then make it possible. If they say you can't, then show them you can. Chase your dreams, and one day you will catch them.

~December 10~
Laws That Still Exist Today

Horses were the means to keeping a city going and with that came a series of new laws that judges put in place to protect the horses and people. Many of these laws are crazy and still on the books today.

- Opening an umbrella close to a horse is illegal in New York City.
- Taking photos of horses on Sundays in McAllen, Texas, can get you up to 3 days in jail for disturbing the animal.
- In Pattonsburg, Missouri, "No person shall hallo, shout, bawl, scream, use profane language, dance, sing, whoop, quarrel, or make any unusual noise or sound in such manner, as to disturb a horse." This ordinance was last revised in 1884.
- Fishing from horseback is illegal in many places, including, Colorado, Utah and Washington D.C.
- Tennessee prohibits lassoing fish from horseback. Let this one sink in.
- In Cotton Valley, Louisiana, men can't eat ice cream while riding a horse.
- Only married women are allowed to ride to church on Sunday under the laws in Bluff, Utah. Unmarried, divorced or widowed women doing so may be incarcerated.
- Horses cannot mate within 500 yards of a tavern, school or church in California.
- Charleston, South Carolina requires horses to wear diapers in public areas.
- Riding an ugly horse in Hartsville, Illinois, can result in jail time. This originated from the need to stop the neglect of horses, but the law doesn't constitute what makes an "ugly" horse.

Just a side note - If you do get in trouble, remember that an attorney practicing in Corvallis, Oregon, can be disbarred if he refuses to accept a horse as payment for his services!

~December 11~
Lipizzaner Rescue

It was April 28, 1945, and the mission was dubbed Operation Cowboy. U.S. troops, along with liberated Allied POWs and a platoon of turn-coat German soldiers, were about to go on a mission to rescue a herd of priceless horses. This was all while fighting off attacks by the German army.

The horses were the prized Lipizzaners of the Spanish Riding School in Vienna. The war in Europe was just a few short weeks away from ending, but it had been brought to General Patton's attention that there were several hundred extraordinarily talented and cherished white horses that had fallen into enemy hands. It was of deep concern that the breed would forever be destroyed by the bizarre Third Reich breeding program that was put into place to try and create an "Aryan horse."

General Patton, along with other officers, overnight put a plan into place to rescue the horses. It would mean riding horses in and herding them out while trying to stay alive. American soldiers led the way through enemy lines to reach the town of Hostau, where the horses were located. At dawn on May 12th, the remarkable caravan began. Close to three hundred horses were herded in small groups with American vehicles positioned before and after them, and Americans, Polish, Czechs, and Cossacks rode as outriders on horseback. The evacuation was an organizational masterpiece, and the horses had covered roughly 130 miles to Mannsbach and arrived safely.

George S. Patton spent a lifetime with horses and had penned this, *"On the other hand, it is probably wrong to permit any highly developed art, no matter how fatuous, to perish from the earth—and which arts are fatuous depends on the point of view. To me the high-schooling of horses is certainly more interesting than either painting or music."*

368

~December 12~
American Quarter Horse

The Quarter Horse holds a special place in American history from the 1880's forward, because this little horse helped tame the west! He had the stamina to help move cattle thousands of miles and was faster than lightning for a quarter of a mile. On top of his speed and endurance, this horse had the calmest temperament which made him a pleasure to ride.

But the story of the American Quarter Horse began long before Texans started moving cattle out west. It is said that the origins of the Quarter Horse can be traced back to Colonial America. Our forefathers enjoyed horse racing and ran the same English horses that they used in the fields and rode every day. It wasn't long before the colonial farmers in the Carolinas and Virginia began to trade for faster horses that were being bred by the Chickasaw Indians. The Spanish Barb horses obtained from the Chickasaws were crossed with the English stock as early as 1611. Over the next 150 years, careful breeding would develop new horses with the body and confirmation that we are familiar with today in the American Quarter Horse. One of the great stallions that came from the early cross-breeding was named Sir Archy, and his traits are still found today in the Quarter Horse.

Fast forward to 1844, when a colt is foaled in Kentucky and is a descendent of the great Sir Archy. He was called Steel Dust, and he came to Texas as a yearling, and soon his reputation spread among cowboys driving cattle up the trails. Soon the name Steel Dust came to identify an entire breed of horses called "Steeldusts," after the great stallion. These horses quickly became the favorite among the cowboys. They were heavy-muscled horses marked with small ears, a prominent jaw, and extraordinary intelligence. Steel Dust was an American Quarter Horse. His future babies would reach unbelievable fame as the horses that could do anything.

~December 13~
Sleigh Racing

The song Jingle Bells has been a holiday favorite for as long as most of us can remember. The vision of a beautiful horse with bells jingling as he pulls a happy couple on a sleigh through the woods, gives us all the warm fuzzies. But the song has a different meaning that was kept from the public for decades! The verses we love to sing actually involve drag racing (sleigh racing) and even crashes. The song was written and published in 1857 by songwriter James Pierpont, and it was originally titled, One Horse Open Sleigh, but two years later, the title would be changed to Jingle Bells. Pierpont found his inspiration for the song on a snowy day, when he came upon sleigh races held on the snow-packed streets of Salem, Massachusetts. He had never witnessed anything like it before, and it compelled him to write the now famous song. Sleigh racing was so popular during the winter months in New England that local newspapers would print the winners and their lineage along with the racing conditions.

The horses were fast trotters and sleigh racing was serious business back then. The song goes on about "bobtailed horses" and this is because the tails on the horses were bobbed to prevent tangling with the reins, which could distract the horse and cause a crash. The lyrics, "one horse open sleigh" was actually about racing sleighs called "cutters" designed for two people to ride in and pulled by one horse. The bells that hung on the bobbed tail, harness, and sleigh were there, not as holiday adornments, but because it was the law! Heavy fines were issued if you didn't "jingle all the way" to let people know you were coming their way fast! There were many accidents during these races, especially if a sled hit a snow bank and became out of control. Since those early days, sleigh racing is still popular in many parts of the world, and children still sing this sweet song every year at Christmas.

~December 14~
After The War

It was 1918, and World War I had ended. For the soldiers, this meant they were going home. The fighting was over, but what was to become of all the horses who had served in the war so courageously? It was a problem that every country was going to have to figure out. So many horses had been killed during the war, and many of the horses that survived were injured or just so worn out mentally or physically that they were not capable of working. For the horses that survived, their future was very uncertain.

The horses that were ridden by officers were the lucky ones. Some of those horses were sent back to the countries they came from and given welcome home celebrations and a guaranteed retirement. Much of the fate of the horses depended on their age and fitness. More than 60,000 horses were sold to farmers in Britain since they were strong enough to work for a few more years. The oldest, worn out, or injured horses were sent to the knacker's yard (slaughterhouse) to be used for food. After the war, severe food shortages hit Europe and soon horsemeat was being used to keep people from starving.

But the role of the horse during the war wasn't forgotten. The "Old Blacks," a team of six horses who survived the entire war, were chosen to pull the hearse of the Unknown Soldier to mark the Armistice in 1920. A handful of other horses were retired to stables owned by The Horse Trust. The RSPCA (Royal Society for the Prevention of Cruelty to Animals), which had helped the army care for thousands of horses during the war, opened the Animals War Memorial Dispensary. It treated 6,000 horses after the war and is still a working clinic today.

I have carried on my back the most common of man to five-star generals. I have fought alongside your bravest of men in the darkest hours of history. Please never forget me – the horse. ~Author unknown

~December 15~
Seeing-Eye Mini

Miniature horses have come a long way from the days of working in the coal mines, and that is a good thing. What is so cool is that these awesome little pint-size horses are doing so much good in our modern world, and you can't write a book without sharing some of their accomplishments. Today's Miniature horses are used for so much more than just pulling carts or carrying little ones on their backs. They are helping be the eyes for the blind with success. While it's common to see a person that is blind using a seeing-eye dog, Miniature horses are also making the news as a companion horse for the disabled.

Seeing-Eye horses (also referred to as Guide Ponies or Assistance Animals) aren't as common as seeing-eye dogs, but they are out there. These little horses are trained to assist their blind owners in the same way. There are various reasons why someone would want a seeing-eye horse instead of a dog. In some cases, as in the Muslim religion, where dogs are forbidden, horses make the perfect substitute for the blind person. Some people feel that Miniature horses provide more stability than large dogs. There range of vision is much wider than a dog's vision, making them an excellent prospect for the person with a total loss of vision.

Dogs tend to be the best choice for most people with disabilities, but the Miniature horse has gained popularity over the last couple of decades, and the public is starting to gain acceptance of these horses as assistance animals.

Miniature horses that work as assistance animals are fitted with special boots to help them grip slippery floors, and they can be trained to load into a car or airplane. They can open and close doors and turn off lights, and there have been some cases where a Miniature horse was trained to dial 911 in an emergency. These little equines are truly a gift from God in the cutest package ever!

~December 16~
Skijoring

They call it the extreme winter equestrian sport. Skijoring has the thrill of fast skiing on hard-pack snow and the excitement of the horses that make it all happen. Skijoring has become a huge equestrian sport in the colder climates where it snows a lot. Skijoring originated in Scandinavia initially as a mode of winter transportation using horses. Skijoring (pronounced skee-joor-ing) translates to "ski driving" in Scandinavian.

In equestrian skijoring, a person wears skis and holds tug lines or long reins attached to the horse's harness. Then the skier is pulled behind a horse that is either being ridden by a second person or steered by the skier himself. Skiing while steering a horse is more complicated and requires horse and rider to be familiar with pull-reining. It's like ground driving on skis but much faster! In Europe, Skijoring races are serious business. The horses are outfitted with special winter shoes and race around a snowy track pulling their drivers at incredible speeds. In North America, a fun variation is to have a rider on the horse in a western saddle, and the skijorer holds a line attached to the saddle horn. With this western version of the Scandinavian sport, skijorers compete behind galloping horses, steering themselves over sizable jumps.

The horses used in skijoring need to be strong and have great stamina. Pulling a human over snow is much harder on the horse than just casually taking a ride through the snow. Some serious competitors even put special studded ice shoes on their horses that work as cleats, so the horse can gain traction as he runs at his top speed. One of the most important elements of the sport is finding a horse that feels comfortable and willing to pull a person without becoming nervous. Some horses love it and they excel at it once they learn their job. Some people call it the perfect winter sport!

~December 17~
Strep & Strangles

With the help of the horse, human doctors and equine veterinarians are now getting together to help find a cure for Strep Throat in humans. Doctors have been wondering for years how the bacteria that causes Strep Throat affects the tonsils. Well, it turned out that horses have a few things in common with humans. Doctors in the UK recently found many similarities between the symptoms of Strangles, which is highly contagious in horses and can make them very sick, and the human sickness Strep Throat. Horses will get a nasal discharge, swollen throat, fever, coughing, swelling, and abscesses. Humans will get a sore throat, swollen glands, cough, and high fever, along with other individual symptoms. Both horses and humans feel awful and lethargic, and it turns out that horses and humans get similar throat infections through genetically similar bacteria.

An article was written that stated, *"Researchers at a veterinary and research charity in the UK called Animal Health Trust found a way to test all of the equine strep genes simultaneously. The people studying human Strep at Houston Methodist Research Institute in Texas, on the other hand, were worried that they'd have to test each strep gene one at a time. That's when their veterinary friends reached out and showed them the more efficient route of gene analysis."* ~Newsweek 11/29/17.

The gene analyzing tool that equine vets are using is now something human doctors are looking at to help identify, isolate and test the different bacteria that help advance Strep. The goal is to develop a vaccine to help eliminate Strep in humans. The horse has contributed to the medical field throughout history, but it is incredible how they are helping in finding a cure for today's modern-day illnesses!

And let us run with perseverance the race marked out for us.
Hebrews 12:1

~December 18~
Wild Horse Annie

The horse has been our partner for thousands of years, doing what is asked of him without much fuss or resistance. But once in a while, they ask us for help just by the look in their eyes. Many people throughout history have understood the terrible situations that many horses have endured during their lives. It is important to pay tribute to some that have helped these horses when called. One such person was Velma Johnston, otherwise known as Wild Horse Annie.

Velma Johnston was born in 1912, and as a child she had polio which left her in constant pain. When she became an adult, she got a job as secretary. On the way to work one day, she saw something that would change her life forever. She watched a trailer full of half-dead horses go by, and as she looked at the horses, she had never seen such sad animals. The wild Mustangs were being transported to a factory to be slaughtered and made into pet food. From that point on Velma had a new mission in life. It was to help the Mustang horses. As she started to investigate the round-up and cruel treatment of the Mustangs, she began to devote all her free time to trying to help the Mustangs and ultimately saving them from extinction.

Velma Johnston became a voice for the Mustang horse during a time when women were to be quiet. She took on Congress, fought the powerful ranchers, and went on many vigilante missions to free the penned-up horses. She encouraged children all over to draw pictures and write letters to Congress. More mail from this campaign was delivered to D.C. than any other issue besides the Vietnam War. In 1971, the Wild Free-Roaming Horse and Burro Act passed Congress due to her dedication to the cause. It was a great example of what one person can do if they don't give up. Johnston became a hero for the Mustang when they needed it most.

~December 19~
Bill The Bastard

At the beginning of World War I, the stallion had become the brunt of jokes and bets. Australian soldiers would often talk about who would come back alive, the horse or the rider. He was known as a difficult horse and had a reputation for dumping soldiers. It was during a time when horses were often treated roughly and unmercifully whipped to get every ounce of speed from their worn-out bodies, and then riding them until they collapsed. Horses often broke down mentally if they didn't die first. The soldiers called him Bill the Bastard, and he became known as the unbreakable horse.

Michael Shanahan saw something in Bill that others did not see. He had witnessed the horse in action during a bloody battle, and even after the horse had been shot, he kept going. It is said that Shanahan was a hundred years before his time in how he worked with horses. Bill caught his eye, and Shanahan asked for the horse as his mount. He nursed the horse back to health and treated him very gently. Bill soon turned from an angry horse into a trusted steed who was solely devoted to Shanahan. Bill quickly gained a reputation for being fearless, standing his ground in an ambush, and warning his rider of danger ahead. During one battle, Shanahan was shot in the leg but kept fighting, going up and down the line until he collapsed on Bill. The loyal horse carried his rider almost two miles to a medic, where his leg was eventually amputated.

Bill became famously known as a courageous warhorse, and his bravery and stamina contributed in saving many soldiers' lives. After the war, most Australian horses were shot for fear they would fall into enemy hands. Bill instead, was given the gift of life. He was retired and left with villagers on Gallipoli, the resting place of Australia's fallen war heroes.

To earn the respect from the most difficult horse is to have a bond like no other.

~December 20~
The Christmas Party

During the earliest part of the 20th century, the Humane Society decided that they would throw a yearly Christmas party at different events across the United States, to bring awareness to the inhumane way many horses were treated. The party was also to encourage others to give their horses a day of rest, which was not the case for most working equines during that time.

It all began in 1919 on a very cold winter day in front of Boston's Post Office. A Christmas tree was put up and decorated with corn, ornaments, and long red banners that read, "Massachusetts Society for the Prevention of Cruelty to Animals." There were barrels of apples and bushels of oats for the horses to eat. People brought their workhorses by the Christmas tree and gave them treats. Some people thought it was stupid, but the majority of the people thought it was wonderful. Holiday shoppers pitched in and helped stack crates of carrots for the horses at the foot of the tree, and began cutting the carrots into bite-size pieces. On December 29, 1919, the Rutland News reported, "Altogether, it looked like a big day for the horses of the city."

Inhumane treatment of the workhorses was finally being addressed. Harness sores, severe beatings of horses, overloading the wagons, undernourishment, and making injured or sick horses work was something that needed to change. It was time to improve the workhorse's life, but for many people, they just didn't take the time to notice, so these parties were a positive way to bring awareness to the public. The Humane Societies' efforts to bring attention to the poor living conditions for the workhorse grew, and soon, "parties for the horses" took place in many major cities. The workhorse had been an integral part of growing the vast economy of the United States, and it was time to show how much they were appreciated.

~December 21~
The White House Stables

Before the black motorcades with bullet-proof glass and limousines with dignitaries coming to visit the President at the White House, there were the horses. The first White House stables were built for a very practical purpose—transportation. It was a simple Georgian design constructed in 1800 under the orders of Thomas Jefferson. Here are a few horse stories from the White House.

President Zachary Taylor's horse Old Whitey was a warhorse veteran, but now Old Whitey helped keep the lawns mowed by eating the grass at the White House. Taylor became President in 1849 but died 16 months after his inauguration, and it was Old Whitey who was in the procession following the casket.

The White House stables burnt in 1864, sadly killing the pony of President Lincoln's son Willie along with five other horses. Lincoln tried to save his son's pony by running into the stable. After the fire, Lincoln's aides saw him crying on the east side of the White House. Willie had died that same year, and Lincoln was anguished at the loss of one of the last ties to his son, which was his pony.

In 1871, President Ulysses S. Grant had a stable built to accommodate stalls for 25 horses, tack and harness rooms, along with living quarters for the staff. He loved his horses and kept the stables full, including his favorite warhorses—Cincinnati, Egypt, and Jeff Davis.

President Roosevelt (1901-1909) and his sons enjoyed horses. Once, his son Quinton brought his pony upstairs in the White House elevator to cheer up his sick bother Archie. Roosevelt was the last President to use the horses and stables at the White House. He was offered a car but proclaimed, "The Roosevelts are horse people." In 1911, the White House stables were demolished, as cars became the new horsepower for future Presidents.

~December 22~
The Show Horse

Showing horses for fun or as a professional is relatively new. Up until the 1940's, horses were mainly used as work animals, but as motorized tractors and automobiles replaced the workhorse, people found a whole new way to enjoy them, and for many, it was a new way to make a living with horses. From plows to the show ring, horses have been taken out of the fields and put into nice cozy stalls with deep comfortable bedding and often with no expense spared. Depending on the breed and discipline, the horse has needed to learn to stand quietly during hours of primping, bathing, clipping, brushing, and braiding, and that is only a small part of it all. They are dressed up with fancy bridles, saddles, and show clothes to match. Today's show horse may be a backyard horse that gets cleaned up for local shows or fair, or they may be a horse that is taken all the way to world competition or even to the Olympics.

The equine has evolved from a workhorse pulling a plow to a carriage show horse that knows how to strut his stuff. The show horse knows when it's time to enter the show ring and perform, and it is both exciting and terrifying for the moms and dads watching their child ride. The show horse demonstrates to us what they are capable of doing in a modern-day world, and they are nothing short of amazing.

There is one thing I've learned after years of going to horse shows. When the horses are finally back home and the bands are pulled from the braids, the show sheet is pulled off, and the horses are turned back outside, the horse just wants to be a horse and a good roll in the dirt is the better than any blue ribbon. That is when I humbly remember that they are still a horse above all else that matters, and it was a privilege to take them to a horse show. What a gift the horse gives us each and every day even in the show ring.

~December 23~
Those Beautiful Spots

They're unmistakably unique in color, and it's easy to do a double take when looking at the spot patterns that decorate their bodies. There is something special about the Appaloosa horse and its connection to the Native American Indians and their heritage.

When the Spaniards traveled to the Americas, they brought with them the tough horses of their native land. During this time some of their horses escaped and roamed free throughout Mexico and the Southwest. The Native Indians soon tamed these wild horses and began trading horses with other tribespeople as far as the Pacific Northwest. The Native Indians quickly recognized the value of these large pack and riding animals, but the Nez Percé tribesmen used the horses to their advantage. They became highly skilled equestrians and selectively bred the Spanish horses for great endurance and stamina. What made their horses incredibly unique were the leopard-spotted coats and other distinctive markings found only among a very small number of the Spanish horses. Those spotted horses are what caught the eye of the Nez Percé tribesmen, and they believed the horses were special above all others.

As settlers migrated to the area, they began referring to the spotted horses as "Palouse horses" because they roamed near the Palouse River in Northern Idaho, which crossed the tribal grounds of the Nez Percé people. In time the "Palouse Horse" became the Appaloosa. The Appaloosas of a century ago probably bore a closer resemblance to the horses used by the Nez Percé Indians. There has been a great effort to improve the Appaloosa breed over the last few decades with breeding to Quarter horses, Arabians, and even Thoroughbreds while making sure they keep those beautiful spots.

~December 24~
The Livery Stable

The livery stable was one of the central hubs (besides the saloon) of most towns before there were motorized vehicles. After all, horses were used for transportation and hauling goods, and if you were traveling through, then you needed a place to keep your horse overnight. Not everyone owned horses so the livery stable is where a person would go to rent a horse or team and a wagon. A person would look for the hotel or boarding house, and that is where they would find the livery stable. Usually they were attached or right next to each other, and horses could be boarded for a short time. The livery stable also had hay and water available and a farrier if a horse was in need of a new pair of shoes. Here is an advertisement for a livery stable that appeared in the Sacramento Daily Union in 1881.

Pioneer Livery Stable
Hacks on call any hour, day or night. Coupes, Phaetons, Rockaways, Barouches, Buggies with the best roadsters – the best to be found of any livery stable on the coast for hire. Horses kept at livery for reasonable rates. Livery Stable on Fourth Street, between I and J.

The livery stable was basically your one-stop shop for horses and vehicles. In larger cities, the livery stable was often proper and formal, while the ones out west were simple and said to offer more options. If you were a stranger in town, you would probably be asked to pay in advance to rent a horse, and there could be a deposit involved as well. If you were an upstanding citizen of the town, your word was usually good enough to rent a horse or buggy, and you could pay when you return. Your handshake was your promise that you would bring the horse back. If a person didn't return the horse to the livery stable, they would be considered a horse thief, and the posse would be sent out after them.

~December 25~
Return Of Horse Power

There are many people who would love to bring "real horsepower" back to our daily lives, and in specific industries, they are doing just that. Logging trees with horses is making a comeback on a smaller but more personal level. Newer logging companies are using draft horses to clear properties. It is in no way on the massive scale of a hundred years ago, but there are some huge benefits. Many customers hire a horse logging business because they get to see how it was done long before machines, and there is something peaceful and nostalgic about it. Harnessed horses leave only hoof prints (okay, maybe a few horse apples!), and it has been found that the horses don't push down the valuable soils like machines do. Horses can also easily get into areas the machines cannot.

There are also some smaller-scale farmers who have chosen to go back to horse and harness to till their fields and plant their crops. Sustainable farming practices using horses are popping up in Canada and parts of the United States, and it is growing.

Going back to the days of animal horsepower seems romantic, but it was often a very hard existence for both man and horse. I will admit, I would rather own horses for enjoyment and have the time to spoil them, than to use them as a full-time workhorse. They have given their time and done their duty for thousands of years, and now they deserve to be used in a much more admired and appreciated way. For the companies that are bringing back the horse for logging and other jobs, it is the perfect blend of the past and the future coming together with these powerful horses right in the middle of all of it. It looks like these gentle giants have jobs again and are returning to the workforce, but this time these noble equines will be treated more like celebrities by young and old alike. They deserve the best of both worlds and to be admired for what they can do.

~December 26~
Helping Prisoners Heal

For the men and women in the prison system, horses have helped in the healing for many of these broken people. Horse therapy in prisons is growing in the United States because there is proof now that the relationship between the horses and the inmates is actually helping some of these people.

Many of the inmates have dealt with heavy addictions, behavioral issues, or depression and human-to-human contact in some cases did not seem to work much in helping them. But in a few trials between the inmates and horses, studies showed that the animal brought out emotions and other positive traits that regular therapy could not. What was noticed was that the horses were helping the prisoners heal.

The horse is an incredibly special animal that will clearly show a person how they are feeling if you are willing to take the time and watch. Harriet Laurie, who works with the horses and inmates, has watched many positive outcomes for the inmates trying to get better through her program. She was quoted was quoted in an article saying, "Horses pick up on everything you're feeling. If you're anxious, uncertain, distracted, or aggressive, the horse will back off and turn away or ignore you. If, on the other hand, you're relaxed, focused, assertive and confident, you can get these horses to do anything you want."

Prisoners know what it's like to be confined and controlled, and in many ways they can relate to the horse's life. The pilot programs that have been tried out in the prison system have proven that horses help prisoners heal and move towards a more positive life. In the words of one young offender who participated in the horse therapy program, "I feel hope for the first time. This is just the beginning."

Love – it always protects, trusts, hopes and perseveres. 1 Corinthians 13:7

~December 27~
Because Of The Horse

I hope this book has given you a better understanding of what horses have endured for man's benefit, both in times of peace and times of war. Horses have been by our side through it all. But there are still a few things we haven't talked about in this book that I wanted to share—all because of the horse.

Because of the horse, little boys and girls learned how to care for something much more important than themselves. They learned that the world didn't revolve around them and the horse's care comes before their own wants and needs. They learned to sacrifice for something bigger.

Because of the horse, men and women changed direction in their careers and chose to become veterinarians, horse trainers, barn managers and so many other occupations in the horse industry. They have chosen to dedicate their work to help improve the lives of horses all over the world.

Because of the horse, the dreams of their youth are finally coming true for so many adults who have raised their children or put their career first for so many years. It's the dream they tucked away years earlier, praying and hoping that one day they could live it. Because of the horse a new chapter has opened and they are ready to ride off into the sunset. For the horse that is lucky enough to be owned by an older person, there is nothing more beautiful.

It has shown us that the horse was put on this earth for so many special reasons and some of those reasons come in the simplest and purest forms with no strings attached except our heartstrings. ~Author unknown

Thank you Lord for the gift of the horse.

~December 28~
Epic Fail

It was 1910, and the ship The Terra Nova was supposed to set out on an expedition to the South Pole for scientific research. Instead, it quickly turned into a race to the South Pole after another Norwegian explorer announced his ship was heading out to be the first to reach the pole.

Captain Lawrence "Titus" Oates had signed on for the expedition, but once he came aboard, he was shocked at the nineteen horses that had been purchased for $6.55 each that would help the team get to the pole. A crew member who knew absolutely nothing about horses bought the small grey and white Manchurian ponies that were extremely unfit for the long journey. Oates also quickly realized that there was not enough fodder for the ponies to eat while on the trip, so he purchased two extra tons with his own money. They quickly set off and once they hit Antarctica, the men set up base at Camp Evans, and from there it would be a 900-mile trek on land to the pole. Once the ponies were on land, it was quite evident, given their poor condition; they would not have the strength to walk any distance through heavy snow, even with snowshoes. The ponies were already weak from the long trip and it was suggested that the weaker horses be killed and the meat saved to feed the sled dogs. That never happened and many of the sick ponies died. Then to make matters much worse, during one night, the snow-covered area where the horses were standing broke wide open with nothing but water surrounding the ice. Soon a dozen killer whales were circling the ice and watching the horses. One horse spooked and fell into the water, and more followed to their death. The men tried to save as many horses as they could, but only one survived for a little longer. In the end, every horse and man died, and the Robert Scott Expedition was considered an epic fail due to extremely poor planning.

~December 29~
Dressage

The word dressage means "training" in French, and its goal is to ride in complete harmony with your horse through gentle communication and positive horsemanship. The earliest work on training horses was written by Xenophon. He was a Greek Military Commander born around 400 BC who wanted to teach the military soldiers that they could have a relationship with their horses which would improve both their riding skills and the horse's well-being. He also wanted to teach the men proper care of the horses. He believed that what happens out of the saddle will transfer into the saddle, and they are deeply connected. Dressage was a new way of learning to understand the horse to make the relationship better while also creating a stronger military. Before Xenophon, horses were at the mercy of their riders, and often cruel bits and other means of control were put on the horse to make them obey or face severe pain. Man's fear of these large animals was the motivation behind the harsh equipment used in these early civilizations.

Using dressage training techniques on horses continued to evolve and be developed by the military into the Renaissance period. The riders trained their horses to perform movements that would make them more maneuverable in battle, with the intention to out maneuver, escape, or attack the enemy. Europeans displayed their highly trained horses in exhibitions, and the Imperial Spanish Riding School of Vienna established in the 16th century was pivotal in promoting dressage training. We use those same principles today in modern dressage.

Dressage is unique because it was founded as a way to create great warhorses. Throughout the centuries, dressage has evolved into the elegant dance of the horse and rider that we are familiar with today.

~December 30~
Half Man/Half Beast

The Aztecs held a position of absolute power in the Mesoamerican culture that flourished in parts of Central America from 1300 to 1521. When the Spanish explorer Hernán Cortés landed on the coast of the Gulf of Mexico in February 1519, he came with a small fleet of 11 ships, 490 soldiers, and a few horses. Horses were costly, and Cortés who was an expert horseman, could only acquire 16 horses for the trip.

The Aztecs had never before seen a horse, and the closest animal they could compare it to was the deer, but there were no deer anywhere near the size of the massive warhorses the Spanish rode onto their land. The Aztecs had never seen men transported on the backs of animals, and when the cavalry were first sighted, they were looked upon as supernatural creatures that were half man/half beast. This impression was magnified by the shiny metal armor the horses wore over their head and body, and it made them seemingly impossible to kill.

The horse played an integral role in the Spanish conquests of the Aztecs and Incans. The horse was an unusual and strange creature to the Aztecs who had never before seen such a beast, and the added fact that the Spaniards had tamed these animals and were riding them sent fear into the people. These native tribes believed these horses were mystical, powerful, and even spiritual beasts. The impact these warhorses had on the Aztec warriors gave the Spaniards a unique and strong advantage in battle. It is said that the horses are what helped Cortés be successful in his conquests against the native people. The awe-factor of the warhorses they brought with them set the stage for how future battles would be fought in the new land—with the horse.

And the armies which are in heaven, clothed in fine linen, white and clean, were following Him on white horses. Revelation 19:14

~December 31~
What Will I Be?

As I finished writing the first draft of this book, I found myself both exhausted and inspired. I learned things I never dreamed a horse could experience or endure, and it made me think about this incredible animal that God created. In its most primitive form of domestication, horses were used to pull things with their tails. As civilizations studied the equine, they understood the beast's great power and the military might it could bring if they could harness it. Soon the horse was put into the harshest equipment and made to obey without a quiver so that kings could conquer kings. How did the horse survive the last five thousand years of hard work for man's personal gain? It gives me chills when I think about it. But God knew what he was doing when he created this perfect animal, and now it's my responsibility to make sure the horses at my farm are well-taken care of. Like so many generations before me, the most God-honoring thing we can do is teach the next generation how to be the best horse owners they can possibly be.

What kind of horse owner will I be? I hope to be one of compassion and patience daily, even when at times, it's difficult. I hope to keep learning so I can create a better life for the horses entrusted to me during their short time on this earth. The horse deserves nothing less. The horses of today's modern world may not work as hard as the horses of the past, but they still need to be treated with dignity and respect. My prayer is that this book will have opened your mind to the incredible willingness the horse has given to man since their domestication. There has never been another animal that has helped change the history of the human race like the horse, and for that, I am thankful to the Lord. What a beautiful gift He gave us wrapped up in a long mane, flowing tail, and a willing heart as big as the moon.

"But ask the animals, and they will teach you, or the birds in the sky, and they will tell you; or speak to the earth, and it will teach you, or let the fish in the sea inform you. Which of all these does not know that the hand of the Lord has done this? In his hand is the life of every creature and the breath of all mankind."

Job 12:7-10

References/Sources

Jan. 1 Horse-Powered Locomotive https://www.amusingplanet.com/2021/07/horse-powered-locomotives.html
Jan. 2 Incredible Legacy americasbestracing.net/the-sport/2016-man-o-war-the-measuring-stick-greatness
Jan. 3 The Bond https://www.historynet.com/majestic-mounts-the-bond-between-horse-and-soldier.htm
Jan. 4 Industrial Revolution resilience.org/stories/2013-03-15/the-big-shift-last-time-from-horse-dung-to-car-smog/
Jan. 5 Medical Evacuation https://historyofyesterday.com/the-history-of-the-ambulance-ecc2d63fb1a6
Jan. 6 Trigger -https://horseyhooves.com/trigger-roy-rogers-horse
Jan. 7 The Perfect Design http://www.equineheritageinstitute.org/shaping-civilizations-the-role-of-the-horse-in-human-societies/
Jan. 8 An Angel Among Us -https://www.cnn.com/2018/05/15/sport/sergeant-reckless-warhorse
Jan. 9 The Norse Horse skemman.is/bitstream/1946/16675/1/Horses%20in%20the%20norse%20sources%20MIS%20thesis.pdf
Jan. 10 The Russian Troika https://www.rbth.com/history/332458-russian-troika-facts
Jan. 11 The Marsh Tacky explorebeaufortsc.com/the-story-of-the-marsh-tacky-beaufort-born-and-bred/
Jan. 12 Little Bighorn https://www.thevintagenews.com/2017/12/18/horse-named-comanche
Jan. 13 The Queen's Horses https://horseyhooves.com/queen-elizabeth-horses/
https://www.induehorse.com/celebrity-lists/10-facts-about-the-queen-and-her-horses/
Jan. 14 Ponies At The Poles www.horsetalk.co.nz/2012/12/29/ponies-at-the-poles-proud-history/
Jan. 15 The Harness http://www.equineheritageinstitute.org/horses-in-history/
Jan. 16 The First Fire Horse firehistory.weebly.com/a-history-of-horses-in-the-fire-service.html
Jan. 17 Losing Their Jobs https://livinghistoryfarm.org/farminginthe40s/machines_13.html
Jan. 18 Ship In Distress httpsrnli.org/about-us/our-history/timeline/1899-launch-from-porlock-weir
Jan. 19 Leroy https://www.atlasobscura.com/articles/the-1976-great-american-horse-race-was-won-by-a-mule-named-lord-fauntleroy
Jan. 21 The Rodeo https://worldsoldestrodeo.com/history/
Jan.22 Logging https://digitalcommons.library.umaine.edu/cgi/viewcontent.cgi?article=1055&context=mainehistoryjournal
Jan. 23 Pit Ponies horsejournals.com/popular/history-heritage/pit-ponies-ghosts-coal-mines
Jan. 24 Horse Latitudes https://oceanservice.noaa.gov/facts/horse-latitudes.html
Jan. 26 Tea For Horses https://discoverplaces.travel/en/the-horse-in-china-history-culture-legend-and-sport-of-kings-the-polo/
Jan. 27 Horse Training horsebreaking.wordpress.com/2009/05/20/the-history-of-horse-breaking/
Jan. 28 Mercury thewarhorsememorial.org/100-hero-horses/hero-horse-number-30-mercury-the-gentle-giant/
Jan. 29 It's Now The Law https://goodnewsforpets.com/history-of-aspca-started-with-a-horse.
Jan. 30 Kings Rode Horses https://grantvillegazette.com/article/publish-341/
Jan. 31 The Status Symbol https://www.medievalists.net/2011/11/horses-as-status-symbols-medieval-icelandic-horses-as-symbols-of-masculine-honor-in-a-one-sexed-world/
Feb. 2 Marengo https://horse-canada.com/horses-and-history/marengo-napoleons-favourite-horse/
https://gustavomirabalcastro.online/en/horses/marengo-napoleon-bonapartes-horse/
Feb. 3 The Bell Marehttps://buckarooleather.com/blogs/buckaroo-johns-blog/history-of-pack-

animals worldwar1centennial.org/index.php?Itemid=292
Feb. 4 Koumiss https://www.centralasia-travel.com/en/countries/uzbekistan/cuisine/kumiss
Feb. 5 Tremendous Machine https://www.horseracingnation.com/news/The_Tremendous_Size_of_Secretariat_s_Heart_123https tcdhorseracing.com/secretariat/
https://www.secretariat.com/secretariat-history/
Feb. 6 Mexican Charro Horse apimagesblog.com/blog/2014/10/15/mexicos-charro-horse-tradition
Feb. 7 It's A Hanging Offense https://truewestmagazine.com/when-did-they-stop-hanging-men-for-horse-theft-also-what-was-the-penalty-after-hanging-was-outlawed/
https://ezinearticles.com/?Horse-Stealing---A-Hanging-Offense&id=6478962
Feb. 8 First Natural Horsemanship worksofchivalry.com/bitless-equitation-in-ancient-times-2/
Feb. 9 Doctor Peyo https://sjm-patterson.medium.com/doctor-peyo-the-horse-doctor-775685e0318b
Feb. 10 The Earliest Olympics https://omahaequestrian.org/equestrian-history-at-the-olympics/
Feb. 11 The Long Day .farmcollector.com/farm-life/farming-with-horses-zm0z22janzram/
Feb. 12 Strongest Of Them All https://horseyhooves.com/strongest-horse-breeds/
Feb. 13 Jousting horse-canada.com/horses-and-history/knights-and-horses-of-the-middle-age
Feb. 14 Campdrafting https://itsmypony.com/horsing-around/campdrafting
Feb. 15 Horseshoes https://dressagetoday.com/horse-health-/history-of-horseshoes
Feb. 16 The Cavalry Blacks thefield.co.uk/country-house/queens-horses-black-beauties-knightsbridge-31908
Feb. 18 The Riderless Horse https://theskeletonkeychronicles.com/2021/05/18/the-riderless-horse
Feb. 19 Merlin https://madridbullfighting.com/blog/merlin-the-bullfighting-horse/
Feb. 20 Milk Delivery https://faceintheblue.wordpress.com/2009/11/26/milkman/
Feb. 21 The Bedouin Legend https://www.stepbystep.com/Arabian-Horses-in-Bedouin-Legend
Feb. 22 Jim Key kellykazek.com/2020/01/04/the-story-of-beautiful-jim-key-the-horse-that-could-read-and-do-math/
https://ilovehorses.net/history-2/beautiful-jim-key-the-lost-history-of-the-worlds-smartest-horse/
Feb. 23 Deep Scars https://equusmagazine.com/blog-equus/blood-trail-endurance-escape-history-horse-54038/
Feb. 24 Nelson & Blueskin https://www.mountvernon.org/library/digitalhistory/digital-encyclopedia/article/nelson-horse/
https://www.horsenation.com/2015/02/16/nelson-and-blueskin-the-first-horses-of-the-united-states/
Feb. 25 Warhorses Missing https://allthingsliberty.com/2018/08/war-horses-gone-astray/
Feb. 26 Snow & Mud https://www.hhhistory.com/2019/02/horses-wearing-snowshoes.html
Feb. 27 World War One https://primaryfacts.com/5369/horses-in-world-war-1-facts-and-information/
www.historyhit.com/the-role-of-horses-in-world-war-one/
Feb. 28 The Arabian https://alexarabians.com/arabian-horse-history/
https://horseracingsense.com/discover-the-arabian-horse-past-to-present/
March 1 Rex https://portside.org/2019-12-26/rex-mine-pony
March 2 Seine Fishing countrytraveleronline.com/2021/10/24/the-columbias-fishing-horses/
March 3 Hawaii https://parkerranch.com/legacy/history-of/hawaii/wild-horses-waipio-valley-hi/
March 4 Medical Advancements understandinganimalresearch.org.uk/what-is-animal-research/a-z-animals/equid
https://www.animalresearch.info/en/medical-advances/nobel-prizes/interactions-between-tumour-viruses-and-genetic-components-o/
March 5 They Never Forget https://listverse.com/2014/01/22/10-fascinating-facts-about-horses/
March 6 The Artillery Horse https://www.napoleon-series.org/military-info/organization/France/Artillery/c_artilleryhorses.html

March 7 Mustang https://www.livescience.com/27686-mustangs.html
https://www.namarmustangs.com/history
March 8 That Amazing Nose https://horse-canada.com/magazine/miscellaneous/10-amazing-facts-equine-smell/
March 9 Snowman http://horsestarshalloffame.org/inductees/82/snowman.aspx
March 10 The Horse Action Saddle thequackdoctor.com/index.php/vigors-horse-action-saddle/
March 11 Guns A Blazing! https://sassnet.com/Mounted-What-is-001A.php
March 12 Endurance Racing Today helpfulhorsehints.com/best-endurance-horse-breeds/
March 13 Spanish Riding Schoolvisitingvienna.com/sights/lipizzaner/visitingvienna.com/sights/spanish-riding-school-history/
March 14 The Wagon Train https://www.history.com/topics/westward-expansion/conestoga-wagon
March 15 Horses And Farming https://blog.aghires.com/history-of-horses/
March 16 The Wedding Gift https://www.theknot.com/content/native-american-wedding-traditionshttps://mongolianstore.com/mongolian-wedding/https://www.aaanativearts.com/cherokee-and-sioux-courtship-and-wedding-customs
March 17 The 80-1 Longshot https://www.bloodhorse.com/horse-racing/thoroughbred/rich-strike/2019
https://en.wikipedia.org/wiki/Rich_Strike
March 18 Jigitovka https://www.rbth.com/lifestyle/326541-did-you-know-that-cossack
March 19 The Games As We Know Them https://omahaequestrian.org/equestrian-history-at-the-olympics/
https://www.topendsports.com/events/discontinued/equestrian.htm
March 20 The Roping Horse https://www.silverspursrodeo.com/the-history-of-team-roping/
March 21 Circuit Riding preacher http://afs.okstate.edu/breeds/horses/tennesseewalking/index.html
March 22 Ancient Egyptian Horses www.timelessmyths.com/history/horses-in-ancient-egypt/
March 23 Mini-Me https://angelsforminis.com/history
https://www.theminiaturehorse.com/historyminiatures.htm
March 24 Bucephalus https://horseyhooves.com/alexander-the-great-horse-bucephalus/
https://www.worldhistory.org/Bucephalus/
March 25 Ice Harvesting bigrivermagazine.com/br.story.ice.htmlscugogheritage.com/history/harvest-ice.htm
March 26 The Newspaper https://burlingtonhistory.org/horse-and-buggy-days-runaways-brought-all-excitement-and-danger
March 27 The Cattle Drive https://equitrekking.com/articles/entry/cattle_drive_history/
March 28 Ban'ei https://www.odditycentral.com/events/banei-the-worlds-slowest-horse-race.html
March 29 The Boat Ridehttps://annearundelhorses.blogspot.com/2010/12/transporting-horses.html
https://military-history.fandom.com/wiki/Horse_transports_in_the_Middle_Ages
March 30 The Trolley Car https://movingnorthcarolina.net/horse-trolley/
March 31 Mounted Drill Team https://okeda.weebly.com/history-of-drill.html
April 1 The Sacrifice https://www.adidam.org/adida/religion/ashvamedha.htm
www.ancient-origins.net/news-history-archaeology/archaeologists-unearth-gruesome-site-where-chinese-emperors-sacrificed
April 2 Police Horse Training https://www.haddontraining.co.uk/police-horses-and-natalie-matthews/
https://cowgirlmagazine.com/police-horses-trained/
April 3 The Makeover https://equinewellnessmagazine.com/exterme-mustang-makeover/
https://mustangheritagefoundation.org/about/#history
April 4 The Most Courageous www.horseandhound.co.uk/features/15-famous-horses-775684
April 5 Mounted Orienteering https://www.equisearch.com/articles/orienteering081201a
April 6 Airborne practicalhorsemanmag.com/lifestyle/jim-wofford-history-transporting-horses-31713
April 7 The English Saddle statelinetack.com/statelinetack-articles/the-history-of-the-english-

saddle/9585/
April 8 Polo https://www.polomuseum.com/sport-polo/history-polo
April 9 Mongol Derby https://equestrianists.com/the-mongol-derby/
https://equestrianists.com/guides/mongol-derby/#4-the-horses
April 10 Time To Retire https://www.msn.com/en-us/news/us/duke-the-longest-serving-member-of-the-lancaster-mounted-police-unit-is-retiring-after-18-years/ar-BB1gzEmv
April 11 Stunt Doubles https://www.horsejournals.com/popular/interviews-profiles/horses-hollywood-movies
April 12 The Samurai https://samurai-world.com/kisouma-samurai-horses/
April 13 The Thoroughbred helpfulhorsehints.com/the-thoroughbred-horse-breed-profile/
April 14 The Icelandic Horse https://www.ancient-origins.net/news-history-archaeology/how-vikings-started-worldwide-distribution-gaited-horses-006434
https://www.cnn.com/2016/03/22/sport/gallery/icelandic-horses/index.html
April 15 Public Health hazard
http://www.livingcityarchive.org/htm/living_city/development_lab/develop.htm
https://fee.org/articles/the-great-horse-manure-crisis-of-1894/
April 16 The Four Horsemen https://annehcampbell.com/horse-colors-in-medieval-art-and-life/
April 17 Horse-Pulling https://www.minotdailynews.com/news/local-news/2021/07/team-pulls-13500-pounds-at-state-fair-horse-pull-event/
April 18 Hunting On Horseback sportsnhobbies.org/which-type-of-horse-is-suitable-for-hunting.htm
April 19 Falconry On Horseback cheval.culture.fr/en/page/the_history_of_falconry_on_horseback
https://www.atlasobscura.com/articles/horseback-falconry-lesson
April 20 Horse Car On Rails https://www.american-historama.org/1801-1828-evolution/horsecar.htm
April 21 The Mule https://truewestmagazine.com/article/the-history-of-mules/
April 22 Stroller horsenation.com/2015/03/13/horses-in-history-stroller-the-olympic-wonder-pony/
April 23 Mister Ed http www.ranker.com/list/history-of-mr-ed-horse-bamboo-harvester/cynthia-griffith
April 24 Military Maneuvers https://museumofmoderntheatre.wordpress.com/orphan-essays/313-
April 25 Jesse https://gearjunkie.com/outdoor/hiking/national-forest-service-retired-mule
April 26 Those Beautiful Eyes https://horse-canada.com/magazine/miscellaneous/10-amazing-facts-equine-vision/
April 27 Horse Powered Wine daily.sevenfifty.com/how-farming-with-horses-makes-better-wine/
April 28 Darcy Day https://www.goodreads.com/book/show/10678266-when-sophie-met-darcy-day
https://www.greatwoodcharity.org/about.html
April 29 The Aussie Police Horse https://theconversation.com/from-colonial-cavalry-to-mounted-police-a-short-history-of-the-australian-police-horse-165087
April 30 Ship Ahoy! https://rnli.org/about-us/our-history/timeline/1936-last-horse-powered-launch
http://happisburgh.org.uk/history/sea/lifeboats/?COLLCC=1381643903
May 2 A Time To Honor https://equitrekking.com/articles/entry/famous_horses_in_history_-_the_fire_horse
May 3 The Religious Ceremony buzzsharer.com/2021/09/19/horses-mythology-and-symbolism/
May 4 Ancient Rome https://imperiumromanum.pl/en/article/horses-in-ancient-rome/
May 5 Feeding Horses equinewellnessmagazine.com/
https://medievalbritain.com/type/medieval-life/activities/medieval-horse-what-was-life-like-for-horses-in-the-middle-ages/
May 6 Diphtheria //www.fda.gov/media/110418/download
May 7 Pony Express https://postalmuseum.si.edu/research/articles-from-enroute/the-story-of-the-pony-express.html
https://loneliestroad.us/history/
May 8 Jack & Jack https://equitrekking.com/articles/entry/famous_horses_in_history_-

_the_fire_horse
May 9 Chetak https://myudaipurcity.com/chetak-horse/
May 10 Figure https://www.morganhorse.com/about/museum/morgan-horse-history/
May 11 Reining https://allaboutreining.weebly.com/history.html
May 12 Trading For Power medium.com/history-in-bytes/the-history-behind-horse-trading-in-politics-7c440dd37cfd
May 13 Ancient Greek Life www.colorado.edu/classics/2018/06/19/horses-ancient-greek-life
May 14 The Quest For Wood horsejournals.com/life-horses/horses-jobs-logging-horses
May 15 Horse Of A Different Color sciencedaily.com/releases/2016/12/161207091114.htm
May 16 The Carousel showmensmuseum.org/vintage-carnival-rides/tracing-the-roots-of-the-carousel/
May 17 Humble Beginnings grunge.com/320443/the-history-of-the-budweiser-clydesdales-explained/
May 18 The Best Horses https://www.history.com/news/horses-plains-indians-native-americans
May 19 Opening The American West   https://www.easterndrafthorse.com/history-of-the-draft-horse
https://www.easterndrafthorse.com/history-of-the-draft-horse
May 20 The Flood https://www.metaspoon.com/100-horses-trapped-island-netherlands-rescue/
May 21 Skepticism Of The Automobile saturdayeveningpost.com/2017/01/get-horse-americas-skepticism-toward-first-automobiles/themoderatevoice.com/will-cars-ever-replace-the-family-horse/
May 22 The Stagecoach Horses imh.org/exhibits/past/legacy-of-the-horse/stage-travel-america/
May 23 South Of The Sahara https://blogs.scientificamerican.com/tetrapod-zoology/domestic-horses-of-africa/
May 24 The Space Shuttle http://astrodigital.org/space/stshorse.html
May 25 Carriage Driving https://www.cookscarriages.com/history-of-the-horse-drawn-carriage
https://www.wehorse.com/en/blog/horse-driving/
May 26 The Insane Disguise https://www.wearethemighty.com/articles/military-disguises/
May 27 The Police Horse https://equusmagazine.com/horse-world/mountedpolice/
May 28 Forest Service Mustang https://www.fs.usda.gov/features/wild-mustangs-help-forest-service-wilderness-rangers-do-their-jobs
May 29 Vanning https://www.museumofthehorse.org/a-history-of-transporting-horses/
May 30 The White Horse https://www.nationaltribune.com.au/new-zealand-gifts-white-horse-to-nikko-toshogu-shrine-in-japan/
www.lrgaf.org/military/hirohito.htm
May 31 The Saddles https://www.ofhorse.com/view-post/History-of-the-Saddle
June 1 Jappaloup De Luze https://equusmagazine.com/blog-equus/jappeloup-pierre-durand-olympic-film/
June 2 Time For A Change https://www.horsejournals.com/popular/history-heritage/pit-ponies-ghosts-coal-mines
June 3 The Buffalo Hunt https://www.history.com/news/horses-plains-indians-native-americans
June 4 Horses In The Bible http://equest4truth.com/equus-in-the-bible/122-horses-in-the-bible
June 5 Traveller https://www.historynet.com/robert-e-lees-horse-traveller.htm
https://lovetheenergy.com/traveller/
June 6 The Only Wild Horse Left greenglobaltravel.com/mongolian-horse-przewalskis-horse-takhi/
June 7 To All The Old Cow horses   https://www.pinterest.com/pin/763289836820044442/
June 8 Sharing The Roads https://www.hagerty.com/media/automotive-history/the-harebrained-idea-to-help-horses-get-used-to-horseless-carriages/
June 10 In Times Of Desperation theatlantic.com/technology/archive/2017/06/horse-meat/529665/
June 11 The First Speed Limits todayincthistory.com/2020/05/21/may-21-first-speed-limit-law-in-the-u-s roadandtrack.com/car-culture/news/a29272/the-first-speed-limit-law-was-passed-on-this-day-in-1901/

394

June 12 Sport Of Kings https://ezinearticles.com/?History-of-Thoroughbred-Racing-in-the-USA&id=481513
https://www.allhorseracing.ag/horseracing-history
June 13 The American Indian Horse https://breed-horse.com/american-indian-horse/
June 14 The Western White House presidentialpetmuseum.com/ronald-reagans-ranch-horses/
June 15 Miracle Twins https://www.dailymail.co.uk/news/article-5876215/Identical-twin-horse-foals-born-Exeter-10-000-1-chance-surviving.html
June 16 Horse Crazy Celebrities https://www.doubledtrailers.com/youll-never-believe-these-famous-celebrities-that-love-horses/
June 17 Doma Menorquina https://www.horsebreedspictures.com/menorquin-horse.asp
https://en.wikipedia.org/wiki/Doma_menorquina
June 18 Women And Horses https://www.horsenation.com/2014/11/17/olympic-girl-power-the-incredible-story-of-lis-hartel/
June 19 The Meat Eater https://thehorseaholic.com/the-forgotten-story-of-meat-eating-horses/
https://www.horsetalk.co.nz/2012/04/17/horses-as-meat-eating-killers/
June 20 La Voltige https://www.fei.org/stories/history-of-vaulting
June 21 "Blue" Lakota War horse notesfromthefrontier.com/post/in-honor-of-a-magnificent-warhorse
June 22 The Horse Galloping Ceremony https://www.handzaround.com/journal-1/in-the-heart-of-oromia-horse-galloping-ceremony
June 23 Real Horsepower! https://medium.com/lessons-from-history/why-britain-pulled-aircraft-with-horses-and-trucks-ddd2dbd2aaa4
June 24 Equine Reenactors https://piedmontvirginian.com/riding-through-history/
June 25 This Armor Is Heavy! https://en.wikipedia.org/wiki/Barding
https://www.metmuseum.org/toah/hd/hors/hd_hors .
June 26 Chinese Horse Proverb thoughtco.com/chinese-proverbs-sai-weng-lost-his-horse-2278437
June 28th Harness Racing https://www.britannica.com/sports/harness-racing
June 29 Left or Right Handed http://www.equineheritageinstitute.org/learning-center/horse-facts/
June 30 Cincinnati https://www.horsenation.com/2016/02/29/horses-in-history-famous-horses-of-the-civil-war/
https://www.civilwarmonitor.com/blog/grants-war-horse-cincinnati
July 1 Belle And Sundance https://www.cbc.ca/news/canada/british-columbia/10-year-mcbride-horse-rescue-1.4958619
July 2 The Movies
https://www.salon.com/2012/04/02/hollywoods_long_history_of_animal_cruelty/
July 3 Old wives tales https://theequinereport.com/2016/10/old-wives-tales-about-horses/
July 4 Light Horse Troop https://www.theplaidhorse.com/2017/07/04/the-horses-that-led-us-to-independence/
July 5 The Posse https://www.arapahoegov.com/2116/History-of-Mounted-Patrol
July 6 The Good Death irongateequine.com/education/methodsofeuthanasia
https://horseracingsense.com/how-are-horses-euthanized-where-are-buried/
July 7 Making People Laugh https://www.breyerhorses.com/blogs/famous-horses/pokerjoe
July 8 Palomo https://dbpedia.org/page/Palomo_(horse)
July 9 Equine Therapy https://www.ofhorse.com/view-post/The-History-of-Equine-Therapy
July 10 Love In A Tiny Body https://www.ctvnews.ca/health/hospital-trots-out-mini-horses-to-comfort-sick-patients-1.2132259
July 11 War Paint https://www.animationsource.org/spirit/en/articles/Native-American-Horse-Paint-Symbols/227787.html&id_film=16
July 12 The Cutting Horse artbycrane.com/riding_styles_disciplines/western/cutting.html
July 13 Amish https://ohiosamishcountry.com/articles/the-amish-and-their-horses
July 14 Medicine Hat Horse beautifulbadlandsnd.com/wild-horses-of-the-badlands-are-they-special/

https://cowgirlmagazine.com/medicine-hat-horse/
July 15 The Last Pit Pony https://www.mirror.co.uk/news/uk-news/the-last-pit-pony-704425
July 16 The Hunter/Jumper http://prohunterjumper.com/history-of-hunter-jumper-competitions/
July 17 A Very Special Horse https://www.horsetalk.co.nz/2021/08/30/sixth-sense-para-equestrian-horses/
July 18 Shetland https://www.shetlandwithlaurie.com/the-blog/shetland-ponies-a-brief-history#/
July 19 Chincoteague https://pony-chincoteague.com/history.html
July 20 Copenhagen https://www.globetrotting.com.au/copenhagen
July 21 Tithes, Taxes And Rules https://www.warhistoryonline.com/medieval/11-facts-never-knew-medieval-warhorses.html
July 22 Riding The Rails https://www.museumofthehorse.org/a-history-of-transporting-horses/
https://horsenetwork.com/2017/09/brief-history-horse-transport-thankful-trailers-today/
July 23 Old Billy https://equineink.com/2021/01/18/old-billy-the-worlds-oldest-horse/
https://www.historic-uk.com/CultureUK/Old-Billy-The-Barge-Horse
July 24 Horse Whims https://core.ac.uk/download/pdf/14342686.pdf
July 25 Horsepower https://www.chronofhorse.com/article/james-watt-and-revolution-horsepower
July 26 Sandy https://www.globetrotting.com.au/sandy-australias-only-war-horse-to-return-home/
https://www.awm.gov.au/articles/encyclopedia/horses/sandy
July 27 Chariot Racing https://earlychurchhistory.org/entertainment/famous-horses-in-romes-chariot-races/
http://imh.org/exhibits/past/legacy-of-the-horse/circus-maximus/
July 28 The Capture https://www.americanindianmagazine.org/story/art-capturing-horses
July 29 Chemical Warfare https://www.armedforcesmuseum.com/wwi-gas-mask-for-horses/
July 30 Tent –Pegging https://ustpf.org/history-of-tent-pegging-standards
July 31 The Disney Horses https://disneyparks.disney.go.com/blog/2021/10/meet-the-new-disneyland-horses-at-circle-d-ranch/
Aug. 1 Mackinac Island https://cloghaun.com/2022/04/25/the-horses-of-mackinac-island/
Aug. 2 Babieca www.artbycrane.com/horse_history_articles_tales/thesupremewarhorseofspain.html
Aug. 3 The Parade https://www.usef.org/compete/disciplines/parade-horse
Aug. 4 Never Forget https://www.susanleyland.com/war-horse
Aug. 5 Horse Act 1535https://www.communitiesforhorses.org/blog/feral-ponies-of-wales-/i-know--happens-but-i-do-not-want-to-think-about-it
https://www.ponybox.com/news_details.php?id=3425
Aug. 6 The Horse Stable https://www.italymagazine.com/featured-story/augustus-stables-rome-be-reburied-lack-funds
https://www.primestables.co.uk/blog/a-complete-history-of-horse-stables-through-the-ages/
Aug. 7 Expectant Mothers hatchingcatnyc.com/2021/12/06/holiday-horse-shortage-horse-tales-new-york/
Aug. 8 Gulf Of Mares https://www.oocities.org/colosseum/park/3450/history.html
Aug. 9 Fantasia https://inmoroccotravel.com/fantasia-in-morocco/
https://www.diariesofmagazine.com/the-tbourida-in-morocco/
Aug. 10 Barge Horses https://www.horsejournals.com/popular/history-heritage/horses-jobs-barge-horses
https://www.canaljunction.com/craft/horsedrawn.htm
Aug. 11 Kasztanka https://en.wikipedia.org/wiki/Kasztanka
https://www.warhistoryonline.com/instant-articles/most-famous-horses-in-warfare.html?chrome=1
Aug. 12 The Ferryboat https://www.shipwreckworld.com/articles/horse-powered-ferry-boat-discovered-in-lake-champlain
Aug. 14 Bits equineman.com/the-history-of-horse-bits/
www.sportingcollection.com/bits/aboutbits.html
Aug. 15 Road Rage https://www.geriwalton.com/carriage-accidents-and-remedies/

Aug. 16 Fire Horse No. 12 hoofcare.blogspot.com/2015/04/the-hoof-of-fire-horse-number-12.html
Aug. 17 Xenophon https://www.chronofhorse.com/article/xenophon-forefather-dressage
Aug. 18 Forty Belgian Draft Horses https://archive.jsonline.com/news/obituaries/112641449.html/
Aug. 19 The Jinx historynet.com/majestic-mounts-the-bond-between-horse-and-soldier/
Aug. 20 World War Two https://tishamartin.com/2018/03/30/horses-during-world-war-two/
https://olive-drab.com/od_army-horses-mules_ww2.php
https://834795671654430932.weebly.com/horses-and-mules.html
Aug. 21 Harvesting The Sea https://www.farmshow.com/a_article.php?aid=31492
https://www.horsejournals.com/popular/history-heritage/horses-jobs-harvesting-sea
Aug. 22 The Farm Horse https://www.geriwalton.com/jobs-for-horses-what-work-they-did-in-the-1800s/
https://blog.aghires.com/history-of-horses/
Aug. 23 Circus Maximus http://imh.org/exhibits/past/legacy-of-the-horse/circus-maximus/
https://www.historyhit.com/locations/circus-maximus/
Aug. 24 Black Jack https://www.horseandman.com/horse-stories/black-jack-the-caparisoned-horse-and-caissons-memorial-day/05/30/2021/
Aug. 25 Lewis And Clark https://lewis-clark.org/horses/horse-chronicles/
https://www.papertrell.com/apps/preview/The-Handy-History-Answer-Book/Handy%20Answer%20book/What-was-the-goal-of-the-Lewis-and-Clark-expedition/001137010/content/SC/52caff6a82fad14abfa5c2e0_Default.html
Aug. 26 The Shunting Horse booksandmud.blogspot.com/2016/09/the-fall-of-railway-horse_67.html
Aug. 27 The Gelding https://www.thesprucepets.com/definition-of-gelding-1886645
https://en.wikipedia.org/wiki/Horse_culture_in_Mongolia
Aug. 28 Vonolel thewarhorsememorial.org/100-hero-horses/hero-horse-number-24-vonolel-the-reliable/
https://comeheretome.com/2010/06/22/the-grave-of-vonolel-the-famous-and-bemedalled-horse/
Aug. 29 Faithful Until Death horsejournals.com/popular/history-heritage/real-war-horses-faithful-unto-death
Aug. 30 Dream Alliance https://www.msn.com/en-gb/entertainment/tv/dream-alliance-how-a-horse-born-on-a-slag-heap-went-on-to-win-the-welsh-grand-national/ar-AAKFjqb
Aug. 31 Horses In Art https://www.fei.org/stories/100-years/horses-art-throughout-ages
Sept. 1 Barrel Racing https://wranglernetwork.com/news/the-history-of-barrel-racing/
Sept. 2 Horse Manure Crazies -The little book of horse poop, A collection of tips, truths and tributes
Sept. 4 Big Game And Fast Cats https://www.amnh.org/exhibitions/horse/how-we-shaped-horses-how-horses-shaped-us/sport/the-thrill-of-the-chase
Sept. 5 Long Live The Friesian nwfhc.com/about-the-friesian-horse/history-of-the-friesian-horse/
Sept. 6 Horseball http://www.fihb-horseball.org/
Sept. 7 How Many Hands? https://horseracingsense.com/why-do-we-measure-horses-in-hands/
Sept. 8 Star https://equitrekking.com/articles/entry/sybil-ludington-and-her-horse-star-heroes-of-the-american-revolution/
Sept. 9 Face Protection
metmuseum.org/art/collection/search/25420https://lustandfound.co/2021/04/19/shaffrons
Sept. 10 The Fox Hunt https://allthingsfoxes.com/fox-hunting/
Sept. 11 Vehicle Names Inspired By…https://journal.classiccars.com/2021/05/08/top-11-cars-named-after-horses-which-is-your-favorite/
Sept. 12 Surprising Statistics https://pawsomeadvice.com/pets/horse-statistics/
https://datapaddock.com/
http://www.equineheritageinstitute.org/learning-center/horse-facts/
Sept. 13 Unusual Inventions https://listverse.com/2012/11/23/top-10-bizarre-victorian-inventions/
https://patents.google.com/patent/US20040140643?oq=horse+powered
http://www.lrgaf.org/inventions.htm

Sept. 14 Horses Of The Civil War https://www.earthintransition.org/2012/09/death-and-the-civil-war-not-counting-the-horses/
www.thomaslegion.net/americancivilwar/totalcivilwarhorseskilled.html
Sept. 15 Queen Of Diamonds https://www.hhhistory.com/2022/01/kitty-wilkins-horse-trader.html
https://www.howold.co/person/kitty-wilkins/biographySept. 16 Colonial Life
http://imh.org/exhibits/past/legacy-of-the-horse/colonial-horses/
Sept. 17 Chernobyl's Wild Horses theconversation.com/the-mystery-of-chernobyls-wild-horses-137270
Sept. 18 The Horse Trail americantrails.org/resources/the-history-of-horse-trails-the-fight-for-trails-across-america
Sept. 19 The Ultra-Race https://ultrarunninghistory.com/man-vs-horse/
Sept. 20 Pick-Up Horse https://www.horsejournals.com/life-horses/horses-jobs-rodeo-pick-horses
Sept. 21 Twenty-Mule Team nps.gov/deva/learn/historyculture/twenty-mule-teams.htm
Sept. 22 Buzkashi http://www.afghanistan-culture.com/buzkashi.html
Sept. 23 The Shahzada https://www.horsetalk.co.nz/features/cj-2001shahzada-prev.shtml
Sept. 24 The Fire Horse https://equitrekking.com/articles/entry/famous_horses_in_history_-_the_fire_horse
Sept. 25 Silver https://www.imdb.com/name/nm1791316/bio
Sept. 26 Search And Rescue https://patch.com/connecticut/easthampton-ct/horse-guards-to-become-equestrian-search-and-rescue-team-16
Sept. 27 Off To School https://www.edgarsnyder.com/blog/2015/08/history-of-school-bus.html
Sept. 28 The Circus Horse blog.biodiversitylibrary.org/2015/09/horses-and-history-of-circus.html
Sept. 29 Packhorse Librarians www.appalachianhistory.net/2018/01/pack-horse-librarians.html
Sept. 30 The Vaquero Tradition https://www.horseillustrated.com/western-horse-training-vaquero-way-17722
Oct. 1 Holiday Horse Shortage http://hatchingcatnyc.com/2021/12/06/holiday-horse-shortage-horse-tales-new-york/
Oct. 2 The Omnibus Horsehttps://www.thevintagenews.com/2016/07/31/priority-horse-bus-charming-photos-look-back-time-people-went-work-horse-drawn-omnibus/?chrome=1
Oct. 5 The Farrier https://www.thefarrierguide.com/2015/02/farrier-history.html
Oct. 6 Branded For Life https://www.equisearch.com/discoverhorses/the-history-of-branding
Oct. 7 The Horse's Prayer https://www.ofhorse.com/view-post/The-Horses-Prayer
Oct. 8 Big Ben http://www.millarbrookefarm.com/horses/big-ben/
Oct. 9 The Shire https://shirehorsesociety.com.au/history-of-the-shire-horse/
Oct. 10 Ghost Horses Of The Desert https://saharafragileorg.b-cdn.net/ghost-towns-and-wild-horses-in-the-worlds-oldest-desert/
Oct. 11 To Pace Or Trot https://horsesandfoals.com/harness-racing/
Oct. 12 A Second Chance https://gustavomirabalcastro.online/en/horses/prosthetics-for-horses/
Oct. 13 Funeral Horses geriwalton.com/jobs-for-horses-what-work-they-did-in-the-1800s/
Oct. 14 The Requisition http://ivybridge-heritage.org/horses-at-home-and-at-war/
Oct. 15 Therapy Horses For Veterans https://www.columbiapsychiatry.org/news/horse-therapy-helps-veterans-overcome-trauma
Oct. 16 The First Equine Veterinarians www.civilwarmed.org/animal/
http://www.findalocalvet.com/Featured-News/2018/The-First-Veterinarians-A-Brief-History.aspx
Oct. 17 The Bathing Machine https://www.apartmenttherapy.com/history-of-the-bathing-machine-photos-facts-231324
www.geriwalton.com/jobs-for-horses-what-work-they-did-in-the-1800s/
Oct. 18 Uniting Over Horses https://www.jpost.com/Israel-News/Israelis-and-Palestinians-unite-over-horses-469770
Oct. 19 The Musical Ride horsejournals.com/popular/history-heritage/rcmp-musical-ride
Oct. 20 The Bond https://www.history.co.uk/article/history-of-horses-during-wwi

Oct. 21 Winter In The City https://equusmagazine.com/blog-equus/horses-christmas-tree-george-angells-gifts-bostons-horses-10929/
Oct. 22 Cloning https://ker.com/equinews/cloning-horses/
Oct. 23 The Treadmill https://treadmill-ratings-reviews.com/blog/the-bizarre-2000-year-history-of-thetreadmill/#1851_A_Horse_Treadmill_Powered_Fog_Whistle_is_Installed_at_a_United_States_li ghthouse
Oct. 24 Combined Driving http://www.davidesaunders.com/education.html
www.wehorse.com/en/blog/horse-driving/
Oct. 25 The Golden Horse https://akhal-teke.org/the-breed/
Oct. 26 Train Race https://www.wired.com/2008/09/sept-18-1830-horse-beats-iron-horse-for-the-time-being/
Oct. 27 Hollywood Horses https://www.insp.com/blog/horses-of-hollywood/
Oct. 28 Sefton https://thewarhorsememorial.org/100-hero-horses/hero-horse10/
Oct. 29 Sea Biscuit https://www.pbs.org/wgbh/americanexperience/features/seabiscuit-biography/
Oct. 30 The Horse Logo https://www.wyohistory.org/encyclopedia/wyomings-long-lived-bucking-horse
https://www.brandcrowd.com/blog/history-of-the-ferrari-logo/
Oct. 31 Retirement https://womenofageridinghorses.com/events/news/central-parks-only-dedicated-mounted-patrol-team-retires/
Nov. 1 Horses In Mythology https://petpress.net/mythical-horses/
Nov. 2 Well Fargo Stagecoach https://stories.wf.com/horses-pride-wells-fargo-service
Nov. 3 Baśka https://visitworldheritage.com/en/eu/the-important-role-of-horses-in-the-mines/280899cc-bbda-4213-956d-2c1e43faf69b
Nov. 4 Shipping Warhorses nam.ac.uk/explore/british-army-horses-during-first-world-war
Nov. 5 The Hairless Horse https://horseyhooves.com/do-hairless-horses-exist/
https://wtf-nature.livejournal.com/454042.html
Nov. 6 The Rescue Of 5000 https://www.horsetalk.co.nz/2011/12/16/true-story-britain-war-horses/
Nov. 7 What Bravery Looks Like https://dressagetoday.com/lifestyle/valiant-26921/
Nov. 8 The Scythian's Horse https://blog.britishmuseum.org/horses-a-scythians-best-friend/
https://www.realmofhistory.com/2019/07/01/10-facts-scythians-warfare/
Nov. 9 "The Galloping Horse" https://www.thevintagenews.com/2016/06/27/46591-2/?chrome=1
Nov. 10 The Outrider horsejournals.com/life-horses/horses-jobs-racetrack-outrider-horses
Nov. 11 Hot/Cold/Warm https://www.omegafields.com/blog/horse-myths-debunked-hot-cold-blooded-horses-have-a-difference-in-body-temperature/
https://www.horsefactbook.com/breeds/hot-warm-cold-blooded-horses/
Nov. 12 The Beer Wagon www.geriwalton.com/jobs-for-horses-what-work-they-did-in-the-1800s/
Nov. 13 Horse Fighting jacobimages.com/2012/09/on-mindanaos-lumads-and-horse-fighting
Nov. 15 Horse Bells https://classicbells.com/Info/History.asp
Nov. 16 Bess https://thewarhorsememorial.org/100-hero-horses/hero-horse9/
Nov. 17 Old Charley https://centerofthewest.org/2014/02/21/points-west-buffalo-bill-horses/
Nov. 18 Making House Calls https://www.historynet.com/call-the-midwife-nurses-on-horseback-in-the-appalachian-mountains/
Nov. 19 The Steeplechase https://www.highhopesteeplechase.com/About/Steeplechase-History.aspx
Nov. 20 The Colonial Pacer http://imh.org/exhibits/past/legacy-of-the-horse/colonial-horses/
Nov. 21 The Brumbies www.cerfhorses.org/brumby-horses/
http://afs.okstate.edu/breeds/horses/australianbrumby/
The-History-of-Brumbies.pdf https://ihearthorses.com/australian-brumby/
Nov. 23 Cortés https://animalsofempire.weebly.com/horses-spain/horses-and-the-spanish-empire
Nov. 24 The Last Fire Horse hatchingcatnyc.com/2015/01/24/last-fire-horses-new-york-fire-department/

Nov. 25 Extinct Equines https://returntofreedom.org/wild-horse-nation/extinct/
Nov. 26 That Beautiful Mane https://www.deephollowranch.com/horse-mane/
Nov. 27 Horse Of A Different Color https://www.whats-your-sign.com/horse-color-meanings.html
Nov. 28 Horse Soldiers https://www.militarytimes.com/news/your-military/2019/10/18/How-the-horse-soldiers-helped-liberate-afghanistan-from-the-taliban-18-years-ago/
Nov. 29 The Mounties grunge.com/287553/the-crazy-history-of-the-canadian-mounties/
Dec. 1 Pinto https://cowgirlmagazine.com/horse-20000-mile-trek/
Dec. 2 Horse Hairhttps://johncanningco.com/blog/horsehair-plaster/
https://originalupholstery.wordpress.com/2015/01/21/horsehair-is-it-still-in-use-yes-of-course/
Dec. 3 Coconut Roll https://www.horsejournals.com/popular/interviews-profiles/remarkable-horses-canada-coconut-roll
Dec. 4 Eventing https://www.fei.org/stories/sport/eventing/history-eventing?&list=2&content=2
Dec. 5 Side-Saddle https://www.colindangaard.com/history-of-side-saddles
Dec. 6 The Western Saddle https://writinforthebrand.com/history-of-the-western-saddle/
Dec. 7 Horse Diving! https://www.thevintagenews.com/2022/01/14/horse-diving-wild-west-invention-turned-atlantic-city-attraction/?chrome=1
Dec. 8 The Show Stealer http://imh.org/exhibits/past/legacy-of-the-horse/circus-horses/
Dec. 9 Phar Lap www.artbycrane.com/horse_history_articles_tales/thegreatesthorseraceever.html
Dec. 10 Laws That Still Exist Today https://www.ofhorse.com/view-post/Crazy-Horse-Laws-That-Still-Exist-Today
Dec. 11 Lipizzaner Rescue https://www.historynet.com/patton-rescues-the-lipizzaner-stallions/
Dec. 12 American Quarter Horse https://www.aqha.com/history-of-the-quarter-horse
Dec. 13 Sleigh Racing https://horsenetwork.com/2021/12/the-hidden-history-of-jingle-bells/
Dec. 14 After The War https://bam.files.bbci.co.uk/bam/live/content/zqn9xnb/transcript
Dec. 15 Seeing-Eye Mini https://www.ponybox.com/news_details.php?row=1&id=1923
Dec. 16 Skiijoring https://horserookie.com/horse-skijoring-equipment/
Dec. 17 Strep & Strangles https://www.newsweek.com/strep-throat-horse-research-can-help-doctors-find-cure-human-strep-725064
Dec. 18 Wild Horse Annie https://equitrekking.com/articles/entry/five_cowgirls_who_changed_history
Dec. 19 Bill The Bastard https://www.news.com.au/entertainment/tv/the-legend-of-bill-the-bastard-and-australias-great-war-horses/news-story
Dec. 20 The Christmas Party https://www.smithsonianmag.com/history/when-humane-societies-threw-christmas-parties-for-horses-180979253/
Dec. 21 The White House Stables horse-canada.com/horses-and-history/horses-at-the-white-house/
Dec. 23 Those Beautiful Spots cowgirlmagazine.com/appaloosas-the-ultimate-comeback-story/
Dec. 24 The Livery Stable https://truewestmagazine.com/livery-stables-west/
Dec. 25
Dec. 26 Helping Prisoners Heal positive.news/lifestyle/wellbeing/horses-prisoners-heal/
Dec. 28 Epic Fail smithsonianmag.com/history/sacrifice-amid-the-ice-facing-facts-on-the-scott-expedition
Dec. 29 Dressage https://www.geniusequestrian.com/origins-of-dressage/
Dec. 30 Half Man/Half Beast ancient-origins.net/opinion-guest-authors/spanish-use-animals-weapons-war-00898

Made in United States
Troutdale, OR
11/28/2024